TEMPEST

The Natural World of the Gulf South

Craig E. Colten, Series Editor

TEMPEST

LIZ SKILTON

Hurricane Naming and American Culture

LOUISIANA STATE UNIVERSITY PRESS ▌ BATON ROUGE

Published by Louisiana State University Press
lsupress.org

Copyright © 2019 by Louisiana State University Press
All rights reserved. Except in the case of brief quotations used in articles or reviews, no part of this publication may be reproduced or transmitted in any format or by any means without written permission of Louisiana State University Press.

Louisiana Paperback Edition, 2023

Designer: Michelle A. Neustrom
Typeface: Sentinel, text

A portion of chapter 3 first appeared in "Gendering Natural Disaster: The Battle over Female Hurricane Names," *Journal of Women's History* 30, no. 3 (2018), Copyright © 2018 Journal of Women's History, Inc.

All charts were created by the author.

Library of Congress Cataloging-in-Publication Data

Names: Skilton, Liz, 1985– author.
Title: Tempest : hurricane naming and American culture / Liz Skilton.
Description: Baton Rouge : Louisiana State University Press, [2019] | Series: The natural world of the Gulf South | Includes bibliographical references and index.
Identifiers: LCCN 2018046643 | ISBN 978-0-8071-7117-2 (cloth : alk. paper) | ISBN 978-0-8071-7145-5 (pdf) | ISBN 978-0-8071-7146-2 (epub) | ISBN 978-0-8071-7996-3 (paperback)
Subjects: LCSH: Hurricanes—Social aspects—United States. | Hurricanes—United States—History. | Popular culture—United States.
Classification: LCC QC945 .S6145 2019 | DDC 304.2/5—dc23
LC record available at https://lccn.loc.gov/2018046643

Every theory of the course of events in nature is
necessarily based on some process of simplification of the
phenomena and is to some extent therefore a fairy tale.

—Sir Napier Shaw,
Manual of Meteorology, 1919

CONTENTS

Acknowledgments....ix

Introduction....1

1 Maria and the Birth of Modern Meteorology....6

2 Camille and Cold War Sexual Politics....35

3 Roxcy and the Feminist Resistance....81

4 Andrew and the Business of Storms....119

5 Katrina and Hurricane 2.0....166

6 Tempest: Assessing Current Conditions....214

Notes....233

Selected Bibliography....283

Index....295

ACKNOWLEDGMENTS

Many deserve acknowledgment for their help in the production of this book, but above all, I wish to thank the feminists, meteorologists, reporters, archivists, and historians who helped shape or uncover the history of hurricane naming. I dedicate this book to you. More than anyone, this includes Roxcy O'Neal Bolton (and her children, Bonnie and Buddy), whose memory lives on in these pages and to whom I am eternally grateful. It also includes Karen Leathem at the Louisiana State Museum; Andre Sivels, NOAA's records officer; and Neal Dorst of the NOAA Atlantic Oceanographic and Meteorological Laboratory Hurricane Research Division. Dorst, in particular, provided essential help in tracking down Weather Bureau files regarding the introduction of the naming system after exhausting other efforts. Through Dorst, I corresponded with former directors of the National Hurricane Center Robert Simpson and Neil Frank; meteorological historians and officials including James Rodger Fleming, Gary Padgett, Chris Landsea, Miles Lawrence, Jeff Callahan, and Albert Theberg; and notable weather forecasters such as Bryan Norcross. Finally, this list includes the forecasters and disaster-response experts that work tirelessly to keep us safe, warn of impending doom, adapt outdated systems of hazard identification, and seriously consider the consequences of human response. Many of these individuals provided years' worth of insight on this subject, meaningfully shaping the conclusions made here.

Research on this subject was possible due to generous funding provided by multiple institutions and organizations. Tulane University's School of Liberal Arts Fellowship and Lurcy Travel Grants permitted the completion of a newspaper database to examine the effects of gendered hurricane naming; a New Orleans Center for the Gulf South Global South Fellowship

ACKNOWLEDGMENTS

allowed time to expand the database to include newspapers from countries bordering the Gulf; the University of Louisiana at Lafayette's Early Career Faculty Grant and Guilbeau Charitable Trust Research Awards offered travel funding to collect final pieces in the hurricane-naming history puzzle; the University of Southern Mississippi–Gulf Coast Preparing for the Next Katrina Travel Grant and a Hagley Museum and Library Disaster Conference Travel Grant provided the opportunity to present portions of this work and receive feedback at key conferences; and the J. J. Burdin M.D. and Helen B. Burdin/BORSF Endowment for Louisiana Studies afforded flexibility to examine the impact of recent storms. Finally, a Louisiana Board of Regents Artists and Scholars (ATLAS) Grant furnished a much-needed semester of sabbatical to finish the manuscript.

Next, I wish to express my immeasurable gratitude to series editor Craig Colten and to Margaret Lovecraft of Louisiana State University Press, who saw the earliest iterations of this work and had the foresight to guide it to completion. Along the same lines, Margy Thomas provided keen feedback as a developmental editor on early drafts of chapters, helping me hone my arguments and narrative. Later, the LSU Press editorial staff and freelance copyeditor Stan Ivester worked diligently to polish this manuscript to its final form. Meanwhile, mentors such as Rachel Devlin, Mary Farmer-Kaiser, Emily Clark, Randy Sparks, Larry Powell, Rosanne Adderley, Elisabeth McMahon, Karissa Haugeberg, Renée Sentilles, John Troutman, Sara Ritchey, Michael Dunaway, and JoAnne DeRouen advised me in the process of research and construction of the text. Thanks, as well, to the anonymous reviewers of this manuscript, the editors at the *Journal of Women's History,* and the numerous conference chairs and commentators who provided insight at critical junctures of this work.

Over the years I relied heavily on a variety of writing groups for support in the day-to-day process of putting words on the screen. These include the University of Louisiana at Lafayette coffee-shop crowd of Heather Stone, Ian Beamish, Kathryn Edwards, Beth Stauffer, and Kelly Robinson; my Tulane writing companions, Kristin Condotta Lee, Walter Stern, Rien Fertel, Alex McManus, Brian McGowan, Christopher Willoughby, Vera Gutmann, and Beau Gaitors; a virtual community of book writers, D'Weston Haywood, Lena Suk, and Debjani Bachaara; and an Unstuck writing group led by Kel Weinhold with Cara Jones, Christy Till, Amy Weiss, Katherina Payne,

ACKNOWLEDGMENTS

Marisa Macias, Lydia Tang, and Jenny Briggs. In addition to writing groups, generous colleagues at UL Lafayette offered support, including Chad Parker, Thomas Cauvin, Sophie Cauvin, Hilton Cordoba, Rich Frankel, Elise Franklin, Michael Martin, Rob Hermann, Jordan Kellman, Carl Richard, Bob Carriker, Pearson Cross, Mary Ann Wilson, Jack Damico, and Ramesh Kolluru. Other academic colleagues critical to the completion of this manuscript include those from the Louisiana Historical Association, the Louisiana Research Collection, the Louisiana Sea Grant LaDIA Fellows program, the Institute for Coastal and Water Research, the Louisiana Watershed Flood Center, the National Incident Management Systems and Advanced Technologies Center, and the Natural Hazards Center. I also wish to thank the following institutions for their assistance as I conducted research: the Schlesinger Library at Harvard University, Library of Congress, National Archives and Records Administration II, Princeton University, Florida International University, the National Hurricane Center, North Carolina State University, American University, Florida State Archives, College of Charleston, University of Southern Mississippi, Rice University, Tulane University, Loyola University–New Orleans, and the University of New Orleans.

Moreover, thanks are due to the countless friends and family members whose couches, spare bedrooms, and air mattresses were always available on all-too-short research trips, and who provided food, attentive audiences, and even office supplies. These include: Adam Beauchamp and Sarah Withers, Sara and Andrew Bartlett, Jessica and Brad Brooks, Ann Case, Ansley Charnok, Tiffany Delcour, Kevin Fontenot, Frank Larson and family, Brian and Amelia McGowan, Rich Manfredi, Cait and Nick Meyers, Matt Nemergut, Liz Sparks and Ross Miller, Bobby Ticknor, George and Andrea Turcu, and Cyndi, Hannah, and Chloe Wagner.

Most of all, I wish to thank my parents (David and Christine) and sisters (Kathryn and Madeline). Because of you, this book exists.

TEMPEST

INTRODUCTION

This book started with a simple question: *Why do we name hurricanes?* The question emerged while I completed research on the hurricane history of New Orleans for the Louisiana State Museum's *Living with Hurricanes* exhibit in 2007.[1] The exhibit contextualized the problematical past of New Orleanians' experience with hurricanes up through the latest storm, Katrina. My job was to collect newspaper articles on one particularly devastating 1965 hurricane, Betsy. As I sat at the microfiche reader reviewing articles that tracked the trajectory of the storm's development and accounts of its aftermath—including devastating levee breaks in eerily similar regions of the city that suffered again forty years later with Katrina—I noticed how many times Betsy was referred to as a malevolent woman. "Betsy did that" or "She was no lady" were just a couple of the phrases often repeated in the articles, making me wonder what phrases were in use at the same time but not appropriate to print.

Growing up in "Tornado Alley," where other extreme weather events occur but are not named, I was fascinated by the phenomenon of naming a storm and then describing it as a gendered object. I combed through newspaper articles about storms of New Orleans's past, noting the language used to describe the hurricanes that feature so prominently in American history and searched for the answer to my original question, *Why were hurricane names introduced in the first place?* As I reviewed this history, I noticed how many stories we tell about why we name hurricanes. This question comes up every season with the release of a new season's list of names, and again as the first hurricane emerges. Even though we discuss this question at least once every season, there is no clear answer about the names' origin. Some claim that bored meteorologists are responsible for naming hurricanes, others

1

that the practice comes from popular literature, and many assert it is a relic of associating the natural world with a feminine entity or god. Meanwhile, the National Hurricane Center's website includes minimal information on the naming history, stating that they are named and that the names have changed over time.[2] Even historians have little to say on the issue, relegating the naming phenomenon to explanatory footnotes as peripheral to the effects of devastating disasters.[3] So, I dug deeper.

At each stage of research, I thought I had answered my primary question. But then I unfurled another tangled thread in our complex understanding of hurricanes in American culture and discovered there was more. In searching for why we name storms, I realized just how much these names shape our impressions of storms. From the moment hurricanes appear on the radar screen until long after the storms are gone, hurricane names affect our perception and reaction to them. First, we respond to the threat of the storm, often by recalling previous experiences with others of the like. We assess its potential impact based on a variety of factors built over years of research into hurricane behavior, choosing to risk our lives or flee as a result of our conclusions. Once the storm hits, we survey damage with critical eyes, trying to make sense of what occurred and what is to come during recovery. Years afterwards, we remember these events as if they were equivalent to fundamental historical periods or with as little importance as a blink of an eye. Throughout all of this, the hurricane is identified with a name that both separates it from similar storms and identifies it as something different from other hazards. Thus, in giving a hurricane a name, we give it a different cultural meaning, a "history" that is shaped by the present moment, ghosts of the past, and fears of the future. We make it part of our lives.

Because storm names play an important role in shaping our understanding of hurricanes, it is essential to know their history. In order to unpack the complicated history of hurricane naming, we must first define some basic principles—how hurricanes are named, what these names mean culturally, and how these names became part of our cultural discourse.

A tropical cyclone is named when it is deemed a sizable threat. We currently define this as the point in a storm's development when it reaches a certain wind speed (74 miles per hour). Once meeting this criterion, the threat receives a name from a list of region-specific predetermined names. Compiled up to six years in advance by regional committees of the World

INTRODUCTION

Meteorological Organization, the list of names represents cultural and region-specific naming practices of that area. Lists are evaluated prior to release each season to make sure that they are equally balanced in terms of male and female names, do not contain names of major storms of the past so as to prevent confusion when identifying, and do not contain names that have specific cultural meaning at the moment of use. For example, storm names that describe current or important historical figures (including politicians and world leaders) are filtered out. We will never see a Hurricane Adolf, as it could easily be associated with Adolf Hitler. Names are only officially used for tropical storms such as hurricanes, cyclones, and typhoons so as to distinguish them from other phenomena. All of this is regulated closely by the World Meteorological Organization, in conjunction with regional weather services such as the United States' National Oceanic and Atmospheric Administration.[4]

This custom of naming tropical storms is a relatively recent phenomenon, only in standard practice since World War II. Since World War II, the hurricane-naming system has evolved with the discourse over larger changes in American culture. The US feminist movement, the environmental movement, and the evolution of US disaster management have all affected naming practices. The current naming system is an inherently American tradition, as it was introduced by the US Weather Bureau and only adopted worldwide later on. Reviewing how this custom spread illustrates larger trends in American influence on the development of meteorology, science, and culture.

But while the story of how hurricanes got their names is important, equally so is the tale of what has happened after names were attached. As Americans (and others) interacted with hurricane names—using them, attaching common cultural associations as descriptors, and responding to their use in popular culture—they altered the perception of these storms. Now a hurricane name is much more than just a tag to identify a developing natural event; it comes with a multitude of characteristics and expectations that distinguish hurricanes from other hazards. Thus, tracing the names, and the evolving discussion over everything associated with them, allows us to measure the understanding of hurricanes at moments in time. In this case, hurricane names serve as fingerprints for cultural change, reflecting and shaping it in the process.

One of the unique results of this naming system is the attachment of cultural attributes to an otherwise blank slate, particularly through the use of gender. The names assigned to hurricanes are specifically gendered either male or female, and thus serve as a way of assigning gender to a natural object. This trend of assigning gender to nature has a long past, deeply rooted in human understanding of nature and attempts to categorize that which is unknown in our world.[5] But the way gender is used regularly as a vehicle to describe hurricanes differs from the way it is used to describe other aspects of our natural world. Tracing the evolution of this gendered attachment as well as the various ways it has developed with changes in American culture provides fascinating insights on modern conceptions of gender and society in the latter twentieth and the twenty-first centuries.

This book is structured to focus on key periods in hurricane-naming history by reviewing major storms that fundamentally defined each period. Its central argument is based on research from a variety of sources—newspapers, archival collections, literature, disaster kitsch, television, social media, and cutting-edge multidisciplinary scholarly research—to provide the widest possible perspective on this question that comes up so frequently but is never authoritatively answered. In fact, I named this book *Tempest* because, much like the definition of the word, hurricane names meant and continue to mean different things. At different moments in time, these names have served as labels for wind; reflexive cultural definitions of women and men; the site of debates over science, culture, and technology; and indicators of Americans' understanding of disaster and its natural and anthropomorphic causes. Throughout American history, storm names have evolved, shifting with the people and cultural time periods. Nowhere is this more evident than in the Gulf South, whose people led the way in the adoption, adaptation, and everyday use of these names. The Gulf South is the nation's "hurricane coast," historically prone to these often-yearly storms.[6] This region's people and their experience with grievous key storms have shaped international discourse about hurricanes. And thus, the Gulf South is the best place to look for a baseline reaction to how named storms impact decisions and discourse in the heat of crisis.

The questions posed through this study are inspired by the work of historians of gender and environmental history, particularly hurricane and disaster history. These include Matthew Mulcahy's foundational work on the

INTRODUCTION

Greater British Caribbean storms; Louis Pérez's astute work on nineteenth-century hurricanes and Cuba; Stuart Schwartz's recent tome on hurricane and disaster management history; Raymond Arsenault's essential text on the change in the perception of storms pre- and post–World War II; Theodore Steinberg's and Kevin Rozario's eloquent discussions of concepts of American disasters; Andy Horowitz's scholarship on Hurricanes Betsy and Katrina; Patricia Bellis Bixel and Elizabeth Hayes Turner's book on the 1900 Galveston Storm; Eleonora Rohland's history of the perception of hurricane knowledge and science; and Cynthia Kierner's research on pre–Civil War disasters.[7] This study was also influenced by scholars who focus on the intersection between gender and environment, such as Carolyn Merchant's fundamental scholarship on the history of Mother Nature; Elaine Tyler May's discussion of gender and the atomic bomb in the context of the Cold War; Carol Bigwood's discussion of gender, nature, and art; and Virginia Scharff's review of the development of ecofeminism.[8] It is also informed by the cutting-edge scholarship of culture and the environment such as Greg Bankoff, Joshua Howe, and Ilan Kelman's discussion of the impact of names in the historical discourse of hazards and vulnerability; James Rodger Fleming's review of the history of weather tracking, control, and meteorology; Joshua Blu Buhs's discussion of fire ants in the Cold War; Laura Martin's work on the Eskimo words for snow; and Lorraine Daston's discussion of the science of clouds.[9] Lastly, it is influenced by those that focus on human efforts to control nature, such as William Cronon's books on the interaction of humans and their environment; Craig Colten's work on the efforts to mitigate and control water for urban development; John McPhee's efforts to unpack the myriad of choices in control of the Mississippi River; and Christopher Wells's discussion of the creation of the American transportation landscape.[10]

I hope this book provides insight not only on why we name and gender hurricanes, but also on how this process affects other aspects of American culture. At the end, it draws some preliminary conclusions about the effect of storm naming and gendering and asks the inevitable question that emerges from review of this subject: *Does hurricane naming harm us?*

MARIA
AND THE BIRTH OF MODERN METEOROLOGY

In 1938, a bespectacled, forty-something English professor in northern California started devoting uncommon attention to the weather. George R. Stewart, a scholar of English literature at the University of California, Berkeley, was always interested in the history of the natural world, but recently more so because of his experience with a barrage of odd weather while living in California. For the next three years, he spent time poring over news coverage of deadly winter storms, researching emerging weather-tracking technologies, and plumbing classical literature for references to violent tempests. He even shadowed employees of a newly formed federal agency, the Weather Bureau, to learn their advanced tracking tactics. Finally, his research and his imagination coalesced into the story of a massive, fictional hurricane that swept from California to New York sometime in the mid-century. In November 1941, he published a 349-page disaster novel titled *Storm*. Each of the novel's twelve chapters traced a single day in the hurricane's life and the valiant efforts of a young meteorologist to track its progress. Stewart was so confident of the book's success, so sure of the public's hunger for a story about a cataclysmic "natural" disaster and the human efforts to understand it, that before the book's release, he lined up speaking engagements on both coasts and planned his victory tour. And he was right: not even the shock of Pearl Harbor, which hurled the United States into a world war just two weeks after the novel's release, would quench demand for it. Even as the American public prepared for the largest mobilization effort in history, their fascination with Stewart's fictional hurricane deepened, and sales outpaced Stewart's wildest dreams.

Stewart's confidence of the success of his hurricane novel was well founded, as the field of disaster fiction gained popularity throughout the 1930s. In most disaster novels, the plot centered on the course and effects of a disaster at a specific site and featured a few key heroes who bravely dealt with the disaster and its aftermath. John Steinbeck's *The Grapes of Wrath* (1935) followed a family of tenant farmers through the Dust Bowl, examining the depth of Depression-era despair.[1] Zora Neale Hurston's *Their Eyes Were Watching God* (1937) reviewed the decimation of levees in Lake Okeechobee, Florida, during the 1928 hurricane as an allegory for the Jim Crow South.[2] And in 1941, nine months before Stewart's *Storm*, William Alexander Percy offered a poignant memory on disaster relief during the great Mississippi River Flood of 1927 in *Lanterns on the Levee*.[3] Each of these novels focused on cataclysmic natural events. What set *Storm* apart was that the disaster it centered on—a hurricane—was wholly imaginary.

Stewart knew that his novel's focus on a disaster, real or fictional, was enough to catapult it to the best-seller lists: it capitalized on (or exploited) one of Americans' greatest fears, uncontrollable weather. Although this fear was as old as America itself, it peaked in the mid-twentieth century as technological advancements made the prospect of controlling the weather vaguely possible. With disastrous plagues, floods, storms, and fires in Americans' recent memory, it was easy to visualize the imagined disaster. So it was that, when *Storm* was published, the American imagination was ripe for a story about the human effort to tame a wild storm using the latest in meteorological knowledge and weather-tracking technology. Stewart's novel was up to the task. *Storm* eventually affected the progression of the war, the field of meteorology, the cultural impressions of wind, and pioneered a new genre of ecological fiction. It did all this all because the storm—the main character—was assigned a name.

Fear and Rationality in a Storm World

Extreme weather long fascinated Americans, its power to terrify rising in direct proportion to the level of development that lies vulnerable to its destruction.[4] Hurricane-force winds and rains cannot be intimidated, controlled, or argued with, and no amount of human rationality stops them from wiping out the hard-won growth of a nation that prides itself on continual progress. In a sense, extreme weather is the most terrifying villain in American history, defying the culture's fundamental ethos of progress. Since the earliest European colonists tried to carve out settlements from the wilderness, that ethos was premised on the power of human rationality: using their faculties of reasoning, humans subjected the natural environment to order, classification, and comprehensibility. Indeed, for the first European settlers who built new lives in the frighteningly unfamiliar surroundings of the New World, their powers of reason and language were the single greatest tools for understanding their environment and surviving within it.

The language used by the earliest European settlers in the New World to describe storms and natural phenomena shows how they blended Old World and New World lexicons into a transatlantic natural language. One way they developed this language was by blending taxonomical terminology, linguistically relating new "foreign" species to known Old World species. In detailed, vibrantly illustrated ecological treatises, they defined and categorized the botanical specimens, animals, and native populations they encountered in the New World, using European and native terminology to meticulously label and explain items of interest.[5] The transatlantic natural language that emerged in the contact zone of the New World, as the settlers named the natural phenomena they encountered, served to bind it together with the Old.

The etymology of the term "hurricane" provides a perfect illustration of the new transatlantic natural language. The *Oxford English Dictionary* lists over thirty different spellings of "hurricane" in use from the fifteenth century to the present, all referring to the same phenomenon: a tropical cyclone. Spelling inconsistencies are initially puzzling since the definition remains constant across centuries, but are explained by the hybridization process of the transatlantic natural language.[6] For example, in the pre-Colombian Americas, indigenous populations dealt with the awesomeness of nature by imposing a certain kind of human logic. One key strategy was to imagine (and name) vengeful weather and water deities, which historian Louis Pérez describes as the "malignant forces that took the form of winds of awesome proportions and destructive power." These "powerful demons," spawned by "malevolent" gods, went by a diverse array of names.[7] The Incan gods who summoned floods and winds were called Paricia and Pariacaca. In both Taíno and Mayan societies, a similar god was regularly referred to by the name *huracán*. Taíno natives in what is now Puerto Rico, Hispaniola, and

Cuba believed that the god Juracán (less commonly known as Guabancex) was responsible for bringing hurricanes to the islands, while the Mayan god Hunraqan or Huracán, also known as U K'ux Kaj, was thought to inflict hurricanes on humans as retribution for their disobedience.[8] Given that multiple populations had water deities they referred to as *huracán,* it is unsurprising that Spanish explorers quickly adopted this word to refer to the great storms they encountered in the New World.

Vengeful water deities were also familiar to Europeans arriving in the New World in the 1500s. Almost every ancient society of the Old World had some form of mythical creature or god connected with the sea. Poseidon was the Greek god of oceans; Neptune, his Roman equivalent. And, in Hebrew, Leviathan was a sea monster or dangerous aquatic creature. Thus, European settlers easily embraced these hurricane labels. By 1555, translated indigenous documents printed in multiple European languages used the word *huracán* in various forms. Some forms of the word included "herycano, furicano, huricano, hurricane, heuricane, and huracán." These varied spellings appeared in text until eventually standardized to the present, English-sounding form, *hurricane,* in the late seventeenth century.[9]

Soon, the word *hurricane* spread back to the Old World. William Shakespeare, for example, refers to hurricanes using various spellings in three plays within a single decade. In *The History of Troilus and Cressida* (1602), Shakespeare uses *hurricanoes;* in *King Lear* (1606), he uses the English form *hurricane.*[10] Then, in *The Tempest* (1611), a play set in the backdrop of the 1609 Jamestown hurricane, he uses an older English term for violent winds—*tempest. Tempest* or *tempeste* in Old English (including the addition of an "e" at the end of the word) referred to violent or stormy winds, often associated with whirlwinds or gales familiar to English residents.[11] Shakespeare's inclusion of the new transatlantic terminology in combination with older references to storms serves as a poignant reminder that the language used at the time to refer to hurricanes fluctuated as reports from European explorers and colonists filtered into popular culture. Shakespeare's fascination with these storms was akin to the public's growing interest and fear of this type of unfamiliar hazard.

Another significant seventeenth-century cultural response to hurricanes included efforts to develop accurate technical illustrations of them. English scholar and scientist Ralph Bohun was the first to attempt such an illustration in 1671, despite never having viewed a hurricane in person. Bohun relied on the descriptions given in accounts of sailors and explorers to map the hurricane in reference to other winds found in nature such as vapors, tornados, and cumulus clouds. While crude, the illustration was fairly accurate. It included notations on the speeds of rotating winds, a clearly defined "eye," and a rough documentation of the size and scale of a typical storm. Bohun even tried to illustrate the decimation caused by these storms by including a textual description. As described by Bohun, "sometimes you shall have a sudden Puffe of wind, driven from between two Clouds, with a violence Displosion of the Air; that descends almost Perpendicularly to the Earth" that generate "Whirlwinds and Tornados."[12] As illustrated by Bohun's technical drawing, Europeans attempted to subject scary, uncontrollable hurricanes to human rationality, relying on old conceptions of nature to ground modern understanding.

Meanwhile, in both the Old World and the New, storms frequently were explained in religious terms as unstoppable acts of God against which the human's only recourses were behavior modification and prayer. This perception of storms as divine intervention is reflected in early hurricane-naming practices as some storms were named ex post facto for saints' feast days as a way of appeasing God.[13] The notion that hurricanes are instances of divine intervention is linked to the understanding of weather (and nature in general) as God's weapon. As Carolyn Merchant argues, Europeans perceived God's actions as carried out by a mythical Mother Nature figure, who acted both independently and in the form of divine retribution.[14] This female figure is one way cultures imagined hurricanes as mythical creatures who loom large and strike with sudden devastation. Whatever the causes ascribed to hurricanes, these events were terrifyingly unpredictable. Even as other environmental mysteries succumbed to human understanding throughout the seventeenth century, hurricanes remained enigmatic, holding sway over the humans each June through November, as one after another, these cyclopes of the sea would snarl their way up the Atlantic coastline, often devastating new settlements. As historian Eleonora Rohland explains, the early settlers of the Gulf South region were particularly ill equipped to react to the frequency of storms that impacted the region. From 1700 to 1855, the Atlantic Basin suffered through an astounding 338 unique storms, ravaging New Orleans, Charleston, and Jacksonville, among other cities.[15] In responding to the regular threat, Gulf South residents led the nation in introducing levee-construction projects, relocating to higher ground if necessary, and implementing community disaster relief efforts. Despite this, prediction methods remained slow at best, reliant on a system of warning flags, word from incoming ships, and old-fashioned eyesight.

By the end of the nineteenth century in the United States, efforts to track and predict devastating winds expanded with the advancement of technology like the telegraph. In 1849, a joint telegraph network controlled and funded by the Smithsonian Institution raised hopes that the telegraph lines would "solv[e] the problem of American storms" by "furnish[ing] a ready means of warning the northern and eastern observers to be on watch for the first appearance of an advancing storm."[16] For the first time it was possible "to collect reports of the current weather over a wide area."[17] In doing so, weather became "more than a local phenomenon," expanding to a national concern. The Smithsonian Institution relied on a growing contingent of unofficial weather observers to connect this network. By the Civil War, over 500 weather-observation stations reported to the *Washington Evening Star*, which compiled and printed the reports daily.[18]

Despite the momentum of this grassroots network, the Civil War wrought havoc on weather reporting. With the destruction of railroad and telegraph lines during the war, the combined system of weather reporting stalled. Yet, as historian James Rodger Fleming points out, the Civil War further stoked Americans' desire to control the weather.[19] Throughout the war, a parallel battle raged over the control of weather-related information, including the documentation and transmittance of reports. Control of weather information turned into a military tactic as the ability to predict cold or rain conferred advantages in preparing and waging battle. It was also widely speculated that gunpowder residue triggered rain. Thus, new theories circulated on the control of atmospheric elements as a strategy of war. While these theories were only peripherally tested, they formed the lore of strategic weather-control efforts years later.

After the Civil War, the federal government sought to reform the fragmented weather network by passing a joint Congressional resolution to establish a nationwide weather network. The new weather network was placed under the control of the US Army Signal Corps, which implemented new standards for weather tracking and reporting. Across 55 stations in 12 regions, the Signal Corps launched new "cautionary signaling" processes for extreme weather. This included the posting of a red flag with a black square during daylight hours to warn of impending extreme weather, and the use of a red light by night.[20]

The 1890s brought America's first fully funded, standardized, national weather-reporting system through congressional establishment of a weather service via the passage of the Organic Act of 1890. The weather service's responsibilities included the "forecasting of weather, the issue of storm warnings, and the display of weather and flood signals."[21] Due to the Spanish-American and Philippine-American wars in the late 1890s and early 1900s, Cuba, Hawaii, and the Philippines were also incorporated. With this weather network in place, Americans for the first time had the capability of communicating across hundreds of miles that a hurricane had formed in the Gulf and was winding its way up the coastline. While the standardized national weather-tracking system was far more sophisticated than its earlier incarnation that relied on volunteer weather reports, it did not guarantee humans safety from nature or from human error.[22] On September 8, 1900, it was tested as a 145-miles-per-hour storm barreled into the island of Galveston, Texas. Alerts about the impending storm arrived via telegraph through the new weather station in Cuba, but Galveston weather officials, anticipating a different landfall in the Gulf, downplayed the alerts. By the time Galveston officials realized their mistake, it was too late.[23] When the storm struck with little warning, an estimated 8,000 people died. This catastrophe proved that, even with the promising new weather-tracking system, the prediction mechanisms and understanding of hurricanes were still primitive.

Subsequent storms followed regularly almost every year while the environmental crises of the 1920s and 1930s compounded the sense of urgency over the weather. Massive river flooding, droughts, and soil exhaustion—combined with technological advancements in aviation that made air flight increasingly common—forced the public to focus on the necessity of a more modernized and better funded meteorological organization.[24] One final wallop, the Labor Day Storm of 1935, drove home this need when it hit the Florida Keys. In theory, storm damage should have been minimal because the Keys were sparsely populated and developed. But in reality hundreds of Great Depression–desperate World War I vets, members of President

Herbert Hoover's "Bonus Army," populated the islands to work on the train lines meant to prepare the area for future development. With no evacuation plans and only tents and ramshackle huts for shelter, veterans were left defenseless against the hurricane.[25] When the storm cleared, survivors found vets buried in the sand next to train tracks, waiting for rescue.[26] Newspapers across the country published horrifying photographs of the victims, inciting public outrage and disgust. Amongst the outraged public was Ernest Hemingway, acclaimed author and a resident of the Keys, who published an editorial titled "Who Murdered the Vets?," a diatribe against President Hoover and the disorganized weather services.[27] Proclaiming that authorities willfully abandoned the veterans to die during hurricane season, Hemingway's call to action elicited anger over the mismanagement of weather warnings.[28]

In the aftermath of the storm, Congress passed the "Storm Patrol Bill" in 1936, establishing a Hurricane Warning Service in Jacksonville, Florida, to avert future disasters and situating the Gulf South as the home of hurricane tracking and severe weather concern.[29] After thousands of storm deaths, Americans prioritized weather understanding. Hurricanes were of utmost concern, but meteorologists also focused on the science behind other forms of extreme weather. In fact, a new "scientific method of meteorological analysis known as air mass analysis was being adopted by meteorologists throughout the world."[30] Air-mass analysis measured the highs and lows of temperatures and humidity across the United States to predict likely shifts that produced strong weather. The method relied on reports of accurate and consistent weather readings at regular intervals by a vast network of observers.

While the United States invested in new meteorological standards, their meteorology system lagged behind that of other countries. Part of the problem was that the Weather Bureau itself was deeply underfunded and unorganized. Since the creation of the US Weather Bureau in the 1840s, weather had been classified under a multitude of federal departments. With each change, funding and personnel transformed. In 1940, as the government refocused energy on meteorology, the Weather Bureau was transferred from the Department of Agriculture to the Department of Commerce.[31] This transfer, under the Reorganization Plan No. IV, "recognized that the role of the Weather Bureau in the general economic life of the nation required great emphasis in non-agricultural fields," particularly in civil aviation.[32] A key reason for the emphasis on civil aviation was the introduction of intercontinental and transcontinental flight routes. Between 1930 and 1938, the number of air travelers grew from around 6,000 passengers to 1.2 million, not including freight shipments, while companies like Delta Airlines (1924) and Pan American (1927) gained transportation market share.[33]

By 1940, the year before the novel *Storm* appeared in print, the US Weather Bureau, a branch of the Department of Commerce, included a voluntary weather-reporting network and official offices that used meteorograph equipment and airplanes to track weather daily in Chicago, Dallas, Cleveland, and New Orleans.[34] Located in Jacksonville, Florida, and in effect since 1935, the Hurricane Warning Service was now reliable and well staffed. In addition, the Army, Navy, and Coast Guard each had their own weather divisions, responsible for relaying weather information. Meanwhile, the study of climatology matured as a field with the publication of the first textbook on climatology, *Physical Climatology*, by Helmut Landsberg in 1941.[35] Overall, in the decades between 1840 and 1940, the American weather service grew from a disconnected network of amateur observers into a full-fledged professional field, a feature of everyday conversation, and a commodity, ripe for exploitation.

Despite the gains in American meteorology, the weather never lost its deadly potential, or its power to threaten American progress by crippling the nation at a moment's notice. The attempts to rationalize, track, and define nature in the United States exemplified the inherent tension in how humans encountered it. As familiarity with these hazards grew, and technological and scientific developments increased, linguistic variation in description was bureaucratically regulated. The effects of this regulation were soon felt.

The Collision of Fact and Fiction:
Constructing *Storm*

The deep roots of the American fear of nature, particularly extreme weather, are an essential context for understanding George Stewart's aesthetic choices in constructing *Storm* as it was in 1938. Halfway between the devastating Florida Keys hurricane of 1935 and the relocation of the US Weather Bureau to the Department of Commerce in 1940, Stewart started researching his novel. Stewart was fascinated by nature, spending vacations exploring the natural parks of the Pacific coast, with their deep ravines, soaring mountains, and seismic wonders.[36] But in 1938, after finishing his latest book, on the life of a whale fisherman, his interest in the Weather Bureau compelled him to study its history.[37] He found the meteorological changes of the previous half-century profound and exciting, particularly the advancements in weather-tracking technology for large storm systems. When he commenced research for the novel, originally titled *Life and Death of a Storm,* he only expected to spend a few months on it. He assumed the short period would provide him enough time to write knowledgeably about an imaginary storm and the weathermen who tracked it. Instead, he spent two years delving into the history and science behind hurricane tracking in addition to the literature produced on the subject of storms.[38] By the end, Stewart reviewed sources old and new, literary and popular, in order to construct his storm, a storm he believed would best all others.

Ever the English professor, Stewart began his research by culling references to storms in classical literature. He sought an understanding of the depictions of storms in fictional works such as Shakespeare's *Tempest* and Strepsiddes and Socrates' famous arguments in *The Clouds,* and even in the Psalms. But his attention soon shifted.[39] Delving into the history of weather tracking, Stewart read every text published on the subject available in the University of California libraries, saving the call slips along with meticulous notes to document his journey of discovery as much as his interest in the material.[40] His readings ranged from Aristotle's *Meteorology* and Virgil's *Georgics* to the more recent scientific texts in fields of meteorology and climatology.[41]

Meanwhile, Stewart also corresponded with different groups and organizations to help him craft a book about a hurricane. Obsessed with the previous half-century's meteorological developments, he communicated with the Weather Bureau. Asking to shadow the bureau's meteorologists at the San Francisco regional offices, Stewart built up a network of individuals who shared stories about their experiences at various levels of meteorological jobs, reviewed histories and detailed maps of storms of the Pacific coast from the previous decade, and fact-checked his drafts for accuracy in representation of bureau activities.[42]

In addition to his fieldwork and literature review, Stewart was inspired by his own first-hand experiences with weather-related news coverage.

When he started the project he knew he wanted to write a book about storms, particularly cyclones or hurricanes, but the winters of 1939 and 1940 pushed him to write about a late-in-the-season hurricane-turned-winter-storm in California. A full year into his research on the history of meteorology and with the outline of a draft in hand, he was shocked when a devastating round of winter storms pummeled the California area in 1939, quickly followed by an additional year of deadly storms that wreaked havoc from California to New York. These extraordinary storm systems brought freezing rains, dumping several feet of snow and causing extreme flooding over the preceding springs. Stewart, already into the first draft of his novel, was rapt with attention, saving clipping after clipping of newspaper articles gathered from Honolulu to Princeton. Underlining phrases used to describe the winter storms, Stewart recognized the effectiveness of powerful descriptions in drumming up interest in storm movements as well as the continued interest in Weather Bureau activities.[43] Stewart was also attuned to weather-related narratives playing out in the press, particularly the conflict between public and private meteorology in the coverage of the dramatic storms. One such conflict centered on a war between Weather Bureau officials and private meteorologists such as the colorful professor Irving Krick of Pasadena, "an instructor in Meteorology" who ran a private weather lab at the California Institute of Technology. Krick's predictions on the winter storm of 1940 differed dramatically from those of the US Weather Bureau's.[44] He even produced his own "Weather Service Bulletin," including a "Weather Map of the Day" that rivaled the official Weather Bureau charts, furthering the divide between private and public meteorology.[45] In addition to the coverage of Krick, Stewart noted reportage on storm damage and the subsequent recovery efforts such as the Snow Patrol saving those buried in deep snow; airlines discussing the suspension of new transcontinental flights because of hazardous conditions; railways delaying shipments of necessary goods like milk and causing widespread shortages; and power failures caused by downed wires and famished rodent consumption, cutting telephone communication between loved ones.[46] But most of all, Stewart watched the unfolding public fascination with the winter storms and their calamitous effects. He witnessed the public's glee when discussing heroic rescues, their appreciation when contemplating nature in all of its majestic forms, and their sorrow at the countless lives lost in the disasters.[47]

Following the deadly winter storms, Stewart enlisted his Random House editor's assistance to write representatives of the occupations he noticed responding to the disasters in the news reports.[48] Two years later, he succeeded at shadowing everyone from the highway and snow patrolmen at the California Division of Highways and Department of Motor Vehicles; to the air and rail operators at Southern Pacific Railways, Pan American, and United Airlines; to the lighthouse operators and ship drivers working for the Coast Guard along the California coast; and even the reporters at the National Broadcasting Corporation (NBC) and United Press—all of whom he promised to include as characters in his book.[49] Through the course of his research, Stewart's appreciation for the weathermen at the Weather Bureau only increased. He regarded them as the heroes behind the scenes, directing the movements of those responding to the storms. And that was how he chose to focus his book—with the weathermen and the storm at its center, and with others cast in supporting roles. In this light, Stewart fashioned hurricanes in the best way he knew how—academic-style research. Thus, like those before him, Stewart's rationalization of hurricanes was based on history, fiction, and personal life experience.

To Stewart, the history of weather tracking and prediction was one of mistakes, corrections, and adaptations, animated by a tension between the human fear of the unknown and desire to control nature—or at least accurately predict it. The plot of *Storm* highlights this. Fittingly, the protagonist is a neophyte: an entry-level meteorologist at the California Weather Bureau. The unnamed young man, referred to throughout the novel as "Junior Meteorologist" or "J.M.," participates in the everyday mechanisms of the bureau and is fascinated by the peculiarities of prediction models, air-mass readings, and pressure fronts.[50] Having only been on the job for five weeks, though, he is not yet embedded in the bureaucracy, and has limited power to assuage the effects of storms. The Junior Meteorologist's colleagues in the Weather Bureau also remain unnamed throughout the book. All of these characters were inspired by the individuals Stewart interviewed and corresponded with while researching the book, including the Chief Meteorologist (or "the Chief"), the Navigator, the Chief Engineer, the Road Superintendent, and the Day Foreman.[51] Stewart's choice to focus on a low-ranking bureaucrat and leave the human characters unnamed places the focus on the novel's central character—the vibrant, violent storm. She is the only character in the novel with a name.

The naming of the hurricane is, in fact, a key plot point in the novel, and explains why Stewart centers the narrative around J.M. early in the book, Stewart reveals that as the Junior Meteorologist tracked storms, he surreptitiously assigned them female names, using a secret system he invented himself. As explained in the first chapter, "at first he [the Junior Meteorologist] christened each new-born storm after some girl he had known—Ruth, Lucy, Katherine."[52] But then J.M. moved on to naming storms after girls he had not known, adding an "-ia" suffix to each name as a way of standardizing the names. He did this because "a storm lived and grew; no two were ever the same"; thus, they were like girls he had known.[53] This system, Stewart discloses, was brilliant, as it allowed the Junior Meteorologist to track all of the storms in his system, watching them form and mature, creating story lines for each.

The system was meant to stay clandestine, though, as the Junior Meteorologist thought his superior (the Chief of the Weather Bureau) would not appreciate its creativity. J.M. was careful to only use the names in his head, never writing them on reports. In creating a secret system that J.M. and readers are privy to throughout the novel, Stewart creates intrigue about the naming system. It also provides the opportunity to explain why a naming system is unique and thus deviant. Stewart explains via J.M. that at first the naming system was unofficial, serving no other purpose than to quench the Junior Meteorologist's boredom amidst the monotony of his job. Second, that J.M.'s secrecy is directly related to Weather Bureau changes, efforts to standardize its practices, and professionalize its image.

After the introduction of characters and explanation of the secret naming system, the superstorm plot unfolds. J.M. is the first to spot the storm when it appears in his territory. J.M. proceeds to do his job, tracking the storm methodically using modern air-mass and climatological analysis, and by charting wind speed, temperatures, direction, and predictive strength. In doing so, the Junior Meteorologist demonstrates his proficiency in modern meteorology as he studies the emergence of the "baby storm" that first appears as a blip on the weather map.[54] Like other storms he is tracking—

which he dubbed Sylvia, Felicia, Cornelia, and Antonia—he gives this new storm a name: Maria.[55] Stewart explains that J.M. felt like he "had been a minister who had just christened a baby, [as] he found himself smiling and benign, inchoately wishing it joy and prosperity."[56] This storm is different, although he cannot say why. "Good luck, Maria!" he exclaims as he stares mesmerized at the radar.[57] Soon, Maria grows into a massive hurricane of unprecedented proportions. With increasing awe, J.M. tracks "her" progress, describing the storm as a "fast mover," "advanced," a "gigantic creature of the atmosphere," and even a "hussy." The Junior Meteorologist continually confirms that Maria is an "individual."[58] Throughout the storm's tumultuous progression, J.M. carefully guards its secret name, imbuing it with a mystical quality.

Midway through the book, it happens: J.M. slips and calls the storm Maria as he reports to his supervisor on the storm's progress. To his surprise, the Chief Meteorologist does not lash out in anger; instead, he commends J.M.'s naming system. The Chief Meteorologist then reveals that he also used a private naming system based on politicized names from history, like Hannibal, Marshal Ney, and Genghis Khan, but that he had discontinued the system when he ran out of names.[59] The Chief then praises J.M.'s system as superior to his own, as it is more efficient and flexible. With this climactic reveal, Stewart does two things: first, he cements "Maria" as a deviant and original name for a storm; second, he provides an example of a commendable and efficient naming system using female names exclusively. Stewart further confirms the uniqueness of this storm by introducing a second, smaller storm that is an offspring of the original, which he dubs "Little Maria." The smaller storm succeeds "her" "mother" by extending its wrath across the United States, beginning on the California coast and petering out days later in the New York region, much like the winter storms Stewart had experienced in 1939 and 1940. At its peak, Little Maria does not supplant Maria in the public's attention. Because of *Storm,* Stewart normalizes the naming of tropical storms. Maria became the face of the first named hurricane, an echoing phantasmagorical force that would forever shape the impression of storms to come.

Stewart's idea to feature a hurricane-naming system in the novel's plot was inspired by his research into the history of weather and meteorology. Although the Junior Meteorologist's fictional system was unlike any used by the US Weather Bureau up to that point, it bore some similarities to other systems used in the past. Through research, Stewart uncovered previous naming systems. His notes, for example, record the array of naming systems he ran across in mythology (for example, storm, wind, and air gods like Zeus and Tlaloc), philosophy (Socrates' "typhon"), religion (Jehovah's "whirlwind"), onomastic or etymological history of wind and storms (evolution of the word "wind" or "cyclone"), and meteorology.[60] It was by studying the latter that he encountered the meteorological lore of a late-nineteenth-century meteorologist named Clement Wragge, who had developed and attempted to popularize a controversial naming system in the 1880s.[61]

Clement Lindley Wragge was the chief meteorologist for Australia's Queensland Weather Bureau from 1887 to 1903. A spry, bearded man known for his "inclement" behavior, Wragge was born in England and quickly moved up the British weather command, taking over a section of Weather Bureau districts in the then-divided Australia. Though allotted limited purview over a portion of the districts, Wragge believed that he controlled all of Australia's weather tracking. The eccentric meteorologist raised eyebrows as he released weather reports containing information on all of Australia, not just the Queensland area. The media openly mocked his imperiousness but, much to the dismay of his fellow weathermen, Wragge's meteorological "kingdom" went unchallenged.[62]

As his weather reports attracted interest from the public, Wragge tested out various systems for storm warnings. First, he tried symbols and standardized warning messages. This included systematizing the reports to include information about various types of wind, rain, or other natural elements so they were reported identically across Queensland. Then, in 1894, the "well-known lecturer on the weather" decided to introduce a new system, naming tropical cyclones after Hebrew letters and Greek gods.[63] In 1896, Wragge tired of these systems and began using a more open-ended approach by giving cyclones female names. The Australian press, who followed Wragge's meteorological kingdom with amusement, weighed in on the new system. "One observes with great pleasure the new departure recently made by the Chief Weather Bureau in regard to the nomenclature of atmospheric depressions," stated an editorial published soon after. "It is hoped that Flora and Irene are only the beginning of a series of feminine names which will help to give a personal interest to the disturbances."[64] The columnist cautioned that the naming system could cause offense, though, suggesting that, before Wragge chose a name, he first contact women by that name for permission. Wragge responded with his typical aplomb, assuring the public that in deference to the women of Australia, he would choose only "soft dulcet names of the dusky beauties of the South Sea Islands" that "bubbled off the tongue." This included names like "Elina," "Mahina," and "Nachon." In fact, he reported, he hoped this approach would encourage mothers in the region to select such names for their own daughters.[65]

Wragge's female-only storm-naming system stirred up considerable discussion in Australia, further heightening interest in the Weather Bureau's actions and increasing Wragge's considerable position as the chief of his tiny fiefdom. But Wragge's perennial restlessness again got the best of him. In 1902, just six years after introducing the female-only cyclone-naming system, he introduced yet another new system.[66] This time, Wragge chose to name storms after well-known Australian politicians, particularly those who recently implemented cuts to the Weather Bureau budget. As a result, Wragge's new naming system quickly escalated into an outright war between himself and the Australian legislature.

One such discontent was Representative Alfred B. Conroy, for whom Cyclone Conroy was named in 1902. Conroy had been a leading critic of Wragge's misuse of Weather Bureau funds and power, openly calling Wragge a "Hottentot rain god," implying that he was primitive and uneducated. Wragge took offense and, in retaliation, named the next cyclone after Representative Conroy.[67] Numerous insults flew between Wragge and Conroy in the Australian press, including the accusation that Representative Conroy "look[ed] black and suspicious."[68] Neither Conroy nor other representatives who fell victim to Wragge's new cyclone-naming system appreciated it. Unfortunately for Wragge, Representative Conroy rallied the government to oust Wragge from the Weather Bureau, arguing that Wragge's antagonistic naming system was reason to call his scientific integrity into question. Within months of introducing the politician-based naming system, Wragge's funding was cut, he was forced out of his job, and his reputation was permanently marred. Unsurprisingly, the next Australian weather chief indefinitely suspended the cyclone-naming system in 1903, and Wragge's legacy faded.[69] But Wragge's creative naming systems became an apologue that reverberated in whispers throughout the global meteorological community for decades.[70]

In 1930s California, George Stewart discovered the cautionary tale of Wragge's cyclone-naming system in the course of his research for *Storm*. Wragge's story was recounted in particular detail in Sir Napier Shaw's 1919 text *Manual of Meteorology,* which was republished in 1938 just as Stewart began his research on the history of weather tracking.[71] The book was a touchstone for Stewart. He even quoted it in bold italics on the first page of *Storm:* "Every theory of the course of events in nature is necessarily based on some process of simplification of the phenomena and is to some extent therefore a fairy tale."[72] And what better fairy tale for Stewart to tell than a storm with a name that could be both villain and victor? In fact, the hurricane-naming system that Stewart uses in *Storm* is a simplified version of Wragge's, built from its most successful elements and filtered through current trends in Stewart's field. Besides, Wragge's female-only naming system for cyclones or large tropical storms in Australia was the most successful of his systems; in use for six years, it was also the longest-lasting storm-naming system to date. It did not have the political explosiveness that his subsequent naming system did, nor the constraints imposed by the alphabetic or Grecian god systems. The only complaint it had provoked was that Wragge should forewarn women whose names might be used for storms. Stewart considered all these points in the system's favor, calculating that the use of a single female name—familiar from classical literary characters like "Miranda" from *The Tempest* and "Daisy" from *The Great Gatsby*—would resonate with audiences.

Stewart recognized that, whatever his rationale for the design of his naming system, he needed to explain it fully in the text. In his detailed explanation of its purpose, features, and continued assessment in text, he confirms its significance and popularity. During the climactic reveal, he acknowledges that, while Maria was a fantasy, the scientific method of tracking it was not, nor was its purpose as a mechanism to explain the destructive power of a storm. Lastly, Stewart distances J.M.'s naming system from Wragge's tainted legacy by hinting that this storm-naming system was not the work of a chief meteorologist lusting for power, but rather by a low-level, eager, reasonable, and well-trained junior meteorologist who has access to the most advanced weather-tracking technology to date. In doing so, Stewart affirms what Wragge had discovered but then backed away from: when naming storms, female names work best. He could not have anticipated just how well received the female naming system, and the fictional storm Maria, would be.

Within weeks of *Storm* hitting the shelves in November 1941, news outlets lauded Stewart for his literary contribution and his masterful construction of a whole new kind of (nonhuman) female character. The *New York Times* proclaimed that "Few Novels Have Been More Minutely Planned Than Was 'Storm.'"[73] It further noted that, despite the years Stewart spent researching the book, "You will agree that he hasn't been wasting his time." In fact, the book was heralded as starting "a new fashion in the 'popularization' of science," particularly meteorology.[74] In 1941 it premiered as a Book of the Month Club choice, was reprinted in mass copies, and featured on bestseller lists.[75] Meanwhile, articles discussing the novel agreed that the main character, Maria, was the real star. According to reporter Walter Bara of the *Washington Post,* "'Storm' has not only a personality but also sex and reproductive power."[76] Other reviewers agreed; according to a brochure for the Book of the Month Club, "[t]he storm is its hero or rather, its heroine," and its heroine was now an American icon.[77] In January 1942, two months after the novel's publication, a major production company, Paramount Studios, announced that it had paid $30,000, a sizable sum at the time, for the rights to develop *Storm* into a movie.[78] The deal soon fell through amidst wartime cutbacks, and Stewart became engrossed in the production of his next book, *Names on the Land,* a detailed history of the place names of towns, cities, rivers, streets, and buildings throughout the United States.[79] Released in 1945, the book was viewed as an "onomastic masterpiece," and Stewart was again applauded for unmasking the "motivation of the namer" in the process of naming.[80] But even as Stewart moved on, *Storm* continued its rise in popularity, with reprinted editions appearing on the shelves every year.[81]

Secret Storms: Weather in Wartime

While Stewart enjoyed the balmy reception of *Storm,* the US Weather Bureau faced a flurry of new challenges brought on by World War II. As troops traversed the globe by land and sea, accurate weather projection was essential. In December 1941, President Franklin Roosevelt consolidated US weather services under Executive Order 8991, "provid[ing] for coordination of meteorological facilities in the prosecution of the war" under a joint Army-Navy task force.[82] This new oversight played a crucial role in the Weather Bureau's expansion of personnel during wartime. From 1942 to 1945, the number of Weather Bureau employees grew by 14 percent, rising from 11,716 employees in 1942 to roughly 16,914 employees by 1945.[83] Many of the new personnel were graduate-educated young men and professional meteorologists groomed in the increasingly standardized methods of weather tracking. Meanwhile, major technological advancements pushed meteorological science to meet the needs of wartime. The introduction of radar, for example, enabled meteorologists to track weather systems with greater precision, using electromagnetic pulses to reflect weather patterns or precipitation trajectories.

Notably, a vast number of the 5,000 new Weather Bureau employees hired between 1942 and 1945 were volunteers and part-time workers, many of whom were women. This hiring strategy was a direct response to the government's 1942 call for female volunteer workers to support the war effort. As stated in the announcement, the Weather Bureau welcomed such applications even though "there has been much prejudice against and few precedents for employing women generally for professional work in meteorology."[84] The statement proposed that the new jobs would present women with "opportunit[ies] to join the vanguard of the many women who [would] find careers in meteorology" in the future. Because of this three-year push to encourage female volunteers, the number of women working in meteorology positions rapidly increased from 2 to nearly 2,000.[85] The positions often involved clerical work, but sometimes also included training in meteorological techniques and measurement systems, as well as time spent as junior weather observers. Much like Rosie the Riveter and Wendy the Welder, the "Weather Woman" became a notable female personality of the wartime years. As women gained positions within meteorology during the war, though, their role was negated as a temporary solution created by wartime exigency. Even in the increasingly diverse weather world, there was no question that the weatherman was male.

Under the joint Army-Navy task force, the new class of (male) meteorological professionals learned to apply military codes, ciphers, and designations to weather patterns. One of these code systems was a brand-new standardized naming system for hurricanes and other tropical storms. The military, specifically US Army and Navy operators, introduced a code-naming system for tropical storms in 1944 as a way to discuss storms of the Pacific Theater during the expansion of US war efforts. Like other codes of the time, it was not released to the general public, nor intended for use past wartime. The code names were all female, chosen from among the names of meteorologists' and soldiers' girlfriends and wives. The names did not follow a particular (for example, alphabetical) order, nor were they ever officially recorded.[86]

While Weather Bureau records contain no formal documentation that confirms a specified reason for the adoption of this naming system, it did bear a striking resemblance to the famous storm-naming system of George Stewart's *Storm*. By 1944, the novel was in circulation for three years, garnering attention for its main character, Maria, and the Junior Meteorologist's catchy naming system. This included a special-edition reprint that appeared as part of the *Armed Services Edition* (or ASE program) ration kits in 1943. The ASE program, designed to entertain deployed soldiers with cheap government-issued printed versions of popular and classic books, doled out over 123 million books during the war. Stewart's *Storm* was among the first round of books sent to soldiers in 1943, just a year before the introduction of the US military's storm-naming system.[87] It is likely that any soldier or meteorologist during the time period read Stewart's *Storm,* and that the real-life naming system they developed was heavily inspired by the fictional storm, Maria.

In addition to Stewart's influence, the female-only code names chosen by the militarized meteorologists studying the Pacific Theater was also rooted in the larger shifts in gender constructions taking place during the war. US mobilization forced both men and women to rethink and renegotiate old gender divides in work, family, and social structures as men left for war and women kept the home front running. The Weather Bureau itself experienced these changes in the influx of female staff between 1942 and 1944, which raised more than a few eyebrows. On the home front, Rosie the Riveter, the Women's Auxiliary Corps (WACs), and the Women Accepted for Voluntary Emergency Service (WAVEs) exemplified a redefinition of femininity in both the private and public spheres. On the war front, as historian Robert Westbrook explains, the US government created more sexualized symbolic images of women for the men at war.[88] Distributed through placards or trading cards, representations of ample-bosomed beauties, known as "pin-ups," served as propaganda to remind the patriotic soldier what he was fighting for and what awaited him back home. Painted on planes, boats, and vehicles, pinups helped attach sexuality to these otherwise sexless objects.[89]

An inverse example of object gendering on the war front is seen in soldiers' characterization of the all-powerful atomic bomb as male. The two most famous atom bombs, dropped on Hiroshima and Nagasaki at the end of the war in 1945, were code-named "Fat Man" and "Little Boy." According to historian Elaine Tyler May, the gendering of the atomic bomb as male was directly related to its characterization as an object that could harness nature's most awesome power, an object that was invulnerable to any other tool produced to control or regulate the natural world.[90] The male gendering of the atom bomb in World War II exemplified the old notion, rooted deep in mythology and history, that man-made forces were undeniably masculine, natural forces were feminine—and that the process of civilization consisted of (male) humans conquering (female) nature. This belief directly carried over to the acceptance of the attachment of feminine names to tropical storms.

Whatever the precise inspirations for the system of code-naming Pacific Theater storms, it was extremely popular. Following the initial test year of 1944, the female-only storm-naming system was continued and expanded for 1945, the last year of the war.[91] This included sustained use of the names of girlfriends and wives as code names, likely inspiring salty behind-the-scenes conversations as the storms progressed and dissipated. In 1945, the code names followed an alphabetical order, featuring female code-names for every letter but "X." (See table 1.)

Table 1
Pacific Theater Female-Only Code-Naming List, 1945

Ann	Grace	Nancy	Tess
Betty	Helen	Nora	Ursula
Connie	Ida	Opal	Verna
Doris	Jean	Peggy	Wanda
Edna	Katie	Queenie	Yvonne
Eva	Louise	Ruth	
Francis	Marge	Susan	

Source: Discussed by Neal Dorst in telephone conversations and correspondence.

Though the female naming system was widely used among meteorologists and the military, it remained, like Stewart's in *Storm*, a well-kept secret during the war.[92] The secrecy of the system was maintained because wartime meteorological reports were subject to censorship rules that might afford the enemy an advantage, allowing them to deliberately attack during a major storm while defenses were weakened. In this context, it is easy to see why Stewart's book was popular with men at war as the secrecy alone drew relatable connections to the novel. Coupled with larger changes in military, meteorological, and gender history, the female gendering of storms in the Pacific Theater during World War II makes sense. How much of a lingering influence Stewart's *Storm* would have on the cultural imagination in the postwar era is undetermined.

We Call the Wind Maria

After the declaration of peace in 1945, weather became the fastest-growing field of federal services as Americans demanded more from their weather service than ever before. As stated in a report on the "use of the Weather Bureau's output" after World War II, "its forecasting services probably touch directly the immediate needs of more people of the United States than do all federal services combined, with the single exception of the Post Office."[93] In response to demilitarization, the Weather Bureau again made changes to its structure and personnel. While the postwar period was a boon for weather services, it also provided a significant challenge—the threat of usurpation by an emerging, privatized field of meteorology.[94] The training in meteorological studies during the war and development of new resources to track it had resulted in a burgeoning private industry seeking to take advantage of this new consumer market and a range of qualified individuals post-demilitarization. The Weather Bureau, recognizing this problem, focused on recruitment. By the mid-1950s, Weather Bureau employment surpassed wartime employment statistics, averaging 32,700 employees ranging from full-time to volunteer observers.[95]

Many of these new (male) employees had received graduate-level training in the field of meteorology during the war and represented a new class of weathermen for the postwar era. With a newly trained graduate-level staff of meteorologists and advanced technology features, such as radar and tracking planes, prediction capabilities increased exponentially. Meanwhile, as censorship bans ended, weather reporting proliferated. Weather-related items like forecasts and maps quickly permeated every facet of American culture in the postwar era. By 1945, nearly every daily newspaper printed weather information on the front page. The same year, the Weather Bureau provided weather forecasts four to six times daily for 700 to 800 radio broadcasting stations throughout the country. Two years later, 157 commercial radio stations broadcast live directly from Weather Bureau offices, no longer waiting for the once-daily report. By the following year, the bureau introduced an automatic telephone service for major cities, where individuals could call in to hear a recorded message detailing their city's current daily weather predictions and warnings. During bad weather, the service received over 250,000 calls per day.[96]

The US Weather Bureau also sought to expand the purview of its weather-tracking capabilities worldwide. The Weather Bureau launched training programs for personnel in Latin America, the Caribbean, and Pacific Ocean regions. The Latin-American Training Program alone trained over 400 weather reporters in American meteorological techniques and terminology.[97] By setting up new weather stations and providing meteorological supplies, these programs contributed to the standardization and worldwide spread of American meteorological terms and weather-reporting practices, not to mention the consumption of American-based cultural products. For example, the US Weather Bureau provided stations with everything from balloons used to take air measurements, to the physical facility of the weather station.[98] The US Weather Bureau also took a primary role in the formation of the World Meteorological Organization (WMO) in 1950, a branch of the United Nations. This new organization, formed during the reorganization of world powers postwar, replaced a previous international organization, known as the International Meteorological Organization (IMO). While the United States trailed other world powers in its meteorological capabilities at its founding in 1873, this new organization signified the rapid, successful growth of US meteorological influence on the global stage.[99]

As the Weather Bureau expanded its services, personnel, and purview in response to increased demand for meteorology after the war, a corresponding cultural trend was also at work: the creation of the "Weather Man" as a cultural icon. With a greater volume of weather reporting on television, and a growing number of televisions in American homes, the Weather Man—part privatized meteorologist, part showman—became a fixture of nightly news broadcasts. A sort of cult of meteorology developed as these weathermen, like titans with chalkboards and weather maps, became favorites of local and national newscasts, often judged for the accuracy of their predictions but rarely for their rhetoric. Americans tuned in to watch their predictions as though they were sportscasters giving play-by-plays on precipitation. Weathermen usually balanced jovial personalities with the gravitas of meteorological training many had received through the growth of the industry and wartime necessities, but also stressed their reliance on the Weather Bureau for confirmation of and consultation on their findings. In this way, the Weather Bureau was positioned as the authority of all weather-related information.[100]

The most significant postwar-era change in the Weather Bureau, though, was the phasing out of the practice of code-naming hurricanes and other tropical storms. The US Weather Bureau decided to end the code-naming practice on the grounds that it was unnecessary for peacetime military communications and never meant for public consumption, especially on the US mainland.[101] But this did not stop word of the naming system from getting out. The postwar years brought several crushing meteorological disasters, raising questions over storm-naming systems and lists used secretly during the war. Storms in 1947 and 1948 wreaked havoc in the Gulf South states, with annual identical landfalls dates, creating some confusion in the multitude of weather reports about the storms.[102] In Louisiana, "The 1947 Ripper" caused considerable damage to property and life, shredding the coastline over Labor Day weekend.[103] The following year, another storm appeared on the horizon as the holiday weekend approached, while mass confusion ensued as weathermen struggled to report on the current storm's path. Reports on the "September Storm" or the "Labor Day Storm" confounded listeners as weathermen tried to describe the differences from "the hurricane of September of last year" with the "current hurricane."[104] Citizens of the Gulf Coast openly proclaimed their dislike of this reportage, calling for a solution to this confusing predicament while pointing out that this was both a regional and a national concern of utmost importance as this part of the country was both the home of the National Hurricane Center and in the path of a higher frequencies of storms.

After the confusion created by the storms of 1947 and 1948, the Weather Bureau implemented an unofficial naming system for all internal communications, the Joint Army/Navy Phonetic Alphabet.[105] (See table 2.) This system mimicked the wartime code-naming system that used only female names, by using standardized military names (beginning with "Able, Baker, Charlie") to ward off any assumptions of misogyny. It contained no references to gender, was standardized, and was familiar to weather officials trained during the war. To make it easy to remember, the same names were repeated each year, starting at the top of the list and working down one by one, through all letters of the alphabet, including "X." Names were only assigned to storms that reached a specific strength (fully formed), and were only used to refer to tropical storms like hurricanes or cyclones. Even though the Weather Bureau designed this system to be less controversial, it was still intended for use for the purposes of identification in internal weather reports and not for communication with the public.

The Weather Bureau used the new Joint Army/Navy Phonetic Alphabet Naming System internally for the next four years due to its popularity, altering it slightly from its original form. Then, in 1951, the Weather Bureau implemented it publicly, introducing the first storm of that year as "Hurricane Able."[106] The following year, though, the naming system hit a snag. In the postwar demilitarization, the Weather Bureau was reclassified from a subsidiary of the military to an independent organization. This change meant that the organization was now free from military oversight. Weather Bureau

Table 2
Joint Army/Navy Phonetic Alphabet Naming System, 1948, for Internal Use

Able	George	Mike	Sugar	Yoke
Baker	How	Nan	Tare	Zebra
Charlie	Item	Oboe	Uncle	
Dog	Jig	Peter	Victor	
Easy	King	Queen	William	
Fox	Love	Roger	X-ray	

Source: L. J. Rose, "Aviation's ABC: The Development of ICAO spelling alphabet," *ICAO Bulletin,* November 2, 1956, 12–14, Records of the Weather Bureau, 1735–1979, Record Group 130, National Archives and Records Administration, College Park, MD.

officials decided to distance the bureau from the military, particularly in the naming and labeling processes. This meant replacing the Joint Army/Navy Phonetic Alphabet system with the less militaristic International Phonetic Alphabet.[107]

While the list otherwise remained the same, slight revisions to the storm-naming system lists grossly affected the media's attitude toward it. Weather reporters throughout the country, confused by the fluctuating name lists, often misprinted the names, mistakenly used old name lists, or deliberately substituted other names out of dislike for the new names chosen. These problems—coupled with the growth of the privatized meteorology industry using their own phonetic alphabet lists, like the International Air Transport Association list and International Civil Aviation Organization list—meant that the processes for naming storms quickly got out of hand.[108] (See table 3.)

As the Weather Bureau was growing into its postwar independence, and the multiple-storm seasons of 1947 and 1948 put hurricanes firmly back in the spotlight, George Stewart's *Storm* still gripped the public imagination. As a result, Stewart was asked to write a new introduction reflecting on the book's popularity in 1947. In the 1947 edition, he reinforced the cultural significance of his femme fatale, specifying that Maria's name is pronounced as if there is a silent "h" at the end, like Maria(h).[109] Four years later in 1951, a hit new Broadway musical about the California Gold Rush, *Paint Your Wagon,* premiered, featuring an iconic single that was clearly inspired by *Storm*. The song, "They Call the Wind Maria," proclaimed that rain was known as "Tess," fire known as "Joe," but that the wind was forever known as "Maria." In a slow, melodic crooning, "Maria" is repeated twenty times in a sixteen-line stanza.[110] The musical, written by newly famous lyricist Alan Lerner, best known for *Brigadoon* (1947), and featuring music by Frederick Loewe, who would later collaborate with Lerner on *My Fair Lady* and *Camelot,* debuted on the same Broadway strip as *The King and I* and *A Tree Grows in Brooklyn*.[111] Its song was an immediate hit, and, one of the most memorable aspects of the play.[112] By the end of the year, a recording produced with the unmistakable baritone of Vaughan Moore became one of the most popular singles of the year.[113] While the "Maria" described in the song and play was not the Maria of Stewart's fantasies, it was certainly inspired by it. They even pronounced the name correctly in the song, singing it over and over again for repeated effect. By the start of 1952, Warner Brothers

Table 3
Phonetic Alphabets Used for Storm Names, 1948–1952

Joint Army/Navy Phonetic Alphabet Naming System, 1948 (internal use)	WMO International Phonetic Alphabet, 1951 (public use)	International Civil Aviation Organization Phonetic Alphabet (ICAO), 1952 (industry use)
Able	Alfa	Alfa
Baker	Bravo	Bravo
Charlie	Coca	Charlie
Dog	Delta	Delta
Easy	Echo	Echo
Fox	Foxtrot	Foxtrot
George	Golf	Golf
How	Hotel	Hotel
Item	India	India
Jig	Juliet(t)	Juliett
King	Kilo	Kilo
Love	Lima	Lima
Mike	Metro	Mike
Nan	Nectar	November
Oboe	Oscar	Oscar
Peter	Papa	Papa
Queen	Quebec	Quebec
Roger	Romeo	Romeo
Sugar	Sierra	Sierra
Tare	Tango	Tango
Uncle	Union	Uniform
Victor	Victor	Victor
William	Whiskey	Whiskey
X-ray	Extra	X-ray
Yoke	Yankee	Yankee
Zebra	Zulu	Zulu

Sources: L. J. Rose, "Aviation's ABC: The Development of ICAO spelling alphabet," *ICAO Bulletin,* November 2, 1956, 12–14; "Aeronautical Telecommunications: Annex 10 to the Convention on International Civil Aviation," vol. 2, chap. 5; International Telecommunication Union, "Appendix 16: Phonetic Alphabet and Figure Code" (Geneva: ITU, 1959), 430–31, all from Records of the Weather Bureau, 1735–1979, Record Group 130, National Archives and Records Administration, College Park, MD.

Note: There is at least one variation in each cycle of name between all three lists. For example, for the "A" storm, one list includes the name "Able" while the others use "Alfa."

Studios contracted to produce *Paint Your Wagon* as a movie, while Walt Disney bought the rights to make *Storm* into a made-for-TV special. This time, Stewart's movie came to fruition, premiering as part of *Walt Disney's Wonderful World of Color* programming in full Technicolor. It was even renamed *A Storm Called Maria* to feature the storm more prominently.[114]

"They Call the Wind Maria" did more than just entertain the masses infatuated with Stewart's *Storm;* it reinforced the growing twentieth-century concept of the wind as gendered. It also inspired a Weather Bureau struggling with a confusing naming system to alter its course definitively. In 1953, the US Weather Bureau introduced a new naming system for hurricanes and other tropical storms. This system included a naming list that diverged from the traditional phonetic alphabets used since 1948, using female names, beginning with "Alice."[115] It also included new standardized rules for name use. Each name on the list was to be used once and spelled identically to the name on the list in all announcements made about the storm. New lists featuring different female names were published yearly. Reports on the new naming system quickly proclaimed that the "namers"—vaguely identified as "weather officials"—were merely attempting to "avoid confusion" in using this new sex-specific naming system.[116] The Weather Bureau chief, Ivan Ray Tannehill, was quick to point out that this system differed from the problematic systems of the past in that "only two names were picked with real people in mind"—"Orpha," for a girl in one of the Weather Bureau's offices, and "Wallis" for the scandalous Duchess of Windsor.[117] While the Weather Bureau officials noted that the female-only naming list was in a test phase, they expressed optimism that it might provide the long-sought solution to the problem of hurricane naming. In any case, excitement over the new system proliferated.

No evidence has been found to suggest that George Stewart was consulted about the new female-only naming list before its debut in 1953. However, he definitely received comment requests from reporters as soon as the announcement was made. While he continued to publish other works, including a postapocalyptic science-fiction novel called *Earth Abides*—which topped *Storm* on the best-seller lists and later inspired authors like Stephen King—he never forgot the attention *Storm* garnered. Seeing outright change take place in Weather Bureau processes was a highlight of his career, one that he documented with careful attention. In 1942, before the book had grown to its eventual popularity, he donated his extensive notes from *Storm*'s research and clippings about his cherished Maria to his alma matter, Princeton University. He knew he had impacted the perception of storms through his book.

And Stewart could not have been more right about the impact, not just because of the book's contents but more because of its timing. In creating his fictitious character Maria, Stewart utilized a destructive feminine character—the femme fatale—to place his work within other popular literature of the time. In doing so, he connected his own personal obsession with meteorological history and his professional training as a literature professor. Pushing Stewart's own motivations aside for a moment, the book's popularity both within the war and after also signify a key moment in American (and more particularly, Gulf South) cultural responses to disaster. *Storm* was published at a critical juncture of meteorological, gender, and cultural change occurring during the war and postwar period. Built on a longer history of the anthropomorphization and feminization of nature, the desire to conquer and control fearful natural hazards, and the growing fascination with destruction, the book provided both fact and fiction. Coupled with wartime needs on every level of society including gender politics that encouraged the adoption of a similar naming system for storms within the war, its increasing popularity within the cultural period is not only easily explained but expected. But what makes it even more fascinating is that, even with postwar changes in bureaucratic systems, the unique naming system inspired by Stewart's Maria never faded into the background. Largely due to the popularity of *Storm, Paint Your Wagon,* and the hit song "They Call the Wind Maria," the secret was out: everyone now knew that *we call the wind* Maria. What effect this new naming system would have on the perception of storms in the future, though, was largely up in the air.

CAMILLE
AND COLD WAR SEXUAL POLITICS

In August 1969, the eyes of Americans were on the skies. Just weeks before, the world was transfixed by grainy television footage of Neil Armstrong's slow-motion dance across the surface of the moon. Now, a different sky drama played out in even slower motion as a massive storm loomed over the Gulf Coast. The growing blip on a radar screen, representing a soon-to-be 175-mile-wide swirl of wind and rain, was moving toward the Mississippi River delta. Over four days, the radar blip expanded from a pinprick to a blob. Newscasters soon announced the female name for the storm: Camille.[1] Like every hurricane since 1954, it was selected from an annual list of female names published by the US Weather Bureau. And it was especially fitting, recalling the virgin warrior queen of Virgil's *Aeneid*, Camillus, known for her ability to run so quickly over oceans that her feet remained dry.[2] But as this Camille approached, she was less a noble warrior than a sinister villain, appearing more dangerous than previous hurricanes. Americans, especially residents of the Gulf Coast, were still recovering from the last Big One, Betsy, which hit the New Orleans vicinity in 1965, and their recent memory contained dozens of other massive storms that had destroyed homes, cities, and precious infrastructure of the growing nation while killing thousands—much as World War II had devastated lives and property a quarter-century before.

Since the official adoption of the female-only naming system at the end of 1953, inspired by George R. Stewart's novel and rallied for by the American people themselves, storms were described as decidedly female. Camille was constructed in this way—and by the time she struck the Gulf Coast, "she" was the ultimate Cold War villain: terrifying, unpredictable, and beyond the control of man. Unless that is, a weapon could stop it.

In the case of Camille, the promise of a weapon turned the American public's dread into tense anticipation. The US Weather Bureau, including its research branch, Project STORMFURY, was eager to use their new weapon, years in the making. It was a specially designed "ice" bomb, meant to cool a hurricane's energies by weakening its powerful winds through a process called "seeding." This process included heroically flying into the eye of a storm, "penetrating" its winds while dropping a container filled with silver iodide crystals meant to "freeze" the storm from the inside out. Countless hours were spent developing the seeding process over the past fifteen years, and represented American's latest, greatest hope to tame nature with weaponized science.[3] Science was the hope Americans had pinned their visions of postwar hegemony, reinforced by successes like the moonwalk of 1969, the curing of polio, and the ongoing negotiation of tentative world peace with hostile nuclear-armed nations. In this precarious Cold War climate, hurricanes represented everything Americans most feared: uncontrollable forces of destruction descending from the skies, laying waste the nation's growing infrastructure and booming population. If Americans divined how to tame winds and rains, they could not only save millions of dollars and countless lives; they could also demonstrate their potency and vigor to themselves and the rest of the world. No region was more vulnerable to these threats than the Gulf South; thus, the people of this region led the way in attempts to stop the storms. So it was that in August 1969, Hurricane Camille became a target of Americans' efforts and energies. They had tried hurricane seeding before, but failed. If it worked this time, they would forever be set free from the willful women who served as nature's deadliest weapons. On August 18, 1969, the battle commenced. Reconnaissance planes flew south to measure the growing storm, and over 200 weather experts spaced across the Gulf South region readied their equipment for their greatest seeding experiment yet.[4]

Where did Americans get the crazy idea that they could control a hurricane? This desire manifested during the Cold War as Americans progressed in weaponizing nature through science. The strength of the atomic bomb terrified the globe in Hiroshima and Nagasaki in 1945, with the sheer size of the blast, its subsequent radiation effects, and utilization for ending a global war. Initial reaction to it was one of horror and contemplation over the possibilities wrought by technological advancement. Assessment of the bomb's size and strength rapidly weighed it with other hazards. The American public debated: Was the atomic bomb more or less like a hurricane? An earthquake? Or a flood? And, if it was different, just how different was it? They all came to the same conclusion: the atomic bomb was most similar to the hurricane in terms of its destructive capabilities and lack of control (both in efforts to respond and to mitigate its effects). Thus, the two greatest threats to American lives were the atomic bomb and the hurricane. As attempts were made to control the atomic bomb, additional efforts were made to control the hurricane. Americans poured time, energy, and personnel into this perpetual war against nature, one where humans had a chance at controlling their environment and even repurposing its energies.

Beneath the drive to control nature was a deep anxiety, a fear of disorder and incoherence fueled by the idea that American hegemony depended on its maintaining a monolithic culture. Another way that anxiety manifested was in the need to (re)domesticate women after the chaos of World War II. During the war, gender roles, rewritten to accommodate the departure of husbands and brothers for war, necessitated the creation of two roles for women: the laborer and the idyllic fantasy. Now that the war had ended, and men were back home to rebuild the United States' economic, political, and cultural power, women were expected to "return" to a life they never had. The American woman's job was to remain within the home, physically and psychically, and females across regions and classes were measured against this idea of femininity, reinforced by advertising, television shows, and literature.

Yet this ideal clashed with more transgressive notions of femininity that opposed familiar images of perfect womanhood such as June Cleaver in *Leave It to Beaver*.[5] As a result, transgressive women were painted as abnormal or unwanted. This, for example, is the central tension of the popular show *Bewitched,* in which Samantha, a witch living as a suburban American wife, constantly strives to fit in with her conventional neighbors, and frequently fails with comedic effect.[6] Humor aside, the show's point was clear: in postwar America, sameness and normalcy were good, and difference and transgression were bad. Meanwhile, the publication of subversive texts like Alfred Kinsey's studies of male and female sexual activities (1948 and 1953) threatened the constructed conservative norm.[7] Such expressions of sexual freedom heightened cultural anxieties about the role of women in Cold War America.

In this climate, it was even proposed that the United States was more vulnerable to foreign attack if it were destabilized by the sexual liberties of transgressive women. The threat of such women was likened to that of the atomic bomb or disasters such as hurricanes. This fear was created through a variety of means, most forcefully through legal measures, symbolism, and description. As a result, following World War II, Americans started gendering nuclear debates. The atomic bomb, for example, was originally deemed a masculine object due to its destructive capabilities. However, following the war, it was "domesticated," "tamed," and "harnessed" for peace. The strength of nuclear energy was repurposed back into the home.[8]

At the same time, the term "bombshells" emerged as a way to refer to sexually expressive women.[9] While the term arose in the 1930s, its usage and general acceptance grew in the postwar period as emphasis on sexually deviant behavior of women was a primary concern. Comparisons of sexualized women with atomic bombs—and vice versa—linked destructive and uncontrollable behavior to national destabilization. And like the atom bomb, bombshells needed to be "tamed" by force back into the suburban American home. Just as bombs were developed to control and harness nuclear energy, women needed to be domesticated in order to contribute to the building up rather than the destabilization of the nation. After the introduction of the female hurricane-naming system, the use of female names for hurricanes became one cultural site for the postwar rhetorical domestication of women. And beginning with the hurricane season of 1954, the epicenter of that response was the Gulf Coast. It was there that the US Weather Bureau was situated, and there that the greatest hurricanes of the Cold War made landfall.

The drive to tame nature, so characteristic of the Cold War, manifested in specific ways in the Gulf South. World War II brought an expansion of wartime military bases, while postwar economic growth fueled the expansion of industries, creating a boom in coastal development, especially in Sunbelt cities like Miami, New Orleans, and Houston and their surrounding suburbs.[10] The population increased in these Sunbelt cities by over 1.2 million people between 1940 and 1970, not including those in adjacent suburbs or counties. (See table 4.) To accommodate this rapidly multiplying population, massive building projects fueled what southern historian C. Vann Woodward called the "Bulldozer Revolution," where bulldozers demolished the old landscape, replacing it with a new one.[11]

Table 4
Population of Selected Gulf South Cities, 1940–1970

City	1940	1950	1960	1970	Total Growth of Population, 1940–1970
Biloxi	17,475	37,425	44,053	48,486	31,011
Houston	384,514	596,163	938,219	1,232,802	848,288
Miami	172,172	249,276	291,688	334,859	162,687
Mobile	78,720	129,009	194,856	190,026	111,306
New Orleans	494,537	570,445	627,525	593,471	98,934

Source: US Census Bureau, Decennial Census, www.census.gov/programs-surveys/decennial-census/data/datasets.2010.html.

Note: All Gulf South cities saw considerable population changes that significantly impacted the size and structure of the region. Miami, home of the National Hurricane Center and Weather Bureau, experienced a significant growth postwar both within and outside of its city limits.

Shaping these changes was the ideology of the American Dream, an idealized yet attainable goal of postwar wealth and prosperity unparalleled in previous eras. Reshaping of one's personal and physical surroundings to meet modern standards was an integral part of the American Dream, also a particularly arduous goal for residents of the Gulf South, who had a long and fraught history of attempts to control their natural world. While their picture-window lifestyle expanded, Gulf South residents fervently sought to eliminate all threats from within and outside of the home. They deployed biological, technological, and cultural weapons to combat the forces that threatened the future of their region. Their fight to tame nature ultimately influenced the rest of the country as hurricanes of not only the Gulf South became targets of these pursuits.

Efforts to combat nature in the Gulf South and make it more inhabitable had been a priority since the region's earliest residents settled there. In the eighteenth century, colonists had struggled to build levee structures and drainage systems, fight rampant disease and insects that thrived in the perpetual warmth, and live in a region prone to quick-onset disaster.[12] As the

Industrial Revolution brought steam-powered technology, so followed efforts to drain swampland and create elaborate pump systems to rid the land of water.[13] By the twentieth century, efforts to dry the land centered on the construction of flood-control structures like the Galveston, Texas, seawall, dams, and spillways, intended to prevent water from encroaching again.[14] But Gulf South residents, try as they might, never could completely control their natural world. Over the first half of the twentieth century, pesky animals and waters continued to seep in through backed-up drainage routes and levees that had displaced them.[15]

The Gulf South's quest to tame nature, or at least carve out comfortable homes and habitations amidst the marshes, bayous, and beaches of the nation's southeastern coast, saw a victory in 1951. That year, the first modern air-conditioning window unit hit the shelves. As historian Raymond Arsenault explained, this new product was quickly incorporated into southern homes, hospitals, and government buildings in order to prevent the natural world from encroaching on the human-built environment. By the late 1960s, over half of the homes in the South included air conditioning, with the highest percentage of use in Gulf South states. This number would only expand in the following decade, as Gulf South residents were freed from a sentence of perpetual sweat.[16] In a related technological innovation, modern refrigeration came to simplify the process of acquiring and preserving food through products like General Electric's classic Frigidaire, International Harvester's "7-Climate Refrigerator," and Kelvinator's "Foodarama."[17] These two cooling technologies, air conditioning and refrigeration, did much more than make a hellish climate more bearable. These technologies made possible the growth in population and industry that created the Sunbelt cities. With the climate now under control, postwar production peaked at unprecedented levels, driving the movement of people into the region—and increasing the concern over the control of the newly bulldozed surroundings.

Another wartime technological advancement that contributed to the development of the Gulf South in the 1950s and 1960s was pest control. The chemical Dichlorodiphenyltrichloroethane, or DDT, debuted to a consumer market in 1945 as an insecticide meant to revolutionize Gulf South homes. Produced in liquid, powder, and aerosol form, it had the power to kill bugs, rodents, and other vermin that encroached on human habitations. As described in advertisements and PSAs, DDT was the weapon of choice against every pest from roaches to mosquitoes. One promotional ad even exhorted Gulf South residents, "DDT: Let's Put It Everywhere."[18] With this powerful weapon to extinguish pests, residents could rid their homes of unwanted elements of the natural world and live comfortably in a space under human control. Meanwhile, outside the walls of the prefab suburban structure, southerners sought to sculpt the landscape itself. Developers cut down large swaths of trees, displaced wildlife, implemented weed-eradication programs, and defended the turf by spraying chemicals such as DDT on areas prone to mosquitoes, fire ants, roaches, and other pests plaguing the fields, waterways, and homes.[19] In the minds of Gulf South residents and Americans at large, this war on the natural world, waged with tools of weaponized science, was closely related to the wars being fought abroad against human armies. As explained by historian Joshua Blu Buhs, residents of the Gulf South often described the infamous red fire ants—the hymenopterous annoyance of the everyday and nemesis of agriculture, cattle, and bare feet— as "communist aggressors" who threatened to infiltrate America from the ground up.[20] These "red menaces" of southern lawns and fields were averted, though, with the right chemical, time, and care, giving hope to the once-hopeless residents.

Other tools in the postwar arsenal included medical advancements such as broad-spectrum antibiotics like penicillin and vaccines for diseases such as polio, all proving that humans had the ability for the first time to stave off anything that might influence their ability to obtain and enjoy the American Dream.[21] For a region historically cursed by a high mortality rate due to disease, these advancements allowed Gulf South residents to view everything as an obstacle that could be tackled with time and human ingenuity. Despite all efforts to control nature in the Gulf South, residents of the region could never quite forget their vulnerability—as they were forcefully reminded every time a hurricane blew through.

The desire to control nature fueled the study of hurricanes as early as the late 1940s through efforts to track and harness its terrifying power. Throughout World War II and into the postwar era, much had changed in Americans' understanding of the hurricane. Professionalization programs trained weathermen at graduate levels, new tracking technology such as radar made storm imaging available to the masses, and the public came to value weather-tracking reportage and expected to access it in their everyday lives.²² Still, much about the hurricane remained mysterious and therefore threatening. The government got in front of this threat, as it had with the atomic bomb, chemical pesticides, and medicines, by sponsoring programs devoted to the study of hurricanes. In 1947, the still-militarized Weather Bureau formed a research project known as Project CIRRUS.²³

As military-sponsored scientific research, Project CIRRUS relied on the same ideology that had driven the development of the atomic bomb. That is, nature was a weapon to harness, and the implications of doing so were not just political but also moral. In theory, the purpose of the project was to study the trajectory of storms by using radar and plane tracking, and eventually, to discover a way to lessen storms' effects. It was a natural progression for a military recently reminded of the significance of accurate weather predictions and destructive hazard mitigation.²⁴ Project CIRRUS took the concept of weather mitigation further, positing that weather control was possible through a "seeding" process. As proposed, "seeding" hurricanes with ice would cool their core and decrease their strength. Planes would drop the equivalent of "ice bombs" into a hurricane's "eye," causing a rapid cooling that slowed the storm's movement, redirected it, or dissipated it all together.²⁵

The impetus for Project CIRRUS was a September 1947 storm known to the public as "The 1947 Ripper."²⁶ The fourth major storm of the season had pummeled the Gulf Coast, causing $160 million in damages ($1.7 billion in 2018) as it swung across Florida's peninsula and pummeled the southern coast of Louisiana, overtopping levees in New Orleans. Unofficially codenamed "George" using the Joint Army/Navy Phonetic Alphabet Naming System, the code name was never released in public bulletins or used in announcements but shaped meteorologists' favorable impression of the naming system and led to the broader introduction of the phonetic-alphabet name list the following year.

A month after "George," Project CIRRUS launched. A joint effort by the US Army Signal Corps, the Office of Naval Research, the US Air Force, and General Electric Corporation, Project CIRRUS represented a collaboration among the military, the meteorological profession, and industry—a true example of the combined scientific and militaristic concern of the postwar nuclear-influenced world. The project employed a new, dedicated unit of aeronautical weather trackers provided by the Air Force known as "Hurricane Hunters," who flew daily weather-watching missions in their fleet of well-equipped weather aircraft. Supporting the Hurricane Hunters were newly staffed weather operations centers spread across the United States and the Caribbean. Like other postwar heroes, the Hurricane Hunters were quickly deified as weather warriors hell-bent on chasing storms and reporting their every movement to the public in detail.[27]

The Project CIRRUS team wasted no time in testing its new experiment. On October 13, 1947, a storm, informally code-named "King," formed in the Atlantic that met the minimum criteria for a modification attempt: it veered eastward off the Atlantic coast and was unlikely to strike land or inflict direct damage. As the Project CIRRUS team mobilized, Americans watched their televisions in gleeful anticipation as news programs reported details of a B-17 plane that dropped 80 pounds of crushed dry ice into the eye of the hurricane. At first, it appeared that the process worked; the hurricane continued away from the shoreline. The public's delight soon turned to horror as the storm suddenly veered towards the Atlantic Seaboard and made landfall near Savannah, Georgia. It brought with it a 12-foot storm surge that caused considerable flooding and damage. The public was outraged, with many Georgia residents blaming the storm's track change on the seeding process, even threatening to sue the government for the damage caused by the storm. Amidst the fury, Project CIRRUS was shuttered.[28] The notion of hurricane modification, however, would die a much slower death.

In 1954, a renewed push to track and control hurricanes emerged. Between 1947 and 1954, the Weather Bureau was tasked with navigating the transition from military wartime procedures to peacetime needs, while also meeting the increasing demand for weather services. Through this period, the popular consumption of weather services grew exponentially. Severe weather became increasingly important to the day-to-day operations of an ever-expanding population along the Gulf South coastline, and was the central focus of millions of residents as dozens of devastating storms made landfall. Another factor drew attention to hurricanes: they had just received new (female) names.

Controlling Hurricanes through Rhetorical Gendering: The Bad Girls of '54

The first female-named hurricane season was off to a listless start. In June 1954, Hurricane Alice blew through Mexico, veered towards Texas, and dissipated at the Texas-Mexico border. Even in its short lifetime, the storm prompted reporters and weathermen across the country to play with the imaginative possibilities of naming a storm. They agreed that "Alice" was a fitting choice for the first storm named in this system, as the Walt Disney movie *Alice in Wonderland* debuted three years before. The storm was like the spirited young fictional character in that, in the end, everything turned out fine.[29] Given the relatively limited damage caused by the storm—disastrous flooding in the Rio Grande Valley—the public quickly lost interest in fleshing out its character. The next month brought another hurricane, dubbed "Barbara," which was similarly anticlimactic. As Barbara "blew out harmlessly" into the Caribbean, reporters wondered whether the new naming system would catch on after all.[30]

Their doubts reversed when a third storm, Carol, came ashore in the first days of September. Forming off the northern Bahamas, it had ample time to gain strength in the warm Atlantic waters before heading up the Eastern Seaboard toward Boston. The storm's landfall in Long Island was deadly, leaving behind 54 fatalities and $462 million in damages ($4.3 billion in 2018).[31] As the first major storm of the 1954 season, Carol left reporters clamoring at the opportunity to describe its nature and impact in newly personified terms. From Miami to Boston, reporters pronounced Carol a fierce "howler" who "maul[ed]" the East Coast after having "wallow[ed] aimlessly" for days, and then turned into a "runaway hurricane," that retreated into the sea with "much of its fury spent."[32] These terms were not original; hurricane accounts of the past had also used words like "howler," "mauling," and "wallowing." But some of the terminology Carol inspired was decidedly new. For the first time, reporters described a hurricane as having distinctly feminine attributes, even referring to it as "she." Reporters at the *Raleigh News & Observer* were some of the first to use such gendered descriptors, reporting that Carol was "everything *but* feminine as she blew out of North Carolina's area."[33] "Her" "whirling body" and "furious" sweep left the Eastern Seaboard devastated, reporters in Boston and Baltimore concurred.[34] Meanwhile, "her" "sister" storm, Dolly, followed on her "heels," creating even more chaos.[35] Dolly was a disappointment compared to her older sister, though, petering out near New England and Nova Scotia.

Before the wounded eastern coastline recovered from these "sisters," another storm formed on the horizon, this one designated as Edna.[36] The fifth storm of the season, Edna initially seemed "skittish" and developed slowly.

Soon, though, Edna escalated into a "carbon copy of Hurricane Carol," and followed the same trajectory up the Eastern Seaboard.[37] As Edna geared up, it "slapped" Florida and split into "twins" near North Carolina, giving no indication of diminishing.[38] The country watched the storm's progress anxiously as "Edna wept her violent meteorological tantrum" for "seventeen hours" over New York City.[39] As it lingered over New York, Massachusetts, and Maine, reporters took the opportunity to spin ever more sensational descriptions. The *New York Times* noted that Edna "maintained the prerogative of changing her mind."[40] The *Miami Herald* depicted the storm as a drunken "freak of nature" that seemed to stall, flirt with Miami, and wave at the entire Eastern Seaboard before selecting its impact zone, Maine.[41] The sultry-heeled female storm carried 125-miles-per-hour winds, leaving tears in its wake. As described by the *New York Times*, the storm even stopped to take "her 'portrait'" with radar as "she" moved, an exhibitionist that was little concerned about privacy.[42]

After more than $40 million in damages ($401 million in 2018) and 29 fatalities, the storm eventually dissipated in Canada.[43] The *Baltimore Sun* declared that "she had been rent by her own violence," which was a relief as she was one "angry woman!"[44] The *Richmond Times-Dispatch* quipped that she was an "erratic lady," if she could be called a "lady."[45]

Within a month of Edna, a third major hurricane, Hazel, "altered" course to follow its predecessors. This October monstrosity was a "nightmare," reported the *Houston Chronicle*.[46] "She" had "dawdl[ed] in her early days" before "wickedly menacing" the coast, pausing briefly to "rejuvenate" before "galloping" to deliver a "terrific battering" during "her last fling."[47] In the end, the storm left over 150 dead in the United States and Canada, while behaving "like Calamity Jane," twisting, turning, and shooting at the coastline with abandon.[48] Hazel "left her calling cards scattered along the coast and inland," leaving no area untouched, stated the *Raleigh News & Observer* in the aftermath.[49] Meanwhile, the *New York Times* declared that Hazel was "one of the worst-tempered brats in an all-girl family," a sneering reference to the storm's predecessors, Carol and Edna.[50]

As in their reporting on Carol and Edna, newspaper writers devised novel ways of describing Hazel's feminine deviance. Three newspapers used the term "wicked," and the *Baltimore Sun* went so far as to caption a cartoon image of Hazel with the phrase, "You Were Certainly No Lady!"[51]

Figure 1. "You Were Certainly No Lady," *Baltimore Sun,* October 17, 1954, 1. Reprinted with permission from the *Baltimore Sun.*

The cartoon portrays Hazel as a witch, hideously ugly, with a crooked nose and wart-covered face. While riding her broom up the coast, she sweeps past the Carolinas, Virginia, Washington, Maryland, and Pennsylvania. Across the bottom, a small figure references the new naming system publicly introduced that year as she declares, "'Ida,' 'Janet,' and 'Kate,' or whatever they'll call you, stay way from our door!" (See figure 1.)

Of all the hurricanes that formed in the 1954 season, none topped the storms known as Carol, Edna, and Hazel in damage caused or colorful descriptions inspired. Together, these storms would cost $751.6 million ($8.3 billion in 2018) and be the subject of 484 newspaper articles spinning vivid characterizations of the storms as though they were characters in a drama.[52] The announcement of the new naming system at the start of the season left reporters eager for a chance to test out new ways to tell the story of deadly storms, and these three hurricanes did not disappoint. Carol, Edna, and Hazel, known as the "Bad Girls of '54," provided reporters a rich source of material to feed increasing public interest. Granted, the public's collective imagination was already primed for anthropomorphic descriptors by literary works such as George Stewart's 1941 novel *Storm* and the musical *Paint Your Wagon*. Indeed, reviewing the 484 articles written about the Bad Girls of '54 across twelve major US cities, some written by those in the affected regions, others not, it is obvious that they are strikingly familiar in description to Stewart's Maria. The fictional storm's femme fatale qualities were almost certainly used as an inspiration in characterizing the new storm systems. They howled, shrieked, split into separate storms like Maria, and played coy with meteorologists who were avidly tracking them. In the media, these gendered characters were both affable and odious. Unlike in Stewart's novel, though, the names of these storms were no secret. The public shared in the naming and character-building, making them all the more exciting.

Underlying the acceptance and usage of the names and descriptions by weathermen, reporters, and the public was the thirst for meteorological news. This thirst only increased in the 1950s, with the Weather Bureau's rapid postwar expansion of operations. The hype over the new storm-naming system was also amplified by the burgeoning field of television meteorology. By the 1950s, weather was a central feature in nightly newscasts. Leading these forecasts were two distinct characters: the distinguished "Weather Man" and the flippant "Weather Girl." It was up to them to provide accurate predictions and comedic relief in a world ever tense with the latest Red Scare. The "Weather Girl" was both a reflection of the wartime training of women in weather roles and the postwar redefinition of women's roles. She was not meant to be the expert; stations had trained meteorologists (men) to do that. Instead, she was relegated to the role of chipper assistant, drawing "weather maps on Plexiglass, don[ning] hats to match the forecast or [rising] yawning from bed in skimpy lingerie to deliver late-night forecasts." Carol Reed, of WCBC New York was the first of the "Weather Girls." Reed debuted on the WCBC station in 1952 with minimal qualifications except her young age (twenty-six), large smile, and happy demeanor. She was a fan favorite with her heels and sign-off slogan that told viewers to "have a happy" following her delivery of the temperatures for the following day. Due to the success of Reed at WCBC, by 1961 the *New York Times* estimated that nearly three-quarters of the 466 television stations in the United States employed a weather girl like Carol.⁵³ It is also little wonder why the name "Carol" was added to the 1954 hurricane-naming list.

In corollary image to the Weather Girls was the refined male meteorologist, or Weatherman, who was consulted when major weather occurred. These weathermen represented the best training available at the time in the field of meteorology and were equipped with the latest technology and research to back up their warnings, emphasizing the seriousness of violent weather with gravitas. The 1954 hurricane season, in particular, brought a new and thrilling challenge for the weatherman: reporting on hurricanes in real time as the storms of 1954 were the first covered live on television. Assisting the weathermen in their live reporting were the Hurricane Hunters based in Florida. These bold young men were presented as thrilling fighter pilots at war with Mother Nature herself. The Hurricane Hunters and television weathermen alike helped emphasize the storm as a central attraction, and Americans as the ticket holders to nature's most devastating sideshow. Hurricanes presented a pulsating drama of potential destruction as well as a celebration of the heroic pursuit of frontline meteorological efforts to tackle the latest threat to peace in the postwar era. With the era's increased appetite for dramatic meteorological news coverage, it is no wonder that the naming system inspired a descriptive struggle filled with illustrious characters, all viewed through the lens of gendered debates.

The creativity inspiring this reportage reflected larger changes in American culture, particularly regarding gender expectations of men and women. In reporters' descriptions of the storms as female, and particularly their attribution of negative gendered traits, they tapped into deeply rooted cultural anxieties regarding acceptable feminine behavior in the aftermath of World War II. Gendering hurricanes, and disparaging them on gendered grounds, amounted to a project of harnessing or even taming an unwieldy and destructive natural force, analogous to the harnessing of nuclear energy into the atomic bomb. The hurricanes of '54 were described as "witches," "erratic ladies," and "furious" or "violent sisters," all popular negative stereotypes of women in the 1950s. And the gendered hurricane descriptors grew increasingly profane as the season progressed and growing numbers of coastal residents were harmed and displaced by the storms. When Edna and Hazel were called "no lady," this was a slur indeed, evoking a lack of voting rights, social status, and sexual restraint, and even suggesting racialized stigma.⁵⁴ Used in hurricane reports, the phrase was meant as the ultimate insult to these storms and an oblique insult to all women whose character might be likened to theirs. In this way, the 1954 hurricane season marked a shift in the American public's perception of storms. Hurricanes were not just female—they were exemplars of the worst kind of womanhood imaginable.

Still, while most members of the media and the public were on board with the use of female names for hurricanes and the creative, albeit negative gendered descriptors names inspired, one newspaper in the Gulf South stood up against the naming system: the *Houston Chronicle*. Throughout the 1954 season, several editorials in the *Chronicle* expressed that the naming system was ill-advised, even immoral. In the aftermath of Hurricane Carol, the *Chronicle* ran an editorial that argued it was "time the storm experts grew up and quit using 'cute' language" to describe tropical disturbances. The authors lambasted meteorologists and reporters for their rapid adoption of the new system of names, declaring that, even though it was "possible to list hurricanes without such silly nomenclature" for "a great many years," it did not "seem right" to "use this juvenile playfulness in naming a cataclysm of nature [that had] the intensity of 100 hydrogen bombs." The *Chronicle* editors opined that the playful naming system represented a "curse of the age," namely "a loss of virility in an effort to be cute."[55] As further evidence of its claim, the editorial cited the rampant use of "cute" gendered language in the advertisements that glutted the consumer-driven postwar culture. According to the editorial, such advertising was larded with an assortment of gendered rhetorical gimmicks, deployed cynically in an effort to sell content or products. So thoroughly did the *Chronicle* staff disapprove of this system that they refused to use it. "Why not simply call them hurricane No. 1 or hurricane No. 2 of 1954," and so forth, the staff wondered.[56] For the rest of the season, the *Chronicle* did just that, replacing all the names with numbers in articles, charts, and even official Weather Bureau bulletins.

One month after, in September 1954, the *Chronicle* staff again registered its refusal to employ the naming system as Hurricane Edna made headlines around the country. While dozens of other newspapers ran stories of Edna's skittish flirtation with the Florida coast, the *Chronicle* pointedly and persistently referred to the storm as Hurricane No. 5. When their refusal to use the storm names raised the eyebrows of the national press, the *Chronicle* issued a new editorial while it took an even stronger stance. It reported that the Weather Bureau had "begun to come under fire for giving deadly hurricanes such lovable names as Carol and Dolly."[57] Then it cited interviews with weathermen asserting support for changing the naming system for the following year. In fact, an interview with then–assistant chief of operations for the Weather Bureau, Ivan Ray Tannehill, quoted the chief as saying that "[the system] isn't necessarily a permanent system; [but] it was the best thing we've come up with thus far." When bluntly asked whether hurricanes were not designated by the number system proposed by the *Chronicle* staff (for example, Hurricane No. 1 of 1954), Tannehill was quoted saying that he "didn't know," but, quickly added, "that you probably would run into the same trouble with numbers as with letters of the alphabet—they could be misunderstood over networks." Tannehill thus rejected the *Chronicle*'s suggestion.[58] The *Chronicle*'s concerns about the Weather Bureau's female naming system and the gendered rhetoric or "cute" language used to describe the storms provoked others to issue similar complaints. The *New Bedford Standard Times,* for example, made the strong claim that "the use of feminine names [to describe hurricanes] is inappropriate, facetious, and devoid of logical reason."[59] The newspaper, located in Carol-affected Massachusetts, was still suffering as a result.

In September, editors at another newspaper in a hurricane-affected area, the *Miami Herald,* responded with an editorial arguing the names were ultimately immaterial: "Hurricane Carol would have been no more or less facetious if named Cornelius or Caliente." While "the Weather Bureau [did not show] much originality in selecting the names for this year's hurricane litter," for reporters it was "a matter of writing headlines." The editors remarked wryly that "the real names we call a hurricane when it gets to town cannot be used in a family newspaper," and concluded that no matter what name a hurricane was given, "the wind still blows the same."[60] In short, the naming system might as well stand because it simply did not matter. Just two days later, the newspaper expressed a different opinion in a column entitled "As We See It." "We think the naming of hurricanes after women should be dropped," the columnist stated. While "the practice of calling" storms "Alice, Carol, Dolly, and Edna and the like grew out of their capricious behavior," this was where "the similarity ends." In retrospect, they argued, "you can't convince anybody in New England that Carol had any ladylike qualities." In fact, the article concluded, "the way they're behaving calls for some strong old Biblical names like Goliath, Jonah, or Samson." "When nature works itself into a mighty wrath, we should not incur further woe with misleading descriptions," and female-named hurricanes would do just that.[61] The *Miami Herald*'s reversal of its previously supportive stance toward the naming system, which we see in its editorials about Edna and Carol, exemplifies a larger trend in how the new naming system was discussed throughout the country in its opening year. Initially, during the first few days of a storm, reporters delighted in the ability to curse the storm through gendered expletives. Then, as storm damage was tallied and lamented, newspapers softened their rhetoric. Even in future hurricane seasons, discussion of storm naming and gendering continued to follow this cycle. Another factor to consider when looking at the *Herald*'s reversal of their previous stance was the proximity of Edna to Florida. While earlier storms brushed Florida on their way up the coast to New England, Edna severely impacted Miami. As a result, their support of the naming system waivered as their experience with the storm changed from provocative fun to deathly horror.

Two weeks after the *Herald*'s reversal, the *New York Times* brought up the issue of the naming system again in an article that refuted the *Herald*'s concerns, siding instead with the Weather Bureau. Titled "Why Gales Are Gals: Hurricane Namers (Male) Prove It's to Avoid Confusion," the *Times* emphasized that the decision to use hurricane names was not a rash choice implemented by weathermen for a quick fix in the naming system.[62] Instead, considerable time and effort had gone into choosing the names. In fact, the Weather Bureau stressed that they chose names to both interest the American public and reflect the changing cultural period. Before further discussion of the *Times*'s support of the hurricane-naming system or the Weather Bureau's critique, the season concluded. The Weather Bureau, realizing it had faced criticism of the new system, particularly by residents in the regions most affected by storms (like Houston and Miami from the hurricane-prone Gulf South, and New Bedford in Carol-affected Massachusetts), decided to implement another nationwide "test" year in 1955. Again, the bureau released all-female names, and weathermen and reporters across the country prepared for the opening of the next year's hurricane season.

Weaponizing Rhetoric: The "Two Windy Sisters" of 1955

By the time the first storm of the 1955 season appeared on the horizon, the disputes of the previous year (led predominantly by two Gulf South newspapers, the *Houston Chronicle* and *Miami Herald*) had faded. Even the skeptical *Houston Chronicle* adopted the 1955 names for regular use. The first two storms of the season, Alice (reusing the name of the first 1954 hurricane) and Brenda, were again a disappointment, much like Alice and Barbara were the year before. But the third storm, Hurricane Connie, was a whopper. Emerging at the beginning of August, the storm traveled parallel to the Eastern Seaboard, causing the evacuation of 14,000 people as it brushed the coastline. When it finally reached the North Carolina coast, it brought with it significant rain and flooding, leaving considerable crop damage and 74 people dead.[63]

As in the previous season, reporters across the country eagerly exercised their literary chops in describing Connie. By the time the storm stopped "lurk[ing] lazily," reported the *New Orleans Times-Picayune,* it was clear that this was a big one. Soon, it spun "like a mad top," evoking fear amongst the residents of the Eastern Seaboard. But residents were enamored with the "capricious" girl who had a "dangerous flirtation" with the coastline. Unfortunately, as Connie "swished her windy tail" and "swirled her skirts," she also delivered a "kiss" that packed a "punch," declared the *New York Times*.[64] In battered North Carolina, the *Raleigh News & Observer* described Connie as "lack[ing] Hazel's wallop," but showing great "persistence."[65]

But in a shift from the previous year, the hurricane reportage now included explicit allusions to the Cold War. Connie was by turns an ominous atomic bomb and a devious Communist. One article reported that this "erratic lady" had not "made up her mind," and instead appeared to stand "still and growl," while having force "equal to thousands of H-Bombs."[66] Eventually referred to as a "menace," Connie quickly was associated with larger Cold War tensions such as the "Red Menace" or "Red Threat." The storm was a "threat" or a "scare," proclaimed articles throughout the nation. Fortunately, "The Connie Scare" passed, as the *Charleston News & Courier* announced when Connie wound its way up the coastline.[67] In the end, even the *Miami Herald* breathed a sigh of relief that the wandering storm dissipated. "Connie's No Lady And Her Temper Proves It," they decreed as they spotlighted damage left to the coastline through a series of images.[68]

Connie's deadliest act, though, was the formation of a subsequent storm, Diane. Four days after Connie's dissipation, Diane emerged along the same, newly cleared path, building momentum toward the North Carolina coast. Striking just south of Connie's landfall location, the storm weakened slightly over the North Carolina mountains before gaining strength and veering upwards toward New England. In Connecticut, Diane wreaked havoc, producing increased sea temperatures and peak rainfall in the region.[69] By its conclusion, Diane was the costliest storm on record, with an estimated $754 million in damages ($7.1 billion in 2018) and 184 casualties. Diane's duplication of Connie's path, technically known as a "Fujiwara Effect"—following the current and low-pressure path already laid out by a preceding storm—was a source of particular indignation for the media and the American public alike. As the *New Orleans Times-Picayune* reported, the "fickle female" had performed some enormous "foot-dragging" as it followed its sister storm.[70] The *New York Times* described the two storms as playing a "cat and mouse" game with the coast, one receding while the other "invaded" and plundered.[71] When "dying," the storm exercised "all the punch of a powderpuff," "weeping" as it went, stated the *Raleigh News & Observer*.[72] In the end, concluded the *Times-Picayune*, the hurricane no longer deserved the "dignified" classification of "hurricane." Instead, it was an "ex-hurricane," losing both its identity and its power.[73]

From the newspaper reports on the "two windy sisters" of 1955, it is clear that, by this second year of the female naming system, reporters were more comfortable in their gendered characterizations of storms. Storms were identified as singularly feminine creatures through terminology like skirt swishing, flirting, and references to their unladylike qualities. Reporters were also more likely to use a gendered reference like "she," "her," "sister," "girl," "lady," or "woman" to describe these storms. As evidenced by the *Houston Chronicle*'s own adoption of the naming system in its second year, Americans now thought of the hurricane as a gendered object, more so than any other hazard in their natural world. This amped fear is easily seen when reviewing the discourse on storms in coastal regions like the Gulf South and the frequency of gender use. Coastal areas, in particular, feared the impact of storms and thus were most likely to adopt gendered rhetoric to describe them. In addition to describing storms as feminized objects, newspapers again printed representations of storms as women. The *Mobile Press-*

Figure 2. "Meteorological Optometrist," *Mobile Press-Register*, August 14, 1955, 8. Reprinted with permission from the *Mobile Press-Register*.

Register, for instance, depicted "The Hurricane 'Girls'" Connie and Diane as angry women under inspection by Air Force weather pilots or Hurricane Hunters who sized up their impact and radius. (See figure 2.)

Gendered characterizations of storms were also heavily laden with Cold War analogies. Hurricanes were personified villains against which reporters and the public could vent their anger at all Cold War anxieties in colorful and emotionally charged language. Thus the gender identification given to storms was used more frequently than with the atomic bomb, as it was consumed on a regular basis with the advent of each storm season. As a menace with the strength "equal to a thousand H-Bombs," the hurricane was the new atomic outlier, a danger waiting in the water for murderous deployment. But the constructed rhetoric of hurricane as female Cold War villain inspired significant public debate about the practice of calling hurricanes by female names. While the debate in 1954 had been confined to the appropriateness of the test system, by 1955 the question was whether the Weather

Bureau should continue to use the naming system indefinitely. Leading the campaign to discontinue the system were two unlikely allies: a famous jazz singer from Georgia named Jane Pickens and a moderate Republican and minority-whip senator from California, Thomas Kuchel.

Jane Pickens was among the first to openly critique the new naming system and the gendered descriptors it inspired. Pickens rose to fame in the 1930s as a member of the "Pickens Sisters" ensemble, eventually going solo to star on Broadway and television shows. By 1955, she was the host of *The Jane Pickens Show* on ABC. It was at this stage that Pickens first publicly declared her disapproval of the newly implemented female-only hurricane-naming system. Pickens asserted that the stereotypes applied to storms damaged the perception of women in American society, especially considering that every major news outlet from Miami to New England used the stereotypes. In an episode that aired in the fall of 1955, Pickens declared, "The association of women's names with 'tragedy and havoc created by hurricanes' is 'a personification of extremely poor judgment.'" She suggested that, in order to avoid perpetuating misleading stereotypes of women, storms should be designated "A, B, C or 1, 2, 3."[74]

In response to Pickens, weathermen quickly jumped to defend the naming system, now in its second year. They again assured the public that the assembled list of names allowed the Weather Bureau to "avoid confusion" when identifying hurricanes in public broadcasts and warnings. The names were not intended as an implicit insult to women.[75] In fact, they reminded the public, "only two names were picked with real people in mind": "Orpha" for a girl in one of the Weather Bureau's offices, and "Wallis" for the Duchess of Windsor, who became infamous in 1936 for her divorce and extramarital affairs that caused the reigning English monarch to abdicate his throne.[76] Further, the weathermen insisted, there was "no other [storm-naming] system that had the same advantages of brevity, ease of pronunciation and recognition."[77] Systems of the past—using names from the Greek Pantheon, the military, phonetic alphabets, and numerals—proved untenably confusing and too exhaustible in nature, but the all-female scheme provided flexibility.

Despite the arguments against Pickens's position, the media avidly reported her protest of the naming system. "Well, once again this year a lady is protesting against the tagging of hurricanes with girls' names," gossiped the editors of the *Raleigh News & Observer* in August 1955. The editors granted that the "notable" singer from Georgia "had a right to protest," but certainly no credibility as a decider of hurricane names. That task was better left to the highly skilled meteorologists at the Weather Bureau, who assuredly intended "no insult to a whole sex." Besides, the editors added, the system could be construed as a testament to women's potency: "most of us can speak with more real feeling about a wind named after a girl than a letter or number."[78] In short, the editors concluded that the Weather Bureau was right to continue to "christen the powerful, capricious things with girls' names" as a reminder "to never underestimate the power of a woman."[79]

The response by the Weather Bureau and media to Jane Pickens was unsurprising in light of the reactions to other outspoken women of the 1950s. At the time, the ideal woman was one who blended into a homogenized suburban America, and Pickens's protests were perceived as unwanted and unwarranted. Her attack on the naming system only reinforced assumptions that Pickens herself was abnormal, and by extension that any woman who protested the naming system was abnormal.

For all the dismissals she encountered, Pickens did find support in one unlikely ally: US senator Thomas H. Kuchel of California, who read about Pickens's protest in the newspaper. In 1955, Kuchel wrote a formal letter to the head of the Weather Bureau, Dr. Francis W. Reichelderfer, in which he emphasized the limitations of the female sex as a metaphor for hurricanes. In the letter, he acknowledged that women were often "stirred to fury," but pointed out that "their rages seldom last as long as Hazel's in 1954, or wreak such vengeance." Similarly, he emphasized that women "can be moody and unpredictable" and "now and then excitable," but "few of them show the wrathfulness of Barbara in 1953 or Edna last summer" or are "rarely as determined as Connie this year."[80] Kuchel concluded that he hoped the Weather Bureau would recognize that storms and women were not analogous, and would devise "a new system of identification" "before the 1956 hurricane season arrives." Kuchel even suggested several alternative naming systems. "How about adjectives which would be descriptive and meaningful?" Like "'acrimonious' or 'aggressive' followed by 'belligerent' or 'bilious' and 'capricious' or 'corrosive.'" The Weather Bureau could also use the names of mythological characters (like "Achilles" and "Zeus") or even aboriginal sources (such as "Algonquin" or "Blackhawk"). Really, "the possibilities of an intriguing and impersonal scheme of meteorological nomenclature appear limited only by human resourcefulness and imagination," he argued. "Perhaps the Weather Bureau could achieve a dual or triple purpose—alert the populace in endangered areas and simultaneously inspire a search of encyclopedias or even broaden the people's knowledge of geography or history," he concluded.[81]

On August 29, 1955, thirteen days after the Pickens story hit the news, the *Washington Post* published Kuchel's letter to Chief Reichelderfer verbatim. Having made similar points in an interview shortly after Pickens's statements made headlines, the senator's letter came as no surprise to the public. Still, the publication of the full text of the letter garnered widespread interest. In addition to offering support for Pickens's controversial statements, it provided specific suggestions for alternative naming systems that were then picked up and repeated in newspapers across the country. Because Kuchel was a US senator (and a man), his argument received a more respectful hearing than Pickens's. Still, he too received mostly negative reactions. *Washington Post* columnist George Dixon wrote, "I had always considered [Kuchel] a serious man." But now that opinion had been called into question. The *Baltimore Sun* criticized the senator's suggestions for alternative naming systems, noting that, even though most of them could fit the Weather Bureau's requirement that storm names be "short, easily pronounced and readily recognized," they did not meet the criterion of being "readily recognized," even with the aid of an encyclopedia. Also, they concluded that a system using mythological character names would "have to skip such sweet, dispositioned characters as Apollo and Eros," thus providing endless complications.[82]

Pickens's and Kuchel's protest of the naming system, and the American public's different responses to those protests, reveal a key difference in the treatment of men's and women's opinions in the 1950s. Kuchel's beliefs were seriously considered in light of his esteemed position, and refutation of his arguments was based on specifics. At no point was his right to criticize the naming system questioned, even though he had no training as a meteorologist. Meanwhile Pickens was refuted on the grounds that she lacked the skills and the right to protest meteorological decisions. Nevertheless, both Kuchel and Pickens attracted considerable media attention for their protests, demonstrating just how closely the American public followed the story of hurricanes and hurricane research. Sadly, both saw their protests of the hurricane-naming system fade into the background as the next year the Weather Bureau released lists of female-only names for both the 1956 and 1957 hurricane seasons. From this point onward, the feminized naming system was widely treated as permanent.

Taming Tempests: Hurricane Modification and the National Hurricane Research Project

The Bad Girls of '54 and the windy sisters of '55 left coastal areas devastated, with millions in damages and significant fatalities. By late 1955, concern about the potential impact of future hurricanes, especially to rapidly developing coastal areas such as the Gulf South, led to increased discussion of the serious scientific study of these weather patterns. It was no longer enough to just name and characterize hurricanes. They needed to be predicted, measured, and tracked more effectively. Just as nuclear energy was domesticated from the atomic bomb—a weaponization of science that put nuclear power under human control—Americans urgently desired to tame the hurricane. By the end of 1955, Congress established a new hurricane-research division specifically dedicated to this area of research. The National Hurricane Research Project (or NHRP, established in 1955) expanded the efforts undertaken with the previous Project CIRRUS, which attempted to tame the hurricane. For the time being, though, the NHRP shied away from weather-modification experimentation.[83]

The NHRP's hesitancy to explore hurricane modification was understandable given the controversy over the attempted seeding of the October 1947 storm, which unexpectedly veered into Savannah, Georgia. Still, the federal government had several strong incentives to risk reestablishing such a controversial program. First, between 1947's Project CIRRUS and the formation of the NHRP, the national broadcasting of named storms and the widespread attention paid to them created a considerable increase in demand for weather services. Second, the devastation wrought by the storms of 1954 (Carol, Dolly, Edna, Hazel) and 1955 (Connie and Diane), particularly on growing coastal regions, garnered significant national attention. Finally, the advancement of technology revolutionizing Americans' interactions with the natural world had created support for efforts to stop what many considered the next "menace."

The NHRP's explicit focus was to improve the prediction and tracking of hurricanes through reconnaissance and scientific measurement. Based in Florida at the West Palm Beach Airport, the NHRP was ideally located to measure the development of storms in both the Atlantic and Gulf waters. On staff were a number of meteorologists, who had at their disposal US Air Force B-49 fighter planes and pilots, as well as the latest in meteorological equipment. The first director of the NHRP, Dr. Robert H. Simpson, was an ambitious meteorologist and researcher. He received his degree from Emory University and rose through the ranks of the Weather Bureau during the new age of meteorology. Like George Stewart's "Junior Meteorologist," Simpson was part of the newer cohort of meteorologists trained during the war, though he had now reached "Chief" status. Simpson's own background had inspired his meteorological interests. At the age of six, Simpson nearly drowned in Corpus Christi, Texas, during the devastating 1919 storm. The experience encouraged him to pursue research on storms, leaving his home state of Texas for Georgia. Following the completion of his master's degree he joined the Weather Bureau in 1940 just before the war and devoted his energies to studying hurricanes. After a year working on Swan Island in the Caribbean and three years at the hurricane center in New Orleans, he moved to Miami, where he became part of the newly burgeoning postwar hurricane trackers. While in Miami, he convinced Air Force and Navy pilots to allow him to ride piggyback in their planes on reconnaissance missions using newly developed tracking technologies. This flight experience provided him the basis to ask for the creation of a specialized hurricane tracking and research unit, the NHRP. For the next three years, as director of the NHRP, he accompanied pilots on flights into every hurricane that formed in the Atlantic, every day for the duration of the storm, all while overseeing the research and operations of the NHRP.[84] As the 1956 season progressed, data collected from storms was incorporated in weather reports and storm broadcasts, and later in scientific studies. By 1958, the NHRP recorded an all-time high of twenty-three missions flown and copious scientific publications on subjects ranging from storm-surge heights to rainfall-distribution expectations, with Simpson as its lead.[85]

Reporters applauded the NHRP's (and Simpson's) research for its veracity, only furthering the support and interest in Weather Bureau hurricane-hunting operations. The daring Hurricane Hunters, including men like

Simpson, now made famous by the media, became culturally recognizable icons, their fleet of planes ever ready to take on nature's greatest challenge. The hunters even had their own magazine, featuring a different pinup on the monthly cover, dubbed "Miss Hurricane Hunter." The women, reminiscent of World War II pinups, usually posed seductively next to the planes used for tracking another gendered object, the hurricane.[86]

As the NHRP received recognition and attention from their research through the 1950s, expansion efforts continued. In 1959, the NHRP migrated to a new facility in Miami, known as the National Hurricane Center (NHC). It included an improved location that shared facilities with the US Air Force and US Navy Hurricane Hunters and, most significantly, a new IBM 650 computer for use in plotting trajectories and impact in record speed. The Miami-based NHC, headquartered at the center of meteorological activity between the booming Gulf South, Gulf of Mexico, and Atlantic Ocean became the headquarters for all hurricane research and reportage on storm movements.[87]

Finally, in 1960, the NHRP turned to a mission that had not been attempted in the United States since Project CIRRUS in 1947: hurricane modification.[88] In April 1960, a group of organizations including NASA, the Weather Bureau, and Radio Corporation of America launched the first in a series of ten satellites designed to measure the Earth's atmospheric conditions. Each satellite, or Television Infrared Observation Satellite (TIROS), was meant to broadcast images of the Earth from space. Over the next five years, the United States launched nine additional satellites, ten in all, nine of which still orbit the Earth as of today. The US government's commitment to developing the TIROS program was part of its larger effort to prove the United States' hegemony over Russia, in what became known as the "Space Race." Since 1954, US and Russian governments raced to launch satellites into space; Russia's *Sputnik 1* had been the first to make it, in October 1957, and the United States' *Explorer 1* had followed three months later, in January 1958. Losing to their Cold War enemy drove the United States to invest in scientific study and education, especially focusing on the exploration of outer space, the development of military weapons, and the promotion of domestic commerce. The TIROS program represented the intersection of all three interests. Efforts to launch satellites and humans into space, including TIROS, fueled the development of military weapons as well as the creation of massive space-exploration facilities across the Gulf South. Between the 1940s and 1960s, the Kennedy, Johnson, Michoud, Stennis, and Marshall space centers were opened in the region, drawing people and industry with them.[89]

With all of these expensive new TIROS facilities located in a hurricane-prone zone, it is unsurprising that NHRP staff redoubled their efforts to track hurricanes more effectively. New satellites now made it possible for meteorologists and the American public to view images of storms brewing miles from the coast and then track the storms' movements with extreme accuracy. Between the imaging technology and the visible tracking of the Hurricane Hunters, Americans had a clearer perspective on what storms looked like and how they moved, removing much of the mystery that shrouded previous storms. The improved imaging capabilities fueled new attempts to develop ways of controlling the weather. The TIROS and NHRP facilities' geographic placement also cemented the impression that the Gulf South was the active war "theater," with battle stations ready to deploy weaponry on the enemy.

From 1961 to 1962, efforts to place TIROS in orbit increased as tensions flared between the United States and Cuba. In April 1961, the CIA sponsored a paramilitary operation to overthrow the Cuban government that failed miserably, to the embarrassment of all. Known as the Bay of Pigs, the event soured relations between the United States and Cuba's Communist leader, Fidel Castro.[90] Meanwhile, research at the NHRP, using TIROS imagery, yielded a new potential method of hurricane modification. The method intended to decrease the hurricane's strength by dropping silver iodide crystals into the eye of a hurricane instead of ice crystals used in 1947's Project CIRRUS. They tested the method secretly in 1958 with Hurricane Daisy.[91] During the storm, silver iodide dispensers were dropped outside of the hurricane's wall, opening up to release their contents. In this initial test, the goal was not to change the direction of the hurricane or even weaken it, but merely to test the effectiveness of the equipment. The result of the test was positive, the equipment and method of delivery worked, and, inspired by the launch of TIROS and fearful of the tensions heating up in the Cold War, the NHRP was ready to test the hurricane-modification process again.[92]

The new method of using silver iodide crystals to tame a hurricane was further developed by none other than Dr. Robert Simpson, who had recently started a doctoral program at the University of Chicago. While in Chicago, Simpson worked under Dr. Herbert Riehl, who specialized in meteorological research. One of Riehl's recent students was Dr. Joanne Malkus, the first American woman to receive a PhD in meteorology, in 1949.[93] Malkus was a product of training programs in aviation at the University of Chicago, where she became interested in meteorology and cloud formation. Having booked an appointment with the professor of her required meteorology course as part of the aviation program, she expressed her interest in his work and his new Institute of Meteorology at the University of Chicago (a part of a number of meteorological training programs and research centers established with the growth of the industry). Within ten minutes Professor Carl-Gustaf Rossby admitted her to the doctoral program and told her that he thought the formation of clouds was a good subject "for a little girl to study" as no one was really interested in it as a research subject.[94] As one of only 7 women in the meteorological graduate degree program of 200 during the war, the young twenty-something Malkus received hostility and guffaws from the all-male students and faculty as she completed her coursework and research. Completing her doctoral dissertation on the subject at age twenty-six in 1949, she became the first woman in the program to do so, and was a rare phenomenon in a world that was adjusting to postwar gender roles. Despite the rarity of her research and her publication history, Malkus faced discrimination at multiple junctures of her work, first as she looked for jobs in the 1950s and quickly found that no faculty or meteorologically trained position hired women for anything but the role of "Weather Girl," let alone a woman like herself who was twice married, with a child.

She finally secured a position at the Illinois Institute of Technology as an assistant professor of physics, moving a few years later to the University of California–Los Angeles. Then she faced complications finding collaborators for projects related to her interests (cloud formation), as many meteorological researchers were uninterested in cloud formation, instead focusing on what occurred after clouds formed. This changed once Malkus published a coauthored work in 1958 with her former advisor, Herbert Riehl, on what became known as the "Hot Tower" hypothesis of tropical convection. In the article, Malkus and Riehl posited that specific clouds draw warm, moist air from the ocean upwards. These clouds were thus essential to understanding how tropical systems emerged and moved.[95] This discovery led Malkus to receive funding from the Office of Naval Research to track the movement and development of Hot Tower clouds at Woods Hole Oceanographic Institution in Massachusetts. Unfortunately, when Malkus arrived in Massachusetts to do research at Woods Hole, she was quickly told that women were not allowed to ride in the planes at the facility. Seeking help from the Navy research staff, the Navy officer in charge reportedly told the director of Woods Hole, "No Joanne, no airplane."[96]

Robert Simpson, who had recently become an advisee of Herbert Riehl, was well aware of Malkus's role in the discovery of these new ideas of cloud formation and movement, as well as her research at the Woods Hole facility. As part of the research he was doing while at the NHRP using TIROS imagery, he stumbled across a report on Hurricane Donna (1960), where he noticed that a pilot mentioned the hurricane sucked up air like a chimney.[97] This chimney "seemed to be the primary energy cell of the hurricane," causing it both to develop and to move. Simpson connected this chimney description to Malkus's work on "Hot Towers," and believed that it directly related to seeding efforts. As explained later by Simpson, "[it] seemed to me that if we seeded the chimney [using silver iodide crystals], we would change the dynamics of the storm."[98] Thus, Simpson invited Joanne Malkus to join him to test this new hurricane seeding model. By 1961, the NHRP now had advanced tracking technology (TIROS), a weapon (silver iodide crystals), and a plan (drop the crystals inside the "chimney" or eye of the storm) based on scientific evidence and research. They just needed a hurricane.

On September 16, 1961, the Florida-based NHRP staff, including Simpson and Malkus, used TIROS technology to track the development of Hurricane Esther, following it from its development at the Cape Verde Islands towards North Carolina. As Esther reached a significant stage of development, "the flying weathermen" took to the sky in planes to drop silver iodide capsules on the storm in hopes of modifying its course or weakening it.[99] For the NHRP staff researching storms for years, the result felt like a victory: several silver iodide dispensers were successfully dropped into the eye wall of the storm, where they opened up to release their contents into the winds, and within a few hours, Esther showed a 10 percent reduction in wind speed, appearing to slow down. The following day, they deployed a second batch of silver iodide capsules in a further attempt to decelerate Esther's path. This time, the silver iodide containers did not end up in the eye wall, and Esther showed no reduction in wind speed. Still, based on Esther's response to the first batch of silver iodide, NHRP staff deemed the experiment a modest success.[100]

The promising results of the Hurricane Esther experiment could not have come at a more opportune moment. Esther represented an important win for a program that had invested years and millions of dollars in congressional spending to develop storm-tracking technology. Now, with the Esther test, there appeared a real, valid, reliable way to manage the meteorological menace that had plagued the American coastline for so long. An article co-authored by Robert Simpson and Joanne Malkus about the results of the Esther experiment quickly caused ripples in the meteorological community. Notably excited about the results, the chief of the US Weather Bureau, Dr. Reichelderfer, addressed the press in a statement, proclaiming that "man stood on 'the threshold of possible control,' of one of nature's most powerful and destructive phenomena—the hurricane."[101] Dr. Reichelderfer cautioned that, in order to obtain further success, the policy banning the administrative use of nuclear weapons or experiments with hurricanes needed adjustment, and the Weather Bureau needed increased funding for this mission. As subsequent hurricane Hilda wrought havoc on the Gulf Coast two months later, residents proclaimed that there was no better time to invest in efforts to combat these tempests. A *New Orleans Times-Picayune* cartoon depicted their thoughts on this issue, pointing out that "defense against disaster" required "cooperation by all of us," including state, local, civic, and civil defense efforts.[102] Hilda and all other angry female hurricanes were the enemy, the battle was under way, and the Gulf Coast was the site of danger. (See figure 3.)

It was this investment that inspired the launch of a new program in 1962 to investigate the possibility of hurricane modification. Known as Project STORMFURY, it became the longest-running weather modification program in American history.[103] Even as the project produced some of the most debatable weather-modification results to date, it reshaped the way Americans perceived and reacted to storms. And one of those changes was the way in which Americans described and characterized these now-feminized objects.

The beginnings of Project STORMFURY were auspicious. With a congressionally funded budget, a directive to deploy every possible tool in their mission of taming storms, potentially replicable results from the modification of Hurricane Esther, and a staff that consisted of cutting-edge researchers

Figure 3. "Hilda and the Gulf Coast," *New Orleans Times-Picayune*, October 3, 1961, 8. Reprinted with permission from the *New Orleans Times-Picayune*.

like its director, Robert Simpson, and meteorological consultant, Joanne Malkus, the stage was set for a thrilling first year. The problem was with the storms themselves. The NHRP had recently established guidelines to prevent another Project CIRRUS-esque scandal, in which hurricane tampering supposedly steered a storm onto an even deadlier course than it had followed naturally. According to the new guidelines, a storm was only selected for "seeding"—the deployment of silver iodide into its eye—if it had a well-defined eye to drop crystals, a large enough diameter to measure changes in strength or wind speed, and less than a 10 percent chance of impacting the mainland.[104] Disappointingly, no storms developed in 1962 that fit Project STORMFURY requirements, so the staff kept tinkering with their formulas, waiting for the ideal storm to materialize.[105]

Meanwhile, as Project STORMFURY researchers waited, others were hard at work studying the influence of silver iodide crystals on different types of clouds, particularly those that developed into rain or storms. At a field site in Arizona, researchers for Project BATON seeded cumulus clouds, measuring them for changes in rainfall or direction. Over the course of several months, the researchers experimented with a variety of chemicals in an underpopulated region, reporting their findings back to Project STORMFURY staff for future use.[106] That October, when the Cuban Missile Crisis led to a thirteen-day standoff over nuclear weaponry positioned 90 miles south of Florida, Americans' attention turned to the nation's increasingly tense relations with Communist Cuba. As a result of the crisis, government leaders began to consider the hurricane's potential as the next great weapon that could be harnessed to defend the nation. If nothing else, the ability to direct a storm away from a populated Gulf South coastline was a real asset that would both protect Americans from storm damage that could, in turn, make them more vulnerable to other, more human threats. Sparking this idea was the interference of Hurricane Ella during the Cuban Missile Crisis. Ella grossly impacted both US and Russian naval operations during the crisis, first by muddling the blockade of Cuba, and then by damaging Soviet nuclear-armed submarines en route to the island.[107] While Ella missed striking the US East Coast on its way out to sea, the confluence of fears of atomic and meteorological weapons was enough to shake the United States to its core, inscrutably linking storms with bombs like never before.

The United States was not the only country impacted by the growing fear of new-age weaponry. For years after, the STORMFURY program would rankle Fidel Castro, as he accused the United States of miraculously steering any storm that impacted Cuba.[108] Castro's paranoia was not entirely ridiculous, as Project STORMFURY was funded by the US government, departmentally housed under the joint oversight of the US Department of Commerce and the US Navy, and physically located at the NHC headquarters outside of Miami and later in Puerto Rico, pointing right at Cuba.[109] Still, even if the United States wanted the hurricane as a Cold War weapon, it did not mean they had figured out how to make it so.[110]

In the second year of Project STORMFURY, during the 1963 season, a new era of hurricane modification dawned with the successful seeding of Hurricane Beulah.[111] When Beulah was first spotted, it did not have a well-developed eye as per the project's selection criteria, but it was far enough from the coastline and large enough to meet the other criteria. Project

STORMFURY staff, having waited in vain throughout the previous storm season, were eager to test new equipment for modification. In time between experiments, new silver iodide canisters had been developed by Drs. Lohr Burkart and William Finnegan, part of the STORMFURY staff, that contained larger amounts of silver iodide crystals and delivered it easily into a hurricane's eye at a faster pace. As explained in newspaper articles across the country, "prior to 1961, [the old method] could put out about 2 or 3 ounces of silver iodide in an hour." The new method, or NOTS technique (named for its development by researchers at the US Naval Ordnance Test Station in China Lake, California), could "disperse a ton of silver iodide crystals within four minutes!"[112] The canisters used in the NOTS technique even came with a name to describe their shape, which included a single hole to deliver and steer the crystals. They were called Cyclops 11, "after mythical Greek giants, who, like hurricanes, had but a single, centrally located eye," and Alecto, "named after one of the Three Furies of Greek Mythology."[113] Now, Cyclops 11 and Alecto canisters were deployed to fight Beulah in an epic battle of man (humans) versus nature (Beulah).

In addition to newly developed methods of seeding, Project STORMFURY staff had also refined their standards for safe seeding experiments. "Beulah was deemed just right for the experiment because she had a relatively stable structure and couldn't possibly have hit the coast within 48 hours of the chemical attack," reported Ann Cook of the US Department of Commerce in a press statement. This new rule of 48 hours and several miles from the coastline was meant to protect coastal residents from a hurricane that is "tampered with." "It's like trying to tame a wild animal," Cook explained in the press briefing, but it would be worth it if the Weather Bureau's "flying laboratories" are able to find the "Achilles heel" of a hurricane with the "silver iodide 'bombs.'" In the end, Cook assured reporters, the unladylike "Beulah [could be] bombed into submission."[114]

The day of Beulah's first seeding, ten planes were deployed with NOTS Cyclops 11 and Alecto canisters full of silver iodide crystals. Three planes patrolled and probed Beulah at 7,000, 18,000, and 41,000 feet; a fourth remained at the edge of the storm to record temperature, wind, barometric pressure, and other factors; two planes made a photographic record; and with everyone in "hurricane battle position," the command plane gave the "go-ahead signal" to the tenth plane or "the sender," a Navy A3B Skywarrior plane, to release the NOTS canisters.[115] Unfortunately for the waiting weathermen, the first seeding of Beulah was an obvious failure, as the iodide dispensers dispersed well outside the ill-constructed eye. Not only did Beulah's wind strength stay constant; it gained speed overnight. The next day, Beulah's eye was more clearly developed, and planes again seeded the storm with silver iodide crystals. This time, their efforts appeared effective; pilots tracking Beulah gaily reported that the storm experienced a 20 percent reduction in wind speed, and exhibited a weakening of the developed eye. As described excitedly in the press, "Beulah had been 'hurt'" by the seeding process. "She never regained her maximum wind speed of 120 miles per hour," reported the *Los Angeles Times*.[116] The encouraging results aligned with those observed with Hurricane Esther and thus appeared to confirm that Project STORMFURY's mission of hurricane modification through seeding was sound. But the next venture into seeding was not so well received.[117]

Less than two years after the successful seeding of Hurricane Beulah, another plausible test storm emerged on the horizon. The second storm of the season, Hurricane Betsy, was described as "erratic," developing slowly and spending ten days "wandering" around the Atlantic.[118] Betsy was far enough out to sea that the NHRP director, Robert Simpson, and his staff, now officially including Joanne Malkus Simpson (whom he had convinced to join the NHRP research team in 1964, and then married a year later), deemed the storm appropriate for "seeding." Americans watched excitedly as Project STORMFURY staff organized their operators. The *New Orleans Times-Picayune* reported the details as they unfolded: "Fifteen planes stood ready" to "drop silver iodide crystals into her moisture-laden winds," and reconnaissance aircraft made "a thorough study of conditions."[119] "If a hurricane can be tamed, Uncle Sam intends to do it," reported the *Christian Science Monitor*, enthusiastically watching Betsy develop. And storms like Betsy could have devastating effects on the Gulf Coast as a hurricane could average power "equivalent in energy to 10 Hiroshima-type A-bombs every second."[120] But then Betsy suddenly veered left, away from the open ocean, and headed into the Gulf of Mexico.[121] The storm beelined for the Louisiana coast, gathering strength before hitting Grand Isle, Louisiana, with winds of roughly 130 miles per hour.[122]

As Betsy traveled inland from Grand Isle, the storm kept to its northwestward path. On September 9, it "slashed and pummeled" New Orleans, wreaking catastrophic damage to the city's levees.[123] The *Times-Picayune*, one of the first newspapers to applaud Project STORMFURY's seeding attempts, was now quick to bemoan Betsy's impact. Although "there is always a big element of unpredictability with hurricanes," a storm like "Belligerent Betsy" with "her" "tempestuous wandering" was "the kind that makes these hurricanes the more hateful the more one sees of them."[124] In fact, "Betsy's rape in the night" was "too powerful to fend off completely."[125] This "irrational lady" ought to be *tamed,* and it was unfortunate that Project STORMFURY was not able to do it sooner, they concluded.[126] Still, just as nuclear energy was harnessed from the atomic bomb, there was hope that hurricanes could be tamed. On the day Betsy struck land, the front page of the *New Orleans Daily States/Item* declared, "Man, learning more yearly about the intricate nature of hurricanes, may soon be able to defang them." This was even more impressive than the taming of nuclear energy, since "Betsy and her ill-gotten sisters [contain] an unbridled force which makes a nuclear arsenal seem puny."[127] The *States/Item*'s front-page story is suffused with the hope inspired by Project STORMFURY, declaring that Americans (referred to as "Man") were closer to discovering the "secrets" of storms through scientific discovery, and that notwithstanding the controversy over the purported seeding of Betsy, hurricane seeding was worth the risk to a city so vulnerable to hurricanes' impact.

As the first storm of its scale, Betsy leveled over a billion dollars in damage to the Gulf South and earned the posthumous nickname "Billion Dollar Betsy." As residents of Louisiana and surrounding Gulf states considered how and why Betsy had inflicted so much damage, their discussions simmered with hostility and blame. First, there was the issue of preparedness, as residents wondered whether meteorologists could have better prepared them for the hurricane's dramatic change of course. The second issue was the post-storm response by the city of New Orleans, as flood victims speculated that not only were levees faultily constructed, but the city may also have bombed the levees protecting lower-income or racially segregated neighborhoods to alleviate floodwater pressure on higher-income areas, as was done with the great Mississippi River Flood of 1927.[128] The third point of discussion involved a conspiracy theory that Weather Bureau officials and Project STORMFURY staff had secretly seeded Betsy in their haste to provide results for Project STORMFURY. Although New Orleans residents supported hurricane-seeding efforts before and during Betsy's course, their support quickly turned to outrage at the idea that Betsy might have been secretly seeded.[129] The rationale for this conspiracy theory was that Betsy's escalation and dramatic turn to the Gulf after days of wandering in the Atlantic was so abnormal that the only reasonable explanation was seeding. This conspiracy theory was fed by several sources: old rumors about the 1947 Georgia storm that had followed a similar pattern after a test seeding process, the well-publicized Project BATON experiments with multiple cloud-seeding chemicals in Arizona, and the widespread newspapers reports that the Weather Bureau had selected Betsy for seeding.[130]

The Weather Bureau naturally responded to the accusations denying having seeded Betsy. The bureau further insisted that the case of Betsy provided a perfect illustration of why careful precautions must be taken in selecting hurricanes for Project STORMFURY modification efforts. They emphasized that the extent of Betsy's damage served to show why hurricane modification was such a necessary project, especially in the Cold War era, when as New Orleans's own *States/Item* had pointed out, hurricanes presented an even greater threat to the nation's strength and security than Russia's or Cuba's nuclear arsenals. The Weather Bureau statement noted that the increased development in the Gulf States meant that storms like Betsy now had greater industrial impact than ever before. The storm had wrought considerable damage on Louisiana's burgeoning offshore oil industry, sinking multiple oil platforms that were later valued at millions of dollars. The storm also impacted many of the barges carrying goods up the Mississippi River, one of which contained over 600 tons of chlorine gas, a chemical used as a weapon during war. In Alabama, the storm stripped roughly 25 percent of the state's pecan trees of their fruit, while crops across the Gulf South suffered from the effects of wind, storm surge, and floodwaters. This was nothing compared to the number of homes destroyed (164,000 in the New Orleans area alone), or individuals lost to the storm (81 total).[131] In an era of rapid population growth in the Gulf South region, any of these devastating factors motivated efforts at prevention. But much like the response to the 1947 Georgia storm, speculation over Betsy's seeding was not dispelled quickly. Time was of the essence for the staff at Project STORMFURY to again prove that hurricane modification was possible and advisable.

If the rhetoric around Hurricane Betsy was any indication, Project

STORMFURY had a profound effect on the American public's perception of storms. While reporters criticized the failed seeding experiments, they also reflected the public's desire to "tame" hurricanes, which increased dramatically with the efforts of the project. The media coverage even blended feminized descriptors—like "rape," "irrational lady," "belligerent," and "tempestuous wandering"—with Cold War containment language, suggesting that, just as nuclear energy had been tamed in the atomic bomb, so too the hurricane could be neutralized as a threat, or even harnessed into a weapon for use against the United States' enemies. Surely Americans would tame the hurricane, and surely Project STORMFURY would lead the way. Success was only a matter of time.

A Triumph or Tragedy? Camille and Debbie

The rumor mill surrounding the purported seeding of "Billion Dollar Betsy" placed pressure on Project STORMFURY officials to reexamine the storm-selection criteria. The project had undoubtedly led to advancements in the scientific understanding of hurricanes and their effects, but still, the project had failed to show conclusive results regarding control of hurricanes.[132] For the next two hurricane seasons after Betsy, the project leadership continued to watch the skies, awaiting a suitable storm for their next seeding effort.[133] This time they were extra cautious to select storms that fit their criteria.[134] But this caution did not slow their efforts to identify a potential storm for seeding. Robert Simpson, having left his position as director of the project in 1966 to become director of operations for the Weather Bureau and then deputy director of the National Hurricane Center, ceded control of Project STORMFURY to his now-wife, Dr. Joanne Simpson (née Malkus).[135] As director of Project STORMFURY, Joanne Simpson continued to test the hypothesis behind hurricane seeding for an additional two years.[136] Unfortunately, no suitable hurricanes developed, and speculation over the effectiveness of the seeding hypothesis only grew. Deciding to move on, Joanne Simpson left her position with Project STORMFURY at the end of 1967 but continued to work with NOAA on cloud experiments in Florida related to rainfall.[137]

The following year was one of transition for Project STORMFURY.[138] At the end of the 1968 season, Project STORMFURY staff—now led by Dr. R. Cecil Gentry of the Weather Bureau/NHRP Laboratory assisted by Captain R. J. Brazzell, commander of the Fleet Weather Facility at Jacksonville, Florida, and overseen by Dr. Robert M. White, Environmental Science Services Administration (ESSA) administrator and Captain E. T. Harding, head of the Naval Weather Service Command—implemented a 48-hour alert for STORMFURY staff to deploy at any chance of storm development.[139] This meant that project scientists, airplanes, and flight crews were on call and ready to deploy on a 48-hour notice should a storm develop before the end of the season in October.[140] Unfortunately, no such storm emerged. By the start of the 1969 hurricane season, Project STORMFURY staff were anxious to find another storm that could be seeded.[141] Their eagerness mounted as the first moonwalk was televised on July 20, 1969. The event was a culmination of the decade-long push to invest in science and American ingenuity, and represented American strength in persevering over feared Communist aggressors in the Space Race. It was in this context that, the next month, the third hurricane of the 1969 season was identified. It was imaged and tracked using the satellite technology that had been developed in the Space Race.[142]

This latest hurricane grew seemingly overnight to a massive storm in the Gulf, following patterns of previously devastating hurricanes. Its name was Camille. Unfortunately, Camille escalated too rapidly for Project STORMFURY efforts to commence, aiming directly at a large swath of the coastal Gulf South. Despite the time and money invested in a weapon to tame storms of its magnitude, all coastal residents could do was pray, or flee. The frustration with this was made all the more upsetting in reference to the conquering of the moon a month earlier. Man had failed. Camille had won.[143]

In expressing human failure to tame the hurricane, newspapers across the country used explicitly gendered rhetoric. The hurricane was the woman who could not be tamed, no matter the science developed to try to understand it, and she had an arsenal of power that made her frightening. The storm "came alive with a bang," springing "suddenly to life" to "prowl over the watery jungles of the tropics until the time came when she was to vent her fury on some luckless coastline," reported the *Austin Statesman*.[144] Once at the Gulf Coast, Camille "shrieked" through the coast "like a woman in labor," reported the *Mobile Press-Register*.[145] She "howled," "whipping the Gulf of Mexico into an angry white froth," all the while "mopping up" the coastline with 175-miles-per-hour winds, the second storm in US history to strike at that magnitude.[146] When it eventually made landfall near Bay

St. Louis, Mississippi, it packed a "Titanic punch," proclaimed the *Miami Herald,* referencing the dramatic deaths of hundreds at sea.[147] In total, damages from "Camille the Terrible," as the *Houston Chronicle* called "her," were estimated at $1.4 billion, topping the previous record-holding storm, Betsy.[148] "It was like Hiroshima," declared reporters in the *Atlanta Journal-Constitution* when surveying the Gulf coastline.[149] But this Cold War–esque apocalyptic aftermath was expected, replied the *New Orleans Times-Picayune,* as "during her lifetime, Camille's total energy equivalent exuded several thousand megatons of TNT, making her a storm of superlatives."[150] In the end, the *Times-Picayune* concluded, Camille made "Betsy and the 1915 storm seem like child's play," as she "was a much stronger-willed 'lady.'"[151] And they were right: the cost to the Gulf Coast had been unbearable, the worst hurricane damage ever seen. This was due not only to the size of the storm, which was "notable" for its "compactness" that allowed it to target an area with "furious" winds, but also to the growth in coastal population and industry that had put more people and infrastructure in the path of hurricanes.[152] While Camille was a small storm in size, its powerful 175-miles-per-hour winds left a disastrous wake. As death counts totaled over 250, injury counts tallied at 8,931, and the $1.4 billion ($9.5 billion in 2018) in damages (including over 19,000 homes destroyed), the catchphrase of the post-storm period became "Camille Was No Lady."[153] Popular culture soon claimed the expression, using it in everything from charity booklets to raising money for storm relief to made-for-TV movies about the horror experienced by the thousands affected.[154] As the costliest storm to date and with this phrase percolating through popular culture, Camille left Americans more motivated than ever before to find a way to tame this Cold War vixen.

Gulf residents did not have long to cope with the trauma of Camille; even as this storm was ravaging the Gulf Coast, a "sister storm" was developing in the warm Caribbean waters. "Husky Hurricane Debbie" emerged on the "heels" of Camille, but mercifully "play[ed] second fiddle" in both strength and interest.[155] Drifting in the Atlantic, the storm initially headed toward the eastern Florida coast, but hooked right to veer further from the shore, having reached a solid 115-miles-per-hour wind strength. Debbie stalled in the Atlantic away from most populated areas and soon curved further into the open sea. Many on land breathed sighs of relief. But this relief soon turned into nervous watchfulness as Project STORMFURY announced they had determined that Debbie fit the criteria for seeding. The sense of urgency over seeding Debbie grew as Camille's unprecedented damage was tallied. With Camille fresh in their minds, Americans around the country tuned in to watch weathermen take on nature. The *New Orleans Times-Picayune* reported, "Meteorologists and pilots declared themselves Tuesday night ready to go with people, planes, and pyrotechnics."[156] The Weather Bureau had the best technology and resources they had ever had at their disposal, including over 200 scientists, Nimbus III satellite imagery, and the well-staffed Hurricane Hunter division that had been practicing flying into the eye of the storm for over a decade.[157] Seven years into Project STORMFURY, there finally was a "suitable storm" in the form of Hurricane Debbie.[158] As Americans held their breath, though, the *Charleston News & Observer* cautioned that the final decision to use Debbie as a case study "depends on Debbie herself."[159] Much like with Betsy, the mission could be aborted up until the last minute.

After much suspense, the head of the National Hurricane Center, Robert Simpson, reported that the seeding of Debbie would commence. "Debbie seems ideally constructed and positioned for seeding," he said. In fact, "she comes as close in filling the bill as I could describe."[160] On August 18, 1969, the same day as Camille made landfall in Mississippi, thirteen aircraft took off from Miami, flying high and far to drop the silver iodide crystals into the eye wall of Debbie.[161] The Project STORMFURY staff then proceeded to monitor the effectiveness of the experiment, tracking the storm's course and strength. "Seeding Starts Today," the *New York Times* happily reported.[162] "Will Debbie Freeze to Death?" wondered the *Raleigh News & Observer*.[163] "Chemical Dropped On New Hurricane To Lessen Force," reported the *Washington Post* in an article explaining the process and quoting key project scientists as stating, "we can now modify a hurricane [and recent efforts] might indeed cripple it."[164] Before long, reports of Debbie's behavior started trickling in. "Seeded Debbie Slowing," the *Miami Herald* exclaimed the next morning.[165] And slowing it was, Debbie had experienced a 31 percent reduction in wind speed overnight, a true feat for the STORMFURY staff.[166]

As the American public continued to watch Debbie, Project STORMFURY staff readied for the second round of seeding. The *Times-Picayune* reported that, even though the Gulf South was still reeling from the damage caused by Camille, the Weather Bureau had "Debbie's location and makeup," and the "prospects for a repeat attack by US Navy jet planes, look pretty good."[167] On the first day of seeding, over 200 weather experts and 17 planes took part in the experiment, a gross increase in personnel from previous seeding experiments.[168] This was because scientists believed that "attacking [a hurricane] with an even larger fleet of planes might indeed cripple it."[169] "Flying went really well with Debbie," reported Weather Bureau officials to the press after the experiment. The Navy pilots involved showed no "fear of a hurricane" after "Vietnam," stating that seeding was "almost a milk run."[170] Two days after the first seeding experiment, fighter pilots again dropped silver iodide crystals into Hurricane Debbie's eye wall and waited for the results. The *Times-Picayune* reported that initially, after "penetration of the eye," "Debbie seemed to calm down."[171] The second seeding reduced it an additional 15 percent. Despite weathermen's efforts to give Debbie the "cold treatment," this "sister" of Hurricane Camille did not dissipate entirely. As newspapers put it, "Debbie goes on despite iodide."[172] Disappointingly, newspaper articles the next day reported "Defiant Debbie" "won't be tamed," as the storm continued to "stalk" Bermuda.[173]

Although Debbie was not exterminated by the iodide pyrotechnics, a 31 percent and 15 percent wind reduction after two seedings was considered a true success.[174] Reporters and weathermen throughout the country quickly reviewed the statistics of previous experiments and hurricane-prediction models to determine just how much of a success it was.[175] Ultimately, they concluded that Debbie had indeed acted atypically after seeding: its winds had decreased, while its trajectory had remained the same. It appeared that the Project STORMFURY staff was onto something, albeit it was possible that Debbie was a fluke. All agreed that duplication of the process was the next step in proving the success of hurricane modification.[176]

Though the seeding of Debbie was only a vaguely qualified success, it did not dampen the celebratory mood. In a joint statement reporting the effects of the experiment months after Debbie's seeding, two Cabinet officers from the Weather Bureau and the Navy stated emphatically: "We believe that the force of Debbie was weakened by our seeding on August 18 and August 20, since this occurred in accordance with our scientific understanding of how seeding would affect a hurricane." They continued, "We want to share with the public the hope we feel from an experiment which appears to be tremendously promising."[177] Debbie had proven that a "Hiroshima-like" hurricane was a "tropical tiger [that could be] tamed into a pussycat" or at least "defang[ed]." Project STORMFURY "gave mankind a weapon" against the violent tropical terrors that had plagued them for years.[178] And they were going to continue to invest in this program, even going so far as to suggest that "the federal government may attempt to seed all hurricanes threatening the nation's shores [in 1970]."[179] As put succinctly by Dr. Cecil Gentry, head of the NHRP Laboratory, "if federal hurricane modification research continues at the present level for a decade and if, in that time, one severe hurricane such as Camille in 1969 can be weakened so that its damage is reduced by as little as 10 percent, the investment will have been returned tenfold."[180] With any luck, Americans would never have to experience another Camille.

The Impact of Hurricane Taming

The seeding of Debbie in 1969 did indeed appear to be a moment of perennial possibilities. Success in building a weapon to defeat or control nature's shrewdest obstacle was indicative of much more than just hope for preventing another Camille. It represented the culmination of the investment in American ingenuity to solve global problems. It also helped to soothe fears in an era where atomic tensions percolated in everyday discourse while juxtaposed with a rapidly expanding technological revolution that threatened demise at every discovery. The battle to control hurricanes was thus seen as the final battle at the close of the decade of discovery—and all hope of achieving this goal had rested in the hands of Project STORMFURY.

The postwar hurricane-modification experiments and government-sponsored research programs had a profound effect on the cultural understanding of hurricanes. In a new era of prediction and televised reporting, the American public was introduced to terminology by the US Weather Bureau that defined everything from storm makeup to prediction path. Hurricanes were no longer illusory cyclones forming from the sea; they were fixed weather patterns that could be identified, monitored, and presumably attacked with troops or weaponry. In defining the hurricane (and everything that went along with it), Americans altered their perception of what a storm was. This alteration, however, extended past the identification of a hurricane's parts, leading to the cultural redefinition of a storm. Because names were assigned to storms, it was easy for the American public to apply new characteristics that described the qualities of hurricanes that were most frustrating in an era where scientific definition was of growing importance. Similarly, while anthropomorphic names fed the associations with human characteristics, the exclusively female-only selection of names impacted the assignment of an exclusive gender to hurricanes. From this point on, hurricanes were intrinsically feminine entities.

The drive to control hurricanes also directly affected the acceptance and use of the hurricane-naming system. There is a definitive correlation between the experimentation to control storms, the Cold War–era hostilities that escalated fear of weaponry of any type, and the shifting cultural changes (gendered expectations and population growth) that fed into the creation of a new type of imagined storm. Fueled by the gendered politics brewing in the backdrop, including those experienced by Joanne Simpson and the "Weather Girls" within the field of meteorology, the rapid adoption of gendered language to describe Carol, Dolly, Edna, and Hazel is not a surprise in a culture obsessed with femininity. Nor is it surprising that the worst characteristics for women were included in the descriptors of storms annually. Americans became more accustomed to the practice and dependent on the efforts to control or tame them due to their devastating potential to impact a postwar coastline flush with industry and population growth. As a result, names were no longer just names, a signifier or title. Instead, they personified storms as beings with emotions, feelings, and lives all their own, a recognizable target to attempt to obliterate.

Due to their association with devastation, however, these feminized storms both reflected the most negative stereotypes of women from the postwar era and helped to produce new harmful descriptors. Between 1954 and 1969, feminized hurricanes were associated with a litany of negative characteristics usually assigned to women who transgressed social norms. When measuring their use and acceptance, few negative reactions are found. In fact, the use of these expletives only increased over time, growing in frequency and creativity. If one were to measure the perception of transgressive women during this era or the hostility toward social change, one need only look at the hurricane descriptions printed in hundreds of newspapers across the country. By 1969, hurricane descriptions became the cultural repository for Americans' descriptions of their "bad girls," used frequently in newspaper articles discussing their impact. Leading the use of these gendered descriptions was the Gulf South, home of the site of all action related to hurricanes. (See figure 4.)

Overall, the descriptions used with Debbie and Camille represented the ongoing negotiation of female roles in society. These descriptors were extremely negative, leaving no doubt about the perception of the transgressive woman within Cold War society. The work of Project STORMFURY correlates with this process. The hurricane, as described, was "attacked" in the process of "seeding," and only appeared to "calm down" once "penetrated." These references within public newspapers are all shockingly sexualized for their time. The fact that they were printed in an era when media censorship laws were gaining ground indicates just how badly the American public wanted this seeding process to work. They were willing to do everything—deploy weapons, manpower, and language—to achieve victory over this enemy. In this way, the description of hurricanes also provided a rare public forum in which people could acceptably flirt with sexual language.

The introduction of the hurricane-naming system, the research that supported hurricane-modification efforts, and the cultural acceptance of hurricane gendering emerged from one region of the United States—the Gulf South. Not coincidentally, this was also the region most adversely affected by storms. But even beyond the Gulf South, the gendered characterizations of storms saw rapid adoption. Broadcast through bulletins, articles, and on television, these images of women were reproduced and commodified for a market that extended far past the geographic boundaries of the United States. They crossed the globe, perpetuating American images of gender appropriateness. By 1969, all regions of the world bestowed human names to tropical storms such as hurricanes, cyclones, and typhoons, as the US Weather Bureau increasingly dominated the production of meteorological knowledge. Transferring with these names were American gendered characteristics attached to female-named storms.[181] Much like other cultural commodities in the Cold War era, no region of the world went unaffected by the hurricane-naming system adopted by the United States in the early 1950s. It continued to expand around the globe through the 2000s as similar naming systems were adopted for tropical storms in the North Indian Ocean and off the coast of Brazil.[182]

In looking at the original expressed intention of Weather Bureau officials in the adoption of the female hurricane-naming system, it is naive to be-

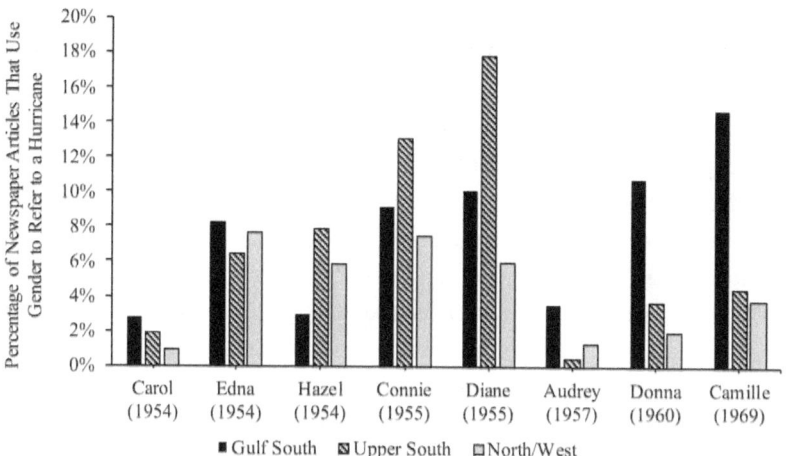

Figure 4. Percentage of newspaper articles that use gender to refer to a hurricane, by region, 1954–69. While the Upper South used gender at a greater frequency between 1954 and 1955, the Gulf South used gender more frequently in the years following, far surpassing all other regions. This was largely due to the location of major storm landfalls, proving that increased gender use correlates with storm impact.

Sources: Measured using qualitative data analysis of 12 US newspapers from five-day periods for nine major storms between 1954 and 1969, or the female-only storm naming period (n = 2,086 in data set as represented here out of 8,915 articles total in book's data set).

Note: Gender was defined by use of gender-specific nouns and pronouns such as woman/man, he/she, to refer to the hurricane (e.g., "*She* was no *lady*"). It does not include the use of gender-specific adjectives, which are more subjective to quantify, but are described in this chapter's text. The Gulf South includes the states bordering the Gulf (Texas, Louisiana, Mississippi, Alabama, and Florida). The Upper South includes states bordering the Atlantic Ocean (the Carolinas, Georgia, and Virginia). The North/West indicates states statistically not prone to repeated hurricane attacks, but which do experience infrequent storms (New York, Maryland, and California).

lieve that these officials did not anticipate the spread of these names or the cultural associations attached to them. It is also erroneous to assume that the Weather Bureau could have known just how well received these names would be, or the negativity they would inspire. Throughout the 1950s and 1960s the Weather Bureau frequently commented that it was surprised how interested the public was in their activities. Even with interest caused by the names, the question of why hurricanes were named never went away.

In articles introducing hurricane names for the upcoming season and reflections published after storms passed through, Americans reconsidered the practice of hurricane naming every year. By 1969, the naming system, in place for fifteen years, had become a fixture of every weather bulletin and news report, and was used broadly in popular culture. Named hurricanes provided Americans with a tangible enemy to scorn, a villain to curse, and a cultural marker of their lives. Meanwhile, American Cold War sexual politics normalized the use of gendered stereotypes with storms.

More importantly, these storms were sites of cultural negotiation where female names and characterizations did more than enable the public (and the media and the government) to identify and describe storms. Seeding efforts helped rationalize the understanding of hurricane movements and impact, and ultimately changed the perception of them. Taming hurricanes was a multipronged effort, involving meteorological description and monitoring as well as government-sponsored modification programs. These efforts were expensive, but the storm names helped justify that expense by fueling two entangled Cold War fears: unharnessed weaponry (and nature) and untamed women. They also placed the practice of hurricane naming squarely in the crosshairs of feminist activists by the 1970s.

ROXCY
AND THE FEMINIST RESISTANCE

Standing on the sidewalk at the doors of the Interdepartmental Hurricane Warning Conference, forty-three-year-old Miami housewife and avowed feminist Roxcy Bolton smoothed an unruly strand of black hair back into her bouffant and looked up at the newly constructed Computer Building on the University of Miami's campus.[1] It was January 1971, and she had had an eventful few months since first writing the letter that brought her here: a terse three-paragraph demand, addressed to officials at the US Weather Bureau's National Hurricane Center (NHC), requesting that they stop giving hurricanes female names. Since then, she had met or corresponded with dozens of Weather Bureau officials and endured incessant press coverage of her quest. Supporting her in her cause was her cohort at the Miami-Dade chapter of the National Organization for Women (NOW). Her cosigner on the letter was the current NOW chapter president, Martha Ingle. But Martha had recently moved out west, and now Roxcy Bolton found herself at the Interdepartmental Hurricane Warning Conference alone, the sole representative of NOW to plead her case for gender equality to the men who controlled the weather. She knew full well that the winds were changing, and so should they.[2]

Roxcy Bolton's quest to reshape public discourse around hurricanes started in December 1969, when she attended her second national NOW conference in New Orleans. There, she brought up recent coverage of the August storms, Hurricanes Camille and Debbie. "I am sick and tired of hearing that Camille was no lady," she stated at the conference. The latest round of coverage, particularly in the Gulf South, was an appalling example of efforts to belittle women in the media. If NOW's mission for the upcoming year was to seek to change the image of women as presented by the media, they need look no further than the hurricane, she implored. In fact, she motioned, NOW should send a letter to the NHC "asking that hurricanes not be named exclusively for women."[3] The members of NOW agreed, passing Bolton's motion. In a press release issued at the conclusion of the meeting, then-president Betty Friedan even went so far as to draw attention to this new issue of NOW concern.[4] Hurricanes and the weathermen who named them were the focus of NOW for 1970, on equal level with efforts to legalize abortion and push for an equal rights amendment, and Roxcy Bolton was to lead the effort.

After Bolton volunteered to spearhead this latest revolutionary mission, she returned home to Florida determined to change the female-only hurricane-naming process. Her first step was to turn to the members of NOW's newly established local Miami-Dade chapter for help. With Martha Ingle, Bolton drafted a statement to the NHC requesting that the system be phased out. The statement's language was fiery; its signatory, newly formidable. The letter comprised three brief paragraphs:

> The National Organization for Women respectfully requests the U.S. Weather Bureau—Hurricane Center, Coral Gables, Fla. to cease and desist from using the names of women as names for Hurricanes. This request includes the 1970 Hurricane season.
>
> The naming of Hurricanes with female names reflects and creates an extremely derogatory attitude toward women. Hurricanes are disasters destroying life and communities, and leave a lasting effect on those affected. Women are human beings and deeply resent being arbitrarily associated with disaster.
>
> *We therefore ask you to refrain from ever designating hurricanes by the names of women.*[5]

They signed the letter "Mrs. David (Roxcy) Bolton, Vice President, National Organization for Women," and "Martha Ingle, President, Dade County Chapter," giving weight to their demand.[6] For Bolton and her compatriots at NOW, the stakes were high. Over the previous decade, they had observed a troubling trend in how newspapers talked about extreme weather: it was now common for news reports to describe storms using a fleet of creative expletives. In the 1969 season, for example, newspapers proclaimed that Camille and Debbie needed to be "seeded," in order to "calm" them. Or that they were uncontrollable "witches," akin to "angry women." For feminists, this trend was symptomatic of larger, systemic problems of the postwar era: the pervasive belittlement of women in public discourse. Bolton and other feminists believed that the use of toxic language to refer to female-named storms should cease.

Bolton was unfazed by the prospect of attending the Interdepartmental Hurricane Warning Conference alone. Growing up in the central Mississippi town of Duck Hill, Bolton learned early to speak up in a crowd and make her point. What was more, this was not her first fight on behalf of women's rights. In her early twenties, she served as a member of the United Daughters of the Confederacy and a volunteer to the American Red Cross, training as a Grey Lady staff aide postwar. After a brief first marriage and quick divorce, she remarried, this time to an officer in the US Navy. Shortly thereafter she took on the US military over the gendered segregation of the swimming pools at her husband's base. As a thirty-something housewife in 1956, she served as the cochair for the presidential campaign of Adlai Stevenson; two years later she became a Democratic national committeewoman; and in 1960, she served as an executive assistant for the US Senate Democratic campaign. In fact, she had fought for equality for as long as she could remember. No, this was not her first fight, and it would definitely not be the last.[7]

Bolton's involvement in NOW began in 1966, when the group passed its neophyte years and started to create ripples of interest nationally. She had joined with a sense of seriousness and destiny. Although Bolton had participated in political organizations before, including those specifically concerned with women's rights, none were as extensive as NOW. At the time Bolton joined it, NOW was little more than a loosely formed group of women, and she its first and only representative of Florida. But the organization quickly grew to become the preeminent organization defending women's liberation in the 1970s. Even in 1970, when Bolton wrote her letter to the NHC, NOW had enough weight to evoke anxiety in any long-standing organization accused of sexist practices. When she delivered the letter, she knew she would receive a reply precisely because she was writing with the heft of the organization behind her. In Bolton's quest, her road was not smooth, but neither was it unique. She was one among many women fighting for equality in twentieth-century America, in a system largely rigged to deny it. How fervently her opponents thwarted her attempts to change one aspect of this system illustrated the larger challenges facing feminism in the twentieth century.

A Storm Brewing: The Creation of NOW

The founding of NOW in 1966 marked the hopeful beginning of a new and more fruitful era in women's rights. For decades after the passage of women's suffrage in 1920, the women's rights movement suffered a frustrating period of minimal successes. The postwar era had brought changes in the definition of gender roles, particularly regarding working women and, by 1961, women's issues started to appear on the national political agenda again. A powerful advocate for women's rights, President John F. Kennedy introduced Executive Order 10980 in 1961 to form a commission to report on the status of women in American society. The President's Commission on the Status of Women included some of the top women in the country, and was initially chaired by former first lady Eleanor Roosevelt. While a Depression-era Women's Bureau existed to study the needs of women, the Commission on the Status of Women was tasked with identifying ways that gender inequality was expressed in postwar American society.

One of the feminist leaders fueling the renewed attention to women's rights and awareness of postwar gender inequality was Betty Friedan, author of a best-selling book, *The Feminine Mystique* (1963). Through analysis of interviews, newspaper articles, and other media commentary on gender roles, Friedan exposed the stark realities of gender disparity in the postwar period. Filling pages with descriptions of boozy, pill-popping American housewives, Friedan proclaimed that American women were "living in a comfortable concentration camp."[8] The book drew millions of readers, reams of commentary, and plenty of criticism. Most significantly, it opened up discussions about women's rights and roles that shaped public discourse for years to come.

By 1963, when the publication of Friedan's *Feminine Mystique* began altering the public conversation on women's roles and rights, American women's rights had hardly advanced since the granting of suffrage in 1920.

Promising civil rights legislation proved disappointing in its execution. For example, the Civil Rights Act of 1964 provided for the creation of the Equal Employment Opportunities Commission (EEOC). The EEOC's mission was to oversee and prosecute any claims of employment discrimination on the basis of race or sex. In theory, the EEOC provided women the chance to voice opposition to employment discrimination practices and the federal support to enforce equality laid out in the Civil Rights Act of 1964.[9] In reality, as Friedan and others soon realized, the EEOC would do little for women's rights in the workplace. Within the first year of its creation, the EEOC was a target of concern for women across the country who had optimistically hoped that women's rights would extend the discussion of equality.

It was in this context of hope and disappointment that an organization called "N.O.W." was formed in 1966. At the Third National Conference of Commissions on the Status of Women in 1966, discussion of the failures of the EEOC reached a tipping point. As twenty-eight women sat in a room discussing these problems, they decided to create a "temporary organization" to address concerns. This organization, formed in the conference's final day, June 29, 1966, was created "to take action to bring women into full participation in the mainstream of American society *now,* assuming all the privileges and responsibilities thereof in truly equal partnership with men."[10] Called "N.O.W." for the National Organization for Women, its first mission was to change the recent EEOC decision to allow the segregation of help-wanted advertisements by sex. This separation into "male" and "female" jobs created an unfair hiring practice—giving less opportunity and variety of jobs, and subsequently affecting pay scales. Other tasks laid out at the organization's founding included equal participation in juries and representation in the Civil Rights Act of 1964.

In October 1966, the group held its first official organizing meeting. Thirty-two women attended as Betty Friedan delivered the opening address. In her address, Friedan compared the organizing meeting to the Seneca Falls Convention of 1848, which spurred the first major push for women's rights, including suffrage. The group then broke out into smaller "nuclei task forces" to discuss potential "Targets for Action" as priorities for the next year. The list of actionable activities went beyond initial discussion of help-wanted ads and the Civil Rights Act of 1964, to include everything from changing Social Security benefits to rights regarding the control of women's bodies and reproduction. The meeting adjourned with a complete list of goals for the next year, including the aim of increasing participation and membership significantly.[11]

In its second year, NOW succeeded on many fronts. Membership grew to 600, with most members hailing from New York, New Jersey, and Connecticut. The organization remained focused on the issues laid out at its founding. Members of the group, including Friedan, had presented arguments in front of the EEOC twice in the last year: first, regarding the help-wanted advertisements that encouraged sex-based hiring practices; and second, regarding the case of airline flight attendants who were fired once they reached the age of 32 or 35, or when they chose to marry. As the group's interests expanded, leaders set up an Educational and Legal Defense Fund to utilize all avenues of change, including legislative. Despite success at garnering attention from the EEOC and setting up a fund to organize a legal revision campaign, NOW was unsuccessful in its proclaimed mission to change "The Image of Woman." Having recently lost their chairman, the Reverend Dean Lewis, to a church mission, this aspect of the NOW mission was flagging. Volunteers were encouraged to suggest new ways to improve the image of women for presentation at the next National Board meeting and "ensure that women are given their rightful place in history."[12]

The following year, as NOW grew to include members from 24 states, the organization felt pressure to standardize not only its membership policies, but also its messaging. One source of pressure was the growth of rival organizations such as the National Women's Liberation Front (NWLF) and SCUM (alleged to mean "Society for Cutting Up Men"). Both NWLF and SCUM tested out extreme definitions of feminism, with SCUM even proposing the total abolition of men. These rival organizations often drew dual members from NOW, especially members who felt NOW was guarded in its positions on key issues like abortion and equal rights. As a result, the messages of NOW, and the more radical NWLF and SCUM, were confusing to news media organizations, which often lumped all of these groups' activities together under the broad term "feminist." The public therefore perceived little distinction between "radical feminist" and "feminist" activities.[13]

Even as NOW grappled with its position in relation to more radical women's rights groups, its overall activities increased. Annual meeting reports show significant progress in court cases regarding state protective laws, equal employment, and working conditions.[14] In addition, NOW encouraged attention to women in poverty, restroom segregation, and women and black power. On the national level, NOW agreed to focus the next year (1969) on the passage of the Equal Rights Amendment and to remove abortion from state penal codes. On the local level, chapters were encouraged to suggest changes to state labor laws, to educate and provide equal opportunities for education of males and females, to tackle abortion penalties, and to examine divorce and alimony laws. The last item for consideration was new approaches to the media, particularly in their construction of images of men and women.

The year 1969 brought nineteen new chapters to NOW while the group experienced both excitement over tasks completed and pressure over those left undone.[15] The organization continued to use sit-in demonstrations, boycotts, and celebratory spotlight events (including one before Mother's Day) to draw the public's attention to its causes. The organization also focused on addressing the perception of women in education; for example, at a collegiate level, courses on women's history were offered at several schools across the country, and community networks were formed to support alumnae of these programs. Also, in more direct attempts to revise the public image of women, volunteers reviewed textbooks and children's books with titles like *Chemistry for Boys,* offering suggestions on how to incorporate female role models, beyond housewives and mothers, into the texts. They also focused on the public discourse of abortion as the debate over repealing abortion laws often folded into debates over ratification of the Equal Rights Amendment. While conservative critique of NOW's efforts increased, a recent study in *Time* magazine showed remarkable shifts in public perception of women's issues, including perspectives on the criminalization of abortion.[16]

Meeting in New Orleans in December 1969, the organization's board members discussed a range of subjects, including the establishment of federally subsidized child-care centers and the support of the Equal Rights for Men and Women Amendment in the next year. One of the board members' top priorities, though, was to develop a response to recent statements by First Lady Pat Nixon that there was "very little discrimination against women in America." NOW suggested that a "personalized cram course on sex discrimination in America" could be provided by the board members for

Mrs. Nixon, the president, and cabinet members if desired. Another issue of concern was President Nixon's initial executive-level appointments. According to NOW, President Nixon appointed only "10 women out of more than 300 high-level White House officials" in his first year in office.[17] As a result, NOW suggested that any upcoming Supreme Court nominations be filled with qualified women and that the president make it a priority to actively select women for future appointments. They also pointed out that the president's denial of sexism in hiring practices for top positions only indicated larger trends in public perception and had dire implications for continuing such behavior.

By the end of 1969, NOW refocused on the perception of women in the media. The group looked for ways to address the belittlement, undermining, and negation of women through everything from textbooks, to role models on television and in jobs, to news coverage of extreme weather. The latter cause was one taken up by an energetic and highly political Miami housewife, Roxcy Bolton, as she attended her first national NOW meeting in 1968.

A Force of Nature: Roxcy Bolton Joins NOW

In 1968, Roxcy Bolton attended her first meeting of NOW's National Board in Atlanta, just a few hours' drive from her home in Coral Gables, Florida.[18] Drawn to the organization's mission of gender equality, Bolton had been a member since its founding in 1966, the year her third child was born.[19] To attend the Atlanta meeting, she had left her husband, David, a lawyer for the US Navy, home in Florida with her two toddlers, Bonnie and David. Bolton later stated that her interest in gender equality was first sparked by the time she spent stationed overseas in Japan with her husband, where she had been amazed by the differences in the treatment of women as compared to the United States in the 1960s. At the NOW meeting in Atlanta, Bolton was fascinated by what she saw and heard.

It was at this meeting that Bolton's political activism was galvanized and clarified. Her attention quickly focused on discussions of the recent actions of the incumbent president, Richard Nixon. In recent weeks, the president had chosen his cabinet members for his upcoming administration, as well as for the newly formed EEOC, largely excluding women from the selections.[20] Bolton took particular interest in conversations about this issue, which was unsurprising given her long-term interest in politics past her early years serving as a Grey Lady staff aide, co-chair of the Dade County presidential campaign for Adlai Stevenson, and as a Democratic national committeewoman. She had also served as the state coordinator for Florida women's activities for President Lyndon B. Johnson upon first moving to Miami in the early 1960s; then, in 1965, she had helped organize the Coral Gables Democratic Women's Club, both respectable positions for a southern Navy wife.[21] Now, at the meeting of NOW's National Board, she went on record expressing interest in forming a task force to urge the president to appoint women to senior positions not only within the EEOC, but within the government as a whole. Women deserved inclusion in the political process, she argued. The NOW board received her proposal favorably and formulated a strategy for how to proceed over the next year.[22] Executing that strategy over the months to follow, NOW sent letters, released press statements, and actively sought out ways to encourage President Nixon to appoint women to positions in the EEOC, Supreme Court, and various governmental departments like the Department of Commerce. These efforts met with minimal success, despite offers from NOW representatives to brief the president and his wife, Pat, on the state of women's affairs in the United States.[23]

After attending the NOW National Board meeting and conference in Atlanta, Bolton returned home to found a state chapter in the Miami area. First known as the Miami Area Chapter, it was quickly renamed the Dade County Chapter, with Bolton officially listed as its president in April 1969.[24] In addition, Bolton agreed to serve on the organization's National Board of Directors the following month.[25] Now that she was deeply involved in the organization on both the state and national levels, she looked for a way to contribute directly to its mission. She found it at the following year's conference, in New Orleans.

When Bolton arrived in New Orleans in December 1969 for the national conference, she had recently given birth to her fourth child in three years, a son named Buddy. Motherhood never slowed her down; frequently taking her young children with her to events and meetings, she was devoted to maintaining her work and taking care of her children.[26] The New Orleans meeting was just another event on her busy activist calendar. Much of the focus of the New Orleans conference was on the political and social climate of the late 1960s, including the establishment of national child-care centers, women's participation on juries, and the extension of protections for Title VII of the Civil Rights Act of 1964 to women.[27] It also featured an extensive discussion of the "New Image of Women" campaign, which sought to "change the stereotyped image and denigration of women in all the mass media." NOW aimed to do this by putting pressure on "networks, advertisers and editors which [had already] succeeded in abolishing the stereotyped images of" other groups like African Americans and Jews. As stated in the meeting's official record, NOW planned to "campaign for the inclusion of images of women which reflect, and thus encourage, the active participation of women in all fields of American society; images which are now completely absent from school books, as well as the media."[28]

This meeting provided Bolton an opportunity to introduce her own project to fit within NOW's overall mission: the southern-bred activist proposed that hurricane naming had created an atmosphere where storms had become avenues for expressing vitriolic sentiments about women. With each year, she argued, the negative gender stereotypes had only grown. She pointed directly to the previous year's storm of concern, Hurricane Camille, which had affected the Mississippi Gulf Coast and New Orleans area. Camille, and subsequent storm Debbie, were described as "unladylike" "witches" and painted as representative of typical women's anger and "erratic" behavior, a troubling connection that Bolton felt misrepresented women and was directly related to their female names. The other board members agreed with Bolton's assessment of the naming system, voting to support her in efforts to suggest changes to the naming policy and assigning her the task.[29]

While Bolton was given the job of pursuing the long-term goal of convincing the Weather Bureau to change hurricane names, President Betty Friedan publicly announced NOW's intention to pursue the issue in the next year. A press statement by Friedan on the final day of the conference went so far as to suggest that the naming system was one of their top priorities for the next year. "Future storms," Friedan reported—based on the discussions spearheaded by Bolton during the 1969 national meeting—"might be named after animals, flowers, or other categories that make just as much sense as women's names; or they might simply be designated by letters or numbers to omit names altogether." These sentiments were expressed in the form of a letter to the National Hurricane Center in Miami, "urging the center to 'choose names other than women's names in designating unwelcome, destructive hurricanes from now on.'"[30] With this, Roxcy Bolton was given a task and the support of a major organization to pursue a mission. It was now up to her to deal with the US Weather Bureau. She returned home from the conference in New Orleans galvanized to achieve her goal.

Change Is in the Wind

When Roxcy Bolton and Martha Ingle, then-president of the Miami–Dade County NOW Chapter, wrote their letter to the US Weather Bureau Hurricane Center, they used two rhetorical strategies common among NOW members. First, they positioned the letter as a hybrid national-local document drawing on NOW's discussion of the naming system at the 1969 national conference. They also emphasized their own role as local leaders interested in the impact of the naming system in both Miami and the larger Gulf South region. In effect, the letter was meant to carry the weight of a national organization while expressing the interest of local constituents. This rhetorical strategy was one frequently used by NOW's members to drive home national issues at a local level, and Bolton and Ingle were aware of this when they signed their letter of protest. Another strategy evident in the letter, and also employed by NOW's National Board and newly established Legal Defense and Education Fund, was the use of legal rhetoric to threaten recourse.[31] Although the letter was not a formal cease-and-desist order, it mimicked the language of one, using phrases such as "cease and desist," "refrain," and "arbitrary" to express the weight of its argument and potential legal recourse.

Following the construction of the letter, Bolton and Ingle prepared for the next step, delivering it into the hands of those who would actually read it. Their goal was to reach an audience high enough in the hierarchy of the Weather Bureau to have influence in the naming process. It was decided that Bolton would deliver the letter in person to the National Hurricane Center in Coral Gables. She arrived on Friday, March 20, 1970, and was received immediately by the director himself, Robert H. Simpson. Simpson led the NHC from 1967 to 1974, having been involved with the Weather Bureau since 1940. He spearheaded research on hurricanes through projects like STORMFURY, and even married the first American woman to receive a PhD in meteorology, leading researcher Joanne Simpson, who had faced her own struggles to find a place in a male-dominated profession. As a result, he was likely aware that NOW had identified hurricane naming as a target of concern in December 1969. Thus, he quickly invited Bolton to meet with him to discuss the topic.[32]

Following his meeting with Bolton, Simpson wrote a memo to his superiors in Washington, dated March 25, 1970, reporting the incident favorably. "We had a very cordial meeting," he stated. He wrote that he found Bolton's "presentation in support of her request ... creditable," and recommended that she be invited to present her request at the next Interdepartmental Hurricane Conference in January 1971. Dismissively, he noted that the reason "we [at the NHC] tend to be sympathetic to her request" was "not for the reason she advances but rather [because] we felt that our present procedure may well have served its usefulness." Simpson added matter-of-factly that he himself had "for several years been considering a proposal to substitute names of mythological characters or infamous characters in history." However, after "brief[ing] Mrs. Bolton on some of the background information on why and how hurricanes are named," Simpson assured his colleagues, "we're sure that she certainly has a better appreciation for the interdepartmental as well as the international aspects and commitments of the National Hurricane Warning Services." By doing so, Simpson indicated to his colleagues that he did not entirely agree with Bolton's claim that changing the names was both easy and necessary. He followed up by stating that NOW's members were in the "minority of women in this particular area of concern"; the majority of women, he stated emphatically, actually requested that "we name a hurricane for them." Simpson closed his memo by noting that Bolton had agreed to provide a list of alternative names "for advance comments" to the committee if she was chosen to present at the conference.[33]

Simpson's letter detailing Roxcy Bolton's initial contact with the Weather Bureau exemplifies the patronizing curiosity weather officials and others would express over the next three years in response to Bolton's crusade to change hurricane names. Like Simpson, many officials expressed support for changing the naming system, even volunteering that they had already considered the issue themselves but only acted upon hearing Bolton's proposed alternatives. In any case, and notwithstanding Simpson's supportive characterization of his meeting with Bolton, and his own background in hiring women, such as his own wife, in meteorological positions, the media portrayed the meeting differently in newspaper coverage over the following month.

The first media coverage of the meeting came within days of Bolton's delivery of the letter. By Wednesday of the following week, articles had appeared in local papers detailing this interchange dispassionately. Bolton's meeting with Director Simpson was described as part of the everyday review of weather-related practices by the National Weather Service. To correlate with this take on the events, segments from Simpson's letter to his superiors in Washington were printed—including the part where he expressed sympathy for her request and suggested that the names were under constant review.

By the following day, the rhetoric in the news stories shifted to focus on the feminists involved in the "protest."[34] The first page of the *Miami Herald* ran an editorial cartoon depicting a trendily dressed woman with a sign in her hand that reads, "Now I ask you ... Do I look like a hurricane?"[35] (See figure 5.) The woman's dress is printed with swirling circles, visually evoking hurricanes while appearing as a fashionable 1960s pattern. Through its use of the word "NOW" in the protest sign, the cartoon points not only to Bolton's debate with the Weather Bureau, but also to the larger feminist connections Bolton was representing. NOW's protest of hurricanes was associated with the larger feminist protest of the late 1960s and depicted as coming from the same feminists responsible for other social and cultural complaints.

Another shift in the second-day coverage was in the characterization of Bolton herself, at the heart of the protest. As reported in the *Miami Herald*:

> Change is in the wind for women in the 1970s, according to the feminist National Organization of Women (NOW), and one of the first items of business is a change in the way winds are named.
>
> It's unfair, unscientific and an insult that hurricanes are named after women, complains Mrs. David Bolton, a Coral Gables housewife who serves as a national vice president of NOW.
>
> "Hurricanes are disasters leaving a lasting and devastating effect on those affected. Women resent the association," she told Dr. Robert H. Simpson, director of the National Hurricane Center at the University of Miami.
>
> [...] "I'm sick of reading headlines such as 'Camille Was No Lady.' It's no longer a joke," said Mrs. Bolton, who says that NOW would take its

Figure 5. "NOW Hurricane," by Dave Cross. From *The Miami Herald,* March 28, 1970, 1A, © 1970 McClatchy. All rights reserved. Used by permission and protected by the Copyright Laws of the United States. Image reproduction by Adam Beauchamp and Nicole Gaudier-Alemañy of Florida State University Libraries.

case to Washington if the center couldn't find another way to name this year's storms.

Mrs. Bolton said she was not suggesting that storms be named for men—or even men and women on a 50–50 basis. "There are thousands of nouns in the dictionary; why can't they be named after trees, birds or other animals?"[36]

Summing up these statements in the first line of the article, the *Herald*'s position was clear—"change is in the wind for women in the 1970s"—and Roxcy Bolton was leading the charge. But, as argued within the article, while Bolton's claims were met with sympathy, the fact of the matter was that hurricane names were already chosen for the year. Thus, as of March, "it would be impossible to revise the 1970 list of names—all female—for the 1970 hurricane season, which begins June 1."[37]

Less than one month later, the public discourse around Bolton's protest altered yet again, taking on a sardonic quality that exaggerated her militancy. Recounting her meeting in detail, reporters now stated that Bolton had "stormed in" to the Weather Bureau offices, "demanding" change in the naming system. In fact, reported one news story, "she threatened her group would march on the Weather Bureau in Washington within 10 days" if her demands were not met.[38] Following an era of civil rights protests, this misrepresentation of Bolton's statement that she would take her case to Washington is key to understanding how opinion on the issue had shifted in a month.[39] Bolton never suggested that NOW would march on Washington; rather, she suggested that they would take their case to the Weather Bureau's superior organization, the Environmental Science Services Administration (ESSA). The newspaper's reporting was meant to be inflammatory. By describing Bolton as "fuming," "demanding, "threatening," and "storming," the article negated her position as a credible and rational protestor as she, and all feminist activity, was likened to a storm of their own making. Indeed, the *Miami News* quickly pointed out that the name "Roxie" appeared on the 1968 hurricane name list, implying that Bolton's concern for the naming process was merely personal. By May 1970, it reported that the Weather Bureau had decided to continue using female names for hurricanes in the 1970 season, "no matter what the women's liberation groups think."[40] Bolton and others would have to wait until the following year to discuss the subject further. And wait they would, eager for the next exchange between the feminists and the weathermen.

No Slur on Women: Roxcy Bolton and the Interdepartmental Hurricane Conferences

When Roxcy Bolton arrived at the University of Miami's campus for the Interdepartmental Hurricane Warning Conference in January of 1971, she was ready. Several months had passed since her first encounter with the Weather Bureau, and she had had ample time to prepare her remarks. Over the preceding ten months, she met several times with weather officials to be "briefed on some of the background information on why and how hurricanes are named," and gave talks in the Miami area to test her rhetoric on hurricane-prone audiences in groups like the Tiger Bay Luncheon Club.[41] She knew she needed preparation for her appearance at the conference, given the hype in the local press following her first interaction. Also in the back of Bolton's mind as she stepped through the doors of the conference hall that morning, besides the words she planned to use to persuade weathermen to change their naming process, was the knowledge that her organization was changing, growing ever more powerful than before, and making significant progress for women's rights. She knew, too, that her own role was changing, becoming more consequential at both the national and local levels. It was largely because of her participation in NOW that Bolton felt ready for whatever came next.

The year 1970 was incredibly busy for NOW's leadership. The organization had grown significantly in size and activity since the conference in December 1969 when Bolton had been tasked with pursuing the NHC's naming system. Now averaging roughly 1,200 members, it was a robust organization with multiple goals. At the national level, NOW's activities varied widely.[42] Beyond encouraging President Nixon to appoint women to cabinet and governmental positions, it was also focused on a tally of the number of states that had sex discrimination laws on the books. This process included gathering information from all states' laws and figuring out which states were violating the Title VI provision of the Civil Rights Act of 1964. At the end of the year, NOW concluded that twenty-three states had policies that needed revision, and organized efforts to agitate for these revisions.[43] In addition to governmental discrimination violations, NOW pursued strategies to address lack of high-level female employees in the airline industry, the automobile industry, and the media.[44] All the while, NOW started to realize that its complaints were falling on deaf ears.

During the busy year between the 1970 and 1971 conferences, Bolton grew more involved in NOW at the national level. Emboldened by the support for her hurricane-naming initiative, she ran for another National Board position, this time the national vice president for fund-raising.[45] Managing fund-raising campaigns for NOW was a considerable task, given all the activities the organization had underway, and required Bolton to attend the national meetings to report on her activities. She also continued her other pursuits in Florida. As Bolton was one of the few board members with small children—three under the age of five—her workload was almost impossible. As a result, Bolton attended the national meeting in Des Plaines, Illinois, in March; by September, her interest in the national proceedings stalled as her efforts in Florida increased, forcing her to send her regrets as she was too busy to travel to the meeting site.[46]

And busy Bolton was. By 1970, Bolton had formed the Miami-Dade chapter of NOW and was assisting with the setup of other local chapters across Florida. In addition, she became engrossed in local efforts for equality. Bolton led boycotts of local businesses, sit-ins at the 700 Club (the penthouse restaurant at the David William Hotel in Coral Gables that refused to serve women), campaigns to allow women to breastfeed in public spaces, and events to mobilize feminists.[47] While her successor, Martha Ingle, took over the daily workings of the Dade County chapter as president, Bolton involved herself in other activities in the area.[48]

Bolton's major 1970 success came from efforts to get the Equal Rights Amendment moving again in Congress.[49] The amendment proposed a constitutional rewrite to state that all women and men were equal. First introduced as a proposed constitutional amendment in 1923, the ERA never passed through a vote in Congress. It was often caught up in larger discussions over funding programs for women and children, concerns over military-service requirements, and gender-role perceptions. In 1969, NOW leaders made it their mission to start pushing for hearings again, with the goal of getting the amendment through the ratification process.[50] Bolton's involvement began when she learned that US senator Birch Bayh, the current chair of the Constitutional Amendments Subcommittee, was in Miami Beach on vacation. She cold-called the senator at his hotel and asked if she could stop by with nine representatives from the Dade County chapter of NOW to discuss the ERA issue. Surprisingly, he agreed. The meeting took place at Bayh's hotel, where Bolton and other feminist representatives detailed the importance of the ERA to Florida women. At the following 1970 legislative session, Bolton cheered as Bayh held the first hearings on the ERA and rapidly drafted a new version of the amendment. The draft garnered support in Congress and was passed by both houses in 1972.[51]

By 1971, both Bolton and NOW had established reputations. NOW had expanded its membership by 5,000 members, averaging 6,000 members in total. At its five-year anniversary, the organization started the process of tallying what was accomplished and what was still left to do. The group's causes ranged from women and the War on Poverty to equal representation of minorities (including women) on television and radio, a national childcare program, and even the Congressional Seniority System. Meanwhile, NOW's attention to major legal cases regarding sexual discrimination in hiring and workplace practices made national news as they worked their way up the legal chain. The organization's main focus, however, was its effort to get the ERA passed and ratified.[52]

As a local activist in Miami, Bolton saw her name become associated with feminist activities gaining attention on the national stage. Bolton gained notable attention for her protests, sit-ins, and boycotting campaigns, and was now a powerful NOW National Board representative in addition to being a local feminist leader. Thus, before she even set foot through the doors of the Interdepartmental Hurricane Warning Conference in Coral Gables in 1971, her stature as a feminist was firmly established, and her campaign to change hurricane names was part of the many ways feminists were addressing social problems.

"Humiliating and Degrading": The 1971 Conference

On Wednesday, January 13, 1971, Bolton stood up before a panel composed entirely of men at the Interdepartmental Hurricane Warning Conference and offered her case for the cessation of hurricane naming.[53] Echoing the language of her 1970 letter to the Weather Bureau, she noted that the naming system was "humiliating and degrading" to women in general, and especially to "women whose names are identical with the names of those hurricanes." In fact, she argued, "the majority of American women would be happier to have a woman named to a top job in the Commerce Department rather than to some hurricanes."[54] After her presentation, the committee of weathermen asked Bolton to propose a different naming system. Suggesting offhandedly that hurricanes be named after birds instead of women, she was immediately shot down on the grounds that "the Audubon Society would object." Bolton had planned for this retort in her preparations for that day's debate, and her response to the weathermen was quick: "You're concerned about the Audubon Society and regard for birds—but not for women?"[55] Nevertheless, following Bolton's speech, the Steering Committee of the Interdepartmental

Hurricane Warning Conference tabled the discussion for further consideration. Four days later, on Sunday, January 17, Director Simpson sent a letter to Bolton to confirm her invitation to attend the conference luncheon the following Wednesday. So it was that, a week after she had first addressed the Steering Committee, Bolton would have a chance to meet with the committee again, this time to plead her case informally. Again, Bolton proposed that alternative names be used, such as those for birds; and again, Bolton's suggestions were dismissed. Bolton was not dismayed by this response, though. She later recounted how the weathermen fell right into her trap: by denying the use of birds' names because of the Audubon Society's objections, they illustrated the negativity associated with the use of names for hurricanes. This was something Bolton pointed out as the debate continued.

Despite Bolton's vigorous presentations, both in the formal debate and at the luncheon, the committee decided to defer the discussion to the following year. Three weeks after the conference ended, the Weather Bureau's Steering Committee chair, Karl Johannessen, responded officially to Bolton's comments. He commended her "calm manner of presentation," stating that the committee members were "sympathetic" to her concerns. Nevertheless, they believed that "the majority of women do not hold Mrs. Bolton's views on the naming of hurricanes."[56] This view was based on the information collected from Director Robert Simpson, who stated that, for every letter the NHC received from women requesting the names be changed, there were ten requesting that their name be added to the list. Nor did Johannessen believe that the hurricane-naming system was flawed: "The committee did not agree that the present practice of naming hurricanes is derogatory to the female sex, or is viewed as being derogatory by people at large." In fact, he further argued, "The practice is widely adhered to by all nations involved with hurricanes and typhoons." Because no "suitable alternative methods" had been proposed, and because "the present practice has the support of the general public, *including women*," the Steering Committee voted to retain the current system.[57]

In the months after Bolton's first appearance at the Interdepartmental Hurricane Warning Conference, newspapers throughout the country applauded the Weather Bureau's decision to keep the current system of hurricane naming. "By maintaining the tradition," declared US Meteorological Director George Cressman, weathermen were simply continuing "a part of American heritage." Getting rid of the system of names that "had a personality" was detrimental to the public, he concluded.[58] The *New Orleans Times-Picayune* agreed: "Betty sounds more powerful than Bob." Moreover, it continued, female names "carry a fundamental message to mankind: 'Ignore us at your peril'"—and that was exactly the effect the Weather Bureau was trying to create.[59] In another defense of the old naming system, a weatherman in a 1971 *Irish Times* interview stated that weathermen, in fighting to keep naming hurricanes after females, "intend no slur on women."[60] The *Los Angeles Times* went so far as to assert that women should see it as an honor to have hurricanes named after them.[61] Why else would the Weather Bureau receive so many letters from women requesting their name be added to the annual list?[62]

Even though Bolton's protest of the naming system garnered considerable attention in the press, her name is surprisingly absent from articles on the subject. As national media reprinted key statistics and quotes from Cressman and others in 1971, they always identified Weather Bureau officials by their proper titles and names, but Bolton was rarely mentioned by name. Headlines proclaimed dismissively that the only people complaining about the naming process were those affiliated with "women's liberation groups." The omission of Bolton from the coverage signals a lack of concern for her role in the naming discussion and reveals the ways in which so many feminist activities nationwide were lumped into a single indistinct conglomeration that was deemed of "little relevance" to the American public as a whole.[63] Similarly, editorial cartoons and newspaper articles mocked feminists outright. In the few cases where Bolton was mentioned by name, it was often with the formal appellation "Mrs. Bolton" and the appositive "feminist," as if to draw attention to her marital status and identification as a feminist.

The intense public reaction to the naming debate and Bolton was not surprising, given the increased interest in feminist activities in 1971. But Bolton was especially remarkable as an anomaly in Florida. This was partially because of her role as a feminist on a national board, which drew national attention to her activism. It was also because she defied the mold of a southern white woman. Bolton was a married housewife and mother of young children, defying stereotypes of feminists as unwed and childless women. She was also focused on issues within her own zip code. The National Hurricane Center (also in Coral Gables) was virtually in Bolton's backyard. The casual observance of the debate soon shifted along with the perception of feminist activities.

Bolton's reception at the 1971 conference did not deter her from her quest to change the NHC's hurricane-naming policy. Immediately, she appealed in writing to Director Simpson, proposing a new solution: "After much thought, I believe I have the most appropriate names possible for the forthcoming season of Hurricanes." Her suggestion: that hurricanes be named after US senators starting in alphabetical order, "or in some method whereby all Senators would have a Hurricane named for them during their 6-year term." By way of explanation, she noted that senators "delight in having streets, bridges, buildings—especially Federal buildings—named for them." So why not hurricanes?[64] "I trust that you will be as enthusiastic about the proposed names for Hurricanes as I am," she concluded. Bolton's proposal that storms be named after senators was both ironic and serious. She preceded her suggestion by pointing out the hypocrisy of the outcry over the previous year's suggestion that storms be named for birds or animals. Thus she both reminded the director of the previous decision and the complications that arose with an offhand remark that disregarded feminist concerns. When at last Simpson's reply to her letter came, it was earnest. He let her know that, while he did find her suggestion a "most interesting innovation," he thought it was "fraught with more political consequences than is implied by [the] conclusion that all Senators enjoy having things named for them."[65]

No Slur on Women: The Second Conference

Before Bolton received the NHC director's response to her proposal to use US senators' names, she was officially invited to attend the 1972 meeting of the Interdepartmental Hurricane Warning Conference.[66] Undeterred by Simpson's concerns regarding her proposed senator-based naming system, she arrived at the conference in January to present the system. But just as at the previous year's meeting, Bolton's request to change the hurricane-naming system was denied, again on the grounds that she failed to provide a sufficient alternative system. While the committee agreed that the use of senators' names was a most interesting idea, they argued that such a course "clearly involves political considerations and individual personalities." The

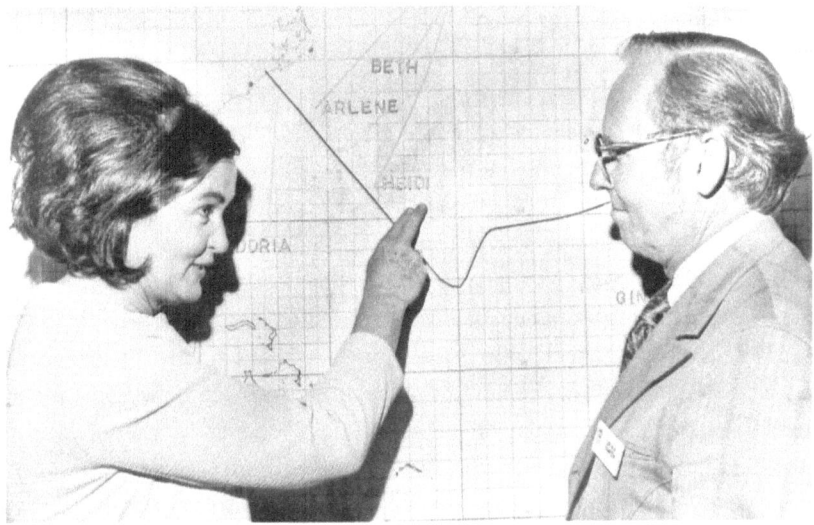

Figure 6. Roxcy Bolton in 1972 with Robert H. Simpson. Image from Associated Press featured in *Los Angeles Times*, January 21, 1972, and the *New York Times*, May 21, 2017.

weathermen further pointed out, "Senators are not uniformly distributed alphabetically." Once again, the issue of hurricane naming was tabled until the next year, forcing Bolton to devise another suitable alternative.[67]

Unlike the previous year, the proceedings of the 1972 conference did not trickle out slowly to the press months later. This time, reports of Bolton's activities were printed immediately. They were also noticeably more condescending. The first evidence of this change came in the description of Bolton herself. Unlike the previous year's reports—when Bolton was either referred to as "Mrs. Bolton" to indicate her status as a local married housewife or, more often, simply left out of the reports—the 1972 newspaper articles not only listed Bolton's full name but included a photo. This image captured Bolton at the 1972 conference, standing with an unnamed "weather service official" who was later identified as the NHC director, Robert Simpson.[68] (See figure 6.)

The day after the *Los Angeles Times* released the photo, Director Simpson's quizzical expression became the subject of dozens of newspaper articles. Journalists characterized the image as an emblem of the annoyance and frustration that weathermen and reporters felt in response to Bolton's campaign. Notably, Simpson is not named in either the photo caption or the article. This omission of Simpson's name and his central role as NHC director gives the impression that Bolton is just a raging ideologue directing her anger at whatever weather official is standing in front of her, rather than a reasonable petitioner explaining her concern to a key decision-maker.[69] This characterization is also subtly reflected in the tagline, which refers to Bolton as "Ms. Roxcy Bolton" rather than the "Mrs. Bolton" of earlier coverage. In replacing "Mrs." with "Ms.," the *Los Angeles Times* turned an idyllic housewife into a bossy feminist. For his part, Simpson later issued an apology to Bolton, sending her a copy of the photo as well as an article from an Alaskan newspaper that had printed it. Simpson explained in an accompanying letter that, to his knowledge, no one from the Weather Bureau had released the picture to the press.[70] While the director's apology was sincere, the fact was that, as soon as media outlets across the country ran the photo alongside articles skewering her statements, the damage to Bolton's reputation had been done.

In addition to the increasingly unflattering visual representations of Bolton in the newspapers, the verbal descriptions of her also turned sour. Gone were the respectful descriptions of Bolton's commendably "calm manner," and in their place were images of a woman giving a gratuitous "warning."[71] As the articles had it, Bolton was "bellicose," "demanded action," and attacked the weathermen as though she were a storm herself, forcing men to "batten their hatches" while pummeling them with absurd suggestions like the one that hurricanes should be renamed "himmicanes."[72] Reporters and weathermen across the country, presenting this version of Bolton, proclaimed that she went too far; just because "hurricane" sounds like "her-icane," they protested, did not mean that the word should be changed. Bolton's request was cast as another example of the so-called "Women's Lib Storm" brewing throughout the country.[73] The havoc wrought by this feminist political storm seemed to confirm why "everyone knows a hurricane is a feminine phenomenon."[74] In the case of Roxcy Bolton, reporters fell back on humor as a mechanism of cultural negation to belittle Bolton and her suggestion to alter the system. On a larger scale, the writers of mass media compared feminist actions in general with negative storm-like behaviors, as a rhetorical strategy for repudiating the feminist movement as a whole. "Hurricane 'Irate Lady' Roars in on U.S. Weathermen," reported one newspaper.[75] As Bolton's cause was conflated with all other feminist debates, it was characterized as part of the larger movement brewing ominously on the horizon—the "Women's Lib Storm."[76]

Bolton's Role Grows: The Mother of Florida Feminism

While Bolton continued her quest to change hurricane names, her activities as part of the NOW organization increased. In 1971, Bolton organized a group of 100 businesswomen, community leaders, and housewives to walk through downtown Miami to promote awareness of the prevalence and harmful effects of rape. The "March against Rape" was wildly successful at drawing attention to the issue. A few months after the march, Bolton founded an organization called Women in Distress that offered lodging, legal assistance, medical care, and supplies to women experiencing "personal crisis."[77] The organization took up much of Bolton's time as she sought resources for the women under her purview. She also continued her work to address the perception of women in the media, taking action with her Miami NOW Chapter to file suit against National Airlines for its "Fly Me" campaign ads featuring stewardesses.[78] In 1973, Bolton spearheaded the establishment of the first rape-treatment center in the country. The Dade County Rape Treatment Center required the cooperation of law enforcement, politicians, and the Miami-area public, later inspiring the creation of similar facilities throughout the country.

While Bolton became widely known in Florida, NOW gained attention nationally. The organization grew to a robust 14,000 members by the end of 1972, and achieved successes in its efforts to revise state sex-discrimination laws, push for decriminalization of abortion, and influence discussion of differences between the sexes.[79] The largest accomplishment was pushing the ERA through Congress. Beginning in 1970, efforts to revise the ERA and present it to the House and Senate were underway. On October 12, 1971, the House of Representatives voted to adopt the amendment. Following soon after, on March 22, 1972, the Senate adopted a revised version led by Senator Birch Bayh, with whom Bolton was in communication. Following its adoption by both houses of Congress, President Nixon signed the amendment. The final step in acceptance was state ratification. As an amendment to the US Constitution, the ERA needed 35 states to accept or ratify it. NOW activists at both national and state levels led massive efforts to push the ratification process along.

At the center of this push for ERA adoption in Florida was Bolton. Within days of the US Senate's approval of the ERA, Bolton and other Florida feminists mobilized to encourage the Florida legislature to ratify the amendment. On March 24, 1972, just two days following the US Senate's approval, the Florida House of Representatives voted in support of ratification. However, the Florida Senate failed to pass it before the session came to a close. In the end, the Florida House introduced, discussed, and even passed the amendment multiple times over the next decade (1972–82), but each time, ratification failed to make it through the state senate.[80] The failure of the ERA in 1972 and 1973 was a crushing blow to Florida feminists like Roxcy Bolton. She and others had thrown considerable effort into keeping the ERA on the agenda for the Florida houses.[81]

So intensive were NOW's efforts to push the ERA through the Florida legislature that other Florida NOW activities were curtailed. Bolton scaled back on her national commitments due to the time the Florida effort was taking, resigning from her position on the NOW National Board in favor of devoting her time to the Florida efforts.[82] Unfortunately, the failure of the ERA in Florida caused division within the state chapter, much as it did with other groups throughout the country. By the end of 1973, after the second year of attempts to push ratification through the Florida legislature, Bolton's own Miami-Dade chapter expressed concern to the national organization about internal divisions, noting a desire to split the chapter into two. A controversial chapter election in 1972 left fractures within the chapter.[83]

At the heart of division within the Miami-Dade NOW Chapter, besides the ERA, was the issue of abortion.[84] The decriminalization of abortion, part of the NOW mission since the late 1960s, remained contentious among women's rights advocates. NOW carefully avoided taking an official stance on the issue, instead leaving it up to members to decide on their own or to join other groups that supported decriminalization, such as the Women's National Abortion Action Coalition (WONAAC). The period between the 1972 and 1973 national conferences brought considerable change to these policies. A court case focusing on the divisive issue, later known as *Roe v. Wade,* made its way to the US Supreme Court. The decision, released January 22, 1973, declared abortion constitutionally protected.[85] Although controversial, the decision was heralded as a major feminist achievement. Many NOW members were highly outspoken about their support for the *Roe* decision, causing frustration in older members who cautioned reservation towards the issue in press.[86]

NOW also continued to press for social change. One of the major areas leaders identified as necessary was the increasingly "false image of women" that spread in the media through television shows, advertisements, and general discussion of women.[87] Coining the term "sexism" to refer to prejudicial stereotyping based on sex roles, NOW and other feminist groups argued that sexism occurred in everyday life in the form of harassment, discrimination, and linguistic representation.[88] Between 1970 and 1972, sexism received coverage by nearly every major news outlet in the country, both on air and in print.[89] As the concept of sexism seeped into public discourse, it emboldened feminists to work toward identifying and remedying gendered language inequities.[90] NOW set up various oversight groups like the Media Reform Committee and organized boycotts of products and services from major companies like Sears Roebuck, Betty Crocker, Red Spoon–Bisquick, and National Airlines.[91] They even formed a task force to review the federal code for instances of sexist language that privileged men over women or defined women as unequal. The "Desexing the Federal Code" project relied on time-consuming volunteer efforts, as participants across the country reviewed all statutes in the federal code for linguistic gender bias and suggested changes to remove it.[92]

Meanwhile, feminists also fought for specific linguistic changes that signified broader cultural equality. With the publication of *Ms.* magazine in 1971, a new title for women appeared: "Ms."[93] As described in the *Washington Post*, "the name of the magazine was chosen to indicate [a] new freedom from traditional roles."[94] As *Ms.* cofounder Gloria Steinem explained, this new title was preferable to "Mrs." or "Miss" because it did not distinguish women on the basis of marital or age-based status.[95] Other gender-neutral terms were also promoted by feminists. In her 1970 work *Sisterhood Is Powerful*, Robin Morgan introduced the concept of "Herstory," initiating a movement of studying history through the eyes of women.[96] Morgan and others argued that history focused on men, leaving women on the periphery, whereas "herstory" focused entirely on women's role in civilization. The term "herstory" was partly comedic, but soon inspired the creation of several women-centered presses, and use by various academics and newspapers.[97] Many college campuses offered courses in women's studies, and celebrated "Herstory Weeks" complete with marches and organized strikes.[98]

The introduction of the terms "Ms." (in 1971) and "Herstory" (in 1970) provoked larger discussions, some quite heated, about the gendered lexicons that frame the ways men and women engage in the world. Not everyone supported these new terms.[99] While some proclaimed the new terms a "feminist fad," others averred that the "Language Lib" was around to stay.[100] Because of the various discussions over women and words circulating in popular culture, between 1974 and 1976, scholars increasingly took an interest in deploying feminist analysis, invigorating every discipline with books and articles that placed women at the center of their investigations and introduced new gender-neutral language. Most noticeable was Casey Miller and Kate Swift's treatise *Words and Women* (1976), which proclaimed that "chairman" could become "chairperson" or even "chair" without inciting linguistic or cultural chaos.[101] Amongst the "chair" discussion, Miller and Swift's work examined the unconscious gendered messages hidden in the language of everyday words, including in names, definitions, and religion. Over time, the changes in discourse suggested through feminist writings were gradually reflected in revisions of textbooks, library catalogs, dictionary entries, official documents, and newspapers' rules of style.

Besides the hurricane-naming debate, which threw the gendered language of weather into a national spotlight, "Language Lib" even affected the meteorological profession. As pointed out in a *Parade* magazine article in 1975 by Detroit-area weathercaster Marilyn Turner, the term "Weather Girl" still plagued women in the profession. Some women, like Diane Sawyer, saw weather reporting as an opportunity to move into larger roles in the industry, gaining necessary airtime to increase popularity. Others, such as Barbara Walters, did not view the role of the female weather correspondent, on the rise again in the 1970s and often relied on for "happy banter" that rarely allowed her to cover more serious news, as a boon in the post-EEOC era. Turner, reflecting on the profession and the stigma surrounding the "Weather Girl," stated in the article, "I don't believe anyone over 21 should be called a girl. You don't call a man a weather boy."[102] Despite Turner's objections to the term, and a brief discussion of its meaning in the press amongst a slew of other proposed linguistic alterations like "chairman," the term "Weather Girl" and "weatherman" did not change. Others, however, were highlighted more frequently, such as gender-neutral terms like "weathercaster," "forecaster," and "meteorologist."

Even as a public discussion of gendered language gained traction, NOW's detractors coalesced into rival groups. Spurred on by NOW's internal disagreement over whether to prioritize abortion, the ERA, sexual discrimination, or media representation, new antiabortion and anti-ERA groups emerged. One such group, STOP ERA, was created by Phyllis Schlafly, a conservative Mississippi activist and published author whose arguments against ratification of the ERA garnered her some notoriety. The "STOP" in the name "STOP ERA" stood for "Stop Taking Our Privileges," meant to reflect the idea that, if the ERA were passed, it would take away gendered privileges that benefited women, such as maternal protections, draft exemptions, and federal assistance.[103] The membership of STOP ERA grew quickly over a few years. As the leading anti-feminist group, it helped to create and perpetuate images of feminists as radicals, heretics, man-haters, and killers of unborn children. And as the US Supreme Court handed down the *Roe* decision, STOP ERA fought vehemently against every feminist activity, pointing out divisions within chapters and leadership of feminist organizations. Meanwhile, in various media, from late-night comedy television shows to anti-ERA campaign posters, feminists were portrayed as one-dimensional, self-centered man-haters who threatened the social order with their extremist and even demonic beliefs.[104]

The growing public distaste for feminism and its leaders trickled into the hurricane-naming debate, inspiring extreme resistance for multiple reasons.[105] First, the naming debate occurred at a cultural moment (1970-73) when some of the most controversial issues related to gender and sexuality in American culture were also under debate, thus heightening the importance of this debate within the context of these discussions. Second, due to these connections, the champions of the debate—Roxcy Bolton in particular— became representative figures of larger discussions of feminist activities, helping to create impressions of feminists and feminism. The naming debate, and its portrayal of those that fought for it, even influenced the terminology used to refer to or negate feminist activities in the future. As a result, hurricane names became the one thing that could be controlled at a time when fundamental aspects of society were up for debate. They were equivalent to the "Last Stand" of gendered change, a perfect representation of the most irrational or irrelevant changes feminists proposed in a slew of significant changes. Thus, in American minds, the hurricane-naming debate came to represent debates over many other controversial issues of the time.

Nowhere is this tension revealed more clearly than in the mutinous response to Bolton's appearance at the 1972 Interdepartmental Hurricane Warning Conference, specifically the uproar over her suggestion of changing "hurricanes" to "himicanes." Bolton had offhandedly remarked at the 1972 conference that the word "hurricane" did sound like "her-icane" and could be altered to "himicane" for equality's sake. Her comment was never meant as a serious proposition. Nor is there evidence that the comment was received by the Weather Bureau as anything more than an aside. Nowhere in her correspondence, in future conversations with the committee, or in supplementary addresses by Bolton is the "himicane" discussion brought up again.[106] Yet the anecdote fueled a bitter public debate about whether to use the term. Perhaps what is most surprising is not the widespread resistance to the neologism "himicane," but the portability of this anecdote into other discussions of naming practices. When put in context, this argument, like many others at the time, is easily connected to the major changes taking place regarding gendered titles, pronouns, and suffixes. The public response to Bolton's offhand comment was defensive, disproportionate, and indicative of other cherry-picked inflammatory remarks made by feminists that were extensively focused on by the media. It would also inspire feminists to push through linguistic changes such as the replacement of the word "chairman" with "chairperson" and "chair."

Weathermen Win: The Third Interdepartmental Hurricane Warning Conference

By the time Roxcy Bolton appeared at her third Interdepartmental Hurricane Warning Conference in January 1973, weathermen had already made up their minds to reject her proposal. Bolton's public image had changed. Her protest was now associated with everything negative about the feminist movement. Bolton was no longer a respectable southern lady raising a concern about her Gulf South community; she was a national figure, an aggressive example of women who corrupted southern belles with radical rhetoric.

With rising opposition expressed openly in the press, the hurricane-naming debate was over, for now. The minutes from the conference, less than one paragraph long, indicate that Bolton appeared for the third year in a row without "substantiating evidence nor acceptable alternative proposals."[107] Despite Bolton's suggestions of changing the names entirely, or later, adding new names to the mix (such as those of senators or wildlife), the delegation was exhausted by the continued debate and deemed it unproductive to review suggestions that had already been denied. They thus decided to table the issue of hurricane naming once and for all. The Weather Bureau would not approach the issue of changing the hurricane-naming procedure again until 1978.

After the Weather Bureau decided to suspend discussion of hurricane naming in 1973, journalists throughout the country promptly proclaimed that weathermen had won this round against the feminists. For their part, feminists involved in the hurricane-naming protest like Roxcy Bolton sensed the battle was a protracted one and withdrew their energies to focus on larger concerns. It took major pressure from a (female) government official, further evolution in American culture, and cooperation from newly formed world meteorological organizations to bring the issue of hurricane naming to the forefront again.

In the Eye of the Women's Lib Storm

In 1973, Roxcy Bolton gave up on the hurricane-naming debate. Firmly shut down by the weathermen and mocked and belittled in the press, she was through fighting for the issue. Apart from the hurricane-naming debate, 1973 was a devastating year for feminists in general. Amid rising anti-feminist protests like STOP ERA, the ERA ratification process stalled both nationally and locally in Florida. Meanwhile, even as NOW's numbers grew, fissures in the organization and individual chapters multiplied. Interestingly, the public continued to associate feminism with storms: opponents used the term "Women's Lib Storm" with increasing frequency in the years to come as a way of dismissing feminist arguments as overly emotional, trivial, and unimportant. In a cultural climate dominated by concerns about the close of the Vietnam War, the Watergate scandal, the environmental impacts of human activity, and growing resentment against the feminist movement, feminists quietly tabled the issue of hurricane naming, regrouping to focus on other concerns.

Over the next few years, Bolton's activities varied widely. Much of her time was taken up by her organization Women in Distress and her efforts to found the nation's first rape treatment center. She also focused on family, organizing the first neighborhood crime watch for her own neighborhood in Coral Gables. In 1973, she attended Florida's first state-level NOW conference, receiving top honors for her work on behalf of feminism in the state. In a memorandum to all Floridian NOW members, the state office proclaimed that "the name 'Roxcy Bolton' is synonymous with women's rights to people throughout the state of Florida." The proclamation declared that, "Despite enduring 'physical and verbal abuse,' Roxcy Bolton has had the courage to stand up and speak when most others remained silent," and "her actions have always demonstrated the ultimate humanistic concerns of feminism." As the *Miami News* editorialized in 1987, "When Roxcy Bolton starts dreaming, potential opponents would do best to step out of her way." As a result of her dreaming, in 1992, the nation's first park "to commemorate women's achievements" opened in Miami and was dedicated to Bolton, following her push to see it built.[108] Despite the multitude of Bolton's accomplishments, for the rest of her life she never stopped receiving questions regarding the hurricane-naming debate and her involvement in it. She remained always "Hurricane Roxcy," a true "force of nature," the woman who took on the weathermen.[109]

Even though some saw Bolton as representative of all feminists and their efforts, she did not entirely fit the feminist stereotype: in her early years on the NOW board, she was one of the few married mothers with small children in the organization. But in another important way, Bolton really did resemble other women who had successfully influenced change. As with Betty Friedan, who faced countless criticism with the publication of *The Feminine Mystique* in 1963, critics focused on her background, education level, and physical attributes in order to negate the arguments she made. Similar critiques were made of Gloria Steinem, founder of *Ms.* magazine, and even of a woman associated more with science than with feminism—Rachel Carson, the author of *Silent Spring*.[110] Published in 1962, Carson's book raised the environmental alarm over water toxicity and dumping practices. Though time would prove her right, at that moment critics negated her research based on her gender. In a sense, then, Bolton's work, and the reactions she experienced, were typical of a feminist of the period. Like Friedan and Steinem with feminism, and Carson with environmentalism, she joined the movement at its origins, contributed greatly to its success, and then faced a lifetime of scrutiny and criticism for her gender and her participation. Also like other feminists of the 1970s, she saw the fruits of her efforts years after her work.

Juanita Kreps Steps In: "Weathermen Bow Down to a Different Storm"

In January 1977, President Jimmy Carter appointed the first female US secretary of commerce, Dr. Juanita M. Kreps, making her only the fourth woman in US history to hold a cabinet position.[111] Kreps was the first female director of the New York Stock Exchange and knew how to assert her authority in a male-dominated business world.[112] As one of an unprecedented number of women appointed to governmental positions by Carter, she was also well aware of the significance of her tenure and its timing in the scheme of other cultural changes.[113] By the time she was appointed to the cabinet position, Kreps was conscious of her role as a feminist and an educated woman.[114] In interviews later in life, Kreps openly stated that she had "always considered [her]self a feminist and [thought her] actions would bear that [out]."[115]

In Kreps's account, there was at the time of her appointment "an important exchange [...] on the question of qualified women," in terms of inclusion and in assessing their roles in shifting workplace settings.[116] She knew people would debate whether she was qualified to make the decisions she did, whether she was simply a "token" female in a position of power, and whether her actions were an extension of perceived radical feminist activities.[117] As her 2010 *New York Times* obituary pointed out, the "Commerce [position] was perhaps the most unglamorous, thankless job in the cabinet" due to its strenuous micromanagement requirements and the wide variety of service and public works projects it encompassed.[118] It did have some significant organizations under its oversight. Commerce regulated the National Oceanic and Atmospheric Administration (NOAA) and the National Weather Service (NWS) or Weather Bureau.

Upon assuming the role as secretary of commerce, Kreps, who considered herself an advocate for women, immediately turned her attention to the hurricane-naming debate.[119] The debate stagnated in 1973 but regained attention in 1975 when Australia decided to introduce a rotating male-female naming system for its tropical cyclones and other storms. Australia, one of the last countries in the since-formed World Meteorological Organization (WMO) to adopt the female-only naming system in 1963, proclaimed the decision to switch to an alternating male-female list as part of a recognition of the United Nations' International Women's Year. Still, the decision was hardly heralded as a grand feminist achievement. As the *Oakland Tribune* reported, Australian feminists were nonplussed by the name change, describing it as "only a gesture" because it "didn't really advance the cause of women."[120] This negation of a national-level policy shift was, according to historian Leila Rupp, typical of the minimization of feminist gains throughout the world.[121] And, with respect to the hurricane-naming debate in particular, the oft-repeated statement that this change meant little to US and Australian feminists suggested that the debate was a thing of the past.

But for Juanita Kreps, the issue was still alive.[122] In 1977, weeks after her appointment, she took a page out of the Australian science minister's book and informed Dr. Bob White, administrator for NOAA, that the agency must adopt an alternating male-female hurricane-naming system the next year.[123] As the secretary of commerce, Kreps had the authority to issue this direct order. A stunned Dr. White informed NHC director Neil Frank of the dramatic policy change. Frank had a significant dilemma to sort through, as the United States had ceded control of the now-global naming system to the broader World Meteorological Organization.[124] In fact, the group had debated global tropical-storm-naming systems the last year, and decided that the names be continued for the 1978 season. Any changes to storm-naming lists for 1978 needed approval by designated regional committees after an extensive discussion and voting process.[125]

Following Kreps's order to change the names no matter what, Frank appeared in front of the regional committee to sway votes for an altered international naming system. While the WMO agreed that it was too difficult to change the naming system for the current 1978 season, it proposed that the global system could change in 1979.[126] But Kreps was not content with this progress and insisted that the change be made immediately for the coming year's hurricane names. To appease Kreps, the National Weather Service worked out a deal with Mexico to change the naming system for the Eastern Pacific Ocean region, or for any storm that might hit the Pacific side of the United States during the interim year. In exchange, they added Mexican-influenced names, such as "Fico," to the 1978 Pacific Coast naming list.[127]

On May 12, 1978, NOAA, overseeing the National Weather Service, announced that Eastern Pacific hurricanes of the 1978 season would alternate female and male names, starting with "Bud."[128] If all went well, all future lists would include male names. In the United States, reactions to the name change decision reflected a mix of witty acquiescence and vituperative denial. For example, in one editorial cartoon printed beside a front-page article in the *New Orleans Times-Picayune,* an obstetrician exclaims to a female hurricane that she "had a son," a male hurricane. But the caption on the cartoon has a more serious tone, expressing the dismay of reporters and weathermen throughout the country: "Feminists Prevail: Storms Now Him and Her."[129] (See figure 7.) The accompanying full-page article was cynically titled, "Meet the Himicane: Liberated Wind That Still Does No Good," a dig at the connection persistently drawn between the feminist movement and a destructive storm.[130]

While NOAA's official reaction to Kreps's decision was supportive, it was also decidedly brief. Director Frank explained in a press release: "There's been some pressure in the United States, no question about it," to change the system. And "we at the NOAA decided that in this day and age it was the sensible thing to do to name some hurricanes after men."[131] Repeating statements he had made in press briefings the year before when discussing the decision to cede control of the naming system to the WMO and potential changes to the names following Australia's decision, Frank said that "names are not really significant to me. [. . .] Hurricanes are death and destruction. I don't want to get involved in a controversy that draws attention away from the hurricane. I'm concerned about the warnings and people responding to the warnings—not what we call them."[132] While Frank's statements made clear that the Weather Bureau was relatively on board with the abrupt policy change, some newspaper editorials reflected much less confidence in the change. "We guess that it was good news" finding out that hurricanes would no longer be solely named after women, stated the *Los Angeles Times,* "but we are not too sure." The editors complained that they did not like either

Figure 7. "Feminists Prevail: Storms Now Him and Her," *New Orleans Times-Picayune*, May 13, 1978, 1. Reprinted with permission from the *New Orleans Times-Picayune*.

the old system or the new, and that "there has to be a better solution." They asked, "Why not name hurricanes numerically [or] after *things*?"[133]

Judgment on the decision also appeared in the "Headliners" section of the *New York Times*, which included a picture of NHC director Frank with the tagline, "Goodbye to Chauvinism." The opening sentence of the article punned, "hell hath no fury like a woman stormed." The final line quipped that the change surely had "nothing to do with the fact [that Frank's] boss, Secretary of Commerce Juanita M. Kreps, is a woman."[134] In interviews on the day of the press release, Frank himself was quick to point out that the pressure he was referring to came from new Gulf South feminists Patricia (Twiss) Butler of Houston and Dorothy Yates of Miami, not Roxcy Bolton or his boss, Secretary Kreps.[135] The irony was on point: the facts all point to the conclusion that the decision was a direct result of Juanita Kreps's influence (and Roxcy Bolton's).

While weathermen were mercilessly teased for losing to feminists, Secretary of Commerce Juanita Kreps was roundly criticized in the national media in explicitly gendered terms for her role in changing the naming process. Reporters likened Kreps's decision to a "storm" of "fury" that had no contextual basis or justification, again comparing feminist activity to irrational, turbulent storms. In fact, as the historical record shows, Kreps was acting within the context of a series of changes occurring on a broader scale in the United States. By 1978, feminists had ushered in sweeping reforms in American law, public policy, and social consciousness: victories in the Supreme Court for women's equality, inclusion in the US military, and even the placement of key women, like Kreps herself, in once male-dominated professions. These advancements, among others, demonstrated that gender equality was important at a governmental level and reinforced that separation or exclusion of the sexes was indeed sexist.

As with other gender-equality changes of the 1970s, once the change finally went through, there was no discussion of a return to the all-female naming system. All agreed that the new male-female system was here to stay. In late 1978, representatives of NOAA "went to the international community" of twenty-one Atlantic Ocean tropical storm–affected countries requesting to change the global naming system. After a trial period in the 1979 season, a standardized system of alternating male-female names was introduced globally.[136]

Winds of Change

A historical account pieced together through archival documents, correspondence, and newspaper articles paints a vivid picture of how gender-based rhetoric changed over a twenty-five-year period in American cultural history. The arguments that women, reporters, and weathermen made about hurricanes during this period reveal how the naming controversy figured into larger concerns within the feminist movement. The most important conclusion drawn from this hurricane history lies in its depiction of feminist protest on an everyday and seemingly mundane level. Within the larger context of complicated debates over workplace sexism, abortion, and sexual freedom at all levels of US society, the hurricane-naming debate became an illustrative example of how ferociously feminists were forestalled as they struggled to accomplish even relatively small changes. Hurricane descriptions became a tool used to negate feminist beliefs, separate ideas of the movement, and conquer its leaders, creating lasting impressions of storms and the movement itself as inseparable feminine objects. Given the protractedness of the hurricane-naming debate, it is a wonder that any change was enacted at all, yet the length of the struggle also makes the feminists' ultimate (qualified) success all the more significant. While the naming debate is critical for understanding the feminist movement and the reactions to it in the twentieth century, the length of that debate speaks to the volumes of pushback and negativity met by any attempt, especially legislative, to redefine sex, sexuality, or gender in the United States.

The experiences of Roxcy Bolton and Juanita Kreps encapsulate key moments in America's gender history. In 1970, when Roxcy O'Neal Bolton first approached the Weather Bureau as a representative of NOW, momentum from the feminist and environmental movements had just begun to build. Bolton's invitation to appear at the Interdepartmental Hurricane Warning Conference was a sign of the era's cultural shifts. As Bolton continued to appear at the conferences, attention to the issue of sexism and the relationship between gender and the environment increased in American culture more broadly. Sympathy for the cause, though, did not increase enough to force change. By the time Dr. Juanita M. Kreps was appointed secretary of commerce in 1977, the US feminist movement was enjoying a moment of triumph, with broad and sweeping changes taking place nationally. Just as feminism had helped Kreps to reach her powerful appointment, she in turn used her position to help the cause of feminism. She enacted critical change in various areas, including the hurricane-naming system. Had Kreps been voicing her concern from a less influential place, as Bolton had before her, it is unlikely the female-only hurricane-naming system would have changed. The change in hurricane names was a fight seen as a regional, national, and international concern. Hurricane names transgressed borders, and with them came descriptors that reflected concerns of the cultural period. Roxcy Bolton grew up in an era where storm names were both introduced and expanded, becoming the foci of the nation's rhetoric. Living in the Gulf South and in the same city as the NHC gave her a front-row seat to these new female-named and -gendered storms, and a unique vantage point to view feminist concerns about the role negative female descriptors played in shaping the perception of women not only in their professions—like the Weather Girls—but also in their personal lives. It was also an issue that affected Bolton personally and professionally, as she would be forever known as the woman who fought the weathermen. Notably, other late feminists leading the push for change were also from the Gulf South region (including Texas and Florida), and key change agent Juanita Kreps herself was a southern feminist hailing from Kentucky and North Carolina. Thus it was this particular breed of southern (Gulf South) feminist who pointed out that this local issue had larger meaning.

    The hurricane-naming debate was just one small part of a complicated and passionate struggle over the definitions of gender and culture in the postwar United States. By reviewing how the debate unfolded, the factors influencing the arguments for and against, and its eventual outcome, we reach a more complex understanding of American definitions of gender and sexuality, culture and politics. Time would tell how this policy change in names would impact the perception of hurricanes, particularly the male-named storms of the future.

4

ANDREW
AND THE BUSINESS OF STORMS

The 1992 hurricane season was off to a slow start. By early August, not a single hurricane had formed in the Atlantic region, a rarity for an area with devastating activity in the years prior. But just as the country relaxed, an "alien" emerged on the horizon as rapidly as the ever-feared UFO.[1] The "beast we named Andrew," reported the *Miami Herald*, "howled ashore" near the Florida Keys as a Category 5 storm, heading straight for Homestead, Florida.[2]

As coverage of the storm shifted to known Florida locales and identified Andrew as the worst of its kind, television meteorologists and reporters geared up for the first-ever 24-hour live coverage of a hurricane. Leading the charge was a new type of television meteorologist, Bryan Norcross, who sat at the helm of Miami's WTVJ–News Channel 4 for 23 hours during landfall, reassuring residents and reporting details to all tuning in to the live broadcast. And watching they were. In the 1980s and 1990s, Americans were obsessed with the weather again, consuming it in new forms in local and national spaces, and participating by sharing personal footage caught with portable video cameras. Part of this obsession stemmed from the coverage's new form—live continuous reporting—which provided growing detail of storm movements and impact complete with sound and image. Through this, hurricanes were grittier, more dramatic, and sensationalized than ever before. These excessively graphic hurricanes were directly supported by new scientific classification for wind speeds like the Saffir-Simpson Hurricane Wind Scale, which delineated categories of intensity, helping to rank storms as larger and deadlier than their predecessors. The increased coverage and newly categorized deadly storms reinvigorated descriptive creativity of storm movements at the same time that Americans culturally redefined the hurricane due to a change in the official naming process. As male-female-named storm lists debuted in the 1980s, becoming part of cultural tradition by the 1990s, hurricanes again became the site of a cultural discourse on gender. As a result, hurricanes yet again became the gender-specific assassins of our nightmares, a place to work out cultural fears, and a reflector of larger debates about gender at the close of the century.

Featured in this discourse was an attempt to redefine an object long described as a feminine entity. Americans wrestled with the new possibilities provided with male-named storms, finally settling on the pattern of hurricane gendering established during storms of the 1950s and 1960s: hurricanes were described with the worst possible gendered adjectives of the time period, fitting with the gendered nomenclature that was attached. These adjectives emerged against the backdrop of the close of the Vietnam and Cold wars, reckoning with environmental changes wrought by human development, debates over new status for women post–feminist movement, new forms of sexual expression and gender definition post–sexual revolution and post–gay liberation movement, and the rise of a new era of conservative politics and pundits focused on family values, morality, and foreign aggressors wielding drugs, war, or threatening American might. Thus, in this context, male hurricanes were aliens from the sky, militarized weapons of war, and unstoppable natural enemies of the state.

Not only did this new breed of male hurricanes fascinate Americans, but so did their aftermath. The growth of discourse through 24-hour news coverage meant the growth of the business of storms, and with it, larger consumption of all aspects of the coverage. Storm coverage was now laid out in granular detail through 24-hour news channels looking for new angles, stories, and details to garner continued interest in their coverage. Increasingly, 24-hour news focused on the storm's aftermath as detailed coverage of bungled evacuation efforts, stalled relief, and mismanagement or lack of relief support served as a way to extend coverage of a storm.[3] As millions of Americans watched Andrew (and other hurricanes in the 1980s and 1990s) and reacted to their detailed coverage, a new consciousness emerged regarding response.[4] Soon after Andrew, calls for changes in federal, state, and local disaster relief policy due to outcry over incidents of mismanagement increased.[5] This spreading sense of responsibility for disaster management extended the definition of not only hurricanes and their aftermath, but also other hazards, forever changing the understanding of what constitutes a disaster.⁶ Most of all, though, this redefinition of disaster occurred as Americans renegotiated the gendered descriptions of hurricanes, providing an opportunity to yet again connect hurricane naming to other changes in American society.

Developments in Objective Measures of Newsworthiness

Twenty-four-hour television coverage fundamentally changed the way Americans viewed and interacted with hurricanes. Its development as a medium in the 1980s and its rise as the primary way Americans received their news by the 2000s in some ways parallel earlier weather-news growth.⁷ As in earlier periods, with the growth in content came growth in interest in everything that made up a hurricane. This growth fueled renewed interest in the names of hurricanes as well as the cultural creativity used with these names to describe storms.

In other ways, though, this new era of weather reporting differed remarkably from the past. First, the number of people consuming this medium changed. Second, the focus of the content of this coverage evolved. As hurricane coverage shifted to defining not only trajectory but impact, it was shaped by several key developments: (a) new storm tracking and prediction technology that provided new objective measures for determining intensity and demonstrating a storm's newsworthiness and refuted old notions of hurricane modification or control; (b) increased interest in relief effort for storms due to the development of 24-hour news; and (c) revisions to disaster policy that changed the way Americans defined disaster and the expected response to it.

The first major change to the perception of hurricane intensity and potential newsworthiness was prompted by the introduction of new objective measures to determine intensity and predict path, particularly the use of the Saffir-Simpson Hurricane Wind Scale. Developed in 1971 by civil engineer Herbert Saffir and then-director of the National Hurricane Center Robert Simpson, the Saffir-Simpson scale was a direct product of the scientific studies of hurricanes that had been under way since the 1950s.⁸ Simpson had led Project STORMFURY, the hurricane-modification program made famous for its efforts to control hurricanes. After its successful seeding of

Hurricane Debbie in 1969, Project STORMFURY efforts stagnated and so had its support.[9] In 1973, the United States entered an economic recession that challenged the postwar prosperity that funded scientific experimentation like STORMFURY.[10] This economic stagnation forced cuts in excess governmental spending and reevaluation of experimental efforts to control hurricanes.[11] A similar effort ensued to decrease the staff support provided by the US Navy as efforts in the Vietnam War increased. Project STORMFURY, costing taxpayers $2 to $3 million a year due to the equipment, flight time, and joint nature of the Commerce and Defense department program, became a targeted program of excess on the Nixon-era chopping block.[12]

Due to a slow hurricane period in the 1970s, Project STORMFURY staff had trouble finding additional storms to seed, leading to problems proving the project's efficacy.[13] STORMFURY staff blamed the Gulf of Mexico, which had frequent activity and was colloquially known by that point as "Hurricane Alley," but rarely met strict requirements that storms be 50 miles away from a populated area in the 18 hours after seeding to prevent unintended effects.[14] With minimal storms to modify, let alone storms that fit the specific criteria of the project, the positive results of Debbie were hard to replicate.[15] The staff tried in 1971 with Hurricane Ginger but had little success. As each year passed, the successes of modification efforts quickly became wishful lore.[16] STORMFURY staff then proposed moving the seeding program west to the Pacific Ocean to study typhoons to compare data to hurricanes but were met with skepticism from other countries in range of potential effects.[17] This did not mean that the entire project's efforts were cut, though. In fact, research on hurricanes increased as newly gained knowledge of hurricane movements (through radar and satellite) developed.[18] Unfortunately, this research further demonstrated that STORMFURY efforts were more myth than reality. By the end of the 1970s, new research on hurricane movements (such as storm-development tracks) refuted the findings of successful seeding experiments.[19] This new research showed that the storms seeded by STORMFURY staff would have behaved similarly even without modification.[20] Thus, the hypothesis that formed the basis of hurricane seeding modification efforts remained invalidated.[21] Because of this, Project STORMFURY was shuttered as its staff was cut, its funding stripped, and its glory days of success refuted.[22]

Even though these results were a disappointing conclusion to a decades-long research project, hurricane research during the 1970s did lead to a reevaluation of the ways Americans interacted with storms, particularly in their understanding of a storm's impact. The active storm period in the 1960s brought new attention to the fact that many storms followed unpredictable patterns and frequently intensified overnight. At the same time, questions raised by feminists like Roxcy Bolton in the 1970s about how meteorologists and reporters stressed the importance and intensity in their reports drew attention to complications with current practices that used gender as a mechanism to define storm intensity.

The Saffir-Simpson scale was a simple solution to this complex problem and was introduced to the public in 1973 after two years of testing.[23] A direct result of Robert Simpson's own research on the subject and interaction with Roxcy Bolton, who had convinced Simpson to revisit the bureau's labeling and classification process for storms, the scale relied on "categories" to label hurricane wind speed and inform the public of the strength of a hurricane.[24] Unlike the naming system for storms, which referred only to a particular storm, the wind scale was meant to distinguish the size of a hurricane throughout its life cycle. It was developed based on an older system of labeling categories of wind (known as the Beaufort Scale) to work in tandem with the hurricane-naming system, allowing for identification of a storm by name and categorization of the fluctuations in its wind speed.[25] For example, the scale took into consideration that many storms changed overnight. Some known changes included wind speed, direction, and intensity of storm surge. To represent these changes, the scale classified storms by a category number. The categories of the Saffir-Simpson scale ranged from Tropical Storm (at the lowest) to Category 5 (maximum intensity).

The scale took the guessing out of the hurricane-warning equation, clearly marking storm strength and danger as linked to wind intensity. As cautioned by Weather Bureau officials, the scale did not replace hurricane naming; it assisted by providing details on storm size. In this way, names and the scale worked in tandem. To receive a name, a storm had to reach a minimum threshold of wind on the scale, thus marking both the significance of a named storm in the public's mind and the scale's importance to its label.

Herbert Saffir's role in developing the Saffir-Simpson scale is also not surprising. As a civil engineer, Saffir was aware of new research taking place in other fields to refine hazard categorization.[26] The Fujita Scale, for instance, was invented in the same year as the hurricane-wind scale (1971) and introduced to the public at the same time as the Saffir-Simpson Scale (1973). Developed by Tetsuya "Ted" Fujita, a professor at the University of Chicago, in conjunction with Allen Pearson, the director of the National Severe Storms Forecast Center, it classified the strength of tornados.[27] This scale added to a previously developed scale that identified earthquake size, known as the Richter Scale. The Richter Scale was developed in the 1930s by Charles Richter and Beno Gutenberg, seismologists at the California Institute of Technology.[28] It was revised in the early 1970s and eventually replaced with the Moment Magnitude Scale (MMS) by the end of the decade. One of the major additions to the MMS was the revision to its categorization of "great earthquakes," updating the ranking and accuracy of its categories.[29]

All of these scales—Saffir-Simpson, Fujita, and MMS—were introduced in the 1970s for public consumption and used numerical classification to signify impact range. For example, in the lowest grade of each scale, hurricanes were identified as a Category 1, earthquakes ranked as a Magnitude 1, and tornados as F1. However, only the Saffir-Simpson scale was meant to work with and not replace a previous method of identifying a natural hazard. Thus, by the end of the 1970s, it was evident that only hurricanes (or tropical storms) were named, even if they were assigned a category of strength. In short, researchers proved that they still considered hurricanes inherently different from other natural hazards, and they felt the public did as well. By the end of the 1970s, the Saffir-Simpson Hurricane Wind Scale became the standard in categorization of hurricane strength and was seamlessly integrated into the existing classification system of naming. These categories of wind strength played a direct role in the perception and description of storms. Reporters now had an easy mechanism for distinguishing the "worst" storm from a weaker storm, especially as other changes emerged in how Americans defined "disaster."

The second major change to the perception of hurricane intensity and potential newsworthiness came with the creation of the Federal Emergency Management Agency (FEMA) in the late 1970s. The establishment of organizations to manage emergencies began with the founding of the country. As explained by historian Kevin Rozario, plans were in place for most local and state areas to respond to fire, flood, and disease catastrophes by the nineteenth century.[30] But much of what had existed before rested on just that: response. And this response was largely left up to state and local or volunteer organizations. But the Cold War provided a new impetus for revisiting these policies. In the 1950s, the federal government took steps to standardize disaster mitigation. From bomb drills to evacuation plans, procedures were implemented to both warn the public of impending disaster *and* help them recover from it. Beginning with the Federal Disaster Relief Act of 1950, the power to declare a national disaster, and thus enable federal response efforts, was placed with the president. The act was meant to support state efforts to respond to disaster, but not supplant them. The act also introduced the key concept of "cost-sharing" disaster relief funds, whereby the federal government would contribute up to 75 percent of disaster relief funding up to a specified amount, and the state(s) affected would contribute the rest.[31]

The declaration of an incident as a "national disaster" had particular significance. First, this official change in policy directly emphasized that disasters were national problems, not just regional ones. Second, it further delineated between disasters of national significance and hazards considered of lesser importance. The designation as a federal disaster meant that an incident was of a certain magnitude and was identified as an extreme event. The threshold of these incidents was set by the president. Once the president had declared the incident a disaster at the behest of the state's governor, federal relief organizations would not need to seek congressional approval to mobilize resources. In a time when federal civil defense and nuclear war concerns were critical, this approach to disaster management centralized control at the executive level. Control at the executive level for disaster designation, in turn, affected not only the response to a disaster, but how all emergencies were discussed, even preemptively. Size, scale, damage, and frequency of repeated impact to a state played a considerable role in the description of hazards and thus became essential to influencing the financial aid decisions following impact.

This perspective on disaster management and mitigation as a federal concern was further expanded by national experience with major hurricanes in the late 1960s and early 1970s. Crisis-management programs for a potential nuclear incident or major hurricane prompted the introduction of the National Plan for Emergency Preparedness (1964), which included programs for large-scale evacuation in addition to fallout shelters.[32] Hurricane Betsy (1965) served as the impetus for the introduction of federal flood relief and mitigation studies and eventual policies, including the National Flood

Insurance Protection Act and National Flood Insurance Program, which provided financial aid to those impacted by major floods.[33] Four years later in 1969, reaction to Hurricane Camille inspired a revision of the Disaster Relief Act of 1950 to introduce a federal coordinating officer to represent the president in organizing disaster relief.[34] Following Hurricanes Betsy and Camille, multiple national initiatives were enacted to mitigate the effect of future storms.

In the hurricane-prone Gulf South, programs like Project STORMFURY, the Florida Area Cumulus Experiment, and the National Hurricane Center received funding as concerns over the effect of storms grew while contemporary research detailed the impact of new factors on current methods for mitigation and response.[35] In June 1972, for example, a nine-state hurricane-preparedness conference hosted over 200 experts to discuss the current issues at stake. The experts' conclusions, printed in newspapers the next day, cautioned that "population density is about to outrun forecasters' ability to provide adequate warnings," dramatically increasing the effect of hurricanes on the Gulf Coast. Identifying "Miami, Charleston, New Orleans, and Texas coastal bend cities as 'amongst the most vulnerable to a major hurricane disaster,'" the conferees stressed that coastal cities should heavily invest in research and planning for the next "Big One." This included the creation of master plans for "hurricane predictions and warnings, evacuation and shelter, and better means of public information and education." They also recommended the implementation of "more stringent land use and building codes, increased medical preparedness, and more exact prediction" to widen the warning time for storms from 12 to 18 hours in advance. "There is a clear and present need for a concerted, carefully coordinated local, state and private approach to the growing menace posed by great storms," the experts proclaimed, and it was necessary to do everything possible to assuage them. One such change resulting from this conference was the public implementation of the Saffir-Simpson Hurricane Wind Scale the following year.[36]

Despite the alert issued by the multistate conference on hurricane preparedness, action to revise federal disaster relief protocol for all emergencies did not occur at a federal level until 1974. The impetus for this change was Hurricane Agnes (1974), which grossly affected six states, placing new emphasis on federal preparation for multistate disasters. As a result of Agnes and risk assessment research done in the early 1970s, the Disaster Relief

Act of 1974 introduced new programs focused on dam safety, earthquakes, nuclear regulation, environmental protection, a national emergency warning system using radio and television messages, and the emerging threat of terrorism.[37]

More significantly, the Disaster Relief Act of 1974 specified the definition of a "major disaster" versus a lesser "emergency" in explicit terms. An "emergency" was "any hurricane, tornado, storm, flood, high water, wind-driven water, tidal wave, tsunami, earthquake, volcanic eruption, landslide, mudslide, snowstorm, drought, fire, explosion, or other catastrophe in any part of the United States which requires Federal emergency assistance *to supplement* State and local efforts to save lives and protect property, public health and safety *or to avert or lessen the threat of a disaster.*"[38] Meanwhile, a "major disaster" was "any hurricane, tornado, storm, flood, high water, wind-driven water, tidal wave, tsunami, earthquake, volcanic eruption, landslide, mudslide, snowstorm, drought, fire, explosion, or other catastrophe in any part of the United States which, *in the determination of the President, causes damage of sufficient severity above and beyond emergency services by the Federal Government,* to supplement the efforts and available resources of State, local governments, and disaster relief organizations *in alleviating the damage, loss, hardship, or suffering caused thereby.*"[39]

These differing definitions were crucial. First, they recognized that incidents vary in size and impact. They could be small emergencies, affecting a single area or state, or they could be major disasters with historically significant multistate consequences. They could also vary in type, cost, or even cause. Second, the 1974 act again placed the sole responsibility for determining the difference between an emergency and a major disaster, and thus federal efforts to assist in relief, with the president. Furthermore, it emphasized that hurricanes ranked at the top of the list of causal hazards both major and minor because there were multiple factors influencing the response and reaction to storms.

With the expansion of the Disaster Relief Act between the 1950s and 1970s, and the growing support of risk-related research, by the late 1970s over 100 different governmental organizations were created to respond to or warn of incidents related to civil defense or disaster management, causing confusion and stress over the process of response.[40] This confusion was made particularly evident during the Three Mile Island nuclear meltdown disaster in Pennsylvania in 1979, whereby the evacuation, handling of cleanup, and process of informing the public of its danger were all questioned. According to the Office of Technology Assessment, which reported to Congress, over 50 percent of the American public was left dissatisfied with the handling of the Three Mile Island disaster.[41] Soon after, the National Governors' Association urged the president to reconsider US policy toward emergency preparedness and response. As a result, on April 1, 1979, President Jimmy Carter officially created the Federal Emergency Management Agency, consolidating all previous organizations under a single agency structure.[42] FEMA, as it would be known, was funded yearly by congressional budgetary spending and was authorized to dictate disaster response orders once sanctioned by the president, acting as the overseeing organization for all efforts. FEMA's mission and oversight in the 1980s would expand significantly as organizational restructuring absorbed previous methods of disaster response. The National Weather Service, and more particularly its National Hurricane Center, headquartered in Florida, assisted FEMA in its efforts to track and mitigate hurricane damage.

Within the National Weather Service, the new policy on federal disaster relief and its specific definitions of incidents, combined with research on storms and the Saffir-Simpson Hurricane Wind Scale, emerged at the same moment the new male-female hurricane-naming system was unveiled. Merged with new definitions of disaster and the categories of wind or intensity, this naming system evolved as Americans attempted to blend older perspectives of hurricane behavior with new understanding. But this understanding was influenced by one final factor: the introduction of a new type of weather news, 24-hour coverage. On May 2, 1982, the Weather Channel (TWC) debuted. Captioned with the slogan "We Take the Weather Seriously, but Not Ourselves," TWC had a revolutionary mission: to broadcast weather news for all regions on a 24-hour cycle.[43] Round-the-clock weather news fit the mold of other emerging news networks of the era.[44] The Cable News Network (CNN), for example, was introduced two years prior (in 1980) and quickly gained extensive viewership. CNN's success spurred other networks into competing for 24-hour coverage. Within five years, other 24-hour channels debuted.[45]

The advent of the continuous news cycle changed the way all news was consumed, produced, and ultimately discussed. The introduction of CNN's

24-hour news network forced newscasts to become increasingly interactive in their coverage of events as stations grappled for coverage in a 24-hour cycle versus a twice- or thrice-daily cycle. Similarly, coverage of events was delivered instantly, or "live," thus changing the way individuals across the globe experienced them. With the demand for 24-hour news only increasing in popularity, these instantaneous or live-coverage events affected viewers as they responded in the moment. This impacted the reaction to the event, the response following, and even the policy or legislation enacted afterward. For example, in the Persian Gulf War, 24-hour coverage from a Baghdad hotel tilted impressions of the conflict. Similarly, response to the search for Baby Jessica, the O. J. Simpson white Bronco chase, and even the 1992 Los Angeles riots was also shaped by news coverage.[46] Political scientists, studying the first years following CNN's debut, nicknamed this new form of consumption the "CNN Effect."[47]

While everyday news coverage changed because of CNN, weather coverage changed because of TWC. First and foremost, the content of weather news changed rapidly after TWC's introduction in 1982. In its initial year, TWC included simple broadcasts with crude graphics. Within one year, TWC expanded these broadcasts to include weather programming and daily weather statistics. As the demand for everyday weather news increased, the expectation that extreme weather events would be covered in new ways live also increased. Take, for example, the trusted weatherman. In postwar form, he became a regular feature report of nightly newscasts. Often showcasing high- and low-pressure systems by using graphs and charts or live reports from the field every once in a while, most weathermen were relegated to a spotlighted feature and no more. TWC revolutionized the perspective on the modern weatherman. In TWC's version, the weatherman was reminiscent of the Storm Fighters of the past. He was in the field, using fancy equipment, and glaringly facing or bracing against a storm. TWC's gimmicks used to highlight the forecaster in the field only increased throughout the next two decades. With features like *Storm Stories* and broadcasts from 24-hour news cycles, the weatherman became a fixture of every major storm. Some stations sent their meteorologist into the field during a major storm just to show him blowing in the wind and rain. Others placed a reporter in the middle of a flooded street to wade through the disastrous region in its aftermath while others included simulation models to showcase damaging winds or hail effects.[48] Such devices were used as a way to garner interest in their coverage.

Despite the increase in weather programming and interest in storm coverage, few channels featured anyone except a male forecaster or meteorologist at the helm, let alone as chief meteorologist. Even TWC's regular programming rarely featured female correspondents, instead favoring men like Jim Cantore for spotlighted segments and modeling gimmicks. While there were exceptions—such as WDSU New Orleans's Margaret Orr—the strong stigma of the "Weather Girl" versus the "Weather Man" persisted nationally past the 1970s, and is still present today.[49] As explained by scholars Nyssa Perryman and Sandra Theiss, while TWC opened doors for women to serve in key roles, including meteorologist or forecaster, in many ways women made more gains covering sports than in weather, to the point that only 19 percent of local weather broadcast positions were held by women by the close of the twentieth century.[50] Americans still consumed their weather news from the same creators in charge since the start, and their impressions of "serious" coverage included a male meteorologist or weatherman in the field, as well as behind the desk. This gendered bent to the field affected the coverage of male-named storms, as impressions of masculinity were formed or reflected by these weathermen and current ideologies of gender.

The introduction of self-made weather videos only added to weather interest after 1983. Beginning that year, Sony introduced the first personal-use video camera, known as the "camcorder." Within two years, videocassette recording, or VHS tape recording, became a popular pastime for Americans, so much so that an entire television show—*America's Funniest Home Videos*—was produced to showcase accidents or dramatic events caught on camera.[51] This new era of recording encouraged active participation in weather tracking in the same way 1950s-era weather prediction had. When fused with 24-hour news, which frequently played these recordings as part of their regular programming, interest in weather and extreme events skyrocketed.[52]

Coverage of weather-based incidents such as hurricanes significantly amplified TWC ratings as it built from its initial year. Alicia (1983), Gilbert (1988), and Hugo (1989) focused eyes on growing coverage and its impact, especially as voices of outraged response slowly started to cause revision in disaster policy. These memorable storms also increased interest in relief efforts to a degree that had only peripherally been reported before. Now that Americans could see storms in detail, react to them live, and influence this reaction, more was at stake.

Like many coastal regions, the Gulf South, particularly prone to hurricanes, experienced significant growth from the 1970s to the 2000s. (See table 5.) This population increase left more people in danger than ever before, making hurricanes ever more threatening. There was also a larger economic value in protecting the region, which was home to major industries like oil and gas. This was made particularly more frightening given the risk reports from the early 1970s about the ill-equipped nature of coastal cities to warn and assist their rapidly growing populations. While advancements such as strength categories, ever-updated evacuation routes, and systems of federal relief were a start, they did not quell fears of chaos arising from memories of past storms like Agnes and Camille combined with growing public awareness of environmental issues such as the effects of a recent nuclear incident, acid rain, smog conditions in cities, rivers on fire from pollution, and rapidly eroding coastlines.[53]

Reporters covering hurricanes in the Gulf South were quick to point out these factors when discussing potential impacts of storms, amplifying the pre-storm hype as well as the post-storm recovery interest. The Gulf South was the place to look for exciting storms, and when the next big one emerged,

Table 5
Population of Selected Gulf South Cities, 1970–2000

	1970	1980	1990	2000	Increase/ Decrease
Biloxi	48,486	49,311	46,319	50,644	▲
Houston	1,232,802	1,595,138	1,630,864	1,953,631	▲
Miami	334,859	346,681	358,648	362,470	▲
Mobile	190,026	200,452	196,263	198,915	▲
New Orleans	593,471	557,927	496,938	484,674	▼

Source: US Census Bureau, Decennial Census, www.census.gov/programs-surveys/decennial-census/data/datasets.2010.html.

Note: All cities except New Orleans saw an increase in the number of residents.

they were ready. A widely varying period of storm activity due to multiple El Niño years (1982–83 and 1986–87) only intensified these discussions as more variability in storm development had a gross impact on the discussion and coverage of the storms that developed.[54] With fewer storms, the ones that did affect the United States were the focus of all eyes, particularly as new hazard definitions and names, systems of categorization, relief and aid organizational structures, and forms of media were introduced.

Meet the Himicane: Masculinized Storms Pre-Andrew

Between the 1970s and 1980s, drastic changes occurred in the way Americans defined and perceived hurricanes. The introduction of the Saffir-Simpson Hurricane Wind Scale and new research on hurricane tracking and prediction provided new meaning to a hurricane's trajectory and potential impact. Meanwhile, systems of federal disaster response and relief emphasized the importance of accurate preparation, response, and description of storms both in the preceding period for accurate warnings and evacuations and in the aftermath as classification of "major disasters" and "emergencies" took on new meaning.

These changes played a direct role in the perception and description of named storms. Initially, the evolved cultural understanding of hurricanes caused a significant decrease in the use of gender as a vehicle to describe hurricane behavior. Storm descriptions from 1974 (after the Saffir-Simpson scale's introduction and updated Disaster Relief Act) to 1983 were increasingly less likely to contain gendered rhetoric, at least in print. One reason for the decrease in gender use from 1974 to 1983 was the attention directed to gendered language by feminists. These concerns ultimately contributed to an official change in the naming system by 1979 to the male-female naming system used today. A second reason for the decrease in gender use was the introduction of the Saffir-Simpson scale, which provided an easy method for categorizing all storms in intensity, making it easy for reporters to describe storms of lesser impact with appropriate terminology. This change in classification for storms was unveiled right at the time Americans were reckoning with language debates, hurricane and disaster relief policies, and a new naming system for storms that included male names in addition to female names.

But the decrease in gender frequency use in newspaper articles during this period does not mean that Americans stopped gendering storms altogether. In fact, a new pattern of hurricane gendering developed between 1970 and 1983: gender was used to indicate the intensity of the storm as spelled out through definitions of its potential impact and its categorical size. Reporters now had an easy mechanism (wind speed and gender) for distinguishing the "worst" storm from a weaker storm, especially as they were testing new language to accompany male-named storms. This grossly affected their description of the storm. If a storm failed to develop, or lacked intensity, reporters used gendered rhetorical description to downplay a storm's newsworthiness. In this way, gendered analogies became critical to shaping the impression of storms. And much like gendered descriptors Americans used in the past, these new (male) descriptors reflected the larger cultural period.

This change in gendered use is particularly evident in the description of hurricanes from 1979 to 1983. Following the introduction of the male-female hurricane-naming list in 1979, reporters speculated as to whether male names would evoke the same type of descriptive creativity and more particularly, fear, as female-named storms of the past. Similarly, many wondered whether hurricanes would ever be considered male, as they had been identified as a feminine object for nearly a quarter of a century. Would they include similar descriptors of aggressive or unwanted behavior? Would these descriptions be linked to cultural standards of masculinity as they were linked with femininity? These questions were well founded in a period of considerable adjustment as the American public grew accustomed to this new naming system.

The first male storm was a bit of a dud. Tropical Storm Bud "barreled" towards Acapulco in mid-June 1978 like a bull in a chute.[55] Described as an untamed stallion, Bud was speculatively described as "big," "bad," and most of all, male.[56] In description, Bud exemplified the ease with which reporters adopted male-named storms the same year that Secretary of Commerce Juanita Kreps ordered that names be changed for the Pacific Ocean region. It was meant as a test system, and initial hesitation to this change faded. Despite the impression that weathermen "bowed" to feminists in this ten-year battle over the names, Bud was welcomed with eager anticipation.[57]

It was fitting that the new alternating male-female naming list was unveiled in the Pacific region because it was there that female names were first introduced during World War II. As with Hurricane Alice in 1954, Bud's name, as well as other male names like Daniel and John, came from the list of top baby names in US popular culture. But Bud was also fitting as the name chosen to represent the first male storm as the name was often used to evoke characteristics of aggressive or bullish behavior. Meteorologists and reporters expected Bud to behave a certain way—masculine—as defined by cultural standards of masculinity in latter-twentieth-century American culture. As a result, Bud ultimately set the tone for male-named storms of the future.

As it matured into a hurricane, however, Bud lost steam, weakening to a depression and dissipating a day later off the southwest coast of California. Reporters rationalized their dismay at Bud's performance.[58] They quickly pointed out that Bud was only a tropical storm on the Saffir-Simpson scale. The next "major storm" would be bigger, badder, and more akin with what they had imagined for male-named storms. Research confirmed that not every storm developed into a beast of epic sagas, and Bud's ranking on the Saffir-Simpson scale proved this. Also, this Pacific storm system was in its test year. Atlantic storms were different, everyone knew, from the research on the Gulf South's "Hurricane Alley." But before reporters and forecasters had time to wallow in their disappointment with Bud the dud, another tropical storm, Carlotta, developed quickly in its wake. Named for the Mexican Empress Carlotta, the storm quickly grew to a 130-miles-per-hour hurricane, wide and strong. Quickly topping Bud's stats, Carlotta gained attention not only due to its size but also its name.

The name "Carlotta," while female, was new in its own right. While Carlotta had been used in storm-naming lists before (1967, 1971, and 1975), its significance this time represented the hasty deal worked out with the Mexican government to switch the Pacific storm-naming system to the newly introduced male-female system within the calendar year. The US/Mexico Pacific naming system not only alternated male and female names, but also included Mexican-influenced names. Carlotta was the first Mexican name included in the mix, with others such as Emilia, Fico, Gilma, Hector, Rosa, Sergio, and Vincente to follow. In total, out of the 21 names on the 1978 naming list, 8 were of Mexican origin. (See table 6.) Despite its formation into a sizable storm, Carlotta did not make landfall, changing direction at the last

Table 6
Male-Female Storm-Naming List, Pacific Region, 1978

Aletta	Gilma	Miriam	Tara
Bud	Hector	Norman	Vincente
Carlotta	Ira	Olivia	Willa
Daniel	John	Paul	
Emilia	Kristy	Rosa	
Fico	Lane	Sergio	

Source: Records of the Weather Bureau, 1735–1979, Record Groups 27 & 130, National Archives and Records Administration, College Park, MD.

moment—but it did surpass previous records as the third largest June storm of all time.[59]

While Bud failed to produce the results desired of his name, and Carlotta veered from land, Hurricane Fico had a dramatic outcome. Fico brushed by Hawaii in July of 1978 with a force of 140-miles-per-hour winds, ranking it higher on the Saffir-Simpson scale than Bud. The longest-lasting hurricane of the Pacific region on record, Fico was everything reporters had predicted with male-named storms. As Fico neared the Hawaiian Islands, the *Los Angeles Times* reported "75 Flee."[60] Twenty days in, Fico was still going, a new record, the paper proclaimed. Despite the initial hype, Fico dissipated. In the end, Fico caused little damage, an estimated $200,000 ($764,000 in 2018)—no comparison to the great storms of the 1960s. Even though its location away from the US mainland and lack of deaths made the storm less deadly, the storm received applause for what it did do: create extreme surf. The "Heavy Surf Will Create Riptide Peril on Weekend," the *Times* cautioned its readers with gravity.[61] "Hurricane Fico kicked up mountainous surf" in its path to the islands, stated the *Chicago Tribune*.[62] This reaction by both the *Times* and the *Tribune* confirmed the power of male storms as opposed to female-named storms. While Fico was more exciting than Bud and Carlotta, the rest of the season passed without major incident, much to the dismay of reporters covering the weather beat.

The hurricane season of 1978 wrapped up lacking male luster just as the male-female naming system tested in the Pacific region was adopted by the World Meteorological Organization (WMO) for the 1979 Atlantic season.

With the WMO announcement that the alternating list was to continue and expand to the exciting amphitheater of "Hurricane Alley," there was little reaction from the public. Unlike the year before, there was no chiding weathermen's decision to incorporate male names, or mention of Secretary of Commerce Juanita Kreps or Roxcy Bolton, and little discussion of the naming debate in general. The announcement was taken as a given, a natural conclusion to a long-ended naming debate. When the 1979 seasonal naming list debuted globally the following June, it included a larger percentage of Mexican-influenced names, as well as other region-specific additions. Meanwhile, another change was made to the naming system. From 1979 on, both the Atlantic and Pacific regions would alternate male-female, but oppositely, whereby the Atlantic system used a female name first, and the Pacific system used a male name first. (See table 7.) This was meant to separate storm reports between regions.

In addition to the change in gendered names, the WMO made other alterations to the naming process. These included the appointment of five regional committees from major WMO-associated weather organizations to select names representative of countries in those areas, representing different dialects and cultural histories. The naming lists would be set up to six years in advance of a season, and names would be recycled or replaced each season based on the committees' suggestions. In addition, any storm names deemed "significant" in popular culture (for example, a storm name used in the past for a major storm or too closely associated with a notable political figure or cultural icon) would be "retired" or replaced. A new hurricane season would officially start on June 1 and run exactly 26 weeks until November 30, or until the last hurricane of the year occurred. Other storm regions would follow separate rules for seasonal lists.[63] With these new naming policies in place, and a test year already completed in the Pacific region, all eyes were now focused on the Atlantic region—the area most impacted by storm activity, and in the first year of the new naming system. What this next storm season would bring was unknown.

The following year, as hurricane season began on June 1, another round of discussion regarding the purported behaviors of male- versus female-named storms ensued in newspaper columns across the country. The results of the 1978 test season did not stop reporters from making predictions on the behavior of male storms, nor from commenting on the cultural period

Table 7
Storm Names for Atlantic and Pacific Ocean Regions, 1979

Atlantic Ocean Region	Pacific Ocean Region
Ana	Andres
Bob	Blanca
Claudette	Carlos
David	Dolores
Elena	Enrique
Frederic	Fifa
Gloria	Guillermo
Henri	Hilda
Isabel	Ignacio
Juan	Jimena
Kate	Kevin
Larry	Linda
Mindy	Marty
Nicholas	Nora
Odette	Olaf
Peter	Pauline
Rose	Rick
Sam	Sandra
Teresa	Terry
Victor	Vivian
Wanda	Waldo

Source: Records of the Weather Bureau, 1735–1979, Record Group 130, National Archives and Records Administration, College Park, MD.

Note: Mexican- or Spanish-influenced names now appear in both the Pacific and Atlantic lists.

influencing this official gender-based naming change. "Hurricane Bob Joins Ladies," reported *Newsday*, three days before the start of the season. "Like McSorley's Bar in 1970, like West Point in 1976, hurricanes in the Atlantic Ocean have joined the ranks of the sexually integrated," summed up the article, referring to the feminist era that was forcing change in multiple systems of culturally separated spaces.[64] As highlighted in this article announcing the 1979 list, male-named storms were "joining" female-named storms;

thus, no matter what, they were considered different. Their results kicked off a renewed "Battle of the Sexes" after a year of sweeping cultural changes.

Sadly for reporters, the first three storms of the 1979 Atlantic season were uneventful. Tropical Storms Ana and Claudette never made it to hurricane-force winds, and while Bob did become a hurricane, it only reached 75-miles-per-hour winds at its peak before striking Grand Isle, Louisiana. David was a different story, though. Emerging from the eastern Caribbean through the Windward Islands, the 175-miles-per-hour storm traveled up the Eastern Seaboard of the United States. When it struck Florida, it weakened slightly, but quickly gained power again to hit Georgia, New England, and even Canada. "Dangerous David" "ripped," "slashed," and "littered" the coastline as "he" went, reported the *New Orleans Times-Picayune* the day after the storm made landfall.[65] The *Raleigh News & Observer* agreed with this assessment, referring to the storm as larger than female storms of the past. "Compared to this, Donna was a pussycat," they proclaimed, referencing the storm that pummeled their state in 1960.[66]

As they gasped for breath following David's "wrath," the country assessed the damages. David was a "menace," proclaimed the *Miami Herald*.[67] The "diabolical storm," stated the *Houston Chronicle,* "razed" the coastline, leaving $1.54 billion in damages (in 1979 or $5.2 billion in 2018) and over 2,000 fatalities.[68] More than that, it locked coastal residents in an epic fight akin to "David & Goliath," where, much like the biblical story, this David won despite the size and numbers along the coast, affirmed the *Los Angeles Times*.[69]

Storms like David were, according to the *New York Times,* "one of the highest of nature's miscreants," and unfortunately, even though the Hurricane Hunters were deployed to "penetrate the eye" of the storm and "the wizardry of satellite photographs provided in-depth detail of its movements," there was little to be done about them.[70] It was exactly for this reason that the *Miami Herald* described David as a harbinger of death, representing it (and the subsequent male storm, Frederic) in a cartoon as pterodactyl-shaped storks, carrying Christian tombstones instead of the usual cherubic baby.[71] Meanwhile, other newspapers described David simply as a "killer."[72]

David was "the most powerful of all storms" affirmed the *New York Times* at the conclusion of the storm.[73] The news-frenzy hype over David's movements was reminiscent of the storms of the 1960s. But unlike the 1960s storms, the language used with David marked a definitive shift in the adjectives associated with storms. In all reports, David was noticeably described using masculine pronouns and characteristics in an attempt to draw comparisons with female storms of the past. Gone were the more feminine adjectives. For example, nowhere in the discussion of David are familiar descriptors like "hugging," "kissing," or even "slapping" the coastline; nor are there aforementioned indecisive qualities like "wandering," "making up their mind," and "erratic." David was diabolical, premeditated, determined, and decided in "his" "attack." He was a menace, killer, and harbinger of death. His actions were dangerous, as he ripped, slashed, battered, and littered the coastline. "He" was God-like, of an era filled with Mesozoic creatures and outside the bounds of scientific recourse, despite all of the tools in human coffers to combat it. In this way, reporters created new images of storms as decidedly male, which they easily expanded as future male storms formed. Amidst an era of the Battle of the Sexes, they removed any doubt that the male storm was distinct. How much of an impact these terms had, and whether they were used again for future male storms, was immediately evident in the two subsequent storms, Elena and Frederic.

Following Hurricane David was Hurricane Frederic, a lesser-strength storm with little impact. Frederic, while lacking the size of David, still inspired panic in newspaper articles. Frederic "rose in the South Atlantic and appeared to following David's approximate path" with determination.[74] The *New Orleans Times-Picayune,* in the direct path of the storm, described it as "a 300-mile-wide major storm that, in its bull's eye between Pascagoula and Mobile, hit four states at once," a true feat of fortitude.[75] Frederic "jackknifed," "sliced," and "lazily lapped up strength from the Gulf's warm waters" until it became a "Gulf Coast Menace" capable of working like a "giant can opener on metal homes" in its path, stated the *Times-Picayune*.[76] While "Frederic did not wipe away Mobile, like Camille did the Mississippi Gulf Coast," the *Times-Picayune* concluded, "he left just enough standing to remind residents how much they had lost."[77] In "his" aftermath, Mobile "resembled a war zone in the early morning hours as merchants literally stood guard" in their own form of Vietnam.[78]

The portrayal of "treacherous Frederic" as the "Gulf Coast Menace," or the cause of a "war zone," along with the descriptions of the storm as a "he" in the *Times-Picayune* articles served to continue separating male-named storms like Frederic from female-named storms of public memory. One aspect of the attempt to separate storms that was clearly illustrated with Frederic was in the differences drawn between types of storm strength. With female storms, strength or devastation was presented as unladylike or unwanted; with male storms, it was revered. A strong male storm was applauded for its ability to harm or maim the coastline; meanwhile, the female storm was said to need taming. Another example is found in the mention of the aftermath of the storm as being akin to a war zone. This association might be familiar to readers remembering the discussion of the female hurricane and the atomic bomb, but the sentiment as used with male storms is noticeably different. As implied, male storms caused the calculated destruction in the same way masculine-dominated armies did, as opposed to the use of uncontrollable weaponry like an atom bomb. Frederic even had the power to stop the press, as the *Mobile Press Register* went offline for two days during the storm.[79] Additionally, placed against the backdrop of the close of the Vietnam War, it is easy to see how these war analogies were attached and evolved.

In contrast to the domineering Frederic, "sister" storm Elena, emerging the same day as Frederic as a tropical storm, was posited as weak and temperamental. "Indecisive Elena sits offshore," confirmed a headline in the *Houston Chronicle*.[80] This behavior was confirmed when it finally hit the Louisiana coastline, as Elena did not matriculate to a full-size hurricane. Immediately, Elena was replaced in interest by reports of Frederic, who followed closely behind. "Frederic and Company," groaned the *Times-Picayune* in a reference to the current popular television show *Three's Company* that featured the antics of two females living with a male roommate (much like the addition of male storms to the female storm mix), was not welcome to knock on the Gulf Coast's door anytime soon.[81]

Even with the welcome sign off, the following year a Category 5 storm emerged on the horizon. Hurricane Allen provoked explicit imagery of what a male-named storm looked like. The *New Orleans Times-Picayune* described Allen as a "typical August storm" at first, "relatively well-behaved."[82] It "teased" the coastline and was "coy" in its choice of direction.[83] This soon changed as Allen developed, "moving unusually fast."[84] He then acted like a "first-time bowler," using the Gulf Coast as an alleyway "500-miles long with Corpus Christi, Texas, as the headpin."[85] As he built up intensity, the "pulsating storm" became guilty of "roiling the Gulf of Mexico with super-charged

ANDREW AND THE BUSINESS OF STORMS

winds and chasing thousands of people inland."[86] Reaching its peak, "Killer" Allen "punished" Texas and "socked" other areas with its winds and rain.[87]

The references to Allen as a bowler, a fighter, and a pulsating storm with supercharged winds were just some of the ways reporters made clear that male-named storm Allen was different from female-named storms. They also did so by illustrating the storm as a male. In one image from the *Times-Picayune*, Allen is depicted as a Prohibition-era roulette dealer grimly manning a table. He is identified by his overweight frame, nonplussed facial expression, and clothing that includes a vest and dealer's green-tinted visor. The caption of the image jokes at the lack of control residents have over a storm's impact zone: "Round and Round It Goes—Where It Stops Nobody Knows."[88] With the table itself clearly representing the center of the hurricane's eye, it is implied that only Allen, the dealer in this scenario, has control over the results of this game. (See figure 8.)

The descriptions of meteorological tracking of Allen also differed from those of female-named storms. Much as with storms of the 1960s, hurricane-tracking planes were sent out to examine the shape of the storm after it was spotted via satellite.[89] This time, though, the Hurricane Hunter squadron sent back reports complimenting Allen's robust movements. As explained in the *Times-Picayune*, "a weather reconnaissance plane flying

Figure 8. "Allen the Roulette Dealer," *New Orleans Times-Picayune,* August 8, 1980, 14. Reprinted with permission from the *New Orleans Times-Picayune.*

into Allen's tight 10-mile eye" reported that "Hurricane Allen, replenished by warm Gulf of Mexico waters," had "rivaled the most intense Atlantic hurricane of all time."[90] As a storm that veered wildly between Category 4 and Category 5 status before striking the Texas coast at Category 3, Allen was enough to scare Texas residents considerably.

But Allen also illustrated something else, besides an example of the robust nature of male-named storms: it displayed a development pattern that mimicked that of 1969's Hurricane Debbie. The rapid development, expanded eye wall, and eerily similar trajectory were impossible to deny. They negated any gains portrayed as a result of the seeding process. By the end of Hurricane Allen, it was obvious that any successes Project STORMFURY staff thought they had gained in seeding Debbie were not really successes at all. Instead, the hypothesis that formed the basis of hurricane-seeding modification efforts was debunked. It was a huge blow to the Project STORMFURY repertoire.[91] With no storms seeded and the seeding process questioned by both scientific theory and visual evidence (from Allen), Project STORMFURY was now obsolete.[92] As a result of Allen (and other cutbacks to the program), by 1983, Project STORMFURY was discontinued, and the era in which man could tame the hurricane concluded. Allen, a male-named storm, ended the decades-long drive to control hurricanes. The irony was not lost on the public, who quickly refocused on what they could control—how other men reacted to storms.[93] The post-1983 era was about disaster management or response, as broadcast live, 24 hours a day.

Storms in the Weather Channel Era

Hurricane Alicia emerged rapidly on the radar in August 1983, a year after the Weather Channel debuted, and three years after Allen's formation and movements officially discredited prior scientific belief that hurricanes could be controlled through seeding. It zigzagged through the Gulf, threatening to strike energy hub Texas.[94] At every moment, 24 hours a day, Alicia was under inspection, not only because of TWC's interest but because Alicia was the first major storm likely to hit the US mainland since 1980's Hurricane Allen. It also drew interest because it was one of the first major storms to impact the region since the creation of FEMA and the era of disaster response. TWC and an enthused media bracket rolled out models and maps to discuss the storm's potential impact zone and spotlight footage of on-the-ground assessments. Using the Saffir-Simpson Hurricane Wind Scale, they classified Alicia as a "fickle" storm with "her" inability to choose a target, but nonetheless deadly based on known size and intensity. As described, the storm had an "unusual birth," puzzling forecasters as it developed.[95] It "stalked the Texas coast" with an "angry woman's 100-plus mph winds" and continued to build, eventually reaching Category 3 right before it "slap[ped]" Texas, southwest of Galveston.[96] Then it continued to Houston, with the media following quickly behind to report on its impact in the downtown area. They were not disappointed as flying debris and rocks shattered windows throughout the energy corridor.

Following Alicia's conclusion, many of the same newspapers applauded the coordinated disaster preparation efforts that had prevented catastrophe on a larger scale.[97] Articles relaying Alicia's damage compared it to previous (male) storms like 1979's Hurricane Frederic. "Frederic holds record for hurricane damage in U.S.," reported the *Houston Chronicle,* emphasizing that, while Alicia had been the first billion-dollar storm in Texas history and the first to hit the US mainland since 1980, response to it was considered adequate.[98] Despite the $1.7 billion (1983) in damages, Alicia's rate of fatality was extremely low, with only twenty-one deaths recorded.[99] Newspapers applauded FEMA's efforts to respond in the aftermath of the storm and noted the increased attention hurricanes received with new forms of media in place.[100] Many observed how this media coverage affected people within the region. One episode that drew considerable attention was the report of thieves encouraging people to leave their homes in wealthy Houston areas unattended by telling them of a newly issued mandatory evacuation order. Although the information was false, the increased media coverage left some speculation as to the widening evacuation routes, causing some to fall into this trap.[101] Other issues with evacuation coverage post-storm raised questions about evacuations and building codes for skyscrapers in downtown Houston that needed revision.[102] For example, post-storm evacuation for Galveston Island following Alicia was delayed when the eye of the storm traveled up through the main evacuation route (Interstate 45). It was agreed that, even with efforts from FEMA, evacuation plans should be updated to include this scenario.[103] Overall, though, interest in Alicia, driven by media surrounding the storm, focused on both the pre-storm and post-storm periods as coverage continued in 24-hour news outlets. This trend only continued as the next major storm threatened the United States.

The year following Alicia was another milder year in terms of storm development because of El Niño conditions but, by 1985, nervous anticipation over storm season amped up coverage once again. That year, three major hurricanes, Gloria, Elena, and Juan, directly impacted the United States. The Gulf South, in particular, felt the effects of both Elena and Juan. Elena was particularly fearsome as it shifted directions multiple times in two days, causing repeat evacuations across the Gulf South. Many residents were forced to leave twice during the course of the storm as the "bad woman," Elena, veered between Florida and Louisiana.[104] Eventually, Elena ended up as a "no show," failing to hit the coast with a significant threat, despite the cautionary warnings.[105] The *New Orleans Times-Picayune* even reported that, "compared to sinister sisters Audrey, Betsy and Camille, which dealt widespread death and destruction in Louisiana and Mississippi, Elena was well-behaved and mild mannered."[106] Juan was no different.

When Hurricane Juan emerged in the Gulf in late October 1985, it was slow to develop. Within two days, its impact zone was clear: it was headed straight towards central Louisiana. By midnight on October 29, it was just offshore directly south of Lafayette, and the governor, Edwin Edwards, had already declared a state of emergency for thirteen parishes. A rare late-in-the-season storm, Juan "batter[ed]" the Gulf Coast, "thrash[ing]" with "winds of 85 miles per hour and waves up to 20 feet."[107] Juan was "the third [storm] to threaten Louisiana this year," reported Louisiana residents, referring to previous hurricanes Danny and Elena.[108] Even though Danny "hit" Louisiana, and Elena "sliced through" the state," Juan shocked residents as it "grew too fast to evacuate offshore [oil] workers," "pounded," and "whirled" in the process.[109] While it weakened as it traveled eastward along the coast, it "backtracked" and struck a second blow in Alabama, bringing 10 to 12 inches of rain to the multistate area of Louisiana, Mississippi, Alabama, and Florida.[110] All things considered, "Juan's four-day rampage" petrified the already soaked region.[111]

The reactions to Juan, Elena, and Danny highlight important distinctions made between female- and male-named storms by the mid-1980s. Descriptions of female-named storms were akin to those of the past, using terminology to illustrate feminine-associated behaviors. In the case of Elena

ANDREW AND THE BUSINESS OF STORMS

(1985) and Alicia (1983), female-named storms "grew" differently, "sliced" the state like desserts, and were "bad women" who were still weaker than their male counterparts in terms of damage. Meanwhile, male-named storms such as Allen (1980), Danny (1985), and Juan (1985) "pounded," "hit," and "rivaled" the most intense hurricanes on record. In this sense, the male-named storms could be likened to a professional wrestler in a period of Hulk Hogan, Macho Man Randy Savage, Andre the Giant, and "Earthquake," out to best other fighters/disasters, proverbial giants, residents, and a particularly vulnerable oil industry alike.[112] This rhetoric of male-female difference only became more accentuated by the end of the decade as subsequent major male-named storms affected the United States.

Over the next two years, 1986–87, the United States experienced a mild version of El Niño, decreasing the number of strong storms that developed.[113] For both seasons, only one major hurricane emerged. Named Emily, the 1987 storm brought little damage to the US mainland, and many wondered whether the end of this El Niño period would spell trouble for the future storm seasons as it had for the 1985 season. Their worries were confirmed when, in 1988, a strong hurricane developed. Immediately, reporters dusted off their male hurricane tropes in an effort to contextualize the storm.

Hurricane Gilbert "blasted" Jamaica on its "rampage" in mid-September 1988.[114] The "brute" formed off the Windward Islands, heading west in a direct line towards the Gulf, before it turned sharply and struck Mexico. "We" really "dodged a bullet" on Gilbert, the *Mobile Press-Register* stated bluntly the day after.[115] The storm turned into the "worst natural disaster" the Caribbean had ever seen, with 600,000 homes destroyed in Jamaica alone, the *New York Times* reported.[116] "Mighty Gilbert" was a "monster" that could have easily swept northward instead of westward while building to the "strongest" storm to date "in [the] fertile territory" of the warm Gulf waters, stated the *Biloxi Sun-Herald*.[117] As it was, "he" "pounded," "slammed," "flayed," and "blasted" the coast.[118] Eventually, the storm transformed into the "incredible hulk," stated the *Raleigh News & Observer*.[119] "Gilberto," as the Mexicans referred to it, reported the *Houston Chronicle*, "deserves to be called Mr. Gilbert," due to size alone.[120]

Compared to coverage for Elena and Juan, the response to Gilbert indicated the size and impact of the storm's radius and winds corresponding with its ranking on the Saffir-Simpson Hurricane Wind Scale. Gilbert was a

Category 5 storm, the highest on the scale. Reporters referred to the storm as the bulky "incredible hulk," "Mighty Gilbert," or "Mr. Gilbert," in an attempt to denote its strength while downplaying storms of the past. While this effort to top previous storms in linguistic representation (through phrases like "monsters" and "strongest storm to date") was not new, there were some new additions to the vocabulary. "Incredible hulk" was a fitting characteristic for a male-named storm at the time. Taken from a Marvel comics character that represented a super-soldier transformed by radiation into an unwieldy ogre, it implied a massive storm made from human-influenced forces in a post–environmental movement era.[121] It was a monster out of the laboratory of scientific making. While Gilbert ended up missing the Gulf Coast, it did cause inexorable damage to the Caribbean and to Mexico. With 318 fatalities and $7.1 billion in damages ($14.9 billion in 2018), it was indeed the largest storm to date, and response to it indicated this.[122]

The panic caused by the size and strength of Gilbert led to yet another revision of disaster management policies. Critique of previous disaster relief legislation lay in the method whereby funding was allotted and a major disaster defined. The Robert T. Stafford Disaster Relief and Emergency Assistance Act, or Stafford Act (1988), sought to clarify this problem by specifying not only what a disastrous incident was, but also the process for doling out funding.[123] Introduced by Robert T. Stafford, a Republican senator from Vermont, this amended version of the Disaster Relief Act of 1974 focused on developing state, local, and federal efforts of disaster relief and response.[124] This included the creation of disaster housing programs (providing temporary rentals and trailers) as well as an expansion of local emergency management efforts funded through federal programs focused on pre-disaster mitigation.[125]

When put in context of the strong storms of the late 1980s combined with the catastrophic Three Mile Island incident (1979) and *Exxon Valdez* oil spill in Alaska (1988), it is easy to see why the Stafford Act was introduced.[126] There is another reason the Stafford Act emerged in 1988: the cultural era shaped its introduction. With TWC broadcasting storms live after 1983, increased attention was drawn to disaster response. Largely emerging during a time when the country was again focused on aggressors impacting the US homeland, and mimicking the rhetoric of the buildup of military strength during the Reagan administration at the close of the Cold War, the ramping up of programs to assuage defensive weaknesses is no surprise.[127] Militaristic hurricanes were weapons that demanded state resources and preparation. While it was impossible to prevent these natural enemies from inflicting damage, FEMA and the Stafford Act were the methods chosen to diminish their impact. Playing a critical role in the success of this process were the 24-hour news networks, armed with the vocabulary to dramatize the weather and mobilize evacuation efforts.

The following September, these processes of disaster relief at the local and federal levels were put to the test as Hurricane Hugo roared towards the Eastern Seaboard. The 1989 storm marked "his passage" by proving that there was "nothing erratic" about its behavior.[128] It had formed off the coast of Africa, headed west toward the Leeward Islands in the Caribbean, and then hooked north at Puerto Rico towards the Carolinas, all while building strength. As it reached the Carolinas, this "Power Boxer" "clobbered" with a "headstrong" method, delivering a "brutal battering" to those in its path, reported the *Baltimore Sun*.[129] Hugo held residents of South Carolina "hostage," acting like a "meteorological wild card" whose victims were unprepared, stated the *Atlanta Journal-Constitution*.[130] By the time it hit, it was a Category 4 storm, having built to a Category 5 initially. But this did not mean that Hugo had weakened. Hugo's "ugly reputation" was largely due to its "muscle," or mass width, which aided in its slow, methodical "blitz," reported the *Houston Chronicle*.[131] After making landfall at Sullivan's Island, South Carolina, it continued to attack the coast for three more days.

In the aftermath, reporters from Charleston to Los Angeles described the storm as again producing a war zone. It left Charleston looking "like a war zone" similar to Vietnam, stated the *Los Angeles Times*.[132] Its impact on the coast was the same as the "war between the states," proclaimed the *Mobile Press-Register*.[133] The bombing it enacted resulted in a visceral reminder of "Nagasaki," offered the *Houston Chronicle*.[134] At the end of Hugo's "march from the sea" the coastline was scorched, stated the *Raleigh News & Observer* in a reference to Civil War General William Tecumseh Sherman's scorched-earth policy that stretched from Atlanta to Charleston.[135] Even Charleston residents agreed. One quote from a Charlestonian, in particular, made the front page of newspapers around the country: "It's like we've survived an atomic or nuclear bomb."[136] The war-specific rhetoric used with Hugo adapted old processes of describing storms as atomic bombs while blending graphic images of the Civil War, World War II, and Vietnam into one apocalyptic incident. In this light, Hugo and other male storms were "total war," and this war was hell.[137]

Reporters also used terminology to indicate the assigned masculinity of Hugo in similar ways to storms of the past. "Mr. Hugo" was a "killer," stated the *Charleston Post & Courier*, employing language to signal excessive respect.[138] But the *Miami Herald* had stronger words: "Hugo the Terrorist," it blasted across the page.[139] The use of the term "terrorist" was new, directly referencing the growing fears caused by an increase in incidents in the 1980s.[140] Its application to a hurricane was meant to signify the lack of control one had in response to these incidents.

The extreme sentiment implied by "terrorist" in its application to Hugo was comparable to the pejorative terminology used with female-named storms of the 1960s like "witch," "slut," or "no lady." The phrase was inherently associated with masculine behavior.[141] Terrorist activities were largely associated with males, as shown by statistics on a rising number of incidents in the 1980s. As emphasized, these men had control over their behavior, or exercised some sort of belief that drove their actions. When used to describe a hurricane, these cultural assumptions would transfer directly, fitting the mold of the masculine hurricane as opposed to the erratic-witch female hurricane. The use of "terrorist" to describe Hugo at the close of the Reagan era was telling. Despite efforts to ramp up disaster mitigation and carefully planned response teams, a single outlier enemy could still wreak havoc. Hurricanes represented a metaphoric terrorist, a guerrilla radical or thug slipping dangerously through the cracks with nihilistic intentions.

The final descriptor used with Hugo that was new to the hurricane vocabulary came from the *New York Times*. While Hugo left "us" wishing for the "glory days of hurricanes on the East Coast," the *Times* stated, its impact surely made it "The Hurricane of the Century."[142] The first to use this phrase, the *Times* would not be the last. The newspaper articles on Hugo reflected a new era of storm description, directly influenced by what was happening in the background, in print and on the screen, one where the male storm had become something new—militaristic, motivated, and unlike anything ever seen before—and most of all, distinctly gendered.

* * *

Andrew and the Changing Culture of Hurricane Description

In 1991, a raspy-throated singer crooned a melody that quickly became an anthem for those experiencing hurricanes. "Thunder, lightning, the wind outside is so damn frightening; but it's alright, alright; stand clear; you're living in the hurricane years," he sang, accompanied by a memorable guitar baseline. The singer was Alice Cooper, and the song was "Hurricane Years." The song was an accurate summation of the hurricane period beginning in the 1980s.[143] Between 1980 and 2000, over 10 major storms (Category 3 or higher) struck the US mainland (including 29 total storms), significantly affecting residents' livelihoods, expression towards storms, and federal perception of response.[144] While storms of the late 1980s inspired a new wave of discussion about hurricanes following an El Niño lull and disaster management changes, the storms of the 1990s, beginning with Andrew, escalated these fears, creating an opening for another round of change in hurricane description, this time almost exclusively gendered. The hurricane was again the number one public enemy, and efforts to mitigate its effects even more dramatic in the era of 24-hour news.[145]

By the 1990s, the explosion of television coverage, in addition to newsprint, expanded the ways Americans were consuming stories of hurricanes. The sheer number of hours covered and people watching was enough to drive increased production of materials related to hurricanes, as well as the creativeness in description. It also created its own version of a CNN effect, where coverage and response to it shaped disaster policy. These trends reached a tipping point with Hurricane Andrew in 1992, where multiple factors placed Andrew as a pivotal moment in hurricane history.

The rush to define the hurricane of the century had started with Gilbert and Hugo, but it was nothing compared to the hell wrought by the early 1990s storm Andrew. The bold killer wrought $26.5 billion in damages ($47.2 billion in 2018) to Florida in particular, topping all previous attempts to describe a hurricane as the worst storm ever experienced.[146] By the time Andrew had dissipated, residents were already proclaiming it the "Storm of the Century."[147] They even produced T-shirts to mark the occasion, saying simply: "I Survived Hurricane Andrew."[148]

When meteorologist Bryan Norcross took his seat to man the live coverage of Hurricane Andrew on WTVJ–News Channel 4, a local affiliate of

NBC, he was taking the lead in a new era of storm tracking. Prior reporters, weathermen, and television personalities had always rotated in shifts of coverage. But Norcross and his team knew this storm was different.[149] His station had been planning a live-coverage hurricane event for two years and, with Andrew headed straight for their home in Miami, the timing was right.[150] They dedicated manpower to cut to live scenes from field sites, had interviewees and specialists lined up to give feedback on the events unfolding, and planned for Norcross to helm the desk throughout the coverage. More than anything, the WTVJ news team banked on this Gulf South storm being memorable and that their coverage would provide something different in the era of round-the-clock news.[151] They were not disappointed.

The season was eerily quiet up until Andrew's formation in mid-August. As the first named storm of the season, Andrew formed almost overnight to a Category 5 hurricane, one of the largest ever seen in the Gulf and in US history. There were only two other storms that topped it in size, the Labor Day Storm of 1935 and Hurricane Camille in 1969. Quickly, associations to the two earlier storms were made in the press. One newspaper called it "Camille II," a souped-up version of the infamous storm of the 1960s, while another assured residents of Florida that the Labor Day Storm of 1935 was a good indication of what was in store for the state should the storm actually make landfall.[152] In short, Andrew was terrifying.

The sheer size of the mass hurtling towards the Florida peninsula was enough to propel mass evacuations. In South Florida alone, evacuation numbers reached 700,000 as its own major newspaper, the *Miami Herald*, published a front-page, above-the-fold article with glaring print describing Andrew as: "Bigger, Stronger, Closer."[153] When it finally rolled into Biscayne Bay and South Dade County to deliver a "predawn pounding," it was only half the circumference of Hurricane Hugo, which devastated South Carolina a few years before, but had winds larger than the entire city of Chicago. Andrew "spun like dice," "leaving marks [. . .] like bullet holes" in the process.[154] Soon after, the "monster" that was "king" of the sky tossed homes like "bath tub toys" in Homestead, Florida.[155] As it "spit shingles," "mowed development," and "methodically" "carved" "giant jig-saw puzzle pieces" out of Florida on its way to the Gulf, it stepped on the "accelerator."[156] Then it began to "throb with agency," and its "ferocious" winds picked up speed.[157] After it "clobber[ed] Florida," the rest of the country watched in horror as "one of the century's most powerful storms" turned westward towards the Gulf, restrengthening in the process.[158] As Andrew continued through the Gulf as a reinvigorated Category 4 storm, it sent a wave of panic through the New Orleans populace.[159]

"Andrew [was] having his way" while "stomping" along, reported the *Biloxi Daily Herald* as it followed the storm's trajectory.[160] The "windbag named Andrew," reported the *Houston Chronicle,* had "set its deadly sights" on Louisiana, and nothing could slow it down.[161] Once in Louisiana, it was like the aliens from the movie *Close Encounters of the Third Kind,* reported the *New Orleans Times-Picayune:* "Andrew came calling in the dark-hours of Monday morning. He came rattling every closed door and banging every taped-up window. He came throwing things at the glass patio doors with menacing winds that issued forth from unexplained places. He came in rivulets of water that crept in over the top of the front door and spat at us through the peephole."[162]

As evidenced by the coverage in the *Times-Picayune,* reporters used a new descriptive reference to confirm Andrew's status in reference to storms of the past. Andrew was different because he was an alien. He had extraterrestrial strength and was set on invading the country via the sky. It was a science fiction novel come true in an era where sci-fi monsters drew recollections of eerie sound effects and untold horror. In the end, Andrew shifted just west of New Orleans to much relief, making landfall for a second time along the western part of the state below New Iberia and Lafayette, bringing with it extensive flooding to a state at sea level. With a "bullseye" strike on Morgan City, Louisiana, "God's explosion" delivered a "big blow" as it "plowed the coast."[163] But "Andrew's maniac circus" was not done yet.[164] "Andy" "bounced back" like a "boxer" and took a "furious swipe" before dissipating.[165]

Throughout the entirety of the storm's formation and through the relief efforts that followed, 24-hour news teams reported on its progress. Besides Miami and its surrounding region, which were on display due to Norcross and his team's efforts, other areas of South Florida became the focal point of national news media because of the devastation left behind as Andrew moved back into the Gulf of Mexico. If they had not watched the live WTVJ broadcast by Norcross, also known by the *Miami Herald* as "the man who talked South Florida through" the storm, or seen the clips on other news networks, Americans soon tuned into the coverage of its aftermath.[166] Meanwhile, other news teams deployed weathermen and reporters into the region to broadcast regularly.[167]

Homestead, Florida, in particular received considerable attention because the 26,000-resident community looked like it had been razed by a massive tornado.[168] Stories of nightmarish scenarios permeated news coverage, focusing on how homes were shattered, power lines were stripped from the ground, and mobile homes—a feature incredibly common in the snowbird retirement capital of the country—became flying shrapnel. In fact, of the 350,000 residents in the South Dade region, 80,000 homes were heavily damaged or destroyed, and 52,000 suffered some damage to their property.[169] In the middle of the storm was the National Hurricane Center, located in Coral Gables (a suburb of Miami), suffering from power outages, wind damage, and flooding due to the catastrophic nature of the storm's path. This amplified fears that a devastating impact on the NHC would somehow slow reporting or warning efforts as the storm shifted track towards the Gulf.[170]

As images of Homestead and South Dade played on repeat, the country watched and responded to horrific live coverage of the storm and its aftermath. In this way, Andrew became a 24-hour national news event, and response efforts a primary focus of concern. Noticeably, gendered descriptions of Andrew's behavior and actions increased across all platforms as discussion continued. In newspapers, in particular, reporters used gender as a mechanism to describe Andrew's actions and aftermath at levels not seen since the 1960s female-named storms. Much like male storms of the prior decade, descriptions of Andrew focused exclusively on its masculine qualities. They represented masculine-associated hurricane norms of the period and confirmed expectations of male storm strength and brutality by using terms like "boxer," "fighter," "soldier," "weapon," "tool," "God," and "male." They also included new descriptors such as "alien." But this gendered terminology also helped shape the rhetoric of storm recovery, fueled by 24-hour news coverage.

Following Andrew, storm recovery did not go smoothly.[171] With all eyes on the meteorological phenomenon, attention did not wane as federal, state, and local disaster relief efforts got under way. Within the same day of impact, reports of looting spread rapidly on news outlets, particularly the looting of the Cutler Ridge Mall, which became the site of a presidential press conference during President George H. W. Bush's visit to the state that afternoon.[172] Despite the interest in incidents of vandalism and lawlessness, however, relief efforts stalled as enactment of FEMA and state-level relief as dictated by the Stafford Act were caught in red tape.[173] The country watched as Dade County's Office of Emergency Management director, Kate Hale, gave public press conferences calling out the slowed response over a three-day period.[174] At one point, Hale exclaimed loudly in a televised press conference, "Where the hell is the cavalry on this one," a reference to not only the war-torn post-hurricane situation she was trying to mobilize funding to respond to, but also the delayed response.[175] The press-conference clips were then replayed repeatedly on stations throughout the country, further likening impressions of male-storm aftermath to war.[176] When relief efforts finally did pour in, the criticism of the response to Andrew and the complications with American disaster management had solidified in public impressions.[177]

The commotion over disaster management policy and the failure of FEMA, the Stafford Act, and other efforts to respond in a timely way kept Andrew (and the events that followed) in the spotlight for long after the storm's impact.[178] Andrew was a household name, the storm a chilling reminder of not only the potential impact of a massive hurricane (let alone a male storm), but also the politics behind disaster management strategies that the American public had struggled with for decades. This would go on to shape the political sphere in the following months as a presidential election cycle further escalated discussion of Andrew's impact. Featuring the incumbent president, George H. W. Bush, versus a new candidate, Bill Clinton, discussion at debates and in the press focused on plans for revamping FEMA, the Stafford Act, and other disaster relief efforts at the same time that reports of hurricane-wounded Florida and Louisiana circulated on 24-hour news.[179] Following the election, the debate continued as President Clinton implemented broad-scale changes to the structure of FEMA by appointing the first professional emergency manager as the director of FEMA, James Lee Witt.[180] Under Witt's tenure, FEMA expanded its focus to include mitigation efforts to major disasters as well as rapid response to disasters occurring live-time.[181] In addition, the number of federally declared disasters increased dramatically with the reorganization of federal processes of response. Through all of these changes, it was clear, hurricanes played a significant role in shaping latter-twentieth-century disaster policy. (See figure 9.)

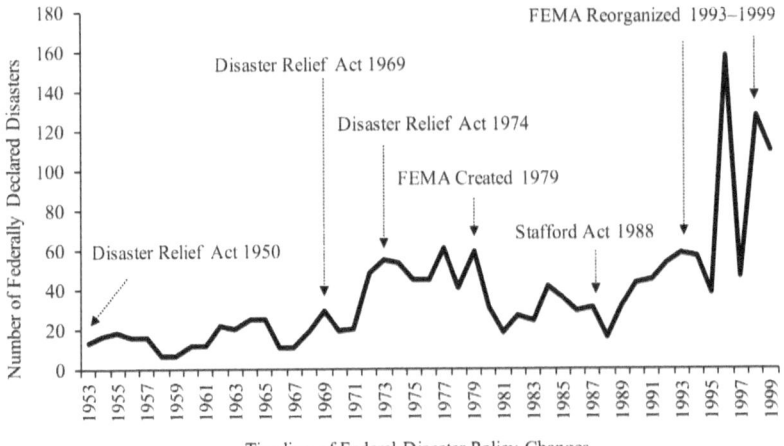

Figure 9. Number of federally declared disasters in relation to policy, 1953–1999. The number of national disasters declared increased with federal disaster relief policy changes (such as the introduction of various Disaster Relief Acts and the creation of FEMA). Policy changes reflected larger debates in the latter twentieth century over how a "major disaster" is defined and who is responsible for disaster mitigation and prevention.

Source: "Disaster Declarations (by Year)," 1953–1999, FEMA.gov, last accessed April 30, 2018.

In the end, Andrew marked a definitive turning point for storms of the future. It had a profound effect on the disaster management strategies in place for the remainder of the twentieth century. It also signified the importance of hurricane descriptions in the era of 24-hour news. Descriptions of Andrew, including the live coverage, had definitely impacted the reception of it and the outpouring of response to relief efforts afterwards to the extent that they influenced a presidential election cycle. Andrew also cemented ideas about hurricane descriptors for male storms. It again positioned the Gulf South in the public eye as the place to watch hurricane drama unfold. Now used for several years, and pervasively in the coverage of Andrew, there was no questioning how to describe a male hurricane. Similarly, the storm strengthened the affiliation of weakness with female storms, as Andrew, Hugo, and Gilbert proved stronger examples of what powerful modern hurricanes could do. Male hurricanes were no longer Camille II; Andrew and its like had replaced Camille.

The "perverse Andrew" had been a "devilish prank" of a storm, reflected the *Miami Herald* as it recovered from what it attributed to a "nuclear winter."[182] With its "God-fearing speed," Andrew left the neighborhoods of Homestead looking like "an enchanted forest on LSD" and the rest of the coast a "modern-day Pompeii."[183] It was an "air bomb" in action, agreed the *New York Times*, a "killer" according to the *Biloxi Daily Sun-Herald*, and a "monster" out of movies like *Close Encounters of the Third Kind* per the *New Orleans Times-Picayune*.[184] Despite the storm's many names and adjectives, one thing every paper agreed on at the end was that "Andrew's punch [was] so strong that there will never be another Hurricane Andrew."[185] Its name was retired by the National Hurricane Center because it was a "storm that will live in infamy."[186] With over $26.5 billion in damages and 65 fatalities, Andrew was the monster the Gulf Coast had always feared.[187] But, following the "storm that will live in infamy," Storm of the Century, or one that was "so strong that there will never be another," how would Americans distinguish other devastating storms of the decade, particularly as efforts to garner response could mean the difference between receiving funding or support, or not? It was a peculiar problem, and one that would only grow over time.

Post-Andrew: The Hurricane as Big Business

In 1998, Hurricane Mitch emerged out of the southwestern Caribbean, building rapidly as it headed first towards Central America and then veered toward Florida. A massive storm, it reached Category 5 status on the Saffir-Simpson scale.[188] The previous year was considered below average in terms of hurricane development, and the coast was rusty in preparations since its last hurricane, Opal, in 1995, which blindsided Florida while the country was watching the O. J. Simpson murder trial verdict come in.[189] Hurricane Andrew had already laid bare the Gulf South's vulnerabilities in terms of geographical location to repeated disaster, infrastructural complications of its sea-adjacent major cities, and political ramifications through election cycles following public outcry—all of which were exposed in new forms of national critique through 24-hour news. In short, hurricanes had caused their own CNN effect, and reporting on them was a profitable business.

In fact, since TWC had debuted, especially with the success of reporting during Andrew, many other networks had invested heavily in their weather segments, including new features and specialists linked to key weather-event programming such as blizzards, tornadoes, and other violent storms. The late "Halloween Nor'easter of 1991," for example, became a sensation for its lack of a name, inspiring the production of a book, *The Perfect Storm,* by Sebastian Junger in 1997, and countless other weather series.[190] All of this led to an increased interest in severe storms and the desire to attract viewers through increasingly distinctive labels, as was made particularly evident in 1998 and 1999.

The 1998 season was already off to a wild start by the time Georges hit in September. At its peak a Category 4 storm, Georges struck seven countries in its path through Gulf waters.[191] Soon, though, an additional storm emerged to follow its path, this one known as Mitch. With descriptions of Georges already floating in print, reporters sought ways to describe the difference between the two storms. Georges was a "lion," an "equal opportunity machine," and a "perfect monster," proclaimed the *Biloxi Daily Sun-Herald.*[192] As "the most serious storm threat in a generation," Georges had aimed for New Orleans directly.[193] It was "like the Energizer Bunny," who just kept going and going with "menace in the air," reported the *New Orleans Times-Picayune.*[194] After a "fateful zig to the east," Georges "showed off its arsenal," but missed New Orleans.[195] The storm then threw a "one-two punch" to the coastline as it veered towards Florida and Georgia.[196] Storms like this serve as "God's hand," wiping the coasts clean as they go, reported the *New York Times.*[197] And the United States needed the reminder, "Yes, It Could Happen Here," but did not experience it this round.[198] The "island hopper" was done when it got to Florida, causing devastation to the Keys, but died on the Georgia-Florida border as a tropical storm.[199]

Although the reaction to Georges was heavily laden with masculine descriptors at the beginning, when Georges hooked right and shrunk in size to a Category 2 storm, this changed. The *New Orleans Times-Picayune,* pausing to reflect on the change in Georges's size, illustrated this change explicitly. Georges "was pretty much a shoo-shoo, as you might expect from the name," they concluded. And this might be because "hurricanes, in any case, have tended to sound less scary since they stopped naming them exclusively for women." And this was a problem. "Bob and Earl might be good ole boys who wouldn't say boo to Betsy, but Georges? The name is more redolent of Parisian hair salons than elemental violence." "Next thing you know," they quipped, "we'll be tracking some effete English aristocrat called Jeremy or Rupert as he saunters across the Caribbean."[200]

The *Times-Picayune*'s reaction to both Georges the storm and Georges the name was telling of a newspaper experiencing a storm en route and then reacting after the fact. It showed how reporters sought to amp up the storm as it was nearing the area, then quickly shifted gears to explain why it did not perform as the "greatest storm of the decade" after the fact. This retraction was made all the more apparent because reporters had shifted their focus to describing the emerging and larger storm, Mitch.

It is noteworthy that the way the *Times-Picayune* writers sought to negate the perceived strength of Georges in an effort to play up Mitch was to belittle the name given to Georges. In doing so, they pointed out assumptions in masculinity as culturally linked to names. By drawing these connections, they referenced cultural ideas of effeminate names equaling effeminate behaviors, and even differences in sexual preference. They explicitly implied that Georges was "weaker" than Mitch because of its name, and that it might even display characteristics often used to describe homosexuality.

This sort of discussion of behavior in reference to sexuality was new to the hurricane-description equation. While there had been brief mentions of names in reference to certain people who held those names, or even behaviors implied by the type of name and its history (for example, Camillus the virgin warrior queen), there had never been a discussion of names that implied sexual preference at the outset. The use of this implication was new. It was a direct result of a time period when reporters struggled to point out in press the difference between one major storm and the next, especially in the post-Andrew era. In an effort to rationalize masculine irrationality in an era when this behavior did not correlate with the image constructed of masculinity, reporters drew on culturally constructed terminology of deviance, particularly sexual deviance.

In 1998, masculine sexual deviance was implied through reference to difference between gay and straight behaviors. Post–sexual and –gay liberation movements, the 1980s brought the era of Reagan-infused masculine bravado, the bomb-throwing anarchist, and the polarity of the forces of good and of dictatorial evil. But it also brought with it the demonology of subversive and sexual difference.[201] At its center was a focus on homogeneous American values that stressed sexual hierarchy and mocked difference with the slur of effeminacy.[202] Combined with the rising threat of an unstoppable virus spreading to the populace despite lack of recognition (AIDS/HIV), this demonology spread fear of the unknown and irreparably linked difference with disaster.[203] By the 1990s, the negatively constructed stereotypes of gay men came crashing into public discourse as activists appeared in television shows and were portrayed in popular culture, forcing Americans to debate policies related to the workplace and military such as Don't Ask Don't Tell (1994).[204] Georges was just one example where these impressions of masculinity blended into weather description. But it is also possible to see this as a moment when hurricane names and descriptors helped create new negative associations of gender deviance. Due to the image created of heteronormative masculine storms like Andrew versus weaker female storms, a new category of storm was invented. Reporters turned to the bifurcated description of masculinity into categories of gay and straight, attaching stereotypes of the first to the storms deemed as behaving "differently."[205] This reinforced ideas about difference between masculinity and femininity in a world obsessed with chromosomal difference.[206] Properly masculine storms were strong, their counterparts weak and feminine. Thus, by default the weakest of all storms was always the female-named storm.

By the time Hurricane Mitch fully formed, the distinction from Georges was clearly set—Mitch was the greater of the two storms, therefore, its descriptors were the epitome of representative male strength. Mitch was a "menace," stated the *Miami Herald*.[207] The storm tore through Honduras, Nicaragua, and Guatemala, bringing an onslaught of rain that created devastating mudslides in the region. As it made its hook to the right to head back out to sea, the death count of the region stood at 11,000, the second deadliest hurricane ever recorded. It had even displaced the Galveston Storm of 1900 in the record books.[208] With these results so far, the Gulf Coast began to panic.

"Diabolical Mitch" was the "Monster of the Caribbean," stated the *Charleston Post & Courier*.[209] It "creeps" towards the coast like a "monster," then "prowls" before "lashing," the *Miami Herald* explained.[210] It was both a "late bloomer" and an "overachiever," agreed the *Mobile Press-Register*, describing the storm's development seemingly overnight into Category 5 strength.[211] And worse yet, even though it lost steam in its trajectory, "it may regain it in the Gulf," depending on what conditions it finds there, emphasized the *New Orleans Times-Picayune*.[212] Luckily, Mitch weakened while over the Gulf. The "eye of the monster," as described in the *Los Angeles Times*, did not end up severely damaging the United States.[213] But the memory of Mitch, infused by the knowledge that the storm could have easily struck the coast, was enough to inspire fear.

In attempting to clearly separate Mitch from Georges during its progression, reporters relied on language used with other male storms of the past—like "monster" and "menace"—to emphasize comparative strength. One of the major reasons they did this was because they had constructed an image of a storm that was the worst of the worst, thus incomparable to other storms, and then subsequently had to backtrack once another large storm formed. This pattern was repeated the following year with another major storm, Hurricane Floyd.

"Hurricane Floyd is huge; he's powerful; he's fast; and he's mean," stated the *Raleigh News & Observer* in September 1999.[214] It was a "Super-Hurricane," stated the *Biloxi Daily Sun-Herald*, something no one had ever witnessed before.[215] "Menacing Floyd" was the stuff of "nightmares," reported the *New Orleans Times-Picayune*.[216] Quickly replacing the "infamous Andrew," "Ugly Boy Floyd" or "Andrew's Big Brother" was a "giant."[217] It had a "menacing eye," and an uncertainty that kept the "East Coast guessing" where it would strike.[218] As the "beast" "stalked," coastal residents predicted that this may be "the Big One."[219] All evidence supported this idea. The "growth factors" for Floyd are "nearly perfect," reported the *Miami Herald*.[220] It was the "Perfect Storm," and thus the "perfect killer."[221] As Floyd continued its path, it was "nastier" than previous storms.[222] It "streaked" like a "vandal," striking a "lethal" blow during its "quick visit."[223] After it "whacked" Florida, it continued toward the Carolinas and Virginia. There, "he" had a "rough flirtation" with Richmond, "kissed Washington," and then "blew the house down."[224] Floyd "neither seduced or enticed," the *Times-Dispatch* reported; instead, "he roared."[225] In truth, the *Times-Dispatch* stated, Floyd was a "bully."[226]

Floyd was definitely worse than Hurricane Dennis, which struck less than a month earlier and "ravaged the coast."[227] In fact, the *Charleston Post & Courier* insisted, Dennis had only served as a "warm-up act" for Floyd.[228] This "unusual storm" "continued his menacing march" as thousands fled.[229] Charlestonians were particularly fearful of monster-hydra storm Floyd's impact. In many ways, the *Post & Courier* explained, the city was still experiencing "heartburn" from Hurricane Hugo in 1989.[230] When evacuation orders were issued, Charlestonians showed no sign of hesitation; they packed up and went. And they were not alone. With nearly all eastern coastal areas from Florida City, Florida, to Plymouth, Massachusetts, under a hurricane warning at some point during the storm's trek north, nearly 2.6 million coastal residents from Florida through the Carolinas evacuated. In Florida alone, 1.3 million people left the coast in less than 24 hours, a first in state history. This rapid exodus, or "hurrevac," as the *Houston Chronicle* described it, could not have been accomplished had the track of the storm been different.[231] The "torture of gridlock" during the evacuation was worth it, reported the *Miami Herald*. The hurricane did "not stray from [its] path," reported the *Chronicle*. And that was a good thing; it allowed effective enactment of evacuation procedures. As residents were evacuating, the *Post & Courier* reported that local radio stations played a plethora of songs about hurricanes on repeat. "Living in the Hurricane Years," "Running against the Wind," "Should I Stay or Should I Go," and "Rock Me like a Hurricane" all provided auditory confirmation of the struggles felt by those packing up their lives.[232] In the end, Floyd turned into the largest peacetime evacuation in US history and marked a new era of hurricane evacuation that continues through the present.

As Floyd struck North Carolina, the coast "took a beating." Floyd "soak[ed] but [didn't] bruise" the North as it "gyrated" up the coast.[233] Finally, the "Monster Hurricane" deemed "Furious Floyd" weakened, "pulling its punch."[234] Like "an exhausted marathon runner," it collapsed between Long Island and Maine, leaving places like New Jersey "muddy and miserable" with the rain that followed.[235] "Floyd fever," or the condition described by the *Miami Herald* as living in a continual state of panic, was finally over.[236]

The rhetoric used to describe Floyd in 1999 was a culmination of a twenty-year buildup of male-hurricane description trial and error. Blending culturally popular favorites such as monsters, menaces, soldiers, beasts, and giants, it was a symbol of the constructed masculine ideal that had been sculpted by science, time, and the environment. Lurking at the backdrop of this overtly physical language was explicitly sexualized language that linked weapons of war to the weapons of culture. While Floyd lived up to its name, asserting its standing in the masculinized status quo, it also went above and beyond to become both superhurricane and titanic brute. As a result, creeping into the subtext in print and in song are references to other issues related to astonishing masculinity, implying sexual aggression and harassment (by rough flirtation and forced contact) and unwanted behavior (such as voyeurism). These characteristics were attached to the hurricane after a decade-long debate on issues related to sexual harassment and normalized behavior extending from the everyday workplace to the Oval Office and Supreme Court.[237] As one newspaper put it, "Floyd never seduced or enticed." He was powerful enough to enact his will. In this way, he was a new type of storm to fear but, as always, built on the current fears of the moment.

The Storm of the Century of the Week

The hyped-up male hurricane had done wonders for ratings, both print and television, which was good because the damage caused by the storms was growing with each subsequent hit to an already devastated US coastline.[238] The Gulf South, in particular, saw $132 billion in damages (in 2018 dollars) for major storms between 1972 and 1999. This was a whopping $98 billion (in 2018 dollars) more than the 1950s and 1960s.[239] Storms in the region were costlier, and so was their relief. But what had these amped-up meteorological nightmares produced? Had they saved lives through their reporting, or influenced funding received post-storm? Or had their descriptions made things worse? Similarly, was there too much pressure to create "The Perfect Storm"?[240] This was the question brought up in a late-night television show after Hurricane Floyd by the end of the decade.

The show opened on a youthful-looking Jon Stewart, gazing seriously at the camera. "Hurricane Floyd turns north up the Eastern Seaboard," he stated matter-of-factly. And like all other news networks in the country, he explained, "our" team of "semi-meteorologists will be providing "up to the minute coverage of *the storm of the century of the week.*" As he said this, a graphic appeared above his right shoulder, screaming: "STORM OF THE CENTURY OF THE WEEK," in bold print with variegated captioning. (See figure 10.)

The studio audience roared with laughter. Continuing with this thread, Stewart introduced his "meteorologist in the field," Stephen Colbert. A wiry-looking Colbert appeared on screen in the field, barely holding onto a lamppost as he was whipped about by pouring rain and wind. Most noticeably,

TEMPEST

Figure 10. "Storm of the Century of the Week." Screen grab by author from Episode 4031 of *The Daily Show with Jon Stewart,* aired September 16, 1999.

Colbert was not wearing a rain jacket. This, he stated, made him a fiercer correspondent than those "pansies at the Weather Channel." As the banter between host and field reporter went back and forth, Colbert reported through snark that New Jersey residents should "brace for [the] burning sensation of cleanliness" inevitably wrought by the Category 4 storm. Meanwhile, Stewart reminded his viewers at the segment's conclusion that this "Storm of the Century" would easily be replaced by the next "Storm of the Century" the following week.[241] In essence, before the winds of the massive storm even died down in late September 1999, Hurricane Floyd was already superfluous.

As a nightly news host of *The Daily Show,* airing weekdays on Comedy Central, the salty comedian Jon Stewart knew how to deliver a punch line with deliberate effect. With his pithy, dry humor, and staff of purposefully misfit "special reporters," Stewart critiqued the obvious through his platform of a mock news show. In highlighting Hurricane Floyd, Stewart commented on the hypocrisy of the amped-up weather reporting he saw develop over the last two decades—one that centered on flair, drama, and of course, panic. The references to the "Storm of the Century of the Week" pointed to the attempts by 24-hour news and weather networks to continually up the ante for each storm, dramatizing the impact radius, scale, and effect for ratings purposes. While jesting at the superficiality of the tagline "Storm of the Century," used frequently with storms in the past decade, Stewart, like many others in the era, struggled to come up with new terminology that attempted to redefine the threat of each hurricane in a 24-hour news world (where punditry equaled screaming declarations) but also adequately represented the threat of these storms. Thus, underlying the subtext of Stewart and his staff's comedy-of-errors approach to reporting was the brutal truth of the newfound complexity of reporting in an age where every storm could be the worst and the demand for weather information was intensifying.

The last thing Stewart showcased was the complication of using new names in the hurricane lexicon. By the time Hurricane Floyd hit in 1999, male names had been in use for twenty years. But so had other forms of scientific identification for hurricanes, like the Saffir-Simpson scale and even federal designations of storm strength used for everything from flood insurance policies to disaster relief aid. With the addition of these systems of identification, names seemed more frivolous than ever—added more as conversation pieces and less for practical purpose. Still, the American public clung heartily to the anthropomorphic naming system of the past. At the same time, another period of cultural renegotiation of gender and sexuality definition was underway, fueled by the remnants of both the feminist and gay liberation movements. As a result, these new names were called into question, this time for their inappropriateness in defining masculinity, not femininity.

Stewart was right to call the process of describing hurricanes (including their names) into question. The adoption of male names in the hurricane-naming system was meant to fix the inequities created by the female-only naming lists. However, Americans still described hurricanes as gendered objects, incorporating new terminology specific to male-named storms. As a result, gender use continued through the close of the twentieth century in all regions of the United States, and was most prevalent in the Gulf South and Upper South due to landfall of major storms in the period. (See figure 11.)

The continued use of gender to describe hurricanes at the close of the century was a direct result of two factors. First, as newspapers sought to compete with continuous-news sources like TWC, they used gendered de-

TEMPEST

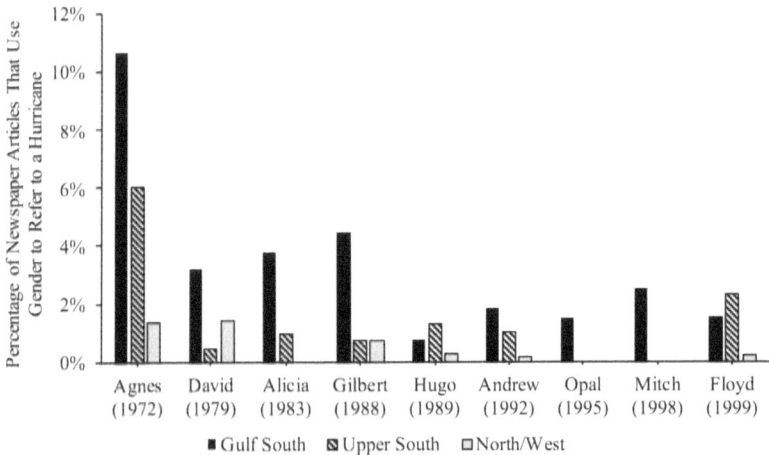

Figure 11. Percentage of newspaper articles that use gender to refer to a hurricane, by region, 1972–1999. Gender use decreased significantly after the introduction of male-named storms to the naming lists because of feminist efforts to draw attention to sexist language practices. Despite this, gender was used to describe hurricanes in all regions of the United States through the close of the twentieth century. Additionally, storm landfall directly impacted the frequency of use of gender (both male or female) to describe storms in all US regions during this period. For example, the Gulf South used gender more frequency *per newspaper article* between 1972 and 1999. Meanwhile, the Upper South used gender more frequently per article when major hurricanes such as Hugo and Floyd struck the Atlantic Seaboard.

Sources: Measured using qualitative data analysis of 12 US newspapers for 5-day periods for 9 major storms between 1972 and 1999 ($n = 2,500$).

scriptors in greater frequency to draw readership. By the end of the 1990s, 9 out of 12 newspapers described storms as gendered objects, at a rate not seen since the early 1970s. (See figure 12.)

Second, due to changes in disaster relief policy, gendered descriptions of hurricanes grew increasingly important to ranking the significance of an event. They were used at multiple junctures of storm development and aftermath to emphasize the severity (or lack of severity) of a hurricane. As a result, storm descriptions mattered more than ever to Americans as gendered descriptions were a way to describe an impending threat and define its impact. This led to the perpetual bloat of gendered terminology associated with the "worst" storm of record, or "Storm of the Century." It also led to

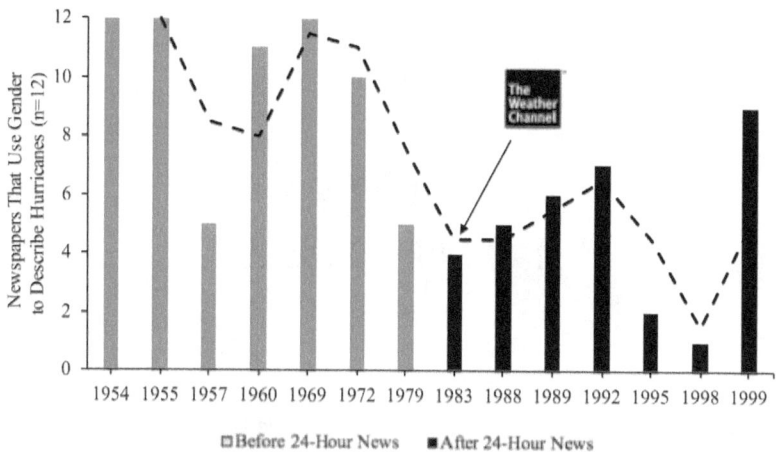

Figure 12. US newspaper use of gender to describe hurricanes, before and after 24-hour news. There was a noticeable spike in the total number of newspapers that used gender to describe storms following the introduction of the Weather Channel. As newspapers tried to compete with 24-hour news like that produced by TWC, they utilized gender more frequently to describe major storms.

Sources: Measured using qualitative data analysis of 12 US newspapers from 5-day periods for 17 major storms between 1954 and 1999 ($n = 4,436$).

the continued attachment of gender-specific terminology invented with the previous storms. In short, once a word entered the hurricane-description lexicon, it was repeated with subsequent storms. It also meant that reporters in the 24-hour news era were always on the lookout for new, culturally relevant, and gender-specific terminology to distinguish current storms from storms of the past.

How the perception of hurricanes and reporting of them would change after the turn of the new century was unknown, but one thing was certain: Stewart and others in the news cycle were at the forefront of influencing it. Stewart's critique of the phrase "Storm of the Century" pointed out a new problem emerging on the horizon. Americans were aware of the growth of gendered hurricane terminology and its effect on the perception of subsequent hurricanes, but that awareness was not slowing their drive to both consume information about storms and participate in the process of creating it. Storms were a business, and business was booming.

KATRINA
AND HURRICANE 2.0

Haunting words of a post–Hurricane Katrina poem are spoken by New Orleans poet Gian Smith as he sits on the stairs of a moldy house in the ill-fated New Orleans neighborhood known as the Tremé. Playing in the backdrop is a gritty soundtrack of a steamboat horn, jazz trumpet, police sirens, and gunfire. The camera cuts to graphic images of the destroyed city: police tape, a dead body, weather-beaten men and women reeling from the surroundings in a hellish modern-day America. As Smith recites the final lines of the poem— "She's the apocalypse heaven sent, a city's extinction-level event. [. . .] O beautiful storm, I won't let you go"—the camera pans over the physical realities of cleaning up after a life-changing disaster.[1] This is the two-minute trailer for the second season of HBO's hit television series *Treme*, which aired for over a million viewers on TV and streaming devices in early 2011, six years after the storm. Averaging 3.2 million viewers per episode, the first season had depicted the storm and its crippling immediate aftermath, and the second season promised to delve even further.[2] As the show became an international hit, winning multiple awards and accolades, *Treme* attempted to showcase events that were largely still unfolding. In doing so, the dramatized narrative not only recounted events that had happened, but influenced the discourse of the post-storm period.

What is striking in Smith's poem is that nowhere does he specify "who" Katrina is, or identify the wide-ranging and dangerous impact it had. Nonetheless, audiences worldwide recognized a surname-less Katrina as the devastating hurricane of 2005. The poem and the television series were a fitting representation of the New Orleans and post-Katrina experience many had grown to recognize in the years following 2005. And as much as the *Treme* series depicted the culture of Katrina post-storm, it also worked to produce that culture.[3] Sales of its commemorative music, episodes on DVD, and merchandise like T-shirts would total in the millions of dollars, which was notable in a city where the $100 million in production spending to film its episodes was desperately needed in a traumatized economy.[4] Thus, the TV show and its teaser trailer featuring Smith symbolized how the widespread consumer culture that formed around Katrina both fueled the rebirth of the city and capitalized on the horror of its experience, in all ways shaping the narrative of what defined *Katrina*.

By 2011, *Katrina* had come to represent more than just a storm. It was both a noun and an adjective. It was a name for the expected experience of living through a hurricane in the twenty-first century; a name for the aftermath and ramifications that followed with structural failures in levees and governmental assistance, physical and emotional loss, and the impact of the largest diaspora in American history; a name for the economics and politics of recovery and relief efforts gone awry in subsequent years; a name for the multitude of people affected by and participating in reaction to it; and a name for the culture that continued to produce, consume, and interact with all of these meanings behind the hurricane years afterward, and via a multitude of platforms, reinforcing the importance of the storm and its definition in memory. In this way, Katrina was different from storms of the past: it was as much a cultural phenomenon as it was a physical storm—a hybrid version of previous iterations, or "Hurricane 2.0"—that in its upgraded form permanently changed the understanding of hurricanes of the future.

It is easy to see how Katrina represents the emergence of Hurricane 2.0 through a review of the material culture around Katrina. This materially and culturally significant storm marked the first time that so many people in different platforms shared and collaborated in the creation of content and construction of meaning for a hurricane, over such an extended period of time. This broad and multifarious construction process and its distribution in the form of objects, experiences, and cultural productions expressed a near-infinite variety of perspectives, ideologies, and viewpoints. More than anything, though, these cultural productions and the extended time period in which they were produced represent the development of a culmination of the culture surrounding hurricanes that was linked to a meta-narrative constructed from their gendered names. In the construction of Katrina as

Hurricane 2.0, all hurricane descriptors, definitions, and associations used in the past were repurposed to provide context. These included the use of language usually reserved for male-named storms, those never associated with a storm before, and those explicitly filled with cultural and political commentary that used the storm and its gender as a mechanism to force reaction.

Katrina was the first and greatest instantiation of Hurricane 2.0 and has continued as a trend with every hurricane since. But it could not have been possible without critical developments in the way Americans were using a new platform—the Internet—and more particularly, the upgraded version of it, Web 2.0. This new platform changed traditional media culture as bloggers and social media commentators critiqued traditional forms of coverage, redefining the hurricane and what it represents in the process. Thus, in many ways, Web 2.0 helped to create Hurricane 2.0, with transformative results.

The Context for Hurricane 2.0

The public's fascination with hurricanes reached new levels by the 2000s, building off interest formed by the hurricane-as-drama 24-hour news media culture of the 1980s and 1990s. Americans now had an incredibly technical understanding of a storm's makeup and movements, and could parrot terminology only vaguely familiar to the average meteorologist decades earlier. Hurricane-specific terms like "storm surge," "category," "cone of uncertainty," "contraflow," and "mandatory evacuation" were commonplace, bringing with them memories of named storm experiences of the past.[5] These terms were regulated and used by a refined group of weather experts, media sources, and educated pundits, who rolled them out with flair through increasingly advanced graphics designed exclusively for mass consumption. But they were also used by producers and consumers on platforms just developed, such as blogs, social media sites, and consumable kitsch.

Meanwhile, in the decade before Katrina, other advances in technology occurred that affected the narration of storms by the traditional media, the new media, and the public. These changes set the stage for Katrina to be the first "Internet storm." Over the mid- to late 1990s, the Internet transformed the static content-delivery media of the 1950s into Web 2.0, a user-generated and highly usable virtual community meant to work across devices—a place for public commentary and interaction. As new communication platforms were released from 2004 to 2006, the Internet became the site of increased accessibility of self-publication, interactivity (social exchange and collaboration), and even marketplace, as blogs, social networks, and e-commerce sites sprang up.[6]

The first harbinger of Web 2.0 was the weblog, or blog. For many, this form provided the first exposure to these new forms of self-publishing and social interaction. The first blog was created in 1994 by Justin Hall, then an undergraduate at Swarthmore College, who referred to his creation as a personal homepage.[7] By 1997, the personal homepage had evolved into the "weblog," or a web-based log of real-world events. The popularity of the blog as both the site of news and personal reaction grew in the early 2000s with the creation of several new free blog sites, such as LiveJournal and Blogger, that made it easier for the public to participate in posting their thoughts on a multitude of subjects. In 2003, with the launch of WordPress (which remains the world's most popular platform), the blog form truly took off. In 1999, when the term "blog" was coined as a shortened form of "weblog," only 23 blogs were on the Internet.[8] By 2006, less than a decade later, the number of blogs had skyrocketed to 50 million.[9] Politicians, corporations, news media, and the general public participated in these forums, and a poll in January 2005 found that 32 million Americans—roughly 10 percent of the American population—read blogs regularly.[10] Many blogs gained so many followers that they were making money (roughly $100 million in ad revenue by December 2005), drawing people to the new medium.[11]

The first blog devoted to hurricane news was, ironically, published by a traditional print-media source, the *Charlotte Observer*.[12] In 1998, one year after the term *weblog* was coined, the *Observer* created a log of live events related to Hurricane Bonnie as it neared the area. The impetus for the *Observer*'s weblog was both the competition from 24-hour TV news and an amassed wealth of information on Hurricane Bonnie. While 24-hour news like that of TWC and CNN drove the creation of ample content and interest in hurricanes, it negatively impacted the popularity of newspapers, which struggled to compete, having only once- or twice-a-day print editions. The *Observer*, recognizing this demand for content, had already deployed reporters and photographers to cover the regional hurricane. Much of the content produced did not make it to the print edition. Instead, the *Observer* staff chose to post it online directly, creating a digital weblog of all content produced related to Bonnie. Their editorial team updated the page every half-hour for a week, posting dispatches from reporters in the field, photographs of the aftermath, and information garnered through tips via phone. They also "gave readers up-to-date county damage assessments, insurance contacts, useful weather links, and the ability to print out a storm-tracking chart."[13] The *Observer*'s weblog soon became one of the most memorable features of Hurricane Bonnie's coverage. By the end of the week, the weblog broke all records for previous page views for the *Observer* and catapulted interest in using weblogs to track response to hurricanes and other news events. Best of all, it provided an avenue where traditional forms of media like newspapers and television could coexist and even benefit from new forms of media online.

The success of the *Observer*'s Hurricane Bonnie weblog also sparked the creation of individual weblogs or weblog entries on storm experiences. The following year, as the term *weblog* was shortened to its now-familiar *blog*, the form expanded to encompass everything from a live news feed to personal written response of individual experience. By the 2004 hurricane season, blogs became an essential form of communication for those affected by multiple storms, including Charley, Frances, and Ivan. For example, in August 2004, as Hurricane Charley gusted through Florida, blogs recorded how those who evacuated did not stop their daily routines. As noted in the *Atlanta Journal-Constitution,* many active bloggers continued to post regular updates about their experiences online, even while evacuating. The print-media outlet reported on this phenomenon as news: "Blogs go on amid storm," proclaimed one headline, marveling at how this new form offered deeper insight into personal experiences of storms unlike any medium that had come before.[14] What seemed like a novelty would eventually come to dominate not only the reportage on hurricanes but how these events were narrated within the broader culture.

As blogs grew in popularity at the turn of the millennium, a new layer of Web 2.0 emerged: social networks. Social networks were dedicated websites or platforms where individuals shared their interests, posted content, or viewed others' content. Early versions included music- and media-sharing sites like Napster (founded in 1999) and friend-based sharing networks such as Friendster (2002), MySpace (2003), and Facebook (2004).[15] These social platforms connected individuals with similar interests, skills, consumer habits, or institutional affiliations through a shared online social network. For example, MySpace allowed users to post content and connect with others interested in similar content, sharing their information publicly to find others interested in the same things. By June 2006, MySpace surpassed Google as the most-visited website in the United States and remained incredibly popular until 2008, when it was overtaken by Facebook. Created by Harvard undergraduate Mark Zuckerberg, Facebook debuted in 2004 as a social networking site that allowed users to post images, short blog posts, and other content to share with their "friends." It built on the concept of a private sharing network established by Friendster, as well as the popularity of MySpace's multi-content format. Initially, Facebook was limited to college campuses in the United States but quickly spread to universities in the United Kingdom and high schools in the United States. By December 2004, it had six million users worldwide. In September 2006, Facebook opened to anyone with a valid email address above the age of thirteen. Its number of active users ballooned, and currently stands at roughly two billion users, or one-quarter of the world's population.[16] The major benefit of Facebook was that it offered users their own private network to post personal content or "posts" without public viewership, thus privatizing the experience of posting except to those chosen to "see" it.

Another social media site, YouTube, debuted in spring 2005, enabling users to upload their videos for public viewing. From its inception, YouTube was conceptualized as an efficient medium for transmitting news of disasters large and small. The inspiration for the creation of YouTube is credited to two incidents in 2004: singer Janet Jackson's infamous Super Bowl wardrobe malfunction, which involved the exposure of her breast on national television, and the Indian Ocean tsunami that formed with little notice after an earthquake and killed more than 200,000 individuals in fourteen countries.[17] The demand for videos of these incidents, both commonly referred to as "disasters," prompted the creation of this video-sharing site, where individuals could post homemade videos or edited clips of a variety of subjects. The sharing platform became so popular that, by November 2005, video viewership reached one million.[18] The popularity of YouTube as a platform to share hurricane videos was a natural progression from the home videos and TWC *Storm Stories* of the 1990s. Between YouTube and other text- and photo-based social sharing sites, the public had a whole new menu of ways to engage in commentary on catastrophic events, beyond letters to the editor, snippet interviews on television news, or even calls for legislation. This form of participation was near-universally accessible, and occurred on multiple platforms with broad viewership.

As social networks like Facebook, YouTube, and LiveJournal expanded between 2004 and 2005, so did the range and number of posts made by its users that discussed hurricane experiences. As Americans consumed these disasters virtually, their interest in them grew, particularly their desire to experience disasters in different ways. By the end of the 2004 hurricane season, many newspaper articles noted the growing social media culture that had become more prevalent online.[19] Newspapers printed articles like "Finding Weather Information on the Web" and "Webcams Keep Coast in View," illustrating their desire to keep up with the new way Americans were consuming the weather. They also printed more content on hurricanes than ever before, with print editions ballooning to include (on average) an additional 118 articles per hurricane.[20]

As blogs and social media networks continued to gain popularity, particularly for tracking severe weather activity, Web 2.0 inspired another form of participatory Internet culture: the buying and selling of products through e-commerce websites, which functioned as online marketplaces for the consumption of a wide range of products. The preeminent online marketplace, eBay, had debuted in 1995, but it expanded dramatically in 2002 with the purchase of pay platforms like PayPal.[21] E-commerce sites provided an avenue for the purchase or sale of "electronics, cars, fashion, collectibles, coupons, and more."[22] Among these new offerings were disaster related items, from clothing to furniture to keepsakes, bought and sold by a variety of consumers around the world. Real-world marketplaces for specially produced disaster items had existed since ancient periods, including pottery from extinct populations or gravesite mines of tombs or catacombs—and more recently pieces of the Hindenburg blimp or Civil War memorabilia.[23] But the mid-2000s explosion of Internet e-commerce supported a rapid expansion in the production and consumption of these items. In the 2004 season alone, a variety of hurricane-related items inspired by the season's storms were listed for sale, including T-shirts that stated, "I survived Ivan the Terrible," "wind in a bottle" from Hurricane Jeanne, and a "Hurricane Frances Sand

Debris Set" that included "five ounces of rainwater or a pound of sand" from an exclusive Tampa Bay seller for $6.99 plus $3.00 shipping and handling.[24] These items were so popular that their producers generated even more supply. By the end of the 2004 season, more than 170 new hurricane memorabilia items were listed for sale on eBay.[25]

Between blogs, social media sites, and online marketplaces—exacerbated by the increased connectivity enabled by advancements in cell phone technology—Americans had more ways to stay in touch and to express their opinions than ever before. They also had more readily usable ways to catch what was happening in their backyards and share it instantly. Similarly, the production of these views, either by a popular blog, social media post, or kitschy product could prove extremely profitable to the "poster" if enough people visited the site. These changes in technological communication served to accelerate preexisting cultural participation in the construction of cultural meaning during and after storms. The Internet became a digital repository for the public's experience and perception of these events, as ordinary people blogged about hurricanes, interacted with each other and each others' content, liking and sharing, and commenting. Similarly, it provided an avenue for old media to capitalize on new media as old media reported on Web 2.0 content creation as news, sharing it to even larger audiences, all while producing their own content.

As the public grew increasingly interested in and knowledgeable about hurricanes, and new technologies emerged for enabling communication about them, new fears about twenty-first-century super-hurricanes proliferated. New data showed historical climate fluctuations, and scientists increasingly discussed the possibility of extinction due to anthropomorphic change.[26] Confirming these fears, the 2004 season brought such a plethora of storms to the Gulf Coast that one commentator remarked that the region should be referred to as "Gulflandia" because the storms knew no state lines except that the states bordering the Gulf waters were the primary target.[27] Another newspaper represented these repeat 2000-era storms as steroid fiends with needles primed full of "Gulf greenhouse doping" drugs.[28] The back-to-back storms of 2004 also emphasized that disasters were growing noticeably larger and more costly, placing burdens on FEMA, even in its expanded form.[29] This was supported by the use of FEMA resources, which had multiplied since its reorganization under the Department of Homeland Security in 2003.[30] Meanwhile, vulnerability studies suggested that engineered levees, water-control structures, and coastal protection zones were weakening rapidly.[31] In short, the public believed that hurricanes were growing stronger and more frequent, while areas like the Gulf South became increasingly weaker with each season.

An important diagnostic effort to study this theory was made in Baton Rouge, Louisiana, in July 2004 in the wake of a close call with Hurricane Ivan, which bypassed New Orleans at the last second. In an experiment known as "Hurricane Pam," the state government, LSU Hurricane Center, National Weather Service, US Army Corps of Engineers, and over 50 other organizations tested resources and response capabilities in an eight-day drill in Baton Rouge. The purpose of the drill was to review planning and response efforts for 13 coastal Louisiana parishes based on a "worst-case scenario" disaster situation. "Hurricane Pam" was a hypothetical, slow-moving Category 3 storm that impacted south Louisiana directly, putting to test the readiness of the various systems of relief. At the conclusion of the eight-day exercise, the agencies involved agreed that, if a hurricane like Pam hit Louisiana, and particularly New Orleans, the damage would be catastrophic. The Pam experiment reinforced evidence of New Orleans's vulnerability, showing that the city would easily succumb to flooding caused by storm surges, levee failure, or even pump failure. Disheartened by these findings, the group quickly scheduled to meet two additional times in 2004, and in July and August of the following year. Even with the revisions to the disaster planning and response procedures, the overall conclusion was that Louisiana was not prepared for even a "slow-moving Category 3 storm," making the possibility of one the following season ever more frightening.[32]

Meanwhile, recent decades brought a broader shift in how Americans defined disasters. In the years following World War II, advances in technology and the scientific understanding of storms gave Americans a new sense of power over nature, including natural phenomena such as the weather. Whereas the Cold War years were dominated by the goal of trying to prevent or control storms, the late twentieth century gave way to efforts to predict them through technical understanding of their causes, constitutions, and movements. The *perceived* destructiveness of a storm was now a significant political question, as it determined the amount of aid or relief that was provided. This trend continued in the 2000s as new types of national crises called attention to the definitions and relief provided in an event.[33] The terrorist attacks of September 11, 2001, and the concerns over larger anthropogenic impact on climate and coastal change, in particular, further widened the definition of disaster to emphasize defining disasters as "major" versus "minor," as well as blurring the line between "man-made" versus "natural" components of causal effects.[34] All of these perceptions affected how Americans saw hurricanes by 2005.[35] A hurricane was now a major or minor event, with natural and man-made causal factors that were multiplying quickly and, even with modern technology to track its movements, was still just as harmful as before. As a result, even the "weakest" storms could have grievous effects, causes, and ramifications in an era when public participation and commentary grew rapidly. The competing agendas and ideologies, continually in conversation among a public who had ideas about what they thought should happen in a hurricane over an extended period of time, also expanded in this era. Added to already varied definitions of storms attached via their gender-specific names, these factors set the stage for the emergence of Hurricane 2.0, which as a culturally defined hurricane was more expansive and multifarious, emerging in 2005 to become Katrina.

Katrina: The Storm We've Always Feared

The storm first emerged on the radar screen like any other. Weather officials placed it on their bulletins, noting its location and size, and eventually bestowed upon it a name from that year's list. This one was called Katrina. It was a sizable storm by late August, and that is when the panic started. The storm quickly "add[ed] muscle" as it "bulk[ed] up" in the Gulf, "curl[ing] north" along the way.[36] Then, it intensified, mushrooming within a few hours of entering the Gulf of Mexico while aiming directly for New Orleans. As it "close[d] in," New Orleans went from being the Big Easy to the "Big Uneasy," "pull[ing] in the welcome mat" and preparing to "rally and wait."[37]

Before it hit land, Katrina did not seem so bad. As coverage looped through the usual media feeds, New Orleans officials assured the public they were ready.[38] But as Katrina "trudged" and "lumbered" towards New Orleans, anxieties rose.[39] The evacuations that were originally precautionary changed overnight as the storm intensified to a Category 5. At 10 a.m. on August 28, just shortly after the National Weather Service upgraded Katrina to Category 5 status, New Orleans Mayor Ray Nagin went live on television to issue the city's first-ever mandatory evacuation order, calling Katrina "a storm that most of us had long feared."[40] As he addressed the public, he urged everyone to get out of "Katrina's way," arguing that the hurricane had the potential to cause death and destruction unparalleled in the city's history.[41] With less than a 12-hour window from the issuance of a mandatory evacuation order and when the storm was set to strike, over 1.2 million coastal residents packed up and evacuated in the largest mass exodus of a region in the nation's history.[42] Meanwhile, weather forecasters declared that Katrina was the "perfect hurricane," feeding into the rhetoric of apocalyptic predictions of a purported "Superstorm" capable of producing a "toxic soup" of problems if it were to attack New Orleans directly.[43] Countless models on television focused on the concept of New Orleans's "bowl filling," or potential for flooding if engineering feats like levees should fail, as well as the vulnerability of the Louisiana coastline based on the known aftermath of storms like Betsy (1965) and Camille (1969) in the region.[44] They also focused on storm-surge possibilities, warning of the economic effects of closing a region so dependent on its coastal production.[45]

While the mass exodus of residents ensued, television cameras positioned themselves to cover the storm live from the historic French Quarter and to interview individuals as they gassed up, packed up, or decided to ride out the historic storm. The footage featured all-too-familiar long lines at the pump, jammed interstates, and large bodies of water that were held back tenuously by man's engineering experiments.[46] At the same time, a countdown clock and satellite image of the storm from space spiraled ominously at the bottom of the television screen, giving visual reference to the doomsday scenario churning closer in the Gulf.[47] Live footage of the evacuation and auto-replayed statements by New Orleans mayor Nagin now proclaiming the storm to be the "storm we've always feared" escalated these concerns further.[48] Viewers all around the country, even those far from the at-risk region of the Gulf South, were exposed to this regular coverage of the storm.[49]

But this hurricane was different as it was narrated and consumed differently from any other storm that had come before it. Even as the traditional media outlets such as TV and print tracked the storm's approach, Web 2.0 was abuzz with a proliferation of accounts from a variety of people.[50] Beyond the traditional media's republication of their coverage in online form (that is, newspaper websites), new content was produced and distributed in Web 2.0 media, including blog posts, social network comments, and further expansion of e-commerce websites that were already selling 2004 hurricane commemorative items. Notable bloggers, independent weather aficionados, and news sources like the online-only *Huffington Post* (which debuted earlier that spring) published accounts through new, digital means.[51] Americans were both consuming *and producing* material about the storm before it had even made landfall.[52] In fact, the first warning of Katrina's potential path shift towards New Orleans was made from a weather-enthusiast blogger in Indiana named Brendan Loy. Loy took to posting his prediction on his blog "irishtrojan.com," strongly urging the New Orleans population to "get the hell out of Dodge right now," which was reposted and shared enough to become the fourteenth most linked-to sites on the Internet by the day the storm hit.[53] Even NOAA, the source of government-issued weather information, published its own online content, including satellite maps of the storm's movements, weather bulletins, and links to historical information on previous hurricanes.[54] With the onslaught of coverage, Katrina was the focus of the entire country, even the world, and this citizenry was actively responding to the decisions made by officials at unprecedented levels through these outlets.[55] Thus, before the hurricane even hit, Katrina had become a sensation: the first major Internet storm.

On August 29, Hurricane Katrina struck the Gulf South near Buras-Triumph, Louisiana, a mere 68 miles south of New Orleans.[56] It had weakened slightly to a Category 3, but not enough to lessen its considerable blow. It was quickly followed by a storm surge of 14 feet at coastal Louisiana and up to 27 feet in Mississippi, with substantial rain and wind.[57] Following its landfalls in Louisiana, the storm moved northeast and made a third landfall at the Louisiana-Mississippi border, then continued towards Tennessee.[58] As the storm ravaged the land with rain and subsequent storm surge, both Louisiana and Mississippi worried about its effects. Quickly, reporters and commentators noted the force placed on vulnerable levees. In horrifying slow motion, the pressure created by the droves of water caused over 50 levee breeches. Within hours of impact in Louisiana, 80 percent of the city of New Orleans lay underwater as the levees failed, flooding the city.[59]

In the real-time coverage of the events unfolding in New Orleans and elsewhere, traditional media coverage and Web 2.0 coverage varied considerably. As in the past, traditional sources of media such as newspapers and their reporters were an essential place of information. Unfortunately, both the *New Orleans Times-Picayune* and *Biloxi Sun-Herald* suffered during the storm.[60] As the waters rose in New Orleans, *Times-Picayune* staff were forced to evacuate their offices. This did not stop their reporting efforts, though. Instead, the newspaper shifted to publishing its content solely online, taking advantage of the Web 2.0 platforms that had developed enough to allow this possibility. Because of their efforts under duress, both the *Times-Picayune* and *Sun-Herald* would win Pulitzer Prizes for journalism, as the prize organization expanded its categories to include online entries post-Katrina.[61] Meanwhile, television coverage of the storm by major news outlets like CNN, Fox News, and TWC spotlighted the hazards caused by the storm in the initial day after it made landfall, positioning cultural meteorological icons like Bryan Norcross, Jim Cantore, Anderson Cooper, and Geraldo Rivera in the heart of the aftermath.[62]

At the same time that traditional news sources were reporting on events unfolding, a separate but connected conversation took place on the web. From the minute the storm formed until long after it was gone, individuals posted their opinions and experiences with the storm, its damage, the response, and the coverage of it.[63] These contributions included the use of public platforms linked with traditional news sources (like CNN's online content to complement their on-air coverage) and public blogs or share sites (such as the AccuWeather blog formed to track Katrina).[64] These shared experiences varied in content and provided multiple narratives of the storm's impact that were soon reused by traditional news sources.[65] Thus, as the storm made its initial impact, the discourse surrounding it started to diversify.[66]

In the aftermath of the storm, the coverage of Katrina only intensified. As reported locally, the region was "under siege by Katrina."[67] It "ravage[ed]" the New Orleans Central Business District and "le[ft] its main artery, Poydras Street, looking little better than a war zone," stated the *New Orleans Times-Picayune*.[68] Its "stinging assault" was felt through "smacks," "stabs," "blasts," and "knockout punch[es]" that were effectively "upend[ing]" life throughout the region.[69] Then the "horror show" stopped its "rampage" and exited, but not before it hovered for hours along the coastline.[70] In the end, it left the region looking like a mixture of "downtown Baghdad" and the aftermath of "Hiroshima."[71] Locally, concerns over Katrina emphasized the power of this storm as a "killer."[72] Through this, reporters from Mobile, Biloxi, and New Orleans concluded that no other storm was as severe as Katrina. In doing so, they effectively distinguished Katrina in the minds of locals as a unique, "perfect storm" to be remembered.[73] The *Times-Picayune* was under duress due to displacement, which limited reporters' reaction to a few articles, but enough to conclude that there had never been another storm like Katrina. The *Biloxi Sun-Herald* confirmed this point. "Cantankerous Katrina" was "Camille II" as soon as it appeared, and even potentially greater, it stated.[74] Meanwhile, the *Mobile Press-Register* scoffed at the notion that Katrina was just "cantankerous"; instead they recommended that the storm could only be called "killer."[75]

By drawing from the rhetoric of war zones (for example, Baghdad), atomic bombs (Hiroshima), and killers, local news blended hurricane descriptors usually affixed to male-named storms as a way of emphasizing the grievous impact of Katrina. Katrina was in this sense "masculinized" in order to stress its catastrophic nature and reporters' uncertainty with how to explain their ravaged surroundings. The above-the-fold emboldened title of the *New Orleans Times-Picayune,* "Help Us, Please," four days after Katrina made landfall further emphasized the vulnerability felt by the horrifying script that was accompanied by a picture of a grief-stricken black woman on her knees crying outside the now globally recognizable overstuffed shelter in the Superdome."[76] The Superdome, where hordes of displaced residents sat waiting for relief as their city lay underwater, was the epitome of the paralyzed and weakened state of a post-Katrina war caused by a combination of natural and man-made forces and a critique of federal response efforts.[77]

Local news also sought to contextualize the storm as representative of its female name. In doing so, they relied on descriptions of the storm as the perfect female storm to both build on linguistic territory that was already familiar and to further drive home their point of the uniqueness of this storm. For example, the use of "cantankerous" as a descriptor not only served as a memorable alliteration, but also an indicator of unwanted or negative feminized behavior. This is further confirmed by imagery of Katrina coming out of the *Mobile Press-Register.* As depicted by well-known *Mobile Press-Register* cartoonist JD Crowe, Katrina fit the image of a woman feared by all. She is represented as a spindly, sharp-nailed voodoo priestess using a needle to inflict severe pain on her target: New Orleans.[78] (See figure 13.)

TEMPEST

Figure 13. "Voodoo Priestess Katrina," *Mobile Press-Register,* August 30, 2005. JD Crowe, *Mobile Press-Register*/AL.com.

Meanwhile, national coverage laid bare for the entire country that the horror-filled speculative predictions had come true: a major city lay underwater, thousands were dead or unaccounted for, and over a million people were effectively stranded far away from their homes at evacuation sites spread throughout the country.[79] Then came the scenes of people trapped by the flooded levees, left to sit on top of their houses with messages scrawled across the rooftops, urging responders to save them.[80] Then the views of underwater interstates cutting pathways out of the city off from the rest of civilization and of people trying to escape only to be turned away or reach a point where no help was to be found (for example, left on the interstate while media choppers flew into the French Quarter).[81] Then, the confusing dichotomy of the already maxed-out shelter and drowned inner-city regions, sitting next to the miraculously dry French Quarter that was surrounded by water on all sides. Soon, reporting turned to speculation, as descriptions of New Orleans "on the brink of anarchy" turned to a city "slipping into chaos."[82] Removed from the impact zone and influenced by the 24-hour news coverage of Katrina's effect on the Gulf Coast region, national coverage of the storm was voyeuristic, gritty, apocalyptically narrated, and heavily laden with gendered references that blended gender analogies used from all previous storms into one to create a master narrative that best described the untold reality abrasively facing them on a multitude of screens.

From the get-go, Katrina was a "doomsday scenario," stated the *Charleston Post & Courier*.[83] The "coastal defenses" were already weakened with the 2004 season, reported the *New York Times*.[84] Now, with "Nature's revenge" in full swing in the following season, it was pure "chaos."[85] The "atomic bomb" finally went off, confirmed the *Houston Chronicle*, as "nearly 80% of [New Orleans was] under water."[86] In the end, the *Raleigh News & Observer* stated, New Orleans looked like "Pompeii," and Mississippi, "Hiroshima."[87] As described, Katrina had behaved like a "Little Andrew" at first as "she churned north" and "slapped the Florida Keys."[88] Then Katrina turned into a "menacing" "monster" that "wreak[ed] havoc," "bearing down" with "full fury."[89] Like "a toxic gumbo" the storm "walloped" with "major blows" on the already "weather-beaten" New Orleans.[90] With "slow and uncoordinated" movements that were both "deadly" and "fickle," the storm then "barreled" past New Orleans and "ripped" up the Gulf Coast.[91] In the end, the region looked worse than an "atomic bomb" "strike zone" as Katrina had "swept" some regions off the map with "a broom."[92]

The gendered language used in national coverage of Katrina mimics that of local coverage. It also undeniably proves Katrina was seen not only as a one-of-a-kind devastating storm, but a gendered one. The use of the phrase "Nature's revenge," for instance, immediately draws to mind connections to the all-powerful association of feminine power with natural attributes. So does the use of gender-action rhetoric such as "sweeping" and "fickle" to link this storm to feminine qualities. Meanwhile, the idea that Katrina was perceived as a "little Andrew" at first links the storm not only to those of the past, but to a preconceived notion that female storms were in some way weaker than male storms until proven otherwise.

National coverage also focused on the visual representation of the storm in terms of its gendered name. Using traditional representations of the housewife to more detailed New Orleans references, the Katrina portrayed on a national scale was a dangerous woman in every aspect and featured prominently as female. The most explicit example of this was in the *Hartford Courant*, where Katrina was blatantly shown stomping across the southern United States, leaving a giant footprint where New Orleans should be, while swinging her skirt blithely along the Mississippi River to the north.[93] In the image, New Orleans is marked with a little sign and rooftops with people sitting on top of them, leaving no room for suggestion as to who has caused this damage to New Orleans—it was a woman, as clearly marked by the Katrina label on the skirt. While New Orleans was the only city marked in the image, the Gulf Coast was illustrated, washed out with the storm surge the hurricane brought with it. Similarly, by depicting Katrina as barefoot and the "land" she is walking on as sand, the cartoon suggested that the task of destroying New Orleans was like a walk on the beach for this bad woman.

Both national and local coverage also introduced new terminology into the hurricane lexicon as attention shifted to the impact of the storm on different races and classes. Indeed, the debate over Katrina, the fate of the famed city, and its mangled recovery efforts that took a week to mobilize provoked other discourse over the economics, class, and racial divisions that notably led to the number of casualties and stranded individuals in New Orleans. The Superdome itself became a visual reminder in all news sources of the chaotic options left to those not fortunate enough to have means of evacuation within a world of mandatory evacuations.[94] The "dome" also became emblematic of the site of wild reporting rumors that would quickly grow as 24-hour news outlets and the Internet would fuel even greater consumption of information about the disaster.[95] Reports about looting exploded as many debated the decisions of those left behind.[96] In upper-class and predominantly white neighborhoods, reporters described individuals as victims of the storm struggling to survive on necessities.[97] Meanwhile, in more impoverished and mainly African American areas of the city, people were described as larcenous individuals who were looting goods in an opportunity to take advantage of a city scarred by the devastating storm and its aftermath.[98] From reports of looting came other stories about racialized violence.[99] Similar issues regarding race and class permeated discussion of law enforcement mishandling of everything from prisoners to suspected looters turned violent.[100] On the flip side, increased reports of violence inspired fearful reaction to those suspected of breaking the law.[101] At the Superdome, these stories coalesced into one, as misreporting covered looting, rape, and murder within the facility, none of which had occurred.[102] And all of these discussions took place in multiple forms of media—on television as 24-hour pundits debated the efforts of recovery and the fate of the city, in print as newspapers updated the public on the current status of Katrina recovery, and particularly, online.[103]

The online forum was a particularly ripe place for discussion, often feeding the coverage within the other media—so much so that 24-hour news guru CNN would credit the blog for documenting "the first American tragedy [...] in real time by its survivors, as they lived it."[104] In this way, the Internet was as critical to shaping ideas of Katrina as photography was to the Civil War. The first blog post about Katrina experience appeared the afternoon the storm struck New Orleans (August 29). From there, blogs became a source of first-person accounts of everything from stories of evacuation to recovery efforts even ten years following.[105]

In all places, pleas for help were present and examples of devastation easy to show on live television and web stream.[106] But support was slow to come.[107] Due to the reorganization of FEMA and revised standards for disaster declaration, miscommunication on all levels of response caused confusion that turned to anger as crucial decision-makers pointed fingers at each other in an attempt to rationalize events unfolding.[108] This tepid response only served to further aggravate situations on the ground, all unfolding live with global viewership and the new realm of social media commentary in the form of shared videos, blogs, vlogs, and posts.[109] By September 2, Katrina as just another devastating storm evolved to become Katrina, the first disaster of its kind. It was "The Storm We Always Feared," not just because it was a hurricane, but because it would leave the nation wondering whether things would ever be the same.[110] "The hellish aftermath of Hurricane Katrina" was to be remembered, all agreed, simply as "catastrophic," separating it and its victims—called "Katrina refugees"—from storms of the past.[111]

Online, Americans consumed coverage of the storm with increasing interest. Through the medium of online news and YouTube, they watched and immediately responded to comments in the days following the storm by the New Orleans mayor, who proclaimed his city to have been left to rot due to long-standing biases of race and class divide all while they were provided with examples of the disarray on the Gulf Coast.[112] It was a "chocolate city," Mayor Nagin argued emphatically, as everyone who was left in this purgatory was African American, poor, prisoner, and old.[113] Americans had abandoned these people in the region, and the slowed recovery efforts were proof.[114] At the same time as the New Orleans mayor was maddeningly critiquing response efforts, former first lady Barbara Bush was visiting the site of evacuees in Houston's Astrodome. Her casual comments on their subpar circumstances caused fury online, provoking musician Kanye West to famously proclaim at a fund-raising "Concert for Katrina" on national television four days after the storm that President George W. Bush "doesn't care about black people," using his mother's comments and slow response to Katrina as the prime example.[115] As evidenced by the rhetoric reflected in Nagin and West's remarks, Katrina had turned into as much a racial discourse on American life as it was an environmental catastrophe.

This discourse only continued as headlines like "New Orleans Slides into Chaos" and reports of looting and "anarchy" in New Orleans appeared in newspapers throughout the country and fueled reaction online, entirely shifting attention on the aftermath of Katrina from the Gulf Coast overall to focus explicitly on the city.[116] As "a city awash in death," now totaling over 1,000, New Orleans "face[d] the fight of its life" after this traumatic experience, stated the *Atlanta Journal-Constitution*.[117] One debate that sparked considerable reaction was the *Raleigh News & Observer*'s question on whether to "Rebuild it or move it?" referring to New Orleans within days after the storm.[118] The *Baltimore Sun* jumped in and asked readers to "Share Your Memories of New Orleans" as it might be gone for good.[119] This debate only continued over the next week as the costs for recovery were tabulated, with statistics shared on all media platforms. In response, New Orleans blogger Ashley Morris posted a blog where he screamed most infamously to critics of New Orleans recovery to "Fuck You, You Fuckin' Fucks," which quickly went viral online, garnering countless views and shares in the weeks following.[120] In this way, while traditional news outlets were focused on the New Orleans that once was, new online forums were full of critique for the New Orleans as it was currently. And in this new discourse the larger impact of the storm on other Gulf South states was forgotten. Katrina was now New Orleans, and the city forever tied to it.

Bloggers were often the first to vehemently debate whose fault levee failure was, how racist media coverage was impacting impressions of victims, the unique experience of individuals affected by the storm and its aftermath in evacuation stories, and the day-by-day feelings of recovery through pictures and on-foot accounts.[121] These blogs were so popular that many blog posts appeared in anthologies published after the storm passed.[122] Fueling this "share" culture were platforms like Facebook and MySpace, in addition to email chains with forward-friendly listservs.[123]

Katrina was the first disaster, and only one to date, to be federally declared as affecting all 50 states.[124] The number of people displaced by the storm caused the most extensive diaspora in American history, at an estimated 1.2 million. This meant that in every state, the number of people affected by the disaster was enough to merit federal aid in response. This does not count the number of people, organizations, and agencies that dedicated resources or time to help with the recovery efforts in New Orleans. It is why the terminology of "refugee" was applied to the people displaced by the storm. They were Katrina's refugees, like other people separated by war, persecution, and disaster. To many experiencing forced displacement, there was no return, their lives officially relocated to these new regions of the country. In this way, Katrina was the first "national" disaster because everyone in the nation experienced it, or provided support following.

Throughout early coverage of the storm and its aftermath, three things remained the same: first, the focus of attention remained almost exclusively on New Orleans in the post-Katrina period, even though areas of Mississippi and Alabama saw similar physical devastation from storm surge. Second, the coverage of Katrina as a major catastrophe was consistent across all platforms of traditional and new media. There was considerable variation in terms of the sensitivity shown to those that were marginalized in mainstream coverage. Web 2.0 narrations of experience with the storm were often more sympathetic to the marginalized, taking it upon themselves to critique coverage in traditional media and elevate the perspectives and experiences of those otherwise overlooked. Third, all of these events—from the racial disparity felt in reporting and representation to the discussion of engineering failure that caused the flooding of New Orleans neighborhoods more prone to occupation by lower-income and African American families to the creation of a new type of victim, the refugee—were described as part of one event. They were Katrina—a conglomeration of storm and reaction, representing larger cultural fissures in the calm following the storm. It was a new type of storm that had been unleashed on the American public and one that did not show a sign of dissipating anytime soon.

This impression of Katrina as a new type of storm was cemented in cultural memory by the storms that followed and the consumer marketplace for Katrina that emerged during recovery. New Orleans's Katrina experience became the symbolic representation of a period and a regional situation. As a result, in popular culture, the name Katrina was forever solidified for a global audience as everything to do with the storm, the aftermath, and the ensuing cultural climate. Fleshed out through mediums of expression in popular culture, Katrina became a social commentary on a multitude of cultural situations that had never entered into a description of a hurricane before. Not even subsequent storms of the same season, Rita and Wilma, surpassed the rhetoric on Katrina, despite the devastation that they caused.

Productizing Katrina

First used as a mechanism to update the public, family, or friends by the media and individuals themselves, Web 2.0 following the storm quickly turned into a place for expression through blogs, fund-raising venues, and social media sites. It also created a place to collect stories of the hurricane as various digital repositories were produced and consumed. The University of New Orleans's Hurricane Digital Memory Bank, for example, served the purpose of providing free-form areas for individuals to record pictures, videos, and written and verbal thoughts.[125] Meanwhile, Think New Orleans and later the Rising Tide Conference hosted lists of over 300 bloggers that wrote about Katrina or its aftermath, forever preserving the digital discourse of those who experienced the storm.[126] The *New Orleans Times-Picayune* even archived their online content produced during the storm and posted cover-to-cover PDFs of their newspaper (also produced online) from August 2005 to November 2005. All of these sites are still accessible online today.[127] With these sites and others, a new type of disaster consumption was created—existing solely in a digital world that was not dependent on a producer, but was instead consumer-driven.

Then, the vast co-construction of Katrina that began with blog posts and social media shares, detailing the local experience of rebuilding and reaction to the aftermath, gave rise to a culture of Katrina-related consumption. In the weeks and months after the storm, this culture evolved into a global marketplace of objects, experiential products, and artworks related to the storm and its aftermath. Although the storms of 2003 and 2004 gave rise to some disaster consumption, facilitated by expanding Internet culture and sale platforms, the number of items produced related to Katrina exponentially exceeded those of the past, and the range of perspectives, experiences, and ideologies that they concretized far outclassed the wind-in-a-bottle keepsakes. These consumer products also further defined Katrina as a gendered event, expressed in a multitude of ways, and for a global audience, providing them exposure to old and new gendered rhetoric that would shape the next decade of storm description.

The first type of Katrina "product" produced and sold was objects related to the storm and its aftermath. Over a decade, thousands of these items were produced and marketed on multiple platforms. These included tours, T-shirts, painted roof tiles, picture frames, furniture, bumper stickers, charity/benefit items, board games, wine, cocktails, costumes, blue-tarp products, Meals-Ready-to-Eat (MRE) products, candy wrappers, lapel pins, Christmas/holiday cards, kitchen towels, umbrellas, coasters, soap, mouse pads, floor mats, koozies, stickers, sew-on patches, flags, key rings, notebooks, beads, and jewelry.[128] The average price of these items varied from "free" to "$1,100"—or more for luxury items—with a median price of $20–25 for most items. While many of these items were marketed to locals affected by the storm—such as tea towels proclaiming that a FEMA trailer could be "Home Sweet FEMA Trailer," a dig on the long-standing trailers located months afterward throughout New Orleans—others were meant for a larger market. Immediately following Katrina, several newspapers throughout the country printed articles about T-shirts for sale that stated that the owner had "survived Katrina."[129] Other websites like Amazon.com and eBay.com listed more objects for purchase—including several "authentic" collectible items such as "MP" military police badges, "Hurricane Katrina Challenge Coins," and, "shoes worn during Katrina."[130]

Overall, the plethora of products produced surrounding Katrina and the rebuilding process were staggering simply because local and national production of these items took place from the beginning. The vast number of disaster related items with Katrina is directly linked to the broad interest in storm recovery and continued focus on New Orleans and the storm in mass media. This broader interest in the disaster caused a wider disbursement of consumer items as there was a more significant demand for them. But what makes Katrina disaster consumption unique are the longevity and continued production of these items today. Of the thousands of Katrina consumer items produced, a vast majority of them are still sold in New Orleans and the surrounding area.[131] Similarly, in addition to the locally produced items, several nonlocal Internet websites sold Katrina-related memorabilia internationally as the Internet provided a place to consume and produce this material and facilitated global distribution of the items. For example, Cafe-Press, a company that prints self-produced images on T-shirts and bumper stickers became a popular site for the production of several items related to the storm. To date, the website lists the availability of 1,880 Katrina-related T-shirts; 2,130 bumper stickers; 344 posters & other art; 2,230 mugs; and, 16 wall calendars. Featured in the designs are quotes from city officials before the storm, images of a city in crisis during, humorous reactions from the locals after, and celebratory gratitude for groups who volunteered assistance as teams in recovery.[132] Other websites created for 2004 hurricane-related swag updated their stock to include Katrina items, and then again with subsequent storms. DopplerDuds.com, for instance, cited over 80 distinct T-shirt designs for Katrina merchandise and 30 designs for other hurricanes. "Before (Katrina) went in, they were standard humorous designs," Cathy Johnson, the owner of the site, stated in a *New Orleans Times-Picayune* interview two months after the storm. "And then [the T-shirts] got political. And then they got sympathetic." Now, "people want to be able to say, 'I did it. I was there.'"[133] Overall, Johnson's website, in addition to others like CafePress, continued the tradition of selling this memorabilia long after the one-year mark of the storm's anniversary.

 This disaster kitsch provides clear insight into the broad impact Katrina had on the country, particularly regarding the breadth of impact felt by the storm. Katrina objects let consumers materially participate in and memorialize the disaster through actual artifacts from the storm site and through consumer goods manufactured to comment on the event itself or on human responses to it. They also provided a way to commemorate the experiences of those who survived and those that were lost to the devastating storm. Finally, they helped further the consumption and use of otherwise inflammatory and explicit rhetoric, mainstreaming its acceptance and attachment to storm descriptors of the future.

 For example, the interest in producing and consuming Katrina disaster kitsch only accentuated the raciness of specific items' popularity, as some of the more popular items were those that were most scandalous. For ex-

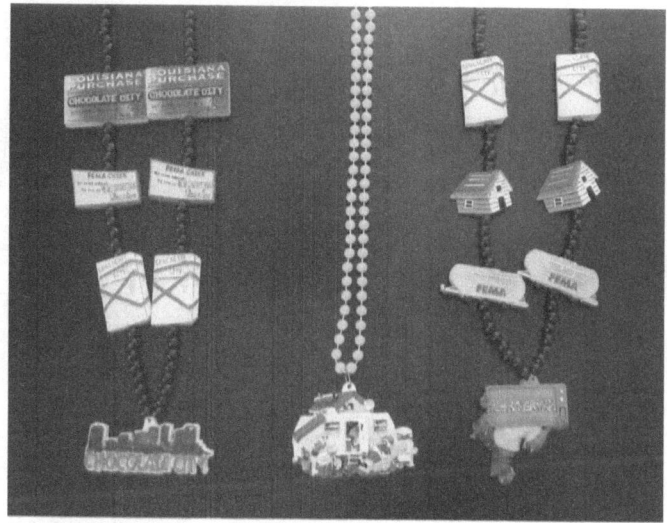

Figure 14. Hurricane Katrina Mardi Gras beads, thrown during Mardi Gras 2006. Themes include Louisiana Purchase Card, FEMA Check, Duct-Taped Fridge, Chocolate City, White Trash FEMA Trailer, Blue-Tarped Roof, FEMA Trailer, and Looterman.

ample, T-shirts that read, "FEMA: Fix Everything My Ass" or "I stayed in New Orleans and all I got was this lousy T-shirt, a new Cadillac and a Plasma TV," were staples for sale in French Quarter tourist shops.[134] But what also emerged prominently in these items was the fixation of storm and relief coverage with Katrina on the issues of race, class, and gender. One example of this was the exclusively produced Mardi Gras "Looterman" beads that illustrate an African American man running while carrying a television in his hands, referencing perceived mass looting and racial stigmatization in the media. Also illustrated are FEMA trailers, blue-tarp houses, and the classic taped-up fridge. A corollary set features "Chocolate City" beads, a reference to the New Orleans mayor Ray Nagin's infamous comment that New Orleans was deserted except for African Americans. Including FEMA checks, Louisiana Purchase Cards, and a cityscape covered in chocolate, the beads illustrate a strong racial and class-related bias linked with storm victims.[135] (See figure 14.)

Other disaster products used explicitly gendered rhetoric to express anger at the storm itself and outrage at its impact. One mass-produced

Figure 15. Hurricane Katrina t-shirts, purchased by author between 2007 and 2011 in New Orleans.

T-shirt—"Katrina Gave Me a Blow Job I'll Never Forget"—depicts Hurricane Katrina performing fellatio on whoever is wearing the shirt.[136] Sold on Bourbon Street, it connected the sin associated with the street to a feminized hurricane's wrath, not only gendering the storm as traditionally fitting to its female name, but hypersexualizing it. A similar T-shirt popularly sold on Bourbon Street represents a younger, more flirtatious, but still sexualized image of Hurricanes Katrina, Rita, and Wilma, portraying the storms as "Girls Gone Wild."[137] This shirt was one of the first to recognize multiple storms at play in the Gulf Coast during this period of disaster. (See figure 15.)

The impetus for many T-shirts often came from post-recovery reaction that was made popular through social media. Popular images of houses spray-painted with the slogan "Katrina You Bitch!" for example, were circulated following the storm and quickly resulted in the production of several consumer products, including bumper stickers, T-shirts, print images, and magnets.[138] While the reference to a hurricane as a "bitch" had appeared offhandedly in print before, the prevalence of this phrase took off in New Orleans post-Katrina. The phrasing "Katrina You Bitch" or "Katrina That Bitch" was indicative of larger cultural shifts that classified "bitch" as one of the worst terms associated with women in the early 2000s. While other words describe women as sexual objects, *bitch* evokes a "sense of feral, hell-hath-no-fury rage" and "visceral fear and anger" that is irrefutable.[139] While the term *bitch*, "applied opprobriously to a woman" had been in use since the 1400s, it became a regularly used slur because of its use on television.[140] Appearing on television sitcoms in the late 1970s, the term was first associated with a female hurricane in print in 1992 following Hurricane Andrew as a way to distinguish the difference between Hurricane Elena (1985) and the current monster storm, Andrew.[141] It was not used again to describe a hurricane until after Katrina.

The reason behind this gap in usage was that the term was not frequently used in modern media due to regulatory standards.[142] Between 1998 and 2007, as standards were relaxed, the use of the word *bitch* on television "tripled from 431 uses on 103 prime-time episodes in 1998 to 1,277 uses on 685 shows in 2007."[143] In fact, with its use to describe Katrina and other subsequent female storms, in addition to relaxed regulatory standards, the use of the word *bitch* has increased by 50 percent on television in the post-2005 period.[144] While regulations regarding the use of the word on television changed, allowing the word to be used more frequently, the prevalence of its use by the media—particularly with Katrina and the disaster memorabilia produced as a result of it—has no doubt contributed to the increased use of the word overall, primarily when referring to hurricanes. It was a modern analogue to the "Camille Was No Lady" slogan that appeared in disaster products in 1969. In fact, many locals can easily meld the two phrases together, filling in the statement, "Camille Was No Lady, *But Katrina Was a Bitch*," when prompted.[145]

Eventually, this popular slogan was made into all forms of discourse, new and old, as products for sale or expression of grief and anger. Meanwhile, frustrated references to FEMA, Katrina, and Louisiana Governor Kathleen Blanco also appeared referencing the hypersexualization of Katrina. One bumper sticker, in particular, stated, "FEMA Sucks, Katrina Blows, Blanco Swallows." The gendered terminology used within represented extremely negative gendered connotations. In the sticker, federal and state leaders are described in hypersexualized language with Katrina located as equal in the mix. The reference to FEMA as effeminate is also easily spotted when placed in conjunction with the image of Louisiana's first female governor as performing a sexual act. Both FEMA and Blanco lacked control in the circumstances of the other destructive female object listed: Katrina. Others continued this trend in linking political figures and sexual proclivities to the current disaster situation with Katrina. One bumper sticker read, "Bill & Monica Is Better Than Bush & Katrina," while another stated, "Had Katrina Been Named, 'Terri Schiavo' Maybe Bush Would Have Reacted Faster."[146] Other T-shirts appeared with similarly sexualized slogans such as: "I Got Blown, Pissed On & Fucked By Katrina/What A Whore," "Katrina Can Blow Me! / She Won't Keep Me Away From Mardi Gras," and, "She Blew Me Like A Cat 5."[147] Images of houses and refrigerators spray-painted with popular sexualized slogans and messages also circulated. Besides the use of the aforementioned "Katrina You Bitch!" phrase that appeared in multiple places, including on the sides of houses, one other such example was the image of a floodwall spray painted with the message "RIP . . . Fuck You Whore Katrina."[148] As circulated in blogs and then as part of video compilations online, the language was undeniably gendered.

The proliferation of these hypersexualized depictions of Katrina, appearing in places like print, on T-shirts, and in parades, represented a larger mutation of descriptors for storms in the Hurricane 2.0 era. In order to one-up the storms of the last century, common descriptors of the storm as both masculine and feminine were merged to create a hypersexual and unquestionably gendered female hybrid storm. These images of the storm as gendered affected the sexualization of other facets of culture impacted by it. FEMA, Governor Blanco, New Orleans, and the Gulf Coast were all victim to these analogies, tied together by Katrina.

The use of sexual slurs and images of a city at war with an aggressive feminine force also linked negative discussions of the city, death, and the politics of recovery to a feminized or weakened New Orleans post-storm. For New Orleans commentators responding to asserted claims that the city should not be rebuilt, one had rebutted in the *Times-Picayune,* "They act as if we are a burden. They act as if we wore our skirts too short and invited trouble."[149] This reference to the city (and its inhabitants) as stereotyped rape victims further scandalized both the storm and its aftermath. The *Mobile Press-Register* also expressed these sentiments through a set of cartoons featuring the Gulf Coast as the purported victim of abuse first by the multiple storms that impacted it in 2004 and 2005, and then as the undeniable victims of a conglomerate "Mother Nature's" abuse after subsequent storm Rita hit the coast following Katrina. In the series of images, the representative Gulf Coast transitions from a battered woman asking "for a restraining order" in 2004, to a series of feminized states warding off sauced-up and gun-toting Rambo-like storms "lookin' for love" in July 2005, to finally crippled men/states begging for protection from a Grim Reaper–esque Mother Nature in late September 2005. Another image from the Georgia-based *Rome News-Tribune* depicts "The Legacy Prom," a dance featuring two presidents, Bill Clinton and George W. Bush, and their dates, "Monica" and "Katrina," furthering the linkage between the sexualized politics of both "crises" and their respective effects on the perspective of their administrations. These images, accessible via the Cartoonist Group, an Internet database of cartoon art used in newspapers, exist amongst over 300 others related to Katrina, and a plethora of others available for consumption, sharing, or sale online, many of which feature feminized versions of Katrina (the storm) and its aftermath as linked.[150] For example, an additional image from Karl Wimer Financial Cartoons showcases Katrina as villainous sea witch Ursula, having taken a "bite" out of the Gulf Coast and the national economy, widening the association of Katrina as gendered and of having a long-term national effect, not just a local or regional impact.[151]

But Katrina kitsch and representation were not just sold through online or product-based one-off consumption; other items were marketed as experientially based consumer products, ones that needed to be or could only be consumed while in New Orleans. These products enabled consumers to have a direct, participatory experience of the disaster on site. As a result, a culture of "dark tourism" or "disaster tourism" sprang up.[152] By December 2005, just four months after the storm, the majority of major tour companies in New Orleans began offering a "Hurricane Katrina" tour.[153] These tours either combined the traditional city or plantation tour with Katrina-specific content or were marketed as a separate tour entirely.[154] Such disaster-based tourism grew out of ecotourism but had shadier foci. Familiar tour routes took visitors through the famous Ninth Ward and Tremé neighborhoods, included stops at controversial sites like the Superdome and Industrial Canal levee, drive-bys to look at "Not as Seen on TV" X-marked and "Katrina You Bitch" spray-painted houses, and showcased volunteer efforts to build houses through organizations like Habitat for Humanity and Brad Pitt's Make It Right Foundation neighborhood in the Ninth Ward.[155] The tours also noticeably excluded neighborhoods that did not see extensive flooding, and updated their tours to showcase sites that became popular through post-storm discourse (particularly as the TV series *Treme* premiered).[156] For example, popular tour company Gray Line offers what they call a "Hurricane Katrina Tour: 'America's Worst Catastrophe'" featuring "an eyewitness account of the events surrounding the most devastating natural—and man-made—disaster on American soil." The tour begins in the French Quarter (blending their original French Quarter/early New Orleans tour) and expands outwards through regions of the city such as Lakeview, Gentilly, St. Bernard, and the Upper Ninth Ward. It ends by discussing not only the storm, but the "connection between America's disappearing coastal wetlands, oil and gas pipelines, levee protection and hurricane destruction," while blending in narratives of those that experienced the storm.[157]

The Katrina tours were controversial from the start, existing on a framework of the discussion of racial relations in the region and the need for a dramatically destroyed cityscape to visit.[158] They also fueled ideas about the geographic specificity of recovery as they focused attention on recovery efforts in some areas of the city and not others. Lastly, the tours were costly—$35 for adults, $28 for children; frequently marketed as offering a percentage of the profits to the neighborhoods most affected, they rarely made such contributions.[159] As a result, in 2006, a New Orleans city ordinance banned official tours-for-profit in regions east of the Industrial Canal, excluding most of the well-known Ninth Ward, which is split by the canal.[160] This did not stop the tour companies from adapting their tours, though. They have since altered their routes and offer voluntary walking-tour segments that correlate the bus-tour sections.[161]

Meanwhile, television shows such as *Treme,* along with music, literature, and art related to Katrina, were also produced in large quantities. New Orleans's vibrant art and cultural community was grossly affected by the storm and became extremely prolific in representing its effect. Musicians were some of the first to receive the spotlight and respond in the post-Katrina era. Many famous musicians suffered considerable losses during the storm, including loss of instruments, property, and even lives. Stories of their experiences permeated news coverage—such as pianist and songwriter Fats Domino, whose bold yellow home was a fixture of the Lower Ninth Ward and was reported missing for a period after the storm—and fed interest in what would happen to the displaced or refugee musicians and New Orleans's music community.[162] Immediately, other musicians and artists sought to help these musicians, offering assistance in the form of donated instruments, funding, time, and places to spotlight their music. For example, New Orleans's own Preservation Hall's New Orleans Musicians' Hurricane Relief Fund gave immediate cash assistance to musicians, Mardi Gras Indians, and social aid and pleasure club members following the storm.[163] Later, Harry Connick Jr. and Branford Marsalis announced plans to build Musicians Village in the Bywater, a collection of Habitat for Humanity homes to house returning musicians.[164]

Others sought to assist in the production of new music inspired following the storm by teaming up with displaced New Orleans musicians, such as producer Leo Sacks's album *Sing Me Back Home*, which featured scattered New Orleans artists.[165] While some musicians such as Aaron Neville performed classic storm favorites like "Sun Is Shining" and "Louisiana 1927" on TV specials and at JazzFest venues, others released new content focused exclusively on Katrina. Anders Osborne, for example, released a song, "Oh Katrina," that described Katrina as a home-wrecking woman who had not only scorned him personally—leaving him and "his 'sweet Crescent City' almost gone"—but prevented him from returning home.[166] Others produced and released records with critical content related to the storm and the relief efforts that followed, using Katrina as a mechanism to assert both anger and critique at a variety of factors the storm had come to represent. One of the first to do this was Fifth Ward Weebie, who released a bounce single titled "F—— Katrina" that popularized the explicit label for the named storm and everything it represented.[167] Rappers Lil Wayne and Juvenile also released tracks critiquing the botched response efforts of everyone from the president (in Lil Wayne's "Georgia Bush" track, a feminization of George W. Bush) to FEMA and Fox News (in Juvenile's "Get Ya Hustle On," that described racialized media coverage and post-Katrina realities).[168]

Within days of the storm, Mos Def released "Katrina Klap," a remix of New Orleans native Juvenile's "Nolia Clap" that called Katrina "a storm for America" because of its broad-sweeping effects and ability to unveil larger tensions related to race, class, and governmental failures.[169] He was later arrested outside of New York's Radio City Music Hall during the 2006 MTV

Video Music Awards for staging an impromptu and permit-less one-song performance of what MTV later called "a freestyle indictment of the Bush administration's slow response to last year's hurricane victims in New Orleans."[170] Lastly, venues across the country opened their doors to the displaced musicians, spotlighting their music and their experience in the process. When New Orleans's own music venues started to come back, they received considerable attention from the press. NPR, for example, broadcast portions of Galactic's first hometown show at Tipitina's, a local venue.[171] Meanwhile, when the New Orleans Jazz Orchestra premiered, an overflow crowd spilled out into the streets as news cameras filmed the homecoming.[172] New Orleans's popular music festivals like JazzFest and Essence Festival received additional attention in their first year back, too, as many famous acts headlined the welcome-back lineup.[173] The opening of music venues, invitations for displaced New Orleans musicians and rappers to perform, in addition to the propulsion of online music sale and consumption platforms like iTunes, Amazon, and YouTube dramatically widened the availability of music-related content focused on interpretations of Katrina. In all of these musical productions, Katrina the storm and Katrina the aftermath are either gendered as a vindictive rampaging woman or used to describe a multitude of social issues (for example, Mos Def's "the storm called America"), reinforcing the connectivity of a multitude of definitions with the storm and its results.

But music was not the only New Orleans community featured in the post-Katrina era; artists were another. The Ogden Museum of Southern Art reopened within a month of the storm to "symbolize the survival of the Crescent City art scene" following the storm.[174] In addition to traditional art venues like the Ogden, other more casual art exhibits sprung up throughout the city. Kirsha Kaechele Projects, pop-up art exhibits in blighted properties in the St. Roch neighborhood, began appearing in October 2006, marking what the *Times-Picayune* has called "the transition from pre-Katrina commercial/museum art establishment to the DIY art vibe that [has become] a part of the city's recovery."[175] The production of art, both for traditional and nontraditional venues, focused on Katrina has since been featured in multiple exhibits throughout the country and notably recognized as inspiring a new period in New Orleans's art history.[176] Meanwhile, several plays debuted featuring Katrina themes and experiences. Like with music tracks, these plays often featured satirical commentary on the federal government's response to Katrina (for example, Larry Gelbart's "Floodgate" and John Biguenet's "Rising Water").[177] Throughout all of this, artists and musicians continued to shape the definition of what made *Katrina*, broadening its time frame and thematic focus.

Another way New Orleanians sought to react and respond to the events that had unfolded since the storm was to commemorate it through the production of Mardi Gras floats, costumes, and entire parades. A Mardi Gras krewe, Krewe d'État, designed an entire parade around their reactions to the storm and called it "Rotten to the Corps."[178] The parade featured riders and walkers decked out in blue-tarp costumes, and floats that made fun of FEMA, the US Army Corps of Engineers, and governmental officials. At its center was a float dedicated solely to the refrigerator-message culture that had emerged as residents disposed of their fridges while spray painting messages along the side. This refrigerator float in particular featured the nota-

Figure 16. "Katrina You Bitch!" float in Krewe d'État parade, 2006. The parade theme was "Rotten to the Corps." Cheryl Gerber Photography.

ble slogan "Katrina You Bitch!" scrolled in bold red letters on its side. As it passed by the parade spectators, it emblematically represented the local and globally recognizable meaning of this expression. (See figure 16.)

Discussion of the city's cultural community frequently turned to the culinary community in the post-Katrina period, as well.[179] While residents noted the return of favorite local eateries such as the Parkway Bakery tavern and po'boy shop or the famous French Quarter beignet spot Café du Monde, others noted the restaurants or establishments that did not return.[180] Well-known Camellia Grill's mysterious closure brought national attention as residents posted signs and notes on its facade, requesting it be reopened.[181] Meanwhile, other New Orleans fixtures like Abita Brewery, Hubig's Pies, and Domino Sugar became examples of businesses that were grossly affected by the storm and forever linked with its economic effects.[182]

In many ways, television show *Treme* tried to capture this diverse and varied Katrina experience through a focus on the musicians, chefs and restaurants/bars, lawyers, bloggers, and educators who were extremely vocal in the post-Katrina era. Each of these groups is represented by characters of the series, which featured storylines based on collected experiences. At its forefront was the event that caused this peculiar set of intersecting circumstances—a hurricane of before-then unimaginable proportions. At its backdrop was the film and television industry expansion in New Orleans and Louisiana during the post-Katrina years.

Beyond the *Treme* series, gruesome depictions of Katrina experience in New Orleans were featured in documentaries like Spike Lee's *When the Levees Broke* (2006) and indie documentary/biography *Trouble the Water* (2008), IMAX films like *Hurricane on the Bayou* (2006), and films such as *Beasts of the Southern Wild* (2012).[183] The films were incredibly popular, acquiring accolades such as Academy Awards, nominations for Oscars, and Emmys, in addition to multiple film-festival grand prizes. The movies also brought up a slew of issues related to the multiplicity of experience with the storm and the representation of post-Katrina New Orleans.[184] Meanwhile, countless television shows, specials, and even full-length movies review the storm's impact on the region and New Orleans's effort to rebuild. Similarly, some of the highest ratings of television shows came from Katrina-related coverage. For example, the New Orleans Saints homecoming at the Superdome on September 25, 2006, provided the highest ratings for sports channel ESPN at the time in terms of viewership.[185] Meanwhile the coverage of celebrities flocking to New Orleans to help with the recovery was notable enough to be spoofed by *Saturday Night Live* in October 2005, just a month after the storm.[186]

Besides films and television shows representing the Katrina experience, the film industry found New Orleans to be a site of interest post-Katrina. Since 2005, the film industry in Louisiana has boomed into a billion-dollar business as economic incentives made filming profitable in the region and interest in the region grew. Major motion pictures like *The Curious Case of Benjamin Button, Jurassic World, The Fantastic Four,* and *Django* were all shot in the state, garnering the state the nickname as the home of "Hollywood South."[187] The state has also hosted reinvigorated filming of Louisiana-related history such as *12 Years a Slave,* as well as television shows that look at Louisiana life like *Duck Dynasty* and *Swamp People*. While these shows did not focus on Katrina, they were shaped by its results and featured episodes connecting their content and cast members to it, even years after the storm had passed, further enforcing the cultural impact of the storm as a marker for the city, state, region, and nation. Coverage of Katrina relief efforts continued to draw interest to New Orleans in the ten years following the storm as recovery is constantly reassessed.

Katrina-related cultural productions expanded in the form of literature, too.[188] As of 2017, there were 2,501 books available for purchase on Amazon.com and over 25.4 million links accessible in a Google.com search on "Hurricane Katrina." Meanwhile, academics are also participating in this cultural production, producing roughly 47,300 peer-reviewed academic articles on the subject. And these numbers only continue to grow.[189]

Overall, music, television shows, literature, art, and cultural productions allowed consumers to make sense of the Katrina disaster through creative expression. These also provided an opportunity for vicarious immersion in the disaster through imagination. These cultural productions drove interest in other aspects of Katrina-related consumption such as disaster objects and experiential opportunities like tours, continuing in relevance through to today. More importantly, the multifariousness of products in the Katrina economy made a variety of narratives visible, and the Web 2.0 platforms gave rise to new possibilities for disaster products. They were marketed via blogs and social media, bought and sold through e-commerce websites, and permeated and drove discourse of the storm's recovery. They have also shaped the perception of the storm as not just a storm, but an experience. Thus, by looking at the products it is possible to see how Katrina was narrated over time, the fissures that were focused on, the contradictions and critiques that appear as subjects of the items, and the dichotomy of old and new forms of media that play a role in Katrina's construction.

There Is No Such Thing as a Natural Disaster: (Re)defining Disaster since Katrina

One of the subsequent results of the in-depth discussion of Katrina's construction was the amplification of interest in the differences between Americans' understandings of natural hazards versus disasters, and the human role in their causes. As Americans wrestled with the complexity of Katrina (its size and radius), the messy response (in an era of federal systems of relief), and its continued impact (even a decade post-storm), they continued to reevaluate what they considered a "normal" disaster, particularly through the use of gendered rhetoric.[190]

Americans' conventional definition of a disaster prior to Katrina frequently described the cause of catastrophes as resulting from either "natural" or "man-made" hazards. This was an easy way to rationalize causes of incidents perceived as preventable or not. Unfortunately, as scholars like Gilbert F. White, Ted Steinberg, and Greg Bankoff are quick to point out, the definition of a "natural disaster" does not account for the fact that all disasters are a result of human behavior.[191] They are junctures of natural and anthropogenic hazards and human (in)action. Most importantly, disasters are only defined as disasters when we choose to label them as such. While this is reasserted in the evolving disaster relief legislation defining major disasters and emergencies, the phrase "natural disaster" persists in popular discourse, particularly in print and online.[192]

The American public got a crash course in disaster history and this particular turn of phrase in 2005 when pundits, scientists, meteorologists, and the courts all tried to make sense of the catastrophe that was Katrina.[193] As explained in detail on blogs, in newspaper articles, on television, and even later in consumable products like wall calendars, T-shirts, music, and literature, Katrina was not a "natural disaster" because "there is no such thing as a natural disaster." Disasters are, according to the authors of one post-Katrina era book, "socially constructed events which are influenced by demographic and socio-economic characteristics, social and cultural norms, prejudices and values."[194] Katrina was tangible proof of this definition. As reiterated across multiple platforms post-2005, there was no backing away from the idea that there was human influence in all factors of the storm and reaction to it. Americans had altered their landscapes, natural world, and perception of vulnerability to their detriment, and all of these things had led up to the incident known as Katrina. And worse yet, as concluded by studies done on the causes for Katrina and everything that it entailed, more Katrinas were likely to happen in the future as a multitude of factors made Americans more susceptible in the twenty-first century.[195] The result was that Katrina was the first of a new era of storms, a Hurricane 2.0 that is representative of the renegotiation of the popularized definition of disaster and the public's impression of the impact it could cause.

The jumbled terminology used to describe Katrina serves as clear evidence of the ongoing redefinition of what a modern disaster as a result of reaction to a hurricane looks like. As shown in representations presented in old and new media, Katrina was both hypermasculine and hyperfeminine, a dichotomized blending of historically separate masculine and feminine descriptors of past storms. It also had notably new descriptors that represented racially and socioeconomically charged themes emerging from the aftermath of the storm.

Thus Katrina set a standard for modern hurricane construction. With every major hurricane since 2005, the public has asked whether it could be the "next Katrina," topping the storm in terms of damage and destruction.[196] And as with Katrina, these later storms were described using hypersexualized, gendered terms that recall the rhetoric established with Katrina as well as additional elements that suggest race- and class-based rhetoric. Finally, because of Katrina, storms are now talked about in a larger and more totalizing way, using gender as a mechanism to highlight difference, by more people, for longer periods of time, long after a storm has impacted a region. The unprecedented culture of participation that grew around Katrina—due to the storm's size and destructiveness, as well as the emergence of Internet-facilitated communication—has become the expected norm. This is readily seen in the communications around the later storms Gustav and Ike (2008),

Irene (2011), and Sandy (2012), and even most recently, Harvey, Irma, and Maria (2017).

The first major post-Katrina threat to New Orleans came in 2008, as Hurricane Gustav veered directly towards New Orleans, threatening a still-vulnerable city. New Orleans mayor Ray Nagin declared in a press conference in the days before impact that Gustav would be the "Mother of All Storms," perhaps an odd choice of words given the male name the storm was assigned. Sources were awash with "apocalyptic predictions" for the storm, anticipating it was bigger and badder than Katrina.[197] This dread was partly attributable to its male name, as there is historic precedent for the perception of male-named storms being more severe than female-named storms. Images of Gustav in coverage before the storm made landfall emphasize this belief, such as in a cartoon from the *Mobile Press-Register* that clearly anthropomorphizes it as a masculine male, with strong muscles, a massive beard, and angry countenance. Whereas illustrations of Katrina had displayed a vindictive or negligent woman, Gustav was presented as a man in charge who knew what he was doing. In the *Press-Register* depiction, Gustav appears as a juggling titan, controlling the deeper politics of the 2008 GOP convention. This imagery was reconfirmed as politicians sought to address not only the current threat to the coast, but how it would impact the recovering region and shape politics of the future. (See figure 17.)

As with previous storms, the fierce, strongly masculine gendering of Gustav in rhetoric and visual representations was contingent upon the strength of the storm. When Gustav dissipated at the last minute at landfall, causing lesser damage to the region than Katrina and disappointing reporters who were ready for the "next Katrina," the characterizations of Gustav immediately shifted. In place of the masculine descriptions, Gustav was described as an effeminate, even homosexual male. The storm made an "impotent" strike at Louisiana with a "bark worse than its bite," claimed one article.[198] The storm, "weaker" in comparison to Katrina, "galloped ashore," stated another.[199] Even jokes about Gustav's appearance during Southern Decadence, the LGBTQ festival held in New Orleans, also made newspapers throughout the country.[200] One comedian even proposed that Gustav might be the first "Gay Hurricane" because of its appearance during the celebratory weekend.[201] Online bloggers also discussed Gustav's impact on Southern Decadence; one, in particular, declared that the Southern Decadence

Figure 17. "Gustav and the GOP Convention," *Mobile Press-Register,* August 31, 2008. JD Crowe, *Mobile Press-Register*/AL.com.

festival had been "tied up, flogged and topped by Gustav."[202] The shift in rhetoric to emasculate or effeminize Gustav following its change in strength follows a well-known pattern of feminizing male storms with disappointing conclusions (for example, Georges in 1998). But in this instance, there was no subtle rhetoric that backpedaled slowly from masculine descriptors. Instead, there was a direct alteration of language to describe the hurricane as "gay" or sexually impotent. The use of these phrases was an extension of the hypersexualized storms of the post-Katrina Hurricane 2.0 era.

The week after Gustav's unsatisfactory show in New Orleans, a similar pattern of hypersexualization was used with Hurricane Ike, which struck Galveston, Texas.[203] Reporters described Ike as a devastating, "infinite monster" or "menace" to the Texas island, all terms associated with male storms of the past.[204] Unlike Gustav, its impact was profound, wiping out Galveston and leaving roughly $6 billion in damages.[205] Still, it was "no Katrina" regarding response, reaction, or even relief efforts. The story of Ike's impact soon faded into the background as it was considered less of a nationwide disaster and more of a regional or city-specific storm due to its singular-state effect. Despite this, the coverage of hurricanes Gustav and Ike reinforced the idea that the Gulf South was still the place to look for mega-storm development.

In 2011, Hurricane Irene became the media-proclaimed "next Katrina" due to its size and potential impact. It traveled up the eastern United States in August, striking North Carolina's Outer Banks. The fact that Irene was a female-named storm played a direct role in the discussion of it, particularly as a new medium of social communication was gaining traction: "Twitter." The platform debuted in 2006, but had grown in use steadily since. One of the unique forms of Twitter communication was the ability to tag various tweets with similar content using a "hashtag." This allowed messages about the same subject to be searchable to broad networks of people. For hurricane communication, Twitter connected those experiencing the event live with the same features of privatized social media feeds, but in a public space. Thus, it quickly became an avenue to produce, post, and share content related to the storm. One of the unique ways Twitter was used during Hurricane Irene was through the creation of a Twitter account or "feed" for the storm itself. The Twitter feed for @HurricaneIrene told viewers that "she" was "the meanest bitch to hit the Jersey Shore," a reference to the opening of a popular MTV television show *The Jersey Shore* which is set on the Jersey seashore, and connected stories about Irene's impact as other users tagged the feed or used #HurricaneIrene or #Irene in posts with photos, videos, and news. Other, similar Twitter feeds developed such as @Irene_Bitch, also featuring reference to familiar attachments of the word "bitch" to hurricanes.[206] Additionally, Twitter's platform allowed for instantaneous commentary on hurricanes that was available publicly in short bursts usually known for pithy rebuttal.[207] Notable celebrities like Kirstie Alley, Piers Morgan, Steve Martin, and Rainn Wilson all tweeted messages on the platform during the storm that described Irene as either a "bitch" or a woman.[208]

In 2012, Hurricane Sandy devastated the Northeast, particularly New Jersey, again. As with Hurricanes Katrina and Irene, Sandy was referred to by traditional feminine descriptors used with past storms as well as Katrina-related descriptors, like "bitch."[209] Notably, though, due to its unisex name, discussion of the storm initially centered on whether it was a male

KATRINA AND HURRICANE 2.0

or female storm. Reporters quickly reviewed the hurricane-naming list for the year, concluding that indeed Sandy was meant to be a female-named storm as it had come after male-named "Rafael."[210] Once confirmed as a female-named storm, creative examples poured in representing its movements as linked to its gender assignment. One example is an illustration of a hurricane-tracking map showing Hurricane Sandy as a character from the movie *Grease*. Like Sandy in *Grease*, the hurricane was illustrated as "maturing" to become a more sexualized and "bad" woman as it neared the coastline. By the end, the new Sandy was a chain-smoking hypersexualized creature wearing blown-out feather-cut hair and spandex, ready for action. The image, while produced by artist Todd Hale, appeared on the *Huffington Post*'s website, TWC, and Bravo television's *Watch What Happens Live with Andy Cohen* show, to name a few places.[211] The use of storm artwork created by news sources illustrates the interplay of old and new forms of media where the cultural construction of a hypersexualized hurricane in the Hurricane 2.0 era is a participatory phenomenon.

Consumer items related to Hurricane Sandy also appeared for sale after the storm. In New Orleans, a T-shirt representative of the same style used with Katrina ("NOLA>Hurricane") appeared with the slogan, "NJ>Hurricane."[212] Another T-shirt for sale at CONSURV, a website selling products dedicated to raising awareness about conservation, had a more sexually explicit phrase, "Sandy's A B*tch."[213] While not as explicit as the New Orleans Katrina versions, using an asterisk in the place of an "i," the sentiment remained the same.

In addition to imagery and kitsch depicting Sandy as a hypersexualized "bitch," Sandy was also referred to as something else—a "Superstorm," because it was both a post-tropical winter storm and a hurricane (arising from a Fujiwara effect). This definition was used predominantly by several media outlets and governmental agencies to distinguish the storm from others of the past, creating the impression that it was worse than Katrina, or at least different. As described by Weather 2000 Inc., a weather-forecasting company in New York, it was a "Frankenstorm," a "monstrous" nor'easter that was only preceded by two other events in hurricane history (and expected to surpass both): the Great Gale of 1878 and Hurricane Hazel in 1954.[214] While "Frankenstorm" would not stick as a label after Sandy struck, the term "Superstorm" would. In its repeated use, multiple platforms, both new and old, explained that "Superstorm" was meant to imply that this was evidence of a new type of storm that was caused by climate change, a blend of all current scares related to hurricanes since Katrina. The term was quickly refuted by others like *Popular Science,* who referred to it as an "imaginary scare-term that exists exclusively for shock value."[215] However, its use was clear: it was meant to separate storms from the legacy of Katrina.

Despite descriptive attempts to separate Superstorm Sandy in popular rhetoric, through mentions of it as the deadliest and costliest storm since Katrina (with 24 of 50 states affected), it did not surpass Katrina in its cultural impact.[216] What Sandy did do, though, was force changes in two areas. First, reporting difficulties related to Sandy caused the National Weather Service to announce that following seasons' hurricane names would be used for longer periods of time, including when a storm became "post-tropical" and "when such a storm poses a significant threat to life and property." This meant that, in all National Hurricane Center advisories, a hurricane like Sandy, once given a name, would retain it until it had dissipated completely and even afterwards if its subsequent effects (like snow) might affect people.

Secondly, Sandy propelled Twitter to become the new "go-to platform for many in an emergency or crisis," in the United States. In the span of five days during the storm, over 20 million tweets were posted on Twitter, nearly twice the usage of the platform in the two days before. According to the Pew Research Center, 34 percent of these tweets discussed the storm, sharing eyewitness accounts, information about governmental relief organizations, and news from news sources or others using the platform. The abrupt increase in the number of tweets also led to complications in the sharing of misinformation as reports of flooding in places like the New York Stock Exchange were retweeted by thousands, even though it was grossly untrue. Imagery also falsely depicted the Statue of Liberty under siege by waves of Sandy's surf, sharks swimming in the streets of New Jersey, and a McDonald's underwater, provoking fear and then humor as it was revealed the images were fake.[217] Also of note in the Pew Center's study of Sandy commentary on Twitter was the roughly 15 percent of tweets that were jokes about the storm and reaction to it, 8 percent on political discourse, and 5 percent of tweets that expressed excitement over the storm.[218] Like past hurricane commentary, many of these joke-themed tweets were references to the gender of the storm, including references to it as a "bitch." One journalist in particular, Jill Filipovic, called out this growing trend of the use of the word "bitch" to describe hurricanes in an opinion piece entitled, "Stop Calling Sandy a Bitch: It Was a Storm, Not a Woman to Hate." Citing instances of references to Sandy as a "whore," providing a "real good" blowjob, and acting as the "most important woman in the swing states" (a reference to the on-going election cycle), Filipovic pointed out that "anthropomorphizing hurricanes helps us master our fear, but [it] often [does so] at the cost of perpetuating fantasies of violent retribution against women." While the piece was shared countless times on social media such as Twitter, and received over 200 comments on the *Guardian*'s forum, the word "bitch" as associated with hypersexualization of female hurricanes persisted.[219]

Responding to interest garnered by the number of tweets and the stories of misinformation that circulated in these tweets, though, Twitter announced the following year that it was implementing a new emergency response feature known as "Twitter Alerts." As described in its press release, Twitter Alerts help "users get important and accurate information from credible organizations during emergencies, natural disasters or moments when other communications services aren't accessible." The alerts appear differently in the timeline of Twitter—using an orange warning-bell symbol—and would help emergency organizations get the word out about a disaster during the incident, appearing with precedence over the flood of tweets produced about a disaster. It would also help filter out content that was not verifiable.[220]

Following the development of the Twitter Alert system, another social media giant introduced its own platform to assist in emergency response. On October 15, 2014, Facebook announced that it would provide the option for users to mark themselves safe during an emergency using a specialized widget that would appear at the top of their main timeline. This program, known as "Safety Check," was only available during a major incident and would immediately broadcast to everyone in each user's social network that users had marked themselves as "safe." Initially, Safety Check was only activated if the Facebook team had identified the event as important enough for a mass Safety Check activation. As a result, in 2015, only four Safety Check activations were deployed. First, during the Nepal earthquake in April, next with Pacific Hurricane Patricia in October, then during the Paris attacks in November, and finally, in March 2016 during the explosions at the Brussels train station. One of the benefits of Safety Check was that users did not need to text, call, or message with their family and friends to assure them of their safety; they simply clicked "safe" in the app, and the message appeared to all of their friends on Facebook. In this way, Facebook's Safety Check attempted to fix problems that arose with Hurricane Katrina when cell towers and networks went down while mass evacuations and rescues were taking place.[221] Following the successful activation of Safety Check with these four incidents, in June 2016 Facebook announced that it had started allowing community-activated Safety Checks. This meant that, if enough people posted on Facebook about an event in their community as an "incident," a Safety Check activated for that community. Safety Checks were as much a participatory activity as a practical necessity, quickly growing in application as more people turned to the Internet as one of their first sources of information during an emergency, no matter their location.

Recognizing the popularity of Safety Check and the increasing number of people using it to connect with those affected by disasters, in February 2017 Facebook introduced the "Community Help" feature to connect providers of relief services with those that need assistance, using the Facebook Messenger app.[222] The Community Help feature provided a way to start fundraisers online and ask for donation assistance. It also expanded on unofficial sources of community-led assistance networks that started to emerge through the use of Facebook profiles. For example, the "Cajun Navy," a group of community volunteers that formed during the 2016 Louisiana floods, used Facebook as their official source of communication to organize boats, volunteers, and resources to assist those stuck in their homes due to an unexpected rain event.[223] The Cajun Navy's inspiration was primarily based on reaction to Hurricane Katrina, where slowed federal relief response had a grievous effect on the flooded population. During the response, interested volunteers viewed the Facebook page for the organization for information on where to gather and how best to assist. Facebook's new Community Help feature (debuting the following spring) built on the fact that Americans had adapted social media post-Katrina to assist with these unofficial and official relief efforts by broadening the scope of these organizations and connecting others offering relief efforts.[224]

The most recent addition to Facebook's disaster relief assistance network appeared on August 21, 2017. On this date, Facebook relabeled its popular Safety Check feature as "Crisis Response" and removed the need for community activism to mark oneself safe from a disaster.[225] The new Crisis Response feature is available at all times, with or without a recognized incident, and allows individuals to mark themselves as safe from any crisis the person deems critical. Individuals can name their incident, broadcast their safety level, and post updates. Once an incident is created, or "named," other individuals interacting with the platform can add their content, too. As described in the introductory press release for Crisis Response, this dedicated tab allows users greater ability to assure others of their safety and, combined with Community Help, connect with critical resources once they are available.[226] Declaring a crisis is now solely controlled by the individual online, marking a significant change in the Hurricane 2.0 era. However, the official designation as a disaster, funding relief, and even processes of response are not individually controlled and are still reliant on federal recognition.

The 2017 hurricane season brought three new examples of the continuing impact of Katrina's legacy and the influence of social media on the perception of storms post-Katrina. The first, Hurricane Harvey, was described en masse as "historic," an "unprecedented crisis," or the "worst storm/hurricane they have ever seen."[227] This was visually confirmed because "Harvey forced the National Weather Service" to add two new colors to its maps to indicate the severity of rainfall in areas like Houston.[228] Meanwhile, Hurricanes Irma and Maria were initially relegated to being called "bitches," both as a way of diminishing their effects and describing their difference from the "historic" male-named storm of the season. Hurricane Maria (not to be confused in pronunciation with George R. Stewart's beloved Maria), was even proclaimed by President Donald Trump to be "not a real catastrophe" in the same way Katrina was.[229] These references quickly caused a social media stir as online commentators, reporters, and governmental officials tried to unpack the discourse of storm stories as they emerged and compare it to the all-encompassing hurricane, Katrina. Discussion focused on whether each storm would wreak the same amount of havoc on a region as Katrina, whether response efforts functioned properly, and whether rebuilding assistance was provided in each of the regions affected. Through all of this, reporters, commentators, and government officials used language of the Hurricane 2.0 era. This included using adjectives associated with gender-specific storms of the past; discussing all three storms' impact on various populations, with particular attention to historic issues of race and class; and the multiplicity of discourses in the millions of tweets appearing as Americans discussed the storms and reconciled them with Katrina.

Social media response during Hurricanes Harvey and Maria, for instance, drew attention because of these connections with Katrina and the evolution of social media disaster relief applications since 2005.[230] Across platforms, many individuals connected events like the historic flood of a major US city, critiqued official response (or lack thereof) through lenses of race and class-based bias, speculated on the total cost of the season as each major storm added up, asked who was to blame for the disasters unfolding, produced content or products from kitsch to music geared at commemorating the events or supporting the victims, and followed live streams of those experiencing the hurricanes.[231] On Twitter, over 7 million tweets appeared about Harvey, with more following about subsequent storms Irma and Maria.[232] On Facebook, the Crisis Response and Community Help features played a new role in response to Houston's flooding. Many used the Crisis Response feature to mark themselves "not safe" or to post their location for rescue by groups like the Cajun Navy. Others shared a database known as CrowdSource Rescue that allowed users to input rescue request information or view those who needed assistance.[233] Meanwhile, others used the Community Help feature to connect thousands with aid organizations. As a result, *Time* magazine labeled Hurricane Harvey the "first social media storm" because not only were a large number of people interacting on various platforms in a multitude of ways, but they were also asking for help during an event via the platforms.[234]

The label of Harvey as the "first social media storm" is interesting when considering the historical implications of Katrina. In some ways, *Time* magazine is correct in assigning this label as the features available on social media and the number of people connected through these elements has expanded dramatically from the initial blogs, vlogs, and social media content available in 2005. It is also correct in terms of the number of people seeking assistance using these new platforms, thus shaping the response to the storm live. However, this grossly underplays the role of Katrina as a new type of storm—the first Internet storm—and the role of social media in the construction of storms between Katrina and Harvey, which was one facet of what made it *Hurricane 2.0*. Victims of Katrina sought help using new forms of social media, posting pictures of their experiences, producing art or consumable products from it, and interacting with the discourse online regarding their experiences.

The ultimate effect of Katrina (the storm) and Katrina (the disaster) then is that it effectively broadened what a modern hurricane looks like, creating a new type of storm: a Hurricane 2.0. The Hurricane 2.0 encourages participation in hurricane cultural construction, including room for people to debate what the hurricane means. As a result, everyone can decide what the hurricane means to them and critique others' meanings that complicate their own understanding. The resulting explosion of forums to discuss and present these meanings has subsequently resulted in marginalized voices gaining more notice than ever before, so much so that they even get picked up in more established media and repeated. It has also resulted in the continued attachment of gender-specific terminology and imagery to describe these storms. With more people participating, the content production, productization, and consumption of these gendered narratives are spreading rapidly, and not just in newspaper text. As a result, the Hurricane 2.0 is a hypersexualized storm from the beginning through years after the aftermath, affecting not only the perception of the storm, but the victims, region, politics, and understanding of comparative incidents.

Of greatest importance in the Hurricane 2.0 era are the places where this discussion takes place, the number of people who participate in it, and the length of time considered to be part of a storm. In newspapers, this has resulted in the continued use of, and even rise in, gender-specific terminology to describe hurricanes since the turn of the century. (See figure 18.)

As important as the review of gender use in newspapers is to tracking the number of individuals participating in and consuming the modern constructions of Hurricane 2.0, also significant is the role of other media. In 2017, the Weather Channel was received by 70 million households in the United States, and at any given moment, has a viewership of nearly 200,000 Americans.[235] When storms like Maria or Harvey occur, channels like TWC, Fox, and CNN receive over 2 million prime-time viewers as the nation tunes in to see the exciting drama as a post-Katrina hurricane unfolds. Similarly, Facebook and YouTube platforms now allow individuals to live-stream public events and users to comment at the same time using a variety of emojis, voting up or down, and asking questions directly of the broadcaster. At the

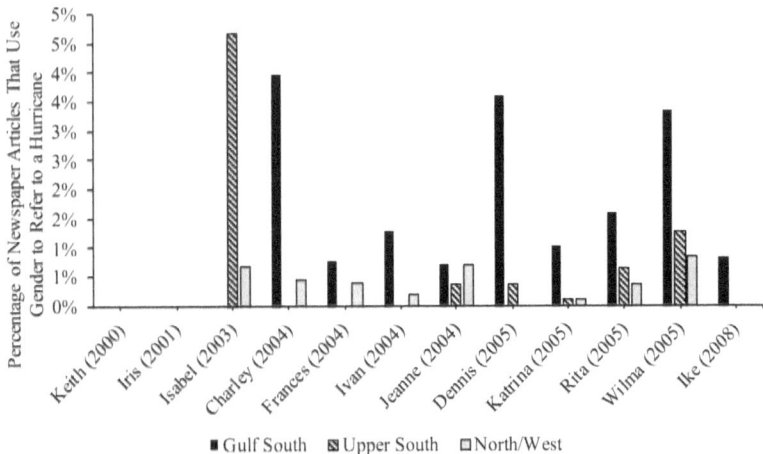

Figure 18. Percentage of newspaper articles that use gender to refer to a hurricane, by region, 2000–2008. Since 2000, the use of gender to describe hurricanes rose in print newspapers, reflecting larger trends in use on social media, television, in consumable products, and in popular discourse as Americans reacted to the particularly devastating storm seasons of 2003, 2004, and 2005.

Sources: Measured using qualitative data analysis of 12 US newspapers' articles from 5-day periods for 10 major storms between 2000 and 2008 ($n = 4,479$).

same time, more than ever, there are a variety of new platforms Americans can receive and interact with weather-related content. A number of apps are available to track and interact with weather information today. According to 42 Matters, a company focused on providing data on digital application use, Apple's App Store and Google Play list 6,127 apps related to the "weather." This includes over 1,000 paid apps.[236] While some are provided by known companies or organizations like NOAA, TWC, Weather Underground, and even FEMA, others are not. All, however, provide a variety of detailed weather maps, data, and reaction to the environment of the every day. With cell phone technology advancements, these apps are available on mobile devices instantly and provide a variety of commentary (and critique) about weather-relevant news or experiences. Many of these build on government-run emergency alert systems, relying on data from the National Weather Service (such as hurricane watches and warnings) and federal emergency management authorities (like FEMA or state programs). As a result, the names and information used by these organizations dictates initial impressions of their use, but are altered afterwards as these apps seek to add their own data or "spin" to the content. Similarly, the content of these apps and alert systems can also report inaccurate information to many instantly, such as the falsely reported nuclear threat to Hawaii in January 2018.[237]

Judging from recent storms and developments in media (both old and new), Americans are consuming, producing, and shaping the understanding of hurricanes in the post-Katrina era. The Hurricane 2.0 as initiated and evidenced by Katrina now means a disaster caused by the combination of natural and man-made forces, one that is all-encompassing, took years to come to fruition and years to recover from, and includes complexities of American historical impressions of race, class, and gender that all ripple to the forefront as the storm unfolds. Similarly, it represents a sum of all of our fears—environmental, cultural, and political—and a combination of all of our parts—local, regional, and national—defined by new and old forms of media, and most importantly, by those experiencing it. These new cultural constructions of hurricanes and the places where they are constructed prove that interest in hurricanes is only expanding in the twenty-first century. While much has changed in the post-Katrina Hurricane 2.0 era, one facet remains the same: we still give hurricanes names.

6

TEMPEST
ASSESSING CURRENT CONDITIONS

Maria. Camille. Roxcy. Andrew. Katrina. For generations these names have taken us back to a time and place, echoing in our heads like people we have known. Yet even with these vivid memories from our past, we still wonder about their origin every June when a new list of names floats ominously into our consciousness while we count the days until the "next Big One" strikes. The uncertainty of their outcome both scares and thrills, encouraging us to create dramatic stories of the possibilities of their impact. It is as if tempting fate is somehow mitigated by giving it a name. But the larger question emerging in these origin inquiries is not just *why* we name hurricanes, but *what is the effect* of these names? This question percolated in the background of naming history in tandem with origin stories, rising to the forefront at different periods as Americans reassessed the naming system. And it is again making headlines today.

To consider the consequences of the naming system, it is necessary to review several issues. First, what was the original motivation for adopting the naming system, and how did the system change over time? Second, what does current research on hurricane names tell us about the naming system's effects? And, relatedly, why do we vehemently defend the naming system's use today? Finally, is the hurricane-naming system still needed, or should we consider adapting or abolishing it?

Regarding the first question—what was the original motivation for adopting the naming system, and how did the system change over time?—when the gendered naming process was introduced in 1953, its original goals were to:

1. Effectively *identify or label storms* for the purpose of public warning;

2. *Indicate a level of severity*, as met by the attachment of a name once a storm reached a certain threshold (wind speed);

3. *Promote brevity and clarity* in communicated information across regions and cultures under the purview of the US Weather Bureau, and later the World Meteorological Organization, throughout the course of a storm's development;

4. *Provide a replenishable source of names* different from those of the past to dissuade cultural confusion.

Over a half-century, Americans questioned the naming system due to various concerns. In reaction to this discourse, hurricane naming changed. This included the alteration of the naming system to:

1. *Standardize the practice of use* to account for the development of new forms of media and discourse;

2. *Introduce male names* to naming lists to correct gender inequity;

3. *Refine levels of severity* through the introduction of parallel but numerically named categories of wind speeds to work in tandem with gendered nomenclature;

4. *Retire hurricane names* of culturally significant storms;

5. *Remove names* that implied additional cultural meanings (such as an association with political, cultural, or historical figures);

6. *Use names as a mechanism to define national disasters* through presidential declaration;

7. *Extend the length of time a name is applied* to warn of continued post-tropical effects.

As a result, the gendered hurricane-naming system in use today is a result of our changing understanding of nature, definition of disaster, and cultural norms of the period—which is also why it is under fire today. As we debate larger issues related to sexism and gender in American society, the role of the uncontrollable natural world, and our evolving forms of social interaction, we are again debating the merits of a naming system that represents a conglomeration of all of these issues. In the same light, it is also easy to understand why many desire to keep the system in place. The current hurricane-naming system took years to construct and was adapted to meet needs in the past, leaving little reason to think it cannot change to meet the needs of the future.

In the last seven years, hurricane naming became a hotbed of debate as new issues emerged with its use. The first wave of discussion appeared in 2012 with the introduction of Hurricane Sandy as a "superstorm." This term provoked questions about the method used to identify the strength and length of named storms. With Sandy, much of the discussion centered on the idea that the storm was not a "typical" tropical system, but instead caused a mass post-tropical cyclone with winter-storm conditions and hurricane-force winds drawn from horizontal temperatures (like cold fronts) rather than ocean water that distinguished it from the regular hurricane.[1] In reports, Sandy's extenuating effects long after its name had "expired" due to its post-tropical status drew attention to the process of hurricane naming.[2] Many wondered why Sandy was named but other storms like winter storms were not.[3]

The frustrations over Sandy's post-tropical impact serve as a logical connection between October 2012 and the next major wave of modern hurricane-naming discussion. This came in November 2012 when the Weather Channel announced its implementation of a new naming system for snowstorms and ice storms for 2012–13 that resembled the hurricane-naming system. TWC's winter-storm naming system used mythological figures and gods as names for storms, such as "Athena," "Dante," and "Nemo." The same day TWC announced its decision to name winter storms, the US National Weather Service issued a statement denouncing TWC's new system.[4] "The NWS does not use names of winter storms in our products. Please refrain from using the term Athena in any of our products," the statement declared.[5] The outright denial of TWC's winter-storm naming system by the National Weather Service was met with curiosity among media outlets throughout the country. Many questioned why the NWS would reject this new system, especially following discussion of the Superstorm Sandy/

Post-Tropical Cyclone with winter-storm conditions the month before. The NWS was quick to clear this issue up. According to NWS statements made in the days following, hurricanes and other tropical cyclones are the only weather forces officially named to prevent confusion in identification. All other storms (winter storms, tornados, floods, earthquakes) do not have names attached in issued warning bulletins. In the case of Superstorm Sandy, a name was attached because it was a hurricane first. In this way Sandy was akin to those of that writer turned meteorological legend, George Stewart, and his beloved Maria, which was, in fact, a hurricane-turned-post-tropical system that wrought winter-storm-like conditions. The NWS response did little to stop TWC's use of the winter-storm naming system, though. During the 2012–13 winter season, TWC covered storms by using their new naming system to identify otherwise labeled "winter storms," rolling out graphics and highlighting public participation in use of the naming system. As memes and gifs of winter storms Dante and Nemo floated around the Internet, it was clear that TWC's winter-storm naming system did what it was intended to do: draw attention to TWC weather coverage and increase public interest in the controversial system.[6] Unsurprisingly due to public interest, other news networks used the TWC names, sometimes clearly identifying it as controversial system and other times presenting the names as standard practice.[7] Due to the popularity of the winter-storm naming system, TWC announced continuation of it in the future, despite the NWS position.[8]

It is interesting that TWC's winter-storm naming system drew such a vituperative response from the NWS, especially considering that it used names selected from a historical system. TWC's naming system used Greek or Roman gods and mythological figures reminiscent of Australian weatherman Clement Wragge's system of the past. It also marked a growing trend since 2010 in the popular labeling of snowstorms by TWC and other media as "snowmageddon," "snowpocalypse," and "snowicane." These labels, much like "superstorm," drew attention to blizzards and winter storms like hurricanes.[9] Despite similarities, the NWS did not budge on their position to reject TWC's naming system. As the 2013 TWC-named winter season rolled to a close and the NWS officially named hurricane season began, the NWS did make one change to its hurricane-naming policy, though, broadening the length of time a hurricane name could be used to describe a storm to include the "post-tropical" period, again highlighting the difference between Sandy and winter systems.

The NWS/TWC debate over names in 2012 and TWC's unapproved use of names to describe winter storms in subsequent years inspired comedic response in the press and online as many wrestled with what hurricane names meant and why they were used.[10] A popular TV sitcom, *30 Rock*, for example, spoofed the recent naming debate during its 2013 season. In the episode, a fictitious storm, "Snowicane White Lady Name Like Dorva or Something," raged towards New York City, much to the dismay of the show's characters.[11] While mocking the storm-naming debate, *30 Rock* pointed out the continued association of negative gendered attributes to storms in the post-Katrina era. In this case, winter storms, much like hurricanes, reflected gendered biases directly related to their names. (See figure 19.)

In 2014, the debate over hurricane naming again eclipsed all other news as a psychological study was published in the *Proceedings of the National Academy of Sciences of the United States of America* (*PNAS*), a leading scientific journal of biological, physical, and social sciences.[12] The study used 1,171 survey responses (from students in university classes) and individuals (who volunteered using the Amazon Mechanical Turk crowdsourcing marketplace), whereby researchers (Kiju Jung and Sharon Shavitt et al.) asked respondents questions about perceived risk and vulnerability to hur-

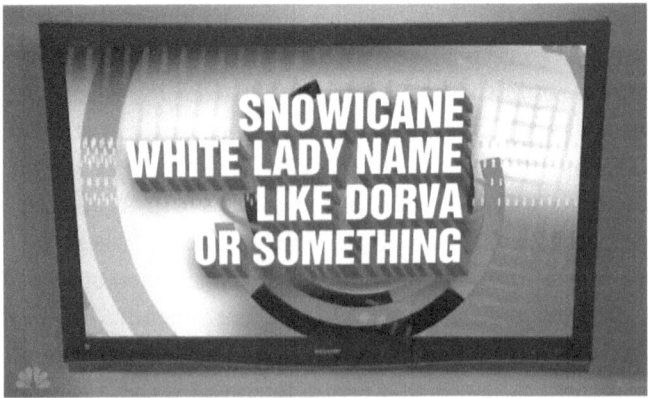

Figure 19. "Snowicane White Lady Name Like Dorva or Something." Screen grab by author from "Hogcock/Last Lunch," *30 Rock* episode that aired January 30, 2013.

ricanes based on storm names. Over the course of six survey experiments, researchers provided names of hurricanes (both male and female) from the 2014 hurricane-naming list and scenarios including varying descriptions of impact, locations, and purported size. They then asked respondents to rank their perceived vulnerability, decision to evacuate (in both mandatory and voluntary situations), and perception of the hypothetical storms. In all experiments, researchers noted an implicit bias in response to the storms: female-named storms were perceived as less deadly than male-named storms, and respondents noted that they were less inclined to evacuate for them. Following the conclusion of the surveys, researchers compared data of known evacuation rates to storm names, finding a similar correlation in historical death tolls and damage related to female-named storms versus those designated by male names. They correlated this research with other studies on risk and disaster, gendered bias and names, and this author's preliminary research on the impact of gendered hurricane names in media description and popular culture. As a result, they published their study under the title "Female Hurricanes Are Deadlier than Male Hurricanes."[13]

The study's results circulated widely in newspapers, on social media, and on air via pundits with every major news network in the country.[14] Over the next week, the psychology of human behavior during hurricanes was the focus of debate across much of the nation. Many emphatically defended the hurricane-naming system, proclaiming that the names provided adequate techniques to identify and describe storms, even with applied gendered bias.[15] Others claimed that the study itself was flawed, citing the number of participants, hypothetical nature, and changes in historical patterns of evacuation.[16] For example, as suggested, the population surveyed was not representative of those living in hurricane-prone regions like the Gulf South in the post-Katrina era.[17] The study even became the focus of several scholarly response papers in *PNAS* and other media, refuting the results.[18] Not backing down from their conclusions, Jung and Shavitt issued rebuttals to these response papers.[19]

In reviewing the reaction to the Jung and Shavitt article, the extreme response is not surprising.[20] The study had prodded a deeply entrenched custom with results that illuminated the system's potential malfunction, suggesting that humans were naturally inclined to respond in an inherently biased way based on a gendered name. It is also not surprising that defense of the naming system through rebuttal struck at the heart of scientific results—by questioning the methodology that was behind the study's conclusions. The response to Jung and Shavitt reveals that it is much easier to rationalize that the flaw in the results lies not with the names themselves, but in the types of people or number of people studied. This study revealed a central fallacy of what Americans have long sought to argue either does not exist or has been mitigated by efforts to equalize gendered associations.

Since the Jung and Shavitt study was published, I revisited my own research in order to provide a different disciplinary perspective to the question, "Does hurricane naming harm us?" As a historian, the question came up frequently as I traced the history behind the naming process and its evolution over time. To consider the impact of gendered names, I completed an exhaustive study of the descriptions of hurricanes in US newspapers. I collected newspaper articles from 12 US cities, for five-day periods of storm development, for 28 major hurricanes (defined by NOAA as the most notable storms of American past), for over 50 years (1954–2008). This included newspapers from three major regions of the United States, including the Gulf South (states bordering the Gulf of Mexico such as Texas, Louisiana, Mississippi, Alabama, and Florida), the Upper South (states further inland from the fall zone but bordering the Atlantic Seaboard such as the Carolinas, Georgia, and Virginia), and the North and West (places that statistically experience major but infrequent storms like New York, Maryland, and California). During each five-day period (including two days before landfall, the day of landfall, and two days following), I analyzed each newspaper article for the type of descriptors (nouns and adjectives) used to describe a storm, the number of times a storm was referenced as a specifically gendered object by nouns like "he/she," and the frequency at which these gendered references repeat in storm descriptions following. The database produced from this multicity newspaper study includes 8,915 articles. I supplemented this with additional newspaper research from 30 other cities (located throughout the United States, Caribbean, and Central America) to cross-check my conclusions.

This newspaper database provides concrete proof of the power of gendered descriptions in the perception of storms before, during, and after an event. It goes beyond just assuming that a few articles' consistencies represent American experience; it tracks just how closely these patterns repeat.

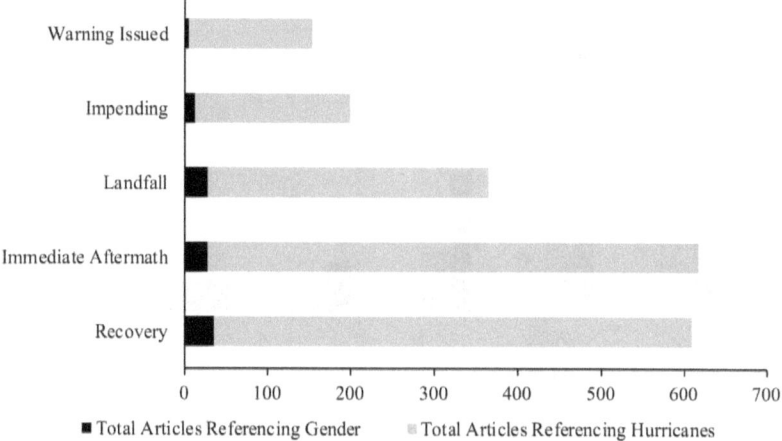

Figure 20. Gender use by day of (select) storms. Gender is utilized most frequently as a mechanism to describe a hurricane's impact and aftermath. Similarly, once gender is attached to a storm, it is more likely to be used again (in subsequent days). This perpetuates the association of gendered attributes to hurricanes throughout the event.

Sources: The five selected hurricanes are a representative sample (n = 2,575 articles) of five decades of American history and each period of hurricane-naming history, including hurricanes Carol (1954), Camille (1969), David (1979), Andrew (1992), and Katrina (2005), as selected from qualitative data analysis of newspapers from five-day periods for 28 major storms, as covered by 12 US newspapers.

Note: Day of Storm was indicated by measuring a five-day trajectory of storm impact. Day 1 is noted as "Warning Issued," Day 2 as "Impending" impact, Day 3 as "Landfall," Day 4 as "Immediate Aftermath," and Day 5 as "Recovery." For storms that had multiple "landfalls," the date of Day 3 was selected based on the most significant landfall and then applied to all newspapers nationally to correlate results.

In reviewing the data, historically, Americans are 2 percent likely to attribute gender to a hurricane within a five-day window of its impact. Within this five-day period, gender is used more frequently post-landfall than before, primarily as a mechanism to describe a storm's impact, not necessarily to warn of its danger. (See figure 20.)

While gender use in articles published about a hurricane has decreased in frequency since its introduction from an average 5 percent to today's 2 percent, it has not entirely dissipated. In fact, hurricane-prone regions like

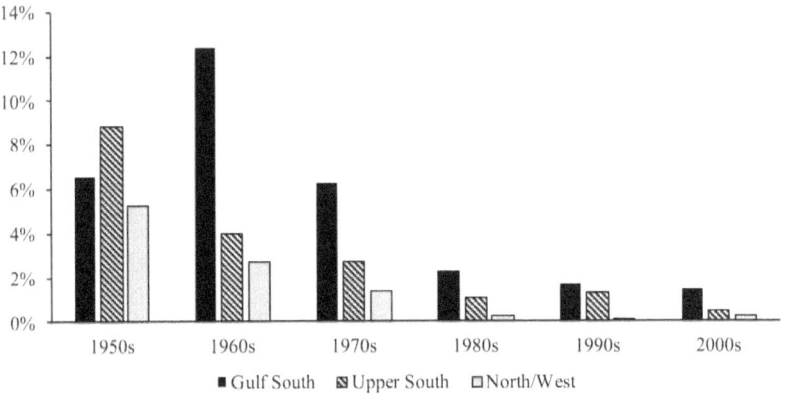

Figure 21. Percentage of newspaper articles that use gender to refer to a hurricane, by region and decade, 1954–2008. Historically, the Gulf South uses gender more frequently to describe hurricanes. However, gender is used in all regions through the twenty-first century, even those not as severely affected by repeated storms.

Sources: Measured using qualitative data analysis of newspaper articles from five-day periods for 29 major storms, as covered by 12 US newspapers ($n = 8,915$).

the Gulf South still use gender frequently to describe storms. Nationally, gender is used to describe hurricanes in all regions in the twenty-first century, even those not severely affected by repeated storms. (See figure 21.)

While a newspaper study of gender use shows significant data on the use of gender through 2008, it does not account for the development of social media and online content available since Katrina. To measure this variable, I examined the effect of social media on hurricane naming and perception in the last decade through a review of content posted on platforms like Twitter, Facebook, and blogs; completed a review of current scientific research on disaster behavior and emergency management; collected oral history interviews with scholars, weather personnel, and individuals affected by storms; and dug through countless archives to uncover the original intentions for the naming system and its evolution over time. As my research shows, the number of times a storm was gendered in the past decreased as we adopted equal-gendered names, incorporated new standards for the process of naming, and further defined the science behind hurricanes. In short, as we came to understand hurricanes better, we gendered them less—

that is, until recently. The number of platforms Americans participate in to discuss hurricanes is increasing, and with it the frequency of gender use to describe storms. While in newspapers this may appear as a slight uptick in results, these results do not adequately represent the discourse emerging on platforms such as Twitter and Facebook. These avenues inspire new forms of creativity for definitions of gendered storms and perpetuate existing descriptors.[21] This historical trend of growth has stayed consistent for the past decade, mounting each season with the increase in the number of people participating in this discourse.[22] But even with this research that clearly states that gender use is on the rise with storms, there is nothing that says this gendered naming system grossly affects the purpose of the naming system—to effectively communicate information about a tropical threat (and everything else as defined in the canon of hurricane naming). Gender bias is not enough to sway our impression that the names hold a larger significance in disaster mitigation.[23]

In 2016, another layer of this discussion emerged as a mass rain event caused approximately $8.7 billion in damages due to flooding in 56 of the 64 parishes in Louisiana.[24] The rains were caused by a "no-name storm" that did not meet the standards to be declared an official system.[25] For eight days, Louisiana was pounded by rain in areas that were least prone to storm-surge flooding, not in designated flood zones, and was sorely underwater in the end. In total, over 7 trillion gallons of water poured into the region, over three times the amount experienced during Katrina.[26] As residents in flooded regions scrambled to get out—often for the first evacuation they had ever experienced, despite having lived through multiple catastrophic storm seasons—a question emerged on the Internet about what to call this freak event. To some, it should just be called a rainstorm; but to others, it was implied that this was a perfect example of why other hazards besides hurricanes should receive names, harkening back to TWC's winter-storm naming controversy. In the year that followed, this question of an unnamed event continued to creep through articles about the Louisiana floods.[27] Most recently, the Louisiana governor, John Bel Edwards, proposed that the lack of a name for the event was one of the reasons why much-needed federal funding for relief was both slow to come immediately following and stalled well into a year later. Had the storm had a name, Edwards implied, Louisiana would have received increased federal funding and at a faster rate. Instead, the Louisiana floods received limited media attention, and thus minimal funding for relief.[28]

Edwards's rationale that naming affected federal funding is an interesting twist in the hurricane-naming saga. As implied by Edwards, the economic impact of names for disasters, or the lack thereof for everything except hurricanes, is significant, particularly if it shapes response to and relief efforts after an incident. Oral history interviews of over 100 Louisiana residents regarding their experience in the 2016 floods shows that a majority of Louisiana residents agree with their governor that the lack of a storm name affected their perception, response, and understanding of the event. (See figure 22.)

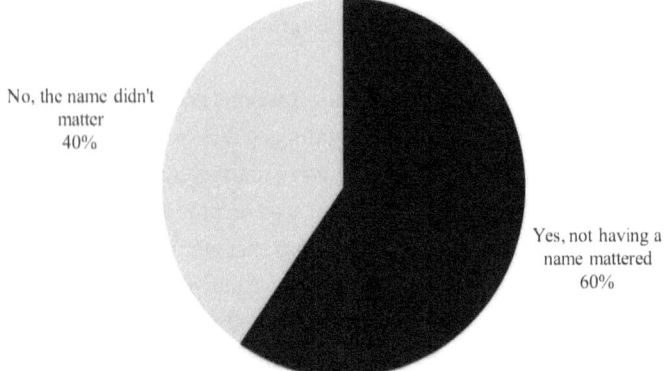

Figure 22. Perceived importance of a name in 2016 flood response. Sixty percent of Louisianans surveyed agreed with their governor that the lack of an official name for the 2016 floods affected their perception of the disaster.

Sources: Liz Skilton et al., "Recent Louisiana Disasters Oral History Project: Memories of the 2016 Floods at One-Year History Harvests," August 12, 2017 (Lafayette), August 13, 2017 (Baton Rouge), and October 21, 2017 (Denham Springs), as part of a collection at the Center for Louisiana Studies, University of Louisiana at Lafayette, and featured in Part One of the *Underwater* podcast, available August 1, 2018, at https://soundcloud.com/ulhistory. The project and podcast are part of a National Science Foundation Grant study (#1637343) measuring the effects of recent Louisiana disasters.

Note: In addition to questions about their experiences with the floods, interviewees were asked, "What do you call this event?" and "Do you think the fact that this event did not have an official name mattered?" "Yes" answers were only tallied if the respondent affirmatively answered yes, the names mattered.

ASSESSING CURRENT CONDITIONS

But still, this is conjectural, based on individuals affected by the unnamed floods. To review whether named disasters are given greater national priority than unnamed disasters, we can turn to the FEMA database on federally declared disasters, as well as the wealth of information on the process of establishing relief funding at a federal level (particularly since the introduction of the Disaster Relief Act of 1950 and the Stafford Act and its various iterations since 1988). Not so surprisingly, it all coincides with the introduction of hurricane names. The FEMA database of federally declared disasters shows that, between 2005 and 2017, hurricanes, flooding, fires, and winter and severe storms took priority in terms of presidential declarations. (See figure 23.)

On average, one in eight disasters declared by presidential order is a named disaster such as a hurricane or other tropical storm, which implies

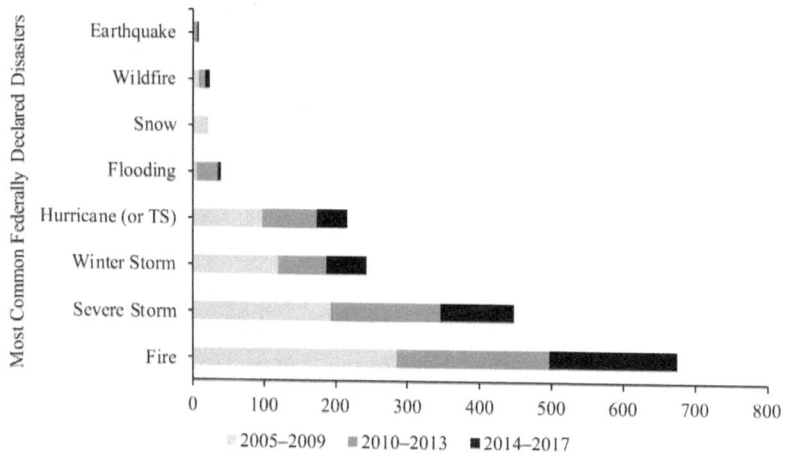

Figure 23. Most common federally declared disasters, by type and frequency, 2005–2017. Between January 1, 2005, and December 31, 2017, US presidents declared 1,650 national disasters at the request of all 50 states and some US territories. Of these, a majority were hurricanes and other tropical storms, flooding, fires, and winter and severe storms.

Source: "Disaster Declarations (by Year)," 2005–2017, FEMA.gov, last accessed April 30, 2018. Efforts were made to synthesize similar data (e.g., "flooding and mudslides" into larger causal labels such as "flooding") and to depict disasters occurring at least three separate times.

Note: TS = Tropical Storm.

TEMPEST

Figure 24. Percentage of all federally declared disasters, named vs. unnamed, 2005–2017. Of the number of federally declared named disasters (such as hurricanes and tropical storms) versus unnamed disasters (like floods, ice jams, and fires) between 2005 and 2017, roughly one in eight were "named" storms like hurricanes.

Source: "Disaster Declaration (by Year)," 2005–2017, FEMA.gov, last accessed April 30, 2018.

that named disasters receive significantly more attention and priority regarding funding. (See figure 24.)

In Gulf South states, named disasters like hurricanes make up an even larger percentage of federal declarations of "major" incidents. Of 254 federally declared incidents between 2005 and 2017, approximately one in four were named. (See figure 25.) In this light, Governor Edwards's suggestion that a name could attract attention and federal relief is probably true. There is a weighted priority towards named hurricanes and other tropical storms expressed in the declaration of federally declared disasters.

Compared to known historical data on gender use and hurricane names, roughly one in four federally declared disasters in the Gulf South is gendered by description, thereby influencing the way an incident is perceived, described, and remembered. This skews the perception of other hazards in the Gulf South as less severe than hurricanes, as gendered hurricanes are more likely to receive federal recognition than non-gendered and unnamed events. As the Gulf South leads the nation in the production, consumption, and continued use of gender to describe hurricanes throughout American history, it sets the standard for hurricane description elsewhere, perpetuat-

ASSESSING CURRENT CONDITIONS

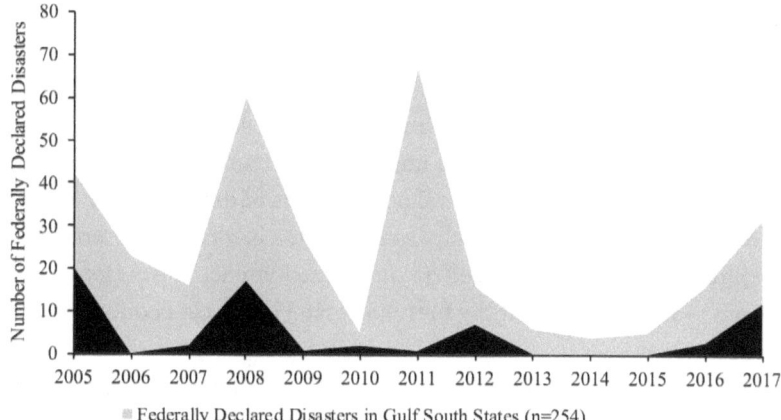

Figure 25. Federally declared disasters in the Gulf South, named and unnamed, 2005–2017. The Gulf South region experienced 254 of the total 1,650 federally declared disasters between 2005 and 2017. Of these 254 federally declared disasters, 65 were named events such as hurricanes (25.6 percent named hurricanes). Based on historical data, named disasters (hurricanes) account for one in four events in the Gulf South recognized by federal declaration as "major disasters," and thus likely described as gendered objects.

Source: "Disaster Declarations (by Year)," 2005–2017, FEMA.gov, last accessed April 30, 2018.

ing the association of gender to hurricanes and the perception of risk associated with named hazards.

The specifics of disaster relief associated with federal disaster declaration is also important data to review, but potentially harder to quantify, as it would need to include the amount of federal aid, state and local aid, and community and volunteer aid.[29] This is essential research to do in the future and should be a priority of historians to assist with as it may well hold an easy answer to the question of economic impact of hazard naming, be it hurricane or not. What I can affirmatively say based on the initial survey of FEMA data on federally declared disasters, combined with longitudinal data collected as part of my newspaper database and archival research, is that names do impact the priorities of federal relief.

Names also affect the privatized markets. Many insurance companies have policies that state that "named" disasters (like hurricanes) qualify for different levels of assistance than "unnamed" hazards such as "heavy rain events" or general "flooding."[30] They also heavily rely on federal disaster declarations and flood insurance policy to set standards regarding qualified disasters, furthering the importance of names as a mechanism to stress significance.[31] Lastly, federal designations of disasters play a role in tax relief, as individuals and businesses are often eligible for tax credits for "qualified disaster losses" based on recognized impact in a region, having an even broader impact on the national, state, and local economies of an affected area.[32]

Coinciding with this discussion of the impact of named hazards is another debate about recent policy changes related to the terminology used with climate- and coastal-change science. The concept of "climate change" is plagued by its name, and often banned from official documents.[33] The use of the term has its own history (not surprisingly also running tandem to hurricane naming), and most recently was removed from the Trump White House website and stricken from Florida state documents by Governor Rick Scott.[34] The discussion of whether climate change exists is often outweighed by the controversy over the use of the polarizing term.[35] The degree to which some Americans avoid the use of the term "climate change" brings up connected debates about the meaning behind the objects we name and the results of giving something a name in our policy debates, cultural perspectives, and even acceptance of science. The climate change–naming debate has inspired its own cry for name changes. Comedian Bill Maher commented offhandedly that the term does not sound scary enough; instead, we should call it something like "Climatica" to inspire the same amount of fear as things like hurricanes.[36] Maher's jest is funny at first, but surprisingly poignant considering the long history of debate over what to call storms and the ultimate decision to introduce gendered names as a way to inspire fear due to their godlike or anthropomorphic associations. This comment is further highlighted by recent research conducted by Yale University showing that Americans perceive the term "global warming" as more threatening than "climate change," suggesting risk-aversion biases linked with the names used.[37]

Following Hurricane Harvey in 2017, additional discussion of naming, climate change, and hurricanes emerged as Americans unpacked the meaning behind a hurricane that seemed to sit atop Texas for an inordinate amount of time, causing devastating flooding and $200 billion in damages as it deposited over 50 inches of rain over the course of 5 days.[38] This storm resulted in a revision of official colors used by the National Weather Service to delineate new levels of rain density. In addition, the 2017 hurricane season was distinguished by multiple other devastating storms that struck the entire Gulf with a ferocity not seen since Katrina, resulting in the costliest storm season in history proclaimed by some as a direct result of climate and coastal change while others argued that they were rare occurrences.[39] In both cases, all parties agreed that these storms were "Storms of the Century" and "so notorious that their names" should never be used again.[40] As one indication of the political and social content associated with the naming conventions of weather events, one political commentator responded "Shouldn't we start naming these repeated Storms-of-the-Century after key climate change deniers? Hurricane Donald. Hurricane Scott." This was in direct reference to the terminology used with the storm, the politics of climate and coastal science, and the cultural understanding of hurricanes in the Hurricane 2.0 period. Within two months, the tweet received 10,000 shares and 31,400 likes. Similarly, in the replies to the CNN commentator's tweet, many added suggested climate abusers to the list of names, such as "Hurricane Exxon" and "Hurricane BP."[41]

As the 2017 season fades in the rear-view mirror of American history, its effects linger, especially in regard to the distinction drawn in coverage of its two major storms, Harvey and Maria.[42] In storm coverage, Harvey received considerable attention from the media, president, and country, while Maria did not. In the year that followed, this fact remained the same, despite new statistics on Maria's death toll and its lingering effects on the people of Puerto Rico.[43] In memory, Harvey and Maria serve as an additional example of the continued persistence of the lopsided perception of female- versus male-named storms' impact and efforts to conform culturally specific gendered attributes to named hurricanes.

Currently, while no official review of the impact of gendered names or named hazards is under consideration, other revisions to the hurricane-naming system are. One suggested change to the hurricane-identification process is to increase the number of categories in the Saffir-Simpson Hurricane Wind Scale to include an additional category that reflects a stronger level of storm. As argued, a "Category 6" could indicate a storm the size of

Hurricane Harvey, for example, which far exceeded the range of the traditional Category 5. Serious discussion of the Category 6 level heated up when Dr. Jeff Masters, cofounder of Weather Underground, posted a blog on the subject that detailed what would constitute a Category 6 storm if the system were adopted.[44] During the 2017 hurricane season, the proposed category expansion confused the public during a crisis as it was discussed on media outlets like TWC.[45] Mistaken as fact, the concept spread so pervasively that some news stations had to issue statements assuring the public that no Category 6 actually exists by the time latter-storm Hurricane Irma formed. Others just called it part of an era of "fake news."[46]

Besides the proposed Category 6 designation, another concern raised with the Saffir-Simpson scale centers on the fact that it primarily addresses wind speed for category level.[47] While it is implied that a storm brings other factors such as rain and storm surge, these are not clearly indicated in the category level. An additional suggestion under review is the inclusion of a different or complementary scale to measure flooding, rain, or storm-surge effects.[48] As proposed, this might assist in hazard warnings for areas that do not see significant effects from wind, but do see damage or potential loss of life from flooding.[49]

In comparing this research, it is possible to see how a multidisciplinary approach both benefits and complicates the simplicity of an answer to the difficult question of whether hurricane names harm us. Psychology shows us that there is implicit bias in the names used with storms. An economic study proves that naming might have an effect on relief funding via declaration of disaster status or insurance funding doled out in the aftermath of an event. Review of current scientific research illustrates that revision is already underway or at least under discussion by a community focused on how to properly identify the evolving threats in a modern era. And a cultural study of the history of the naming system contextualizes the reasons why gender is on the rise in the attachment of storm descriptions through multiple forms of discourse and how naming matters historically to our impression of storms of the past and of the future. Historical data also points out the centrality of the Gulf South as the place to look for discourse on the naming system as its position as both the "nation's hurricane coast"—due to frequency of storms (and other hazards like climate and coastal change), and people affected (from meteorologists to feminists). The region is inte-

ASSESSING CURRENT CONDITIONS

gral to the cultural construction of hurricanes and the decision to continue the gendered hurricane-naming system.

It is clear that the social and cultural consequences of the current naming system transcend anything intended when it was first introduced. It shapes how we think, respond to, and understand hazards of all types. But has it reached a tipping point where it is outdated or out of sync with the greater good of the population? Does it still meet its original goal to effectively communicate information about hurricanes to the public in a way that outweighs negative attributes? Can we overlook or adapt the system for this flaw that has developed due to human-nature interaction? And what would an effective alternative be that would communicate threats to the public, and shape behavior toward preparedness and reaction to dangerous events in positive ways?

In the history of hurricane naming, it is easy to find examples of time periods and situations where the culture surrounding storm naming called for a change in the system. The fact that we ask *Why are hurricanes named?* every single year is significant; it means that, despite more than a half-century of use, we still debate the system's purpose. Until we stop asking this question, hurricane naming is up for reconsideration. To judge whether it is time to do this, we must complete an assessment of the naming system as a systemic practice.

In line with its original goals, the naming system positively meets the purpose of labeling or identifying storms through brevity, clarity, and a replenishable list of names. The World Meteorological Organization now constructs and regulates the list, clearly representing cultures, regions, and predominantly associated genders. A process exists for removal of names that imply larger social and cultural associations to people or past storms. Where the naming system fails, however, is in the larger meaning behind these names and what people do with them once they are assigned. This is where an adaptation of the naming system could easily happen. We could standardize the process whereby we discuss storms after they are named. This has already been done to some extent through the introduction of category levels for wind speed, but might also include a communal effort to remove gendered rhetoric associated with these names in print and in practice. We could also label storms as FEMA currently does, using a numerical ID associated with each disaster, varying only by the letters that represent its type in classification. For example, Hurricane Harvey's impact on Texas was classified by FEMA as incident DR-4332.[50] The potential for catastrophic failure of our current naming system, though, lies not where the naming system is adapting but where the system causes unknown results, or has unintended consequences. Research on storm naming's effect on our perception of other hazards or priorities given to disaster relief is critical for the future, but so is thinking about the larger cultural impacts influenced by rapidly expanding digital interaction.

It is vitally important to know the history of the naming system in order to understand the effect it has had on the way we think about storms, especially as it affects our response or reaction to them in the moment. Even if there is no intended or applied bias with a name, there are descriptors following that circulate to thousands in seconds. These descriptors impact our understanding of not only the storm of the moment, but those of the future, especially as we make decisions based on our knowledge of storms of the past. In this way, named hurricanes are the ultimate tempests because they encourage us to reminisce at moments of crisis, potentially shipwrecking us in the process.

The story of hurricane naming is not finished. Americans are still debating the merit and purpose of the gendered naming system. We are in a new period of naming history, largely shaped by the culture of the current moment. In the long and complicated history of the naming system, answering the basic question of how storms got their names reveals that these names are just as important now as they were half a century ago. Hurricane names matter. They fundamentally shape our impressions of storms, and more importantly, hazards overall—for good and bad—and for that reason alone it is time to assess their merit again.

NOTES

Introduction

1. *Living with Hurricanes: Katrina and Beyond* (New Orleans: The Presbytère, Louisiana State Museum, 2010).

2. This was as of 2007 when I first began my research. It has since been updated to include the results of my research, which was in part assisted at critical moments by the National Hurricane Center's hurricane historian, Neal Dorst.

3. See sections on tropical cyclone names (including PAGSA, Indian Ocean, and Northwest Pacific regions) by Chris Landsea and Gary Padgett in Paul V. Kislow, *Hurricanes: Background, History and Bibliography* (New York: Nova Science Publishers, Inc., 2008); discussion of naming in Raymond Arsenault, "The Public Storm: Hurricanes and the State in Twentieth-Century America," in *American Public Life and the Historical Imagination*, ed. Wendy Gamber, Michael Grossberg, and Hendrik Hartog (Notre Dame, IN: University of Notre Dame Press, 2003), 274–75; and the footnote on naming in Ted Steinberg, *Acts of God: The Unnatural History of Natural Disaster in America* (Oxford, UK: Oxford University Press, 2000), 67–68.

4. For current policies regarding tropical cyclone naming, see the World Meteorological Organization's website (last updated 2018) at public.wmo.int/en/About-us/FAQs/faqs-tropical-cyclones/tropical-cyclone-naming.

5. Carolyn Merchant, *The Death of Nature: Women, Ecology, and the Scientific Revolution* (New York: Harper & Row, 1989).

6. Barry D. Keim and Robert A. Muller, *Hurricanes of the Gulf of Mexico* (Baton Rouge: Louisiana State University Press, 2009).

7. Matthew Mulcahy, *Hurricanes and Society in the British Greater Caribbean, 1624–1783* (Baltimore: Johns Hopkins University Press, 2006); Louis Pérez, *Winds of Change: Hurricanes and the Transformation of Nineteenth-Century Cuba* (Chapel Hill: University of North Carolina Press, 2001); Stuart B. Schwartz, *Sea of Storms: A History of Hurricanes in the Greater Caribbean from Columbus to Katrina* (Princeton, NJ: Princeton University Press, 2015); Arsenault, "The Public Storm"; Steinberg, *Acts of God;* Kevin Rozario, *The Culture of Calamity: Disaster and the Making of Modern America* (Chicago: University of Chicago Press, 2007); Andy Horowitz, "*Hurricane Betsy* and the Politics of Disaster in New Orleans' Lower Ninth Ward,

1965–1967," *Journal of Southern History* 80, no. 4 (November 2014); Patricia Bellis Bixel and Elizabeth Hayes Turner, *Galveston and the 1900 Storm: Catastrophe and Catalyst* (Austin: University of Texas Press, 2000); Eleonora Rohland, *Changes in the Air: Hurricanes in New Orleans from 1718 to the Present* (New York: Berghahn Books, 2018), and "Hurricanes on the Gulf Coast: Environmental Knowledge and Science in Louisiana, the Caribbean and the U.S., 1722 and Beyond," in *Works of Nature: Global Scientific Practice in an Age of Revolutions, 1750–1850*, ed. Patrick Manning and Daniel Rood (Pittsburgh: University of Pittsburgh Press: 2016), 38–53; and Cynthia Kierner, "Awful Calamity: Sentiment, Gender, and the Nation in the Richmond Theater Fire of 1811," Southern Association of Women Historians Annual Address, Dallas, November 11, 2017.

8. Carolyn Merchant, *Ecological Revolutions: Nature, Gender, and Science in New England* (Chapel Hill: University of North Carolina Press, 1989); Elaine Tyler May, *Homeward Bound: American Families in the Cold War Era* (New York: Basic Books, 2008); Carol Bigwood, *Earth Muse: Feminism, Nature, and Art* (Philadelphia: Temple University Press, 1993); and Virginia Scharff, *Seeing Nature through Gender* (Lawrence: University Press of Kansas, 2003).

9. Greg Bankoff, "Rendering the World Unsafe: 'Vulnerability' as Western Discourse," *Disasters* 25, no. 1 (2001): 19–35; Joshua P. Howe, *Behind the Curve: Science and the Politics of Global Warming* (Seattle: University of Washington Press, 2016); Ilan Kelman, J. C. Gaillard, and Jessica Mercer, "Climate Change's Role in Disaster Risk Reduction's Future: Beyond Vulnerability and Resilience," *International Journal of Disaster Risk Science* 6 (2015): 21–27; James Fleming, *Fixing the Sky: The Checkered History of Weather and Climate Control* (New York: Columbia University Press, 2010); Joshua Blu Buhs, "The Fire Ant Wars: Nature and Science in the Pesticide Controversies of the Late Twentieth Century," *Isis* 93, no. 3 (2002): 377–400; Laura Martin, "'Eskimo Words for Snow': A Case Study in the Genesis and Decay of an Anthropological Example," *American Anthropologist* 88 (1986): 418–23; Lorraine Daston, "On the Science of Clouds," Lecture for the Max Planck Institute, Berlin, September 13, 2012, www.hf.uio.no/ifikk/forskning/aktuelt/arrangementer/gjesteforelesninger-seminarer/faste-seminarer/estetisk-seminar/lorrain-daston-on-the-science-of-clouds.html.

10. William Cronon, *Uncommon Ground: Rethinking the Human Place in Nature* (New York: W. W. Norton & Co., 1996), among others; Craig E. Colten, *An Unnatural Metropolis: Wresting New Orleans from Nature* (Baton Rouge: Louisiana State University Press, 2005); John McPhee, *The Control of Nature*, rpt. ed. (New York: Farrar, Straus and Giroux, 1990); Christopher Wells, *Car Country* (Seattle: University of Washington Press, 2014).

1. Maria and the Birth of Modern Meteorology

1. John Steinbeck, *The Grapes of Wrath* (New York: Viking Press, 1935).
2. Zora Neale Hurston, *Their Eyes Were Watching God* (Philadelphia: J. B. Lippincott, 1937).
3. William Alexander Percy, *Lanterns on the Levee* (New York: Alfred A. Knopf, 1941).
4. Rozario, *The Culture of Calamity*.
5. See examples in Richard Hakluyt, "Narrative by Christopher Columbus: Navigations,

Voyages, Traffiques and Discoveries of the English Nation in America," *The Principle Navigations, Voyages, Traffiques and Discoveries of the English Nation* (Edinburgh: E&G, 1884), vol. 12; "Narrative by Bartolomé Las Casas," in *Tears of the Indians: Being an Historical and True Account of the Massacres and Slaughters of Above Twenty Millions of Innocent People...*, trans. J. Philips (London: J.C. for Nath. Brook, 1655); and John Taylor, *Newes and Strange Newes from St. Christophers of a tempestuous Spirit, which is called by the Indians a Hurry-Cano or whirlewind* (London, 1638).

6. Varied spellings of the word *huracán* resulted from both the population's and translators' pronunciations and cultural tradition.

7. Pérez, *Winds of Change*, 17.

8. The history of various deity origins is included in Thomas Besom, *Of Summits and Sacrifice: An Ethnohistoric Study of Inka Religious Practices* (Austin: University of Texas Press, 2010), 66–68; Francis Parry, "The Sacred Symbols and Numbers of Aboriginal America in Ancient and Modern Times," *Journal of the American Geographical Society of New York* 26, no. 1 (1894): 163–207; Adela Fernández, *Dioses prehispánicos de México: Mitos y deidades del panteón náhuatl* (México, DF: Panorama Editorial, 1992); and Kay Almere Read and Jason Gonzalez, *Handbook of Mesoamerican Mythology* (Oxford, UK: Clio, 2000).

9. Peréz, *Winds of Change*, 19.

10. William Shakespeare, *The History of Troilus and Cressida*, act 5, scene 2 (Champaign, IL: Project Gutenberg), search.ebscohost.com/login.aspx?direct=true&scope=site&db=nlebk&db= nlabk&AN=1010700; Shakespeare, *King Lear*, act 3, scene 2.

11. Shakespeare, *The Tempest*, first folio ed. (New York: Thomas Y. Crowell & Co., 1903), via Google Books.

12. Ralph Bohun, *A Discourse Concerning the Origine And Properties Of Wind, With An Historical Account of Hurricanes, and other Tempestuous Winds* (Oxford, UK: W. Hall for Tho. Bowman, 1671), 17–19. Image available online via Google Books.

13. David M. Ludlum, *Early American Hurricanes, 1492–1870* (Boston: American Meteorological Society, 1963).

14. Merchant, *The Death of Nature*.

15. Michael Chenoweth, "A Reassessment of Historical Atlantic Basin Tropical Cyclone Activity, 1700–1855," *Climatic Change* (2006): 69, www.aoml.noaa.gov/hrd/hurdat/Chenoweth/chenoweth06.pdf.

16. "Summary Prepared for the Section of History, World's Congress of Meteorology, Chicago 1893," in Smithsonian Institution, Board of Regents, "The Meteorological Work of the Smithsonian Institution," *Annual Report of the Board of Regents Showing the Operations, Expenditures, and Condition of the Institution* (Washington, DC: Government Printing Office, 1893), 89–93.

17. Ibid.

18. "Weather Is the Nation's Business: The Report of the Department of Commerce Advisory Committee on Weather Services to the Honorable Secretary of Commerce" (Washington, DC: Government Printing Office, 1953).

19. Fleming, *Fixing the Sky*.

20. War Department, "Practical Use of Meteorological Reports and Weather Maps," Office of the Chief Signal Officer, Division of Telegrams and Reports for the Benefit of Commerce (Washington, DC: R. Beresford, 1871), 9–10, openlibrary.org/books/OL23453755M.

21. "Evolution of the National Weather Service Timeline," NOAA Online, nws.noaa.gov/pa/history/timeline.php. Accessed August 25, 2012.

22. Jamie L. Pietruska, *Looking Forward: Prediction & Uncertainty in Modern America* (Chicago: University of Chicago Press, 2017).

23. Bixel and Turner, *Galveston and the 1900 Storm*.

24. For more on environmental catastrophes of the 1920s and 1930s see John Barry, *Rising Tide: The Great Mississippi Flood of 1927 and How It Changed America* (New York: Simon & Schuster, 1998), and Donald Worster, *Dust Bowl: The Southern Plains in the 1930s* (Oxford, UK: Oxford University Press, 2004).

25. Willie Drye, *Storm of the Century: The Labor Day Hurricane of 1935* (Washington, DC: National Geographic Society, 2002).

26. Phil Scott, *Hemingway's Hurricane: The Great Florida Keys Storm of 1935* (New York: McGraw-Hill, 2006).

27. Ernest Hemingway, "Who Murdered the Vets? A First-Hand Report on the Florida Hurricane," *New Masses* 16, no. 12 (1935).

28. Scott, *Hemingway's Hurricane*.

29. "Weather Is the Nation's Business," 8.

30. Ibid.

31. "Reorganization Plan No. IV of 1940," 5 F.R. 2223, 54 Stat. 1238, by act June 4, 1940, ch. 231, §1, 54 Stat. 230.

32. "Weather Is the Nation's Business," 9.

33. "America by Air: Airline Expansion & Innovation, 1927–1941," *Smithsonian Air & Space Museum Online Exhibit,* 2007, www.airandspace.si.edu/exhibitions/america-by-air/online/innovation/innovation15.cfm.

34. "Reorganization Plan No. IV of 1940."

35. Helmut Erich Landsberg, *Physical Climatology* (DuBois, PA: Gray Print. Co., 1958).

36. Donald M. Scott, *The Life and Truth of George R. Stewart: A Literary Biography of the Author of "Earth Abides"* (Jefferson, NC: McFarland, 2012).

37. George R. Stewart, *Take Your Bible in One Hand: The Life of William Henry Thomes, Author of A Whaleman's Adventures on Land and Sea, Lewey and I, the Bushrangers, A Gold Hunter's Adventures, Etc.* (San Francisco: Colt Press, 1939).

38. Bennett A. Cerf, editor at Random House, "Notes on George Stewart's *Life and Death of a Storm,*" George Rippey Stewart *Storm* Collection, Record Group C0128, Rare Books and Special Collections, Princeton University, Princeton, NJ (hereafter cited as Stewart MSS).

39. "Folder 3: Notes (Unsorted in 3 Envelopes) undated," Stewart MSS.

40. Ibid.

41. Aristotle in "Background 2," box 3, "Folder 1: Notes and Storm Outlines, 1922–1935," Stewart MSS; *Georgics* in envelope 2, box 3, "Folder 3: Notes (Unsorted in 3 Envelopes), undated," Stewart MSS.

42. F. W. Reichelderfer (Chief of Weather Bureau) to George R. Stewart, letter, December 22, 1939, "Folder 17: Correspondence, 1939–1940," Box 2, Stewart MSS.

43. "Folders 6, 7, 8, 9, and 10: Weather Clippings, 1938–1940, February," Box 3, Stewart MSS.

44. "Weather Experts Disagree; Fate of Biscuit Doubtful," *San Francisco Chronicle*, February 1940, in "Weather Clippings," Stewart MSS.

45. "Krick Weather Service Bulletin, Pasadena, Calif., Weather Map for Day," "Weather Clippings," Stewart MSS.

46. "Weather Clippings," Stewart MSS.

47. Ibid.

48. Bennett A. Cerf (Random House, Inc.) to William Van Dusen (Pan American Airways), letter, September 22, December 22, 1939, "Correspondence," Stewart MSS.

49. "Correspondence," Stewart MSS.

50. Stewart, *Storm*, 43.

51. Ibid., 23, 24, 33, 37, 41, 43.

52. Ibid., 12.

53. Ibid., 18.

54. Ibid., 16, 17.

55. Ibid., 12, 13, 18.

56. Ibid., 18.

57. Ibid., 18.

58. Ibid., "Fast mover," on 43; "Individualized," "Advanced," and "Gigantic Creature of Atmosphere," on 147; "Hussy" on 91.

59. Ibid., 234.

60. "Unsorted Notes," Envelope 1, Stewart MSS.

61. Gordon E. Dunn and Banner I. Miller, *Atlantic Hurricanes* (Baton Rouge: Louisiana State University Press, 1960).

62. "The Kingdom of Wragge," courtesy of the Melbourne Public Library, as sent in email correspondence with author and National Hurricane Center (NHC) historian Neal Dorst, September 12, 2012.

63. "Names Give Hurricanes Identity," *Charleston News & Courier*, September 22, 1989.

64. Allegreto, "Stenograms," *Australian Queenslander*, February 15, 1896.

65. "The Storm-Eline: Gales and Rain on the Coast, Latest Forecast," *Brisbane Courier*, February 2, 1898.

66. "The Weather Outlook," *Brisbane Courier*, August 5, 1902.

67. Ibid.

68. "The 'Stiger Vortex' in the West," *Brisbane Courier*, August 5, 1902.

69. "Vale! Mr. Wragge," *Brisbane Courier*, August 5, 1902.

70. Peter Adamson, "Clement Lindley Wragge and the Naming of Weather Disturbances," *Weather* 57 (September 2003): 359–63.

71. Sir Napier Shaw, *Manual of Meteorology*, 2nd ed. (Cambridge, UK: Cambridge University Press, 1938).

72. Shaw, *Manual of Meteorology*, 1st ed., 1919, p. 123; rpt. in Stewart, *Storm*, preface.

73. Robert van Gelder, "An Interview with George R. Stewart: Few Novels Have Been More Minutely Planned Than Was 'Storm,'" *New York Times*, December 14, 1941.

74. Robert van Gelder, "George Stewart's 'Storm' and Other Works of Fiction," *New York Times*, November 23, 1941.

75. "Books—Authors," *New York Times*, September 17, 1941.

76. Walter A. Bara, "Life and Times of Howling Maria," *Washington Post*, November 30, 1941.

77. "Excerpt from Book-of-the-Month-Club Brochure," pasted inside copy of Stewart, *Storm*, 1941.

78. "News of the Screen," *New York Times*, January 21, 1942.

79. George R. Stewart, *Names on the Land: A Historical Account of the Place-Naming in the United States* (New York: Random House, 1945).

80. William Bright, "George Rippey Stewart (1895–1980): A Biography," American Name Society website, updated December 29, 2001, www.wtsn.binghamton.edu/onoma/Default.htm#Stewart.

81. Stewart's *Storm* was republished in 1942, 1943, 1944, 1945, 1946, 1947, 1948, 1950, 1951, 1953, 1955, 1957, 1965, 1974, 1975, 1983, and most recently in 2003.

82. "Thirtieth Annual Report of the Secretary of Commerce, 1942," Records of the Weather Bureau, 1735–1979, Record Group 130, National Archives at College Park, MD (hereafter cited as MSS WB).

83. Ibid.; "Thirty-First Annual Report of the Secretary of Commerce, 1943"; "Thirty-Second Annual Report of the Secretary of Commerce, 1944"; "Thirty-Third Annual Report of the Secretary of Commerce, 1945," MSS WB.

84. "Opportunity for Women in Meteorological Work," 1942 Announcement, Weather Bureau, cited in "Women in the Weather Bureau during World War II," NOAA History: A Science Odyssey, updated June 8, 2006, www.history.noaa.gov/stories_tales/women6.html.

85. This figure is calculated from the annual report for 1945. It states that there were 1,074 new female employees hired during the fiscal year, but does not state whether the existing 1,000 female employees were retained or relieved of their position. This puts the number of female employees in 1945 somewhere between 1,074 to 2,074 ("Thirty-Third Annual Report of the Secretary of Commerce, 1945," MSS WB).

86. The Pacific Theater code-naming list was discussed in Neal Dorst, "They Call the Wind Mahina: A History of the Naming of Tropical Cyclones," talk given October 23, 2012, Atlantic Oceanographic and Meteorological Laboratory, Coral Gables, FL. The talk was attended virtually through "Go-To-Meeting" software by the author and was prompted by four months of correspondence regarding the author's initial research in summer 2012.

87. The other book most commonly distributed to soldiers in 1943 as part of this program was F. Scott Fitzgerald's *The Great Gatsby*. Fitzgerald's book features a similarly iconic female character—"Daisy"—and arguably increased in popularity following the war due to its inclusion in the ASE program. Both books are described in Maureen Corrigan, *So We Read On: How "The Great Gatsby" Came to Be and Why It Endures* (New York: Little, Brown, 2014), and *Books in Action: The Armed Services Editions*, ed. John Y. Cole (Washington, DC: Library of Congress, 1984), catdir.loc.gov/catdir/toc/becites/cfb84600198.html.

88. Robert B. Westbrook, "'I Want a Girl, Just like the Girl That Married Harry James': American Women and the Problem of Political Obligation in World War II," *American Quarterly* 42, no. 4 (December 1990): 587–611.

89. The tradition of characterizing ships as female and using feminine pronouns dated back at least to the fourteenth century. Of the many theories that have been proposed to explain why ships have been gendered female through the generations, four of them are most likely to be true, based on vernacularic history. According to the *Oxford English Dictionary*, possible explanations are (1) that sailors were male and named their ships as a token of good luck or tribute to the goddesses; (2) that it was one of many natural objects that was personified as feminine, including the moon, stars, Earth, or planets; (3) that the original root word for ship had a grammatical gender of female, and thus the attachment carried over to the representation of ships later on; and (4) that it was a mistake in the translation and printing of the word that was simply continued over time. While the lexicographical history does not tell us the true origins of the tradition of referring to ships as female, it has continued into the twentieth century. New forms of transportation technology, such as automobiles and airplanes, have also taken on this feminine association. The most succinct history of the reasoning behind ship gendering is discussed in a blog by Patricia T. O'Conner and Stewart Kellerman, "Why did we start 'she'-ing ships?" *Grammarphobia*, December 2, 2010, www.grammarphobia.com/blog/2010/12/ships.html.

90. May, *Homeward Bound*.

91. Dorst, talk and email correspondence.

92. "Restrictions were relaxed on November 1, 1944," in "Thirty-Second Annual Report of the Secretary of Commerce, 1944," 10, MSS WB.

93. F. W. Reichelderfer, Letter to the Undersecretary, "Use of the Weather Bureau's Output," July 25, 1945, MSS WB.

94. "Material for Karl Stefan on Weather Service in Relation to Post-War Problems," General Correspondence of the Weather Bureau, 1942–45, MSS WB.

95. "Annual Report of the Secretary of Commerce," 1945–51, MSS WB.

96. Ibid., 1946, 1947, 1948, 1949, 1950, and 1951.

97. Ibid., 1942, 1943, 1944, and 1945.

98. "Un Proposed Establishment of a Radiosonde Station Un Guadalupe Island," Mexican Meteorological Project File, General Correspondence of the Weather Bureau, 1946–50; "Brief History of Mexican Meteorology Service, 1949," General Correspondence of the Weather Bureau, 1946–50, MSS WB.

99. "Weather Is the Nation's Business" and "Annual Report of the Secretary of Commerce," 1945.

100. "Material for Karl Stefan on Weather Service in Relation to Post-War Problems," General Correspondence of the Weather Bureau, 1942–45, MSS WB.

101. While there is no document of the decision to cease the code-naming system provided in Weather Bureau records, they do not appear in the detailed annual report. These facts have been confirmed through email correspondence with Neal Dorst and former Weather Bureau officials at the National Hurricane Center Library (Dorst, talk and email correspondence; MSS WB; National Oceanic and Atmospheric Association Regional Library, Miami [hereafter cited as NHC Library]).

102. Ralph Sanders, "The Hurricane of September 19, 1947, in Mississippi and Louisiana," Weather Bureau Office, New Orleans, submitted to Weather Bureau Library on January 27, 1950, NHC Library.

103. "West End Takes Brunt of Storm; 65-Mile Winds," *New Orleans Times-Picayune,* September 4, 1948.

104. "New Hurricane Nears Louisiana," *New Orleans Times-Picayune,* September 3, 1948; "Gulf Coast Area Menaced by Wind," *New Orleans Times-Picayune,* September 4, 1948; "Hits 12 Hours Sooner," *New Orleans Times-Picayune,* September 4, 1948; and "September Storm," *New Orleans Times-Picayune,* September 5, 1948.

105. Grady Norton, "Hurricanes of the 1950 Season," *Monthly Weather Review* (January 1951): 8–15.

106. "Hurricane Season Is with Us Again: Scientists Have Two Theories Which Seek to Explain Why the Storms Act as They Do," *New York Times,* September 7, 1952.

107. "What's in a Name? The Phonetic Alphabet Goes International," *Topics of the Weather Bureau* 2, no. 3 (March 1952): 38.

108. L. J. Rose, "Aviation's ABC: The Development of ICAO spelling alphabet," *ICAO Bulletin,* November 2, 1956, 12–14; "Aeronautical Telecommunications: Annex 10 to the Convention on International Civil Aviation," vol. 2, chap. 5; International Telecommunication Union, "Appendix 16: Phonetic Alphabet and Figure Code" (Geneva: ITU, 1959), 430–31; all in MSS WB.

109. Stewart, *Storm,* 1947.

110. Alan J. Lerner and Frederick Loewe, "They Call the Wind Maria," *Paint Your Wagon: The Musical,* album cover, 1951.

111. Sam Zolotow, "*Paint Your Wagon* Will Open Tonight," *New York Times,* November 12, 1951.

112. Claudia Cassidy, "On the Aisle: 'Paint Your Wagon' Has Other Charms, but the Dancers Steal the Show," *Chicago Daily Tribune,* December 17, 1951.

113. "1951 Concludes amid Boom in Real Estate," *Daytona Beach News-Journal,* December 1, 2001.

114. The movie debuted on *Walt Disney's A Wonderful World of Color* as *A Storm Called Maria* (November 27, 1959), 60 minutes.

115. "Hurricane 'B' Sweeps Out over Ocean," *Baltimore Sun,* August 16, 1953.

116. "Why Gales Are Gals: Hurricane Namers (Male) Prove It's to Avoid Confusion," *New York Times,* September 26, 1954.

117. Ibid.

2. Camille and Cold War Sexual Politics

1. "Tropical Storm Camille Forms in Caribbean, Will Touch Cuba," *Mobile Press-Register,* August 15, 1969.

2. Virgil, *The Aeneid,* trans. Robert Fagles (New York: Penguin Books, 2008); George R. Stewart, *American Given Names: Their Origin and History in the Context of the English Language* (New York: Oxford University Press, 1979), 73.

3. "Scientists Seek to Tame Hurricane with Crystals," *New Orleans Times-Picayune*, August 19, 1969.

4. "Atlantic Hurricane Seeded by Planes," *New York Times*, August 19, 1969.

5. Joanne Meyerowitz, ed., *Not June Cleaver: Women and Gender in Postwar America, 1945–1960* (Philadelphia: Temple University Press, 1994).

6. Susan Douglas, "Genies and Witches," *Where the Girls Are: Growing Up Female with the Mass Media* (New York: Times Books, 1995), 123–38.

7. Alfred C. Kinsey, *Sexual Behavior in the Human Male* (Philadelphia: W. B. Saunders, 1948).

8. The *New Orleans Times-Picayune*, for example, depicts the atomic bomb as masculine when in the wild (unharnessed), and feminine when domesticated for energy use (harnessed) ("A New Career for Mr. A," *Times-Picayune*, September 11, 1954, 6).

9. May, *Homeward Bound*, 108.

10. Matthew D. Lassiter and Kevin M. Kruse, "The Bulldozer Revolution: Suburbs and Southern History since World War II," *Journal of Southern History* 75, no. 3 (2009): 691–706.

11. C. Vann Woodward, "The Search for Southern Identity" (1958), in Woodward, *The Burden of Southern History*, 3rd ed. (Baton Rouge: Louisiana State University Press, 1993).

12. Lawrence N. Powell, *The Accidental City: Improvising New Orleans* (Cambridge, MA: Harvard University Press, 2013).

13. Jack E. Davis and Raymond Arsenault, *Paradise Lost: The Environmental History of Florida* (Gainesville: University Press of Florida, 2005).

14. Michael Grunwald, *The Swamp: The Everglades, Florida, and the Politics of Paradise* (New York: Simon & Schuster, 2006).

15. Cindy Ermus, ed., *Environmental Disaster in the Gulf South: Two Centuries of Catastrophe, Risk, and Resilience* (Baton Rouge: Louisiana State University Press, 2018).

16. Raymond Arsenault, "The End of the Long Hot Summer: The Air Conditioner and Southern Culture," *Journal of Southern History* 50, no. 4 (November 1984): 597–628.

17. Sandy Isenstadt, "Visions of Plenty: Refrigerators in America around 1950," *Journal of Design History* 11, no. 4 (1998): 311–21.

18. Thomas Dunlap, *DDT, Silent Spring, and the Rise of Environmentalism* (Seattle: University of Washington Press, 2015).

19. Gregg Mitman, *Breathing Space: How Allergies Shape Our Lives and Landscapes* (New Haven, CT: Yale University Press, 2008).

20. Buhs, "Fire Ant Wars," 377–400.

21. David Oshinsky, *Polio: An American Story* (New York: Oxford University Press, 2005).

22. "Annual Report of the Secretary of Commerce," 1945–51.

23. Ibid.

24. Fleming, *Fixing the Sky*.

25. H. E. Willoughby, D. P. Jorgensen, R. A. Black, and S. L. Rosenthal, "Project STORMFURY: A Scientific Chronicle, 1962–1983," Hurricane Research Division, AOML/NOAA, vol. 66, no. 5, May 1985, NHC Library.

26. H. R. Byers and R. R. Braham, "History of Weather Modification," *Weather and Climate Modification* (New York: Wiley & Sons, 1974).

27. "Weather Men Become World Figures as Forecasting Hits New Peaks," *Christian Science Monitor*, August 30, 1947.

28. "Dispute Cloud Seeding Effect on Hurricanes," *Chicago Daily Tribune*, August 8, 1956.

29. *Walt Disney's Alice in Wonderland*, directed by Claude Geronimi, Wilfred Jackson, and Hamilton Luske (Walt Disney, Inc., 1951).

30. "Alice Struck on July 25, Starting Season of Gales," *New York Times*, October 16, 1954.

31. Parenthetical notation of current US dollars according to Bureau of Labor Statistics, CPI Inflation Calculator.

32. "Fierce" and "howler" in "Hurricane Carol Hits Coast, Fades," *Atlanta Journal-Constitution*, August 30, 1954; "Mauls East Coast" in "Hurricane Mauls East, Killing 37; Loss in Millions: Hundreds of Yachts Smashed," *Atlanta Journal-Constitution*, September 1, 1954; "Wallowed aimlessly" in "Atlantic Storm Losing Strength," *Mobile Press-Register*, August 30, 1954; "Runaway hurricane" and "much of its fury spent" in "Hurricane Rakes East, Kills 47; Batters Long Island; Power Cut," *New York Times*, September 1, 1954.

33. "North Carolina Areas Count Storm Damage," *Raleigh News & Observer*, September 1, 1954.

34. "28 Reported Dead in Hurricane: NE Bears Brunt of Full Wind," *Mobile Press-Register*, September 1, 1954.

35. "On the heels of Carol" in "Hurricane Dolly off North Carolina," *Miami Herald*, September 2, 1954.

36. "The Storm of September 11, 1954 (Hurricane Edna)," US Weather Bureau, submitted to Weather Bureau Library, October 26, 1954.

37. "Skittish" in "New England Braces for Hurricane," *Biloxi Sun-Herald*, September 10, 1954; "Carbon copy of Hurricane Carol" in "Threat of Hurricane Cancels East Events," *Mobile Press-Register*, September 12, 1954.

38. "Sister" in image caption, *Atlanta Journal-Constitution*, September 11, 1954; "Slaps" in "Upper East Coast Residents Flee Inland as Howling Edna Grazes Carolinas, Roars North," *Atlanta Journal-Constitution*, September 11, 1954.

39. "Edna wept in her violent meteorological tantrum" in "Hurricane Skips City, Long Island; With a Wet but Vicious Left Jab," *New York Times*, September 12, 1954.

40. "New York, New England Preparing for Hurricane," *Raleigh News & Observer*, September 11, 1954.

41. "Hurricane Edna," *Miami Herald*, September 11, 1954.

42. "Edna Has Her 'Portrait' Taken on Radar as She Moves up Jersey Coast," *New York Times*, September 12, 1954.

43. Edward Sable, "Hurricane Edna—September 11, 1954," US Weather Bureau, submitted to Weather Bureau Library, January 4, 1955.

44. "Freak of nature" in "Hurricane Dampens Braves," *Charleston News & Courier*, September 11, 1954; "Angry woman!" in "Hurricane Misses Charleston, Steers for New England Coast," *Charleston News & Courier*, September 10, 1954; "Rent asunder by her own violence" in "Hurricane Edna Splits into Sections: 7 Persons Known Dead in Path of Big Storm," *Mobile Press-Register*, September 12, 1954.

45. "Hurricane Edna Passes 100 Miles off Virginia Capes: Heavy Rain, Winds Hit East Coast," *Richmond Times-Dispatch*, September 11, 1954.

46. "Nightmare" in "Raging Floods Sweep Wind-Battered Areas," *Houston Chronicle*, October 17, 1954.

47. "Dawdle[d]" in "Hazel Takes Trail Set by 2 'Sisters,'" *Miami Herald*, October 15, 1954; "Wickedly menacing" in "Hurricane Kills 36 in Northward Path," *New Orleans Times-Picayune*, October 16, 1954; "Rejuvenate" in "Hurricane Hazel Is Expected to Pass near Cape Hatteras," *Charleston News & Courier*, October 14, 1954; "Galloping" in "Hurricane Kills 36 in Northward Path," *New Orleans Times-Picayune*; "Terrific battering" in "Damage Is Wide in Pennsylvania," *New York Times*, October 16, 1954; "Last fling" in "Hurricane's Toll Hits 36 in Canada," *New York Times*, October 17, 1954.

48. "Hurricane Brings Death, Destruction," *Raleigh News & Observer*, October 16, 1954.

49. Ibid.

50. "Hurricane's Toll Increases Toll 8; Toronto Ravaged," *New York Times*, October 17, 1954.

51. "Menace" or "Menacing" appeared in the *New York Times, Raleigh News & Observer, New Orleans Times-Picayune,* and *Atlanta Journal-Constitution*. "Wicked" was used in the *Atlanta Journal-Constitution, New Orleans Times-Picayune,* and *Raleigh News & Observer*. Often the two words appeared together in a sentence.

52. "The Storm of October 15, 1954 (Hurricane Hazel)," US Weather Bureau, submitted to Weather Bureau Library, November 22, 1955.

53. David Laskin, "Television: A Change in the Weather," *New York Times*, February 18, 1996.

54. Linda K. Kerber, *No Constitutional Right to Be Ladies: Women and the Obligations of Citizenship* (New York: Hill & Wang, 1998).

55. "Storms Got 'Cute' Names during War in Pacific," *Houston Chronicle*, September 10, 1954.

56. Ibid.

57. "Time the Storm Experts Grew Up and Quit Using 'Cute' Language," *Houston Chronicle*, September 2, 1954, 2H.

58. Ibid.

59. *New Bedford Standard Times* in "The Town Crier," *Miami Herald*, September 9, 1954.

60. Ibid.

61. "As We See It, 'No Time to Be Capricious,'" *Miami Herald*, September 11, 1954.

62. "Why Gales Are Gals."

63. "Bulletins and Advisories Issued by Weather Bureau Office, Miami, Florida and Weather Bureau Airport Station, Washington, D.C. on Hurricane 'Connie,'" US Weather Bureau, submitted to Weather Bureau Library, December 7, 1955.

64. "Lurked lazily" in "Hurricane Is Churning off Coast of Carolina," *New Orleans Times-Picayune*, August 10, 1955; "Spins like a mad top" in "Hurricane Loafs; City Has a Chance of Avoiding Blow," *New York Times*, August 11, 1955; "Capricious" in "Hurricane's Advance Winds Do Most Damage along North Carolina Coast," *New York Times*, August 13, 1955; "Dangerous flirtation" in "City Alert Ended as Connie Whirls toward Carolina," *New York Times*, August 12, 1955.

65. "Lacked Hazel's Wallop: Persistent Connie Has Gone," *Raleigh News & Observer*, August 13, 1955.

66. "She hadn't made up her mind" in "Big Storm Dawdling off Carolina Coasts," *Mobile Press-Register*, August 11, 1955; "Stood still and growled" in "Connie Dwindles, Leaving 41 Dead," *New Orleans Times-Picayune*, August 14, 1955; "Force equal to thousands of H-Bombs" in "Connie Blows North with Force Equal to Thousands of H-Bombs," *New York Times*, August 13, 1955.

67. "The Connie Scare" in "Hurricane Threat Disrupting Business in Pee Dee Section," *Charleston News & Courier*, August 12, 1955; "No longer a menace" in "Connie Safely Past; Area's Residents Eye Beaches Again," *Charleston News & Courier*, August 13, 1955; "Anemic image of her former self" in "Hurricane Clips City, Then Fades in Pennsylvania," *New York Times*, August 14, 1955.

68. "Connie's No Lady and Her Temper Proves It," *Miami Herald*, August 14, 1955.

69. "Bulletins and Advisories Issued by Weather Bureau Office, Miami, Florida and Weather Bureau Airport Station, Washington, D.C. on Hurricane 'Diane,'" US Weather Bureau, submitted to Weather Bureau Library, December 7, 1955.

70. "Fickle female" and "foot-dragging" in "Hurricane Log," *New Orleans Times-Picayune*, August 18, 1955; "Ex-hurricane" and "dignifying" in "Diane Is Getting Weaker by Hour," *New Orleans Times-Picayune*, August 18, 1955.

71. "Cat and mouse" in "Connie Bows Out," *New York Times*, August 14, 1955; "Invaded" in "Weather," *Houston Chronicle*, August 15, 1955.

72. "Weeping" in "Water Damage Tops Sweep of Hurricane over North Carolina," *Raleigh News & Observer*, August 18, 1955; "All the punch of a powderpuff" in "'Terrific Damage Caused Crops by Wind, Rains of Two Storms," *Raleigh News & Observer*, August 18, 1955; "Dying" in "Other States Feel Effects of Hurricane," *Raleigh News & Observer*, August 19, 1955; "Two windy sisters" in "Business Gives with Wind in Hurricane at Beaches," *Raleigh News & Observer*, August 19, 1955.

73. "Ex-hurricane" and "dignifying" in "Diane Is Getting Weaker by Hour," *New Orleans Times-Picayune*, August 18, 1955.

74. "Why Gales Are Gals."

75. Ibid.

76. "Orpha and Wallis," *New Orleans Times-Picayune*, October 13, 1954.

77. "26 Females in the Wind: Weatherman Picks New Set of Names for This Year's Lady Hurricanes," *Washington Post*, February 15, 1955.

78. "She Blows," *Raleigh News & Observer*, August 16, 1955.

79. Ibid.

80. George Dixon, "Washington Scene," *Washington Post*, August 29, 1955.

81. Ibid.

82. "New Names for Storms? Senator Likes 'Acrimonious' Better Than 'Alice,' 'Connie,'" *Baltimore Sun*, August 19, 1955.

83. Willoughby et al., "Project STORMFURY: A Scientific Chronicle, 1962–1983."

84. Ben Funk, "Hurricane-Chaser Believes Seeding Can Tame Tempests," *Hartford Courant*, February 11, 1968.

85. Willoughby et al., "Project STORMFURY: A Scientific Chronicle, 1962–1983."

86. "Miss Hurricane Hunter 1956," Air Force Weather History Office, Offutt Air Force Base, Nebraska, posted by Lieutenant Colonel Bernard Barris, Retired, Air Weather Reconnaissance Association website, www.awra.us/gallery-feb05.html. Followed up by author with phone interview and email correspondence with Barris, August 14, 20, 22, 2013.

87. Robert Simpson, "Implementation Phase of the National Hurricane Research Project, 1955–1956," Selected Papers 13th Technical Conference on Hurricanes and Tropical Meteorology, American Meteorological Society, Miami Beach, December 1–5, 1980.

88. National Hurricane Research Project, "Objectives and Basic Design of the National Hurricane Research Project" (Washington, DC: Department of Commerce, 1956).

89. Erik M. Conway, *High-Speed Dreams: NASA and the Technopolitics of Supersonic Transportation, 1945–1999* (Baltimore: Johns Hopkins University Press, 2005).

90. Fleming, *Fixing the Sky*.

91. J. A. Colon and staff, NHRP, "On the Structure of Hurricane Daisy, 1958," *National Hurricane Research Project Report*, no. 48, Department of Commerce, 1961.

92. H. Riehl and J. S. Malkus, "Some Aspects of Hurricane Daisy," *Tellus* 12 (1958): 181–213.

93. Joanne Gerould was born in Boston, March 23, 1923. She married three times; thus her name changed from Joanne Gerould to Joanne Starr (1944), to Joanne Malkus (1948), and finally to Joanne Simpson (1965). She is referred to in text by the name she used at each historical moment (usually Malkus or Simpson).

94. John Weier, "Joanne Simpson (1923–2010)," *NASA Earth Observatory* online, April 23, 2004, earthobservatory.nasa.gov/Features/Simpson/simpson.php. Includes information from Simpson's files by Jacalyn R. Blume and Kathy Jacob of the Schlesinger Library at Harvard University.

95. Riehl and Malkus, "Some Aspects of Hurricane Daisy."

96. Weier, "Joanne Simpson (1923–2010)."

97. C. L. Jordan and F. J. Schatzle, "The 'Double Eye' of Hurricane Donna," *Monthly Weather Review* 89 (1961): 354–56.

98. Funk, "Hurricane-Chaser Believes Seeding Can Tame Tempests."

99. "August Test Slated to Find Way to Divert or Dilute Hurricanes," *Washington Post*, July 14, 1961.

100. "Hurricane Curbs Believed Nearer," *New York Times*, October 11, 1961, 49.

101. Ibid.

102. Temple, "Hilda," *New Orleans Times-Picayune*, October 3, 1961, 8.

103. US National Oceanic and Atmospheric Administration, *Project STORMFURY* (Rockville, MD: Department of Commerce-NOAA, 1972), NHC Library.

104. National Hurricane Research Project, "Project STORMFURY, 1963–1973: Annual Reports" (Miami: AOML, 1973).

105. Willoughby et al., "Project STORMFURY: A Scientific Chronicle, 1962–1983."

106. National Hurricane Research Project, "Project STORMFURY, 1963–1973: Annual Reports."

107. Gary E. Weir and Walter J. Boyne, *Rising Tide: The Untold Story of the Russian Submarines That Fought the Cold War* (New York: Penguin, 2004).

108. Schwartz, *Sea of Storms*.

109. As described in later reports, Project STORMFURY's activity was just one of many weather-modification experiments taking place in the United States. This included projects run by Dr. Irving P. Krick (an inspiration for George R. Stewart's meteorologists in *Storm*); rain experiments at multiple locations; and Project Skyfire, an effort to cloud seed in order to reduce or eliminate lightning-caused forest fires. All of these efforts are detailed in "The Weather," *Baltimore Sun*, April 9, 1967.

110. "The Space Age of Clouds and Hurricanes," *Baltimore Sun*, August 4, 1963, 57; "Where Will Cindy Be Born?" *Baltimore Sun*, August 31, 1963.

111. H. M. Hoose and J. A. Colon, "Some Aspects of the Radar Structure of Hurricane Beulah on September 9, 1967," *Monthly Weather Review* 98 (1970): 529–33.

112. Kristine Harper, *Make It Rain: State Control of the Atmosphere in Twentieth-Century America* (Chicago: University of Chicago Press, 2017).

113. "New Experiments Due in Hurricane Control," *Los Angeles Times*, November 4, 1963.

114. "How to Tame a Hurricane: Project STORMFURY," *Hartford Courant*, September 22, 1963.

115. "New Experiments Due in Hurricane Control."

116. "Cloud-Seeding Clue to Control of Hurricanes: Huge Research Program Probes Nature of Destructive Storms, Seeks to Subdue Them," *Los Angeles Times*, November 3, 1963.

117. "Clouds 'Exploded' in Tests; Hurricane Preventative Seen," *Baltimore Sun*, August 7, 1964.

118. "Violently Erratic Behavior" in "Betsy Swings to Northwest in Gulf as Speed Increases," *New Orleans Times-Picayune*, September 10, 1965.

119. "Chances of Seeding Now Are Diminished," *New Orleans Times-Picayune*, September 14, 1965.

120. "Can Weathermen Tame a Hurricane?" *Christian Science Monitor*, August 30, 1965.

121. "Too Big for Usual Defenses," *New Orleans Times-Picayune*, September 14, 1965.

122. "Hurricane Betsy, September 2–11, 1961: Preliminary Report with the Advisories and Bulletins Issued," US Weather Bureau, submitted to Weather Bureau Library, January 4, 1962.

123. Clarence Doucet, "Thousands Flee Flood Threat as Hurricane Slams into New Orleans, Winds above 100 Miles," *Times-Picayune*, September 10, 1965.

124. "Element of unpredictability" in "Betsy Whirls In," *New Orleans Times-Picayune*, September 10, 1965; "Belligerent Betsy" in Carolyn Kolb, "40-Member Staff of U.S. Weather Bureau Busy," *New Orleans Times-Picayune*, September 9, 1965; "tempestuous wandering" in "Betsy in Gulf," *New Orleans Times-Picayune*, September 9, 1965; "the kind that makes . . ." in "Betsy a Big One but Wound Not Deep," *New Orleans Times-Picayune*, September 11, 1965.

125. "Rape in night" in "National Guard Aid Asked to Protect from Looters," *New Orleans Times-Picayune*, September 11, 1965; "Too powerful" in "Too Big for Usual Defenses," *New Orleans Times-Picayune*.

126. "Irrational lady" in "National Guard Aid Asked to Protect from Looters."

127. "Betsy," *New Orleans Daily States/Item/Times-Picayune*, September 9, 1965.

128. Barry, *Rising Tide*.

129. "Can Weathermen Tame a Hurricane?" *Christian Science Monitor*, August 30, 1965.

130. "Seeding of Storm to Be Tried Today," *New York Times*, September 1, 1965.

131. Andy Horowitz, "*Hurricane Betsy* and the Politics of Disaster in New Orleans' Lower Ninth Ward," *Journal of Southern History* 80, no. 4 (November 2014).

132. R. C. Gentry, "Project STORMFURY," *WMO Bulletin* 18 (1969).

133. "The Space Age: Weather Spies in the Sky," *Baltimore Sun*, February 2, 1969.

134. "The Many Factors Which Determine a Storm's Severity," *Boston Globe*, March 2, 1969.

135. "New Study of Hurricane Control Is Begun by Weather Scientists," *New York Times*, August 14, 1966.

136. Project STORMFURY staff tried to tame Hurricane Faith in August 1966, but the storm veered at the last minute to shore, and seeding was called off ("Faith Twists toward Mainland; Seeding Attempt Is Called Off," *Washington Post*, August 31, 1966).

137. Joanne Simpson would participate as part of the Florida Area Cumulus Experiment (1967–74), studying the impact of seeded cumulus clouds on rainfall totals, an offshoot of her research with Project STORMFURY. W.-K. Tao et al., "The Research of Dr. Joanne Simpson: Fifty Years Investigating Hurricanes, Tropical Clouds, and Cloud Systems," *Meteorological Monographs* 29, no. 51 (January 2003): 1–16.

138. "Gentry to Head Federal Project on Hurricanes," *Washington Post*, December 30, 1966.

139. "Storms to Get Intensified Seeding," *Baltimore Sun*, August 5, 1968.

140. "Storm Killers Poise for Action," *Atlanta Constitution*, June 22, 1969.

141. "Hurricane Tamers to Try Again," *New York Times*, August 5, 1969.

142. "Hurricanes under Test," *Austin Statesman*, August 8, 1969.

143. "Holding Back the Fury," *Atlanta Journal-Constitution*, August 20, 1969.

144. "US Hurricane Center Observers Say Camille 'Came Alive with a Bang,'" *Austin Statesman*, August 27, 1969.

145. "Monster" and "Shrieked" in "12-Food Water Rise at Biloxi," *Mobile Press-Register*, August 18, 1969; "Like a woman in labor" in "Great Hurricane Reaps Destruction in Vacation Area," *Mobile Press-Register*, August 19, 1969.

146. "Storm Lashes MS Coast," *New Orleans Times-Picayune*, August 18, 1969.

147. "Erratic Camille Has Titanic Punch," *Miami Herald*, August 17, 1969.

148. "Camille the Terrible Zeroes in on Florida," *Houston Chronicle*, August 17, 1969.

149. "200,000 without Homes," *Atlanta Journal-Constitution*, August 19, 1969.

150. "Mississippi Gulf Coast Suffers Nature's Mightiest Blast," *New Orleans Times-Picayune*, August 19, 1969.

151. "Plaquemines Towns Hit," *New Orleans Times-Picayune*, August 19, 1969.

152. "Timing" and "Compactness" in "Camille Made Notable for Timing, Compactness," *New Orleans Times-Picayune*, August 21, 1969; "Furious winds" in "Furious Winds Damage Coast," *New Orleans Times-Picayune*, August 18, 1969.

153. At the time, Camille was the costliest hurricane to date.

154. Jim Davidson, *Camille . . . She Was No Lady*, fundraising booklet (Batesville, AK: Dav-Mac Publishing, 1969), in "Hurricane Katrina Collections," Special Collections, University of Southern Mississippi, Hattiesburg.

155. "Husky Hurricane Debbie" in "Hurricane Seeders May Tackle Fierce Debbie Today,"

Miami Herald, August 18, 1969; "Tame" in "Will Debbie Freeze to Death?" *Raleigh News & Observer*, August 19, 1969.

156. "Storm Fighters Ready Again: Prepared for Another Attack on Debbie," *New Orleans Times-Picayune*, August 20, 1969.

157. "Atlantic Hurricane Seeded by Planes," *New York Times*, August 19, 1969.

158. "Five year search" and "suitable storm" in "Atlantic Hurricane Seeded by Planes," *New York Times*, August 19, 1969.

159. "Weathermen Will Try to 'Freeze' Debbie," *Charleston News & Courier*, August 18, 1969.

160. "Hurricane Seeders May Tackle Fierce Debbie Today," *Miami Herald*.

161. "Prepare for Debbie, Bermudans Warned," *Washington Post*, August 22, 1969.

162. "Seeding Starts Today," *New York Times*, August 18, 1969.

163. "Will Debbie Freeze to Death?" *Raleigh News & Observer*, August 19, 1969.

164. "Chemical Dropped on New Hurricane to Lessen Force: Position of Debbie," *Washington Post*, August 19, 1969.

165. "Seeded Debbie Slowing," *Miami Herald*, August 19, 1969.

166. "Sister Storm Being Seeded," *Baltimore Sun*, August 19, 1969.

167. "Storm Fighters Ready Again," *New Orleans Times-Picayune*.

168. "Atlantic Hurricane Seed by Planes," *New York Times*, August 19, 1969.

169. "Chemical Dropped on New Hurricane to Lessen Force," *Washington Post*.

170. Ibid.

171. "Storm Fighters Ready Again," *New Orleans Times-Picayune*.

172. Stefan Bechtel, *Roar of the Heavens* (New York: Citadel Press, 2006), viii.

173. "Defiant Debbie" in "Defiant Debbie Stalks Bermuda," *Austin Statesman*, August 21, 1969; "Won't Be Tamed" in "Debbie Won't Be Tamed, Threatens Bermuda," *Globe and Mail*, August 21, 1969.

174. R. C. Gentry, "Hurricane Debbie Modification Experiments," *Science* 168 (1970): 473–75.

175. P. G. Black, H. V. Senn, and C. L. Courtright, "Airborne Radar Observations of Eye Configuration Changes, Bright Band Distribution and Precipitation Tilt during 1969 Multiple Seeding Experiments in Hurricane Debbie," *Monthly Weather Review* 100 (1972): 208–17.

176. H. F. Hawkins and D. T. Rubsam, "Comparison of Results of the Hurricane Debbie (1969) Modification Experiments with Those from Rosenthal's Numerical Model Simulation Experiments," *Monthly Weather Review* 99 (1971): 427–34.

177. "Hurricane Seeding Raises Hopes," *New York Times*, December 5, 1969.

178. Bechtel, *Roar of the Heavens*, viii. The term "pussy-cat" to refer to hurricanes was used later with other female-named storms ("Arlene: A Pussy-Cat," *Hartford Courant*, June 5, 1971).

179. "Successful 'Debbie' Crystal-Test May Be Repeated: Respect for 'Seedy' Hurricane Dims," *Austin Statesman*, December 5, 1969.

180. "They Aim to Tame Hurricane," *Atlanta Journal-Constitution*, August 16, 1970.

181. Example as seen in "Titulares y Titulitos," *El Mundo*, August 9, 18, 1955.

182. See sections on tropical cyclone names (including PAGSA, Indian Ocean, and Northwest Pacific regions) by Landsea and Padgett in Kislow, *Hurricanes*.

3. Roxcy and the Feminist Resistance

1. Interdepartmental Hurricane Warning Conference, *Report of the 1971 Interdepartmental Hurricane Warning Conference, Coral Gables, Fla., January 13–14, 1971* (National Hurricane Center, 1971), NHC Library.

2. A portion of this chapter appeared in my article "Gendering Natural Disaster: The Battle over Female Hurricane Names," *Journal of Women's History* 30, no. 3 (2018). Copyright © 2018 Journal of Women's History, Inc.

3. Roxcy Bolton addresses NOW, recorded in "Board Minutes, 1969," National Organization for Women Records, 1959–2002, MC 496, Schlesinger Library, Radcliffe Institute, Harvard University, Cambridge, MA (hereafter cited as MSS NOW).

4. Press Release, December 8, 1969, "NOW Press Releases, 1969," MSS NOW.

5. Roxcy O'Neal Bolton, letter to Director of Hurricane Center, Roxcy O'Neal Bolton Papers, "Hurricanes," M94, State Library and Archives of Florida, Tallahassee (hereafter cited as MSS Bolton).

6. Ibid.

7. Bolton, letter to Director of Hurricane Center, MSS Bolton; Liz Skilton, interview with Bonnie Bolton, June 10, 2017.

8. Betty Friedan, *The Feminine Mystique* (1963; New York: W. W. Norton, 1997).

9. Nancy Woloch, *Women and the American Experience*, 5th ed. (New York: McGraw-Hill, 2011).

10. "Board Minutes, 1966," MSS NOW.

11. Ibid.

12. Ibid.

13. Valerie Solanas, *SCUM Manifesto* (Paris: Olympia Press, 1967).

14. "Board Minutes, 1967," and "Board Minutes, 1968," MSS NOW.

15. "Board Minutes, 1969," MSS NOW.

16. Ibid.

17. "NOW Press Releases 1969," MSS NOW.

18. "Board Minutes, 1968," MSS NOW.

19. "Hurricane Roxcy," *New Times: Miami's News & Arts Weekly* 13, no. 44 (February 22–28, 1989).

20. "Board Minutes, 1968," MSS NOW.

21. "Hurricane Roxcy."

22. "Board Minutes, 1968," MSS NOW.

23. Ibid.

24. "Florida NOW," Newsletter, October 1, 1973, MSS NOW.

25. "Board Minutes, 1968," MSS NOW.

26. Skilton, interview with Bonnie Bolton, June 10, 2017; and interview with Buddy Bolton, June 12, 2017.

27. "Board Minutes, 1969," MSS NOW.

28. "Task Force 4: Full Human Dignity—New Image of Women," 1969, MSS NOW.

29. Sunday, December 8, vote mentioned in "Board Minutes, 1969," MSS NOW.
30. "NOW Press Releases 1969," MSS NOW.
31. "Board Minutes, 1971," MSS Bolton.
32. R. H. Simpson, letter to Roxcy Bolton, March 25, 1970, MSS Bolton.
33. R. H. Simpson, letter to director, ESSA—Weather Bureau, "Naming of Hurricanes," March 25, 1970, MSS Bolton.
34. "Protest" in "Hurricane Hullabaloo," *Los Angeles Times*, April 6, 1970.
35. NOW Hurricane, *Miami Herald*, March 28, 1970.
36. "Hurricanes' Names Stir Storm," *Miami Herald*, March 28, 1970.
37. "Storm Warning: Bureau: Hurricanes to Stay 'Her-icanes'," *Miami News*, April 1, 1970.
38. Ibid.
39. "Cultural Hurricane Predicted," *Globe and Mail*, July 27, 1970.
40. Ibid.
41. "Notes on Address to the Tiger Bay Luncheon Club," MSS Bolton.
42. "Board Minutes, 1970," MSS NOW.
43. "Desexing the Federal Code," 1973, MSS NOW.
44. "Board Minutes, 1970," MSS NOW.
45. NOW President Aileen C. Hernandez, memo to officers and members of the Board of Directors, 1970, MSS NOW.
46. "Board Minutes, September 1970," MSS NOW.
47. "'700 Club' Again Open to Women," Dade County Chapter Update, January 1971, PR-1, MSS NOW.
48. "Update on NOW Dade Chapter," Florida: Dade County, 1970–73, PR-1, MSS NOW.
49. "Florida NOW," Newsletter, October 1, 1973, MSS NOW.
50. "Board Minutes, 1969," MSS NOW.
51. "Florida NOW," Newsletter, October 1, 1973, MSS NOW.
52. "Board Minutes, 1971," MSS NOW.
53. Interdepartmental Hurricane Warning Conference, *Report of the 1971 Interdepartmental Hurricane Warning Conference*.
54. Bolton, speech before Interdepartmental Hurricane Warning Conference, January 13, 1971, MSS Bolton.
55. Bolton, letter to Dr. R. H. Simpson, January 1, 1972, MSS Bolton.
56. Karl Johannessen, letter to Roxcy Bolton, February 9, 1971, MSS Bolton.
57. Bolton, letter to Dr. R. H. Simpson, January 17, 1971, MSS Bolton.
58. "Hurricanes—No Slur on Women," *Irish Times*, May 27, 1971.
59. Bill Neikirk, "Hurricane Naming after Women to Be Continued," *New Orleans Times-Picayune*, May 27, 1971.
60. "Hurricanes— No Slur on Women."
61. "Female of Species Not More Deadly?" *Los Angeles Times*, January 21, 1972.
62. R. H. Simpson, letter to Roxcy Bolton, March 25, 1970, MSS Bolton.
63. Dick West, "Sexually Balanced Language," *New York Journal and Guide*, February 12, 1972.
64. Bolton, letter to Dr. R. H. Simpson, January 1, 1972, MSS Bolton.

65. Robert H. Simpson, letter to Roxcy Bolton, January 17, 1971, MSS Bolton.
66. Simpson, letter to Roxcy Bolton, January 26, 1972, MSS Bolton.
67. Ibid.
68. "Female of Species Not More Deadly?" *Los Angeles Times*.
69. Dr. R. H. Simpson, letter to Roxcy Bolton, February 1, 1972, MSS Bolton.
70. Ibid.
71. Karl Johannessen, letter to Roxcy Bolton, February 9, 1971; Bolton, letter to Dr. R. H. Simpson, January 17, 1971, MSS Bolton.
72. "Hurricanes—No Slur on Women."
73. Ibid.
74. Art Buchwald, "Stormy Women," *Washington Post*, April 27, 1972. A variation of this by the same author also appeared in "Women and Hurricanes: a Natural Relationship," *Los Angeles Times*, April 30, 1972.
75. "Hurricane 'Irate Lady' Roars in on U.S. Weathermen," *Atlanta Constitution*, April 12, 1970.
76. "Woman Storms on Hurricane Names," *Chicago Tribune*, April 20, 1972.
77. "Florida State Newsletter," December 3, 1973, PR-1, MSS NOW.
78. "Women's Group Sues National for 'Fly Me' Ads," *Boston Globe*, October 28, 1971.
79. "Board Minutes, 1972," MSS NOW.
80. Kimberly Wilmot Voss, "The Florida Fight for Equality: The Equal Rights Amendment, Senator Lori Wilson and Mediated Catfights in the 1970s," *Florida Historical Quarterly* 88 (Fall 2009): 173–208.
81. Joan S. Carver, "The Equal Rights Amendment and the Florida Legislature," *Florida Historical Quarterly* 60 (April 1982): 455–81.
82. "Board Minutes, 1972," MSS NOW.
83. "Florida State Newsletter," December 3, 1973, MSS NOW.
84. Ibid.
85. *Roe v. Wade*, 410 US 113, 93 S. Ct. 705 (*1973*).
86. "Board Minutes, 1973," MSS NOW.
87. Woloch, *Women and the American Experience*, 364–66.
88. See Media Reform Committee [Correspondence and memos], MSS NOW.
89. Woloch, *Women and the American Experience*, 364–66.
90. Ethel Klein, *Gender Politics: From Consciousness to Mass Politics* (Cambridge, MA: Harvard University Press, 1985).
91. "Board Minutes, 1972," and Media Reform Committee [Correspondence and memos], MSS NOW.
92. "Desexing the Federal Code," 1973, MSS NOW.
93. "Liberated Ladies to Have Their Own Magazine," *Chicago Tribune*, October 28, 1971.
94. "Ms. Steinem's 'Ms.'" *Washington Post*, October 28, 1971.
95. "A 'Populist' Magazine for Women: *Ms.*" *Washington Post*, December 12, 1971.
96. Robin Morgan, *Sisterhood Is Powerful: An Anthology of Writings from the Women's Liberation Movement* (New York: Random House, 1970).

97. June Sochen, *Herstory: A Woman's View of American History* (New York: Alfred Publishing Co., 1974).

98. "College Campuses to Offer Range of 'Herstory' Courses," *Los Angeles Times,* September 14, 1970; "Women's Suffrage: Celebrating 'Herstory' Week," *Chicago Tribune,* August 19, 1972; "Coming Wednesday: A Herstory-Making Event," *New York Times,* August 23, 1970.

99. "Can Feminists Upstage Miss America?" *New York Times,* September 8, 1974.

100. "Feminist Fad," *Times of India,* November 23, 1975; "Language Lib," *Chicago Tribune,* September 15, 1970.

101. Casey Miller and Kate Swift, *Words and Women* (Garden City, NY: Doubleday, 1976), 136, 138.

102. Marilyn Turner in *Parade* (1975), cited in Nyssa Perryman and Sandra Theiss, "'Weather Girls' on the Big Screen: Stereotypes, Sex Appeal, and Science," *Bulletin of the American Meteorological Society,* March 2014, 347–56.

103. Donald Critchlow, *Phyllis Schlafly and Grassroots Conservatism: A Woman's Crusade* (Princeton, NJ: Princeton University Press, 2005).

104. Media Reform Committee [Correspondence and memos], MSS NOW. For more on feminist stereotypes, see Alice Echols, *Daring to Be Bad: Radical Feminism in America, 1967–1975* (Minneapolis: University of Minnesota Press, 1989).

105. Woloch, *Women and the American Experience,* 374.

106. See correspondence in MSS Bolton.

107. Interdepartmental Hurricane Warning Conference, *Report of the 1973 Interdepartmental Hurricane Warning Conference, Coral Gables, Fla., January 24–25, 1973* (National Hurricane Center, 1973), NHC Library.

108. "Florida Park Honors an Entire Gender," *Chicago Tribune,* July 5, 1992.

109. Sam Roberts, "Roxcy Bolton, Feminist Crusader for Equality, Including in Naming Hurricanes, Dies at 90," *New York Times,* May 21, 2017, www.nytimes.com/2017/05/21/us/roxcy-bolton-dead-feminist-hurricane-names.html.

110. Rachel Carson, *Silent Spring* (1962), 40th anniversary ed. (Boston: Houghton Mifflin, 2002).

111. "Mrs. Kreps Blunt from the Start," *Baltimore Sun,* December 21, 1976.

112. "Being First Is Kreps' Life-style," *Hartford Courant,* December 21, 1976.

113. "Are Women Eager to Pull Up Stakes and Go to Washington?" *Globe and Mail,* December 25, 1976.

114. "Commerce Secretary Not a 'Liberationist,'" *Globe and Mail,* December 21, 1976.

115. "Interview with Juanita Kreps," by Lynn Haessly, January 17, 1986, Interview C-0011, Southern Oral History Program Collection, University of North Carolina at Chapel Hill, docsouth.unc.edu/sohp/browse/themes.html?theme_id=6&category_id=30.

116. Ibid.

117. "Commerce Choice Is a Business Pioneer," *Atlanta Constitution,* December 21, 1976.

118. "Juanita M. Kreps, Commerce Secretary, Dies at 89," *New York Times,* July 8, 2010.

119. "Warning Given on Weather," *Hartford Courant,* July 13, 1978.

120. "Hurricane Names Turn Bisexual," *Oakland Tribune,* February 25, 1975.

121. Leila Rupp, *Worlds of Women: The Making of an International Feminist Movement* (Princeton, NJ: Princeton University Press, 1997).

122. Eleanor Clift and Tom Brazaitis, *Madam President: Shattering the Last Glass Ceiling* (New York: Scribner, 2000), 107.

123. "Doing Something about the Weather," *New York Times*, August 7, 1978.

124. Dr. Neil Frank, email correspondence with Neal Dorst of the NOAA/AOML/Hurricane Research Division regarding hurricane naming tradition, passed on to author, August 21, 2012.

125. "Other Nations Must Consent: Some Hurricanes May Get Men's Names," *Baltimore Sun*, December 16, 1977.

126. Telephone interview with Dr. Neil Frank by Neal Dorst, August 20, 2012, passed on to author in email correspondence with Neal Dorst and author, August 21, 2012.

127. "Hurricane Bob? Stormy Feminists Sink Tradition of Feminine Storms," *Wilmington Morning News*, May 13, 1978.

128. "Weathermen Blown Over; Hurricanes to Be Unisex," *Los Angeles Times*, May 13, 1978.

129. "Feminists Prevail," *New Orleans Times-Picayune*, May 13, 1978; "Hurricanes to Become Himmicanes in 1979," *Mobile Press-Register*, May 13, 1978.

130. "Meet the Himicane: Liberated Wind That Still Does No Good," *New Orleans Times-Picayune*, May 13, 1978.

131. "Hurricane Watchers Now Prepare for . . . Bud, Hector, Sergio," *Washington Post*, May 13, 1978; "Another Sexist Bastion Falls: Hurricanes Renamed," *New York Times*, May 13, 1978.

132. "Other Nations Must Consent."

133. "What's in a Number?" *Los Angeles Times*, May 21, 1978.

134. "Goodbye to Chauvinism," in "Headliners," *New York Times*, May 14, 1978.

135. "Another Sexist Bastion Falls."

136. "Hurricane Watchers Now Prepare for . . . Bud, Hector, Sergio."

4. Andrew and the Business of Storms

1. "After Andrew, Quakes No Longer So Terrifying," *New Orleans Times-Picayune*, August 26, 1992.

2. "An Awful Howl: Andrew Hits Hardest in South Dade," *Miami Herald*, August 24, 1992.

3. President George H. W. Bush, "Address to the Nation on Hurricane Andrew Disaster Relief," September 1, 1992, *The American Presidency Project*, www.presidency.ucsb.edu/ws/?pid=21401.

4. David Twigg, *The Politics of Disaster: Tracking the Impact of Hurricane Andrew* (Gainesville: University Press of Florida, 2012).

5. "Hurricane Andrew: FEMA Lessons Learned," US Federal Emergency Management Agency, October 9, 1992, Homeland Security Digital Library, www.hsdl.org/?view&did=456174.

6. "25 Years Later: How Hurricane Andrew Impacted Emergency Response," *All Things Considered*, August 24, 2017, NPR.org.

7. Amy Mitchell, Jeffrey Gottfried, Michael Barthel, and Elisa Shearer, *The Modern News Consumer: News Attitudes and Practices in the Digital Era*, Pew Research Center report (July 7, 2016): 5–11.

8. H. S. Saffir, "Hurricane Wind and Storm Surge," *Military Engineer* 423 (1973): 4–5; R. H. Simpson, "The Hurricane Disaster Potential Scale," *Weatherwise* 27, no. 169 (1974): 169–86.

9. "Hurricane Seeding Pressed," *Washington Post*, July 23, 1970.

10. "Hurricane Center Probed on Cutbacks," *Baltimore Sun*, July 27, 1973.

11. "Program to Tame Hurricanes Halted by Budget Trims," *Washington Post*, February 18, 1973; "Hurricane Center Probed on Cutbacks," *Baltimore Sun*, July 27, 1973.

12. "Cloud-Seeding Faces Money Drought," *Washington Post*, September 15, 1974.

13. "Plan Set to Temper Storms," *Baltimore Sun*, August 3, 1971.

14. "14 Planes Join Hurricane Seeding Tests," *New York Times*, September 27, 1971.

15. "North Carolina Coast Braces for Hurricane," *Los Angeles Times*, September 29, 1971.

16. "Project STORMFURY Crew Ready for Storm," *Atlanta Daily World*, July 13, 1972.

17. "Hurricane Fighters in Search of New Action: Stormfury Scientists Now Want to Send Flyers to Seed Pacific Ocean Typhoons," *Los Angeles Times*, December 10, 1971.

18. "Pacific May Get Storm-Taming Project," *Los Angeles Times*, July 6, 1976.

19. "Scientists Now Fly Hurricane Missions: Use Computers to Refine Predictions," *Los Angeles Times*, October 9, 1977.

20. "Dry Mexico Thinks U.S. Hijacked Its Hurricane," *Washington Post*, July 7, 1980.

21. "Searching for Ways to Control Weather," *Chicago Tribune*, June 26, 1974.

22. R. W. Knight and G. W. Brier, "A Technique for Evaluating the Effectiveness of Hurricane Modification Experiments," *Applied Meteorology* 17 (1978): 222–27.

23. "'73 Hurricanes to Be Graded," *Bridgeport Post*, May 9, 1973.

24. Saffir-Simpson Team, "The Saffir-Simpson Hurricane Wind Scale," National Hurricane Center, updated February 2012, www.nhc.noaa.gov/pdf/sshws.pdf.

25. The Beaufort Scale (introduced in 1805) defined different types of breezes for sailors at sea. For example, it specified the difference between a "stiff breeze" and a "soft breeze." The Beaufort Scale did not include a difference between a breeze and tropical storms, nor did it delineate the size of tropical storms when originally introduced. In 1946, the Beaufort Scale was updated to include tropical storms as part of its listing of winds.

26. Debi Iacovelli, "The Saffir/Simpson Hurricane Scale: An Interview with Dr. Robert Simpson," *Mariners Weather Log*, April 1999.

27. Ted Fujita, "Proposed Characterization of Tornadoes and Hurricanes by Area and Intensity," *Satellite and Mesometeorology Research Paper* 91 (1971).

28. C. F. Richter, "An Instrumental Earthquake Magnitude Scale," *Bulletin of the Seismological Society of America* 25, no. 1 (January 1935): 1–32.

29. Thomas C. Hanks and Hiroo Kanamori, "A Moment Magnitude Scale," *Journal of Geophysical Research* 84, vol. B5 (May 1979): 2348–50.

30. Rozario, *The Culture of Calamity*.

31. US Congress, Disaster Relief Act of 1950, Pub. L. No. 81-875, § 64 Stat. 1109.

32. "The National Plan for Emergency Preparedness," Office of Emergency Planning (Washington, DC: Government Printing Office, December 1964).

33. "Senate Passes Omnibus Disaster Relief Bill," *CQ Almanac 1965* (Washington, DC: Congressional Quarterly, 1966), library.cqpress.com/cqalmanac/cqa165-1260010.

34. Andrew Morris, "Hurricane Camille and the New Politics of Federal Disaster Relief, 1965–1970," *Journal of Policy History* 26, no. 3 (2014): 406–26.

35. Tao et al., "The Research of Dr. Joanne Simpson."

36. "Hurricane Season Comes Again," *Atlanta Journal-Constitution*, June 4, 1972.

37. President Richard Nixon, "Statement about the Disaster Relief Act of 1974," May 22, 1974, *The American Presidency Project,* www.presidency.ucsb.edu/ws/?pid=4218.

38. US Congress, Disaster Relief Act of 1974, Pub. L. No. 93-288.

39. Ibid.

40. "The Federal Emergency Management Agency," FEMA, Washington, DC, November 2010.

41. Office of Technology Assessment, "Chapter 8: Public Attitudes toward Nuclear Power," *Nuclear Power in the Age of Uncertainty* (Washington, DC: US Congress, Office of Technology Assessment, OTA-E-216, February 1984), 210–47, OTA Legacy pages, Princeton University, www.princeton.edu/~ota/.

42. Office of the President, Executive Order No. 12,127, 44 Fed. Reg. 19,367 (Mar. 31, 1979), rpt. in 15 USC § 2201.

43. Frank Batten and Jeffrey L Cruikshank, *The Weather Channel: The Improbable Rise of a Media Phenomenon* (Boston: Harvard Business School Press, 2002).

44. Connie Sage, *Frank Batten: The Untold Story of the Founder of the Weather Channel* (Charlottesville: University of Virginia Press, 2011).

45. Scott Collins, *Crazy like a Fox: The Inside Story of How Fox News Beat CNN* (New York: Penguin Group, 2004); Bill Kovach and Tom Rosenstiel, *Warp Speed: America in the Age of Mixed Media* (New York: Century Foundation Press, 1999).

46. Ingrid Volkmer, *News in the Global Sphere: A Study of CNN and Its Impact on Global Communication* (Luton, UK: University of Luton Press, 1999).

47. Stuart H Loory, Ann Imse, and Cable News Network, *CNN Reports: Seven Days That Shook the World* (Atlanta: Turner Pub., 1991); Hank Whittemore, *CNN: The Inside Storm: How a Band of Mavericks Changed the Face of Television News* (New York: Little, Brown, 1990); Steve M. Barkin, "The Impact of CNN," *American Television News: The Media Marketplace and the Public Interest* (New York: M. E. Sharpe, 2003).

48. Alex Berg, "Al Roker, CNN, Weather Channel, and More Hilarious Wind-Blown Reporters," *Daily Beast* (blog), August 29, 2012, www.thedailybeast.com/al-roker-cnn-weather-channel-and-more-hilarious-wind-blown-reporters.

49. This term (along with the stigma associated with it) is still used today. Most recently (2017), three leading female meteorologists—Ginger Zee, Jen Carfagno, and Janice Huff—drew attention to it on national television, citing the stigma this gendered label has on shaping young girls' ideas of women not only in meteorology but in all science, technology, engineering, and math fields. "Stop Calling Us 'Weather Girls,'" they stated on air, quickly inspiring dozens of articles and posts about the subject (and others, such as the comments made about female meteorologists' attire, attitudes, and capabilities). For the current Weather Girl debate, see Maria Gallucci, "Meteorologists to the World: 'Don't Call Me Weather Girl,'" *Mashable,* January 29,

2017, mashable.com/2017/01/29/weather-channel-meteorologists-weather-girl/; for the perception of women in meteorology since the 1990s, see "Sleeveless: The Sheath: A Particular Brand of Female-Anchor Sexy," Slate.com, April 29, 2013, www.slate.com/articles/double_x/doublex/2013/04/female_tv_newscasters_and_the_sleeveless_sheath_dress; for Margaret Orr, see "WDSU Promotes Margaret Orr to Chief Meteorologist," *TVNewsCheck*, December 23, 2008, www.tvnewscheck.com/article/28207.

50. Perryman and Theiss, "'Weather Girls' on the Big Screen," 347–56.

51. Richard Roeper, "The Camcorder Never Blinks," *Chicago Sun-Times*, March 11, 1990.

52. Due to popularity, TWC includes a "Video Submission Agreement" on their website to submit personal videos, www.weather.com/multimedia/agreement.html.

53. "We're Changing the Weather, and Sometimes That's Good," *Chicago Tribune*, November 30, 1980.

54. Jack Williams, "How the Super El Niño of 1982–83 Kept Itself a Secret," *Washington Post*, June 12, 2015.

55. Tropical Storm Bud in Emil B. Gunther, "Eastern North Pacific Tropical Cyclones of 1978," *Monthly Weather Review* 107 (July 1979): 911–27.

56. Don McLeod, "Males to Share the Billing in Names for Hurricanes," *The Day (New London, Conn.)*, May 15, 1978.

57. "Hurricane Bob? Stormy Feminists Sink Tradition of Feminine Storms," *Wilmington Morning Star*, May 13, 1978.

58. "Hurricanes: U.S. Escaped Direct Hit in 'Average' Season This Year, but That Could Change," *St. Petersburg Independent*, December 2, 1978.

59. Gunther, "Eastern North Pacific Tropical Cyclones of 1978."

60. "75 Flee, Homes Damaged as Hurricane Hits Hawaii," *Los Angeles Times*, July 21, 1978.

61. "Heavy Surf Will Create Riptide Peril on Weekend," *Los Angeles Times*, July 14, 1978.

62. "Hurricane Fico Brushes Hawaii," *Chicago Tribune*, July 21, 1979.

63. "How It Works: Beyond Jennifer and Jason," *New York Times*, October 13, 1995.

64. Susan Page, "Hurricane Bob Joins Ladies," *Newsday*, May 28, 1979.

65. "David Hits Cuba; Fla. Is Alerted," *New Orleans Times-Picayune*, September 2, 1979.

66. "60,000 in Dominica Homeless as David Thunders Northward," *Raleigh News & Observer*, August 31, 1979.

67. "50,000 Weather Storms in Shelters; More Leave Their Homes Willingly," *Miami Herald*, September 3, 1979.

68. "Storm Still Threat to Georgia Coast: 'David to Hit Charleston,'" *Houston Chronicle*, September 4, 1979.

69. "Hurricane Batters Miami: Thousands Flee Homes in S. Florida," *Miami Herald*, September 3, 1979.

70. "Flights in Eye Give Best Data on Hurricanes," *New York Times*, September 2, 1979.

71. David and Frederic, cartoon, *Miami Herald*, September 4, 1979.

72. "Hurricane Kills 84; Evacuation of Keys Ordered in Florida," *New York Times*, September 2, 1979.

73. "Hurricane Kills 10 in Caribbean Islands," *New York Times*, August 31, 1979.

74. "National News Summary," *New York Times,* September 3, 1979.
75. "Frederic and Company," *New Orleans Times-Picayune,* September 14, 1979.
76. "Mobile Is Left in Shambles," *New Orleans Times-Picayune,* September 14, 1979; "Gulf Coast Menace," *New Orleans Times-Picayune,* September 12, 1979.
77. "Recovery Begins in Crippled City," *New Orleans Times-Picayune,* September 14, 1979.
78. "Picking Up Pieces of Life," *New Orleans Times-Picayune,* September 14, 1979.
79. "Mobile Press-Register 200th Anniversary: Devastation of Hurricane Frederic's Damages Left Young Reporter Heartbroken, Public Officials Speechless," AL.com, June 23, 2013, blog.al.com/live/2013/06/mobile_press-register_200th_an_22.html.
80. "Indecisive Elena Sits Offshore," *Houston Chronicle,* September 1, 1979.
81. "Frederic and Company," *New Orleans Times-Picayune.*
82. "A typical August storm" in "Hurricanes Don't Go by the Book," *New Orleans Times-Picayune,* August 9, 1980; "relatively well-behaved" in "Texans Flee Coast before Killer Allen," *New Orleans Times-Picayune,* August 9, 1980.
83. "Teased" in "Southwest La. Is Prepared If Allen Turns," *New Orleans Times-Picayune,* August 9, 1980; "coy" in "Stalled Allen Punishes Texas," *New Orleans Times-Picayune,* August 10, 1980.
84. "State Preparing for the Worst," *New Orleans Times-Picayune,* August 7, 1980.
85. "Hurricanes Don't Go by the Book," *New Orleans Times-Picayune.*
86. "Texans Flee Coast before Killer Allen," *New Orleans Times-Picayune.*
87. "Killer" in "Texans Flee Coast before Killer Allen," *New Orleans Times-Picayune;* "punished" in "Corpus Christi Fears Brunt of Storm Fury," *New Orleans Times-Picayune,* August 10, 1980; "socked" in "Hurricane Alley Socked by Storm," *New Orleans Times-Picayune,* August 9, 1980.
88. "Our Opinions," *New Orleans Times-Picayune,* August 8, 1980.
89. "Hurricane Allen Tropical Cyclone Report: July 31–August 11, 1980," NOAA, National Hurricane Center Data Archive, www.nhc.noaa.gov/data/?#tcr.
90. "Allen Could Become Strongest Storm Ever," *New Orleans Times-Picayune,* August 8, 1980.
91. Willoughby et al., "Project STORMFURY: A Scientific Chronicle, 1962–1983."
92. "Dry Mexico Thinks U.S. Hijacked Its Hurricane," *Washington Post,* July 7, 1980.
93. "We're Changing the Weather, and Sometimes That's Good," *Chicago Tribune,* November 30, 1980.
94. "Preliminary Report: Hurricane Alicia, 15 to 21 August 1983," NOAA, National Hurricane Center Data Archive, www.nhc.noaa.gov/data/?#tcr.
95. "Fickle Alicia Puzzled Forecasters," in *Biloxi Sun Herald,* August 18, 1983.
96. "Stalked the Texas coast" in "Hurricanes Pose 3-Way Danger with Storm Surge, Winds, Rain," *Houston Chronicle,* August 18, 1983; "Fickle" in "Fickle Alicia Puzzled Forecasters," *Biloxi Sun Herald;* "slaps" in "Alicia Slaps Texas; Falling Trees Kill Two," *Biloxi Sun Herald,* August 18, 1983; "Angry woman's 100-plus mph winds" in "Ironic Twists of Fate Reported in Fury of Hurricane Alicia," *Houston Chronicle,* August 18, 1983.
97. "Weather Service's New Forecast System Rated High in Its 1st Test," *Houston Chronicle,* August 18, 1983.

98. "Frederic Holds Record for Hurricane Damage in U.S.," *Houston Chronicle,* August 19, 1983.

99. "Damage Report for Texas, La.," *Houston Chronicle,* August 18, 1983.

100. "U.S. Is Mobilizing Disaster Aid to Local Governments, Individuals," *Houston Chronicle,* August 20, 1983.

101. "Evacuation Orders Prove to Be a Hoax," *Houston Chronicle,* August 18, 1983.

102. "Some Experts Fault Houston Code for Glass Buildings," *New York Times,* August 19, 1983.

103. "Despite Technology, Storm Stumps Pros," *Miami Herald,* August 18, 1983.

104. "Elena Calm Compared to Betsy," *New Orleans Times-Picayune,* September 3, 1985.

105. "Elena Is 'No Show' and Mississippi Is Happy," *New Orleans Times-Picayune,* September 1, 1985.

106. "Elena Was Easier Than Most on Gulf Coast," *New Orleans Times-Picayune,* September 3, 1985.

107. "Hurricane Juan Kills 3 as It Batters Gulf Coast," *New York Times,* October 29, 1985.

108. Ibid.

109. "Pounded," "whirled," and "sliced through" in "Hurricane Juan Kills 3 as It Batters Gulf Coast"; "Grew too fast" in "Juan Grew Too Fast to Evacuate Offshore Workers, Officials Say," *St. Petersburg Independent,* October 30, 1985.

110. "Juan Is Waning, but Its Waters Are Keeping Louisiana Flooded," *St. Petersburg Independent,* October 30, 1985.

111. Ibid.

112. Information on the history of professional wrestling and disaster-based nom de guerre provided by historians Christopher Stacey and Charles Pellegrin. Erik Beaston, "WWE Classic of the Week: Hulk Hogan vs. Earthquake from SummerSlam 1990," *Bleacher Report,* August 4, 2015, www.google.com/amp/s/syndication.bleacherreport.com/amp/2539067-wwe-classic-of-the-week-hulk-hogan-vs-earthquake-from-summerslam-1990.amp.html. The Louisiana oil industry suffered a significant blow in the mid-1980s when deregulation upset the local markets. This made hurricanes like Juan all the more frightening. See Jason P. Theriot, *American Energy, Imperiled Coast: Oil and Gas Development in Louisiana's Wetlands* (Baton Rouge: Louisiana State University Press, 2014).

113. "'El Niño' Says 'Adios,'" *Los Angeles Times,* April 25, 1988.

114. "Gilbert Lashes Cayman Islands; Winds Rise to 175 mph," *Baltimore Sun,* September 14, 1988.

115. "Mobile Area Returns to Normal," *Mobile Press-Register,* September 11, 1988.

116. "Hurricane Is Reported to Damage over 600,000 Homes in Jamaica," *New York Times,* September 12, 1988.

117. "Mr. Gilbert" in "Gilbert Rages into Gulf," *Biloxi Sun-Herald,* September 14, 1988.

118. "Pounded" in "Gilbert Pounds Jamaica; Radio Reports 30 Deaths," *Baltimore Sun,* September 13, 1988; "slammed" in "Hurricane Gilbert Slams Jamaica," *Charleston Post & Courier,* September 13, 1988; "flayed" in "Florence Whips Coast, Tapers to Storm," *Houston Chronicle,* September 10, 1988; "blasted" in "Hurricane Rips Caymans; Loss Feared Heavy," *Los Angeles Times,* September 13, 1988.

119. "175-mph Gilbert Threatens Gulf," *Raleigh News & Observer,* September 14, 1988.

120. "Gilberto" in "Next Up: Hurricane Gilbert?" *Biloxi Sun-Herald,* September 11, 1988; "Yucatan Resorts Make Ready for Gilbert's Visit," *Houston Chronicle,* September 14, 1988.

121. The Incredible Hulk was a Marvel comics character popularized in superhero television shows, comics, and movies. One such made-for-television movie was *The Trial of the Incredible Hulk,* which premiered in 1989 on NBC and was based on a popular television series that ran from 1978 to 1982. See "Superheroes' Battleground: Primetime," *New York Times,* October 11, 1988.

122. "National Disaster Survey Report: Hurricane Gilbert, Sept 3–16, 1988," NOAA and Department of Commerce, based on survey completed September 22, 1988, NHC Library.

123. Robert T. Stafford Disaster Relief And Emergency Assistance Act, P.L. 93-288, Washington, DC: Federal Emergency Management Agency, 1988.

124. US Congress, Disaster Relief and Emergency Assistance Amendments of 1988 as part of the Disaster Relief Act of 1974, Pub. L. No. 93-288, 42 USC § 5121 et seq.

125. Francis X. McCarthy, "Federal Stafford Act Disaster Assistance: Presidential Declarations, Eligible Activities, and Funding," Congressional Research Service Report for Congress, June 7, 2011, fas.org/sgp/crs/homesec/RL33053.pdf.

126. President Ronald Reagan, "Executive Order 12657—Federal Emergency Management Agency Assistance in Emergency Preparedness Planning at Commercial Nuclear Power Plants," November 18, 1988, *The American Presidency Project,* www.presidency.ucsb.edu/ws/?pid=35184.

127. "Reagan's Defense Buildup Bridged Military Eras," *Washington Post,* June 9, 2004.

128. "In the Wake of Hurricane Hugo: Hugo Fools Forecasters and Bypasses MD," *Baltimore Sun,* September 23, 1989.

129. "Eye of the Storm: Hugo Rips Charleston," *Baltimore Sun,* September 23, 1989.

130. "Irate Residents Confront Guard at Myrtle Beach," *Atlanta Journal-Constitution,* September 23, 1989.

131. "Southeast Bracing for Hugo," *Houston Chronicle,* September 20, 1989.

132. "Charleston Devastated: At Least 9 Dead as Hugo Levels Buildings, Floods Historic City," *Los Angeles Times,* September 21, 1989.

133. "Mansions Withstand Hugo's Ire," *Mobile Press-Register,* September 23, 1989.

134. "'What Was That?' Hugo Survivor Asks," *Houston Chronicle,* September 24, 1989.

135. "Hugo's March from Sea Churns S.C. Coast," *Raleigh News & Observer,* September 23, 1989.

136. "Worshippers Look to God after Hugo," *Charleston Post & Courier,* September 24, 1989.

137. For the casting of the male body in times of war, see Christina S. Jarvis, *The Male Body at War: American Masculinity during World War II* (DeKalb: Northern Illinois University Press, 2010).

138. "S.C. Coast Braces for Hurricane Strike," *Charleston Post & Courier,* September 21, 1989.

139. "Beachfront Homes Tossed in Wind," *Miami Herald,* September 23, 1989.

140. Global Terrorism Database, National Consortium for the Study of Terrorism and Responses to Terrorism, University of Maryland, created 2009, www.start.umd.edu/gtd/about/.

141. Candice Ortbals and Lori Poloni-Staudinger, "How Gender Intersects with Political Violence and Terrorism," *Oxford Research Encyclopedia of Politics*, February 2018, doi:10.1093/acrefore/9780190228637.013.308.

142. "Devastated by Hurricane, Montserrat Starts to Rebuild," *New York Times*, September 22, 1989.

143. Alice Cooper, "Hurricane Years," *Hey Stoopid*, Bearsville, July 2, 1991.

144. "U.S. Hurricane Strikes by Decade," National Hurricane Center, www.nhc.noaa.gov/pastdec.shtml.

145. William K. Stevens, "More Strong Hurricanes Predicted for East in Next 2 Decades," *New York Times*, September 25, 1990.

146. Ed Rappaport, "Preliminary Report: Hurricane Andrew, 16–28 August 1992," National Hurricane Center, December 10, 1993, www.nhc.noaa.gov/1992andrew.html.

147. "Louisiana Is Hit by High Wind & Water," *New York Times*, August 26, 1992.

148. "Vendors Hawk Hurricane Mementos," *Miami Herald*, August 28, 1992.

149. Bryan Norcross, *My Hurricane Andrew Story* (Bryan Norcross Corporation, 2017).

150. Jason Samenow, "Bryan Norcross, Hero of Hurricane Andrew: Florida Is 'Not Remotely Prepared' for the Next One," *Washington Post*, August 23, 2017, www.washingtonpost.com/news/capital-weather-gang/wp/2017/08/23/bryan-norcross-hero-of-hurricane-andrew-florida-is-not-remotely-prepared-for-the-next-one/.

151. "Channel 4, Norcross Excel," *Miami Herald*, August 24, 1992.

152. "Hurricane Turns Big Easy into Big Queasy—Andrew Stirs Memories of Earlier Killers," *Atlanta Journal-Constitution*, August 25, 1992.

153. "Bigger, Stronger, Closer: South Florida Bracing for Hurricane Andrew," *Miami Herald*, August 23, 1992.

154. "Leaving marks like bullet holes" in "Homestead AFB Devastated," *Miami Herald*, August 26, 1992; "spun like dice" in "Andrew's Death List Spanned Dade County," *Miami Herald*, August 26, 1992.

155. "Monster" in "When a Monster Is on the Way, 'It's Time to Get Out of Town,'" *New York Times*, August 26, 1992; "king" in "A Million Are Told to Flee Hurricane in South Florida," *New York Times*, August 24, 1992; and, "bath tub toys" in "At Least 9 Killed—Houses Left in Splinters," *New York Times*, August 25, 1992.

156. "Spit shingles" and "mowed development" in "Miami Suburb Was 'Just Defenseless,'" *Raleigh News & Observer*, August 25, 1992; "methodically" and "giant jig-saw puzzle pieces" in "800 Louisiana Evacuees Had Close Encounter with Andrew," *Raleigh News & Observer*, August 27, 1992; "carved" in "Andrew Cuts Swath through Louisiana," *Raleigh News & Observer*, August 27, 1992; "accelerator" in "Andrew Is Nasty, Full of Surprises," *Raleigh News & Observer*, August 24, 1992.

157. "Throb with agency" in "Voices of Stoicism, Fear & Revelry as Many Prepare to Ride Out Storm," August 24, 1992; "ferocious" in "Amid Wreckage, Survivors Tell Their Stories," *New York Times*, August 25, 1992.

158. "Clobbers Florida" in "An Awful Howl," *Miami Herald;* "One of the century's most powerful" in "Louisiana Is Hit by High Wind & Water," *New York Times*, August 26, 1992.

159. "Grand Isle, N.O. Begin Hurricane Preparations," *New Orleans Times-Picayune*, August 24, 1992; "Residents Fleeing as Andrew Bears Down on Florida," *New Orleans Times-Picayune*, August 24, 1992.

160. "Bitch Elena" in "Andrew Slides By," *Biloxi Daily Sun-Herald*, August 26, 1992; "Andrew Having His Way" in "Storm Leaves South Florida with Multibillion Dollar Mess," *Biloxi Daily Sun-Herald*, August 25, 1992; "stomping" in "Possessions Not So Important," *Biloxi Daily Sun-Herald*, August 25, 1992.

161. "Windbag Named Andrew" in "Gone with the Wind—Hurricane Andrew Cuts Homecoming Crowd," *Houston Chronicle*, August 26, 1992; "set its deadly sights" in "La. Gets Jump on Storm—Coastal Residents Told to Evacuate," *Houston Chronicle*, August 25, 1992.

162. "After Andrew, Quakes No Longer So Terrifying," *New Orleans Times-Picayune*.

163. "God's explosion" in "'God's Explosion' Devoured S. Florida," *Houston Chronicle*, August 26, 1992; "big blow" in "Getting Ready for the Big Blow," *Houston Chronicle*, August 26, 1992; "plowed the coast" in "1 Million Told to Flee Andrew—S. Fla. Braces for Huge Storm," *Houston Chronicle*, August 24, 1992.

164. "Night of Anguish and Relief," *Miami Herald*, August 25, 1992.

165. "Andy" in "Folks Fleeing Andy Pack Area Hotels," *Mobile Press-Register*, August 26, 1992; "furious swipe" in "Storm Brings Homelessness Home," *Miami Herald*, August 27, 1992; "bounced back" and "boxer" in "Andrew Is Nasty, Full of Surprises," *Raleigh News & Observer*.

166. "The Man Who Talked South Florida Through," *Miami Herald*, August 25, 1992.

167. "Weather Experts Caught in Middle," *New Orleans Times-Picayune*, August 25, 1992.

168. "Homestead AFB Devastated," *Miami Herald*, August 26, 1992.

169. Jay Barnes, *Florida's Hurricane History*, 2nd ed. (Chapel Hill: University of North Carolina Press, 2007), 274.

170. Lizette Alvarez, "From Forecast to Disaster: A Timeline at the National Hurricane Center," *New York Times*, August 30, 2017.

171. "What Went Wrong," *Newsweek*, September 6, 1992.

172. "Bush Inspects Storm Damage in South Miami," *New Orleans Times-Picayune*, August 25, 1992.

173. "We Need Help (Andrew)," *Miami Herald*, August 28, 1992; "Relief Bottlenecks Bring Appeals for More Troops," *Miami Herald*, August 28, 1992; "Recovery Varies Widely across Dade," *Miami Herald*, August 28, 1992.

174. "Hurricane Andrew—During and after the Storm Excerpts WTVJ," August 23–24, 1992, *WTVJ-Miami* clips on YouTube, posted by moviemagg, www.youtube.com/watch?v=qV3HWSDxtC4.

175. "Hurricane Andrew, We Need Help! Part-1, Part-2," *Channel 7-Miami* clips on YouTube, posted by moviemagg, accessed December 2, 2017, www.youtube.com/watch?v=qV3HWSDxtC4.

176. Mike Clary, "Personality in the News: Disaster Official Stands Fast in the Eye of Political Storm," *Los Angeles Times*, August 28, 1992.

177. "Hurricane Andrew Still Haunts Florida 25 Years Later," *USA Today*, August 24, 2017.

178. "Hurricane May Have Exposed Flaws in New Disaster Relief Plan," *Washington Post*, September 3, 1992.

179. "Bush Inspects La. Damage, Says 'It Shows That I Care,'" *New Orleans Times-Picayune*, August 27, 1992.

180. "The Storm: Interview with James Lee Witt," *Frontline*, PBS, November 22, 2005.

181. Naim Kapucu et al., "U.S. Presidents and Their Roles in Emergency Management and Disaster Policy, 1950–2009," *Risk, Hazards, & Crisis in Public Policy* 2, issue 3 (October 2011): 1–34.

182. "Perverse Andrew" and "devilish prank of a storm" in "Devilish Prank of a Storm Steals Our Shade," *Miami Herald*, August 27, 1992; "nuclear winter" in "Fear Invades South Dade's Dark Nights," *Miami Herald*, August 28, 1992.

183. "God-fearing speed" in "Storm at Most Savage in 2 South Dade Cities," *Miami Herald*, August 25, 1992; "an enchanted forest on LSD" in "This Time, the Tragedy Lies Outside My Own Front Door," *Miami Herald*, August 26, 1992; "modern-day Pompeii" in "Andrew Humbled Once-Proud Homestead Base," *Miami Herald*, August 28, 1992.

184. "Air bomb" in "At Least 9 Killed—Houses Left in Splinters"; "killer" in "Hurricane Andrew Begins to Worry Guice," *Biloxi Daily Sun-Herald*, August 23, 1992; "monster" in "Daring the Monster Hurricanes," *New Orleans Times-Picayune*, August 27, 1992.

185. "Andrew's Name Will Be Retired," *New Orleans Times-Picayune*, August 25, 1992.

186. Joaquin Aviro, Dade County manager, qtd. in "Andrew's Name Will Be Retired."

187. "Hurricane Statistics Fast Facts," *CNN*, last updated May 8, 2018, www.cnn.com/2013/05/31/world/americas/hurricane-statistics-fast-facts/index.html.

188. John Guiney and Miles Lawrence, "Preliminary Report: Hurricane Mitch," National Hurricane Center, January 28, 1999.

189. "Opal's Havoc: Panicky Panhandle Stunned—Storm Alert Eclipsed by O. J. Verdict," *Miami Herald*, October 5, 1995.

190. The 1991 storm in Bob Chartruk, "NOAA Meteorologist Bob Case, the Man Who Named the Perfect Storm," NOAA News Online, June 16, 2000, www.noaanews.noaa.gov/stories/s444.htm. The 1997 book by Sebastian Junger, *The Perfect Storm: A True Story of Men against the Sea* (New York: Norton, 1997), was also made into a movie: Warner Brothers Pictures, *The Perfect Storm*, June 30, 2000.

191. John Guiney, "Preliminary Report: Hurricane Georges," National Hurricane Center, January 5, 1999.

192. "Georges Defies the Odds," *Biloxi Daily Sun-Herald*, October 25, 1998.

193. "Georges Plows in with Wind, Water," *New Orleans Times-Picayune*, September 28, 1998.

194. "Energizer Bunny" in "Strong Winds Expected to Rake N.O. by Tonight," *New Orleans Times-Picayune*, September 26, 1998; "Menace was in the air" in "Some Face Storm with Shrug, Smile," *New Orleans Times-Picayune*, September 26, 1998.

195. "Fateful zig east" in "Georges' Wobble Spared N.O. Area," *New Orleans Times-Picayune*, September 29, 1998; "showed off its arsenal" in "The Toll of the Unwelcome Tourist," *New Orleans Times-Picayune*, September 30, 1998.

196. "We're Really Thankful It Wasn't Worse: Rains Still Hammering Coast," *New Orleans Times-Picayune,* September 30, 1998.

197. "Georges Was an Island Hopper: The Hurricane Bypassed Most of the Caribbean; the Unlucky Few Are Now Cleaning Up," *New York Times,* October 25, 1998.

198. "Yes, It Could Happen Here," *New York Times,* October 25, 1998.

199. "Georges Was an Island Hopper."

200. James Gill, "An Ambiguous Farewell to Georges," *New Orleans Times-Picayune,* September 30, 1998.

201. Michael Rogin, *Ronald Reagan: The Movie and Other Episodes in Political Demonology* (Berkeley: University of California Press, 1987).

202. Michael S. Kimmel, *Manhood in America: A Cultural History* (New York: Oxford University Press, 2018).

203. Margot Canaday, *The Straight State: Sexuality and Citizenship in Twentieth-Century America* (Princeton, NJ: Princeton University Press, 2011).

204. John D'Emilio and Estelle B Freedman, *Intimate Matters: A History of Sexuality in America,* 3rd ed. (Chicago: University of Chicago Press, 2013).

205. Randy Shilts, *And the Band Played On: Politics, People, and the AIDS Epidemic,* 25th anniversary ed. (New York: St. Martin's Griffin, 2007).

206. Sarah S. Richardson, *Sex Itself: The Search for Male and Female in the Human Genome* (Chicago: University of Chicago Press, 2013).

207. "Menace in the Caribbean," *Miami Herald,* October 27, 1998.

208. Guiney and Lawrence, "Preliminary Report: Hurricane Mitch."

209. "Mitch Aims at Mexico," *Charleston Post & Courier,* October 28, 1998.

210. "Creeps" in "Jamaica Braces as Hurricane Threatens," *Miami Herald,* October 25, 1998; "monster" and "prowls" in "Hurricane Grows into Monster Storm," *Miami Herald,* October 26, 1998; "lashing" in "Mitch Lashes Central America," *Miami Herald,* October 29, 1998.

211. "Mitch's Gusts Hit 180 mph," *Mobile Press-Register,* October 26, 1998.

212. "Mitch Loses Steam but May Regain in Gulf," *New Orleans Times-Picayune,* October 29, 1998.

213. "The Eye of a Monster," *Los Angeles Times,* October 28, 1998.

214. "'Mean' Floyd Imperils Coast," *Raleigh News & Observer,* September 14, 1999.

215. "Big Storms Fascinate Americans," *Biloxi Sun Herald,* September 15, 1999.

216. "1 Million in Florida Flee Menacing Floyd," *New Orleans Times-Picayune,* September 14, 1999.

217. "Floyd Has East Coast Guessing, but Fleeing," *New Orleans Times-Picayune,* September 15, 1999.

218. "Infamous Andrew" in "1 Million in Florida Flee Menacing Floyd"; "Ugly Boy Floyd" in "Ugly Boy Floyd," *New Orleans Times-Picayune,* September 15, 1999; "Giant" in "Floyd Has East Coast Guessing, but Fleeing," *New Orleans Times-Picayune.*

219. "Beast" and "stalked" in "A Sense of Dread: Florida Braces for Worst as Hurricane Stalks Coast," *Miami Herald,* September 14, 1999; "the Big One" in "Waiting for Floyd: This May Be 'Big One,'" *Miami Herald,* September 14, 1999.

220. "Growth Factors Nearly Perfect," *Miami Herald,* September 15, 1999.

221. Ibid.

222. "Evacuating Charleston, SC, 4½—How Trip Took 12 Hours," *Richmond Times-Dispatch,* September 16, 1999.

223. "Streaked" and "like vandal" in "Floyd Leaves Mess in Va.," *Richmond Times-Dispatch,* September 17, 1999; "lethal" and "quick visit" in "Hurricane's Quick Visit Spurs Lingering Woes," *Richmond Times-Dispatch,* September 17, 1999.

224. "Rough flirtation" in "VA Power Workers to the Rescue—Crews from Other Areas Help Turn Lights Back On Here," *Richmond Times-Dispatch,* September 17, 1999; "Kissed Washington" and "blew the house down" in "Floyd 'Blew the House Down,'" *Richmond Times-Dispatch,* September 17, 1999.

225. "Stormy Weather," *Richmond Times-Dispatch,* September 18, 1999.

226. "Why Don't We Bomb Hurricane Floyd," *Richmond Times-Dispatch,* September 14, 1999.

227. "Storm on Path to Hit Va. by Thursday," *Richmond Times-Dispatch,* September 14, 1999.

228. "Islanders Take No Chances," *Charleston Post & Courier,* September 15, 1999.

229. "Thousands Flood Roads to Flee Storm," *Charleston Post & Courier,* September 15, 1999.

230. "Facing Floyd with Benefit of Experience," *Charleston Post & Courier,* September 15, 1999.

231. "Florida Evacuates 1.3 Million in 24 Hours—Success Attributed to Storm Not Straying from Path," *Houston Chronicle,* September 16, 1999.

232. "Storm Doesn't Stifle Joy-Seekers," *Charleston Post & Courier,* September 18, 1999.

233. "Took a beating" in "Service Industry Hurt by Floyd," *Charleston Post & Courier,* September 18, 1999; "Soaks but doesn't bruise" in "Floyd Soaks but Doesn't Bruise North," *New Orleans Times-Picayune,* September 17, 1999; "gyrated" in "At Least 31 Die—Towns Are Inundated," *New York Times,* September 18, 1999.

234. "Monster hurricane" in "Even before Landfall, Floyd Drives Unprecedented Flooding, Record Evacuees," *Los Angeles Times,* September 16, 1999; "Furious Floyd" in "After Floyd's Fury," *Raleigh News & Observer,* September 17, 1999; "pulling its punch" in "Floyd Weakens, Pulls Its Punch," *Houston Chronicle,* September 17, 1999.

235. "An exhausted marathon runner" in "Northeast Soaked as Floyd Fades Out," *Miami Herald,* September 17, 1999; "muddy and miserable" in "Storm Left N. J. Town Muddy, Miserable," *Miami Herald,* September 19, 1999.

236. "South Florida Restless Evacuate from Doldrums of Floyd Fever," *Miami Herald,* September 15, 1999.

237. This includes the 1998 Bill Clinton–Monica Lewinsky and 1991 Anita Hill–Clarence Thomas scandals. See Starr Commission, *The Starr Report* (Washington, DC: Government Printing Office, 1998); Anita Hill, *Speaking Truth to Power* (New York: Anchor Books, 1997).

238. "Gaze Deeply into My Eye: A Public Fixated on the Weather Is Mesmerized by Floyd," *New York Times,* September 17, 1999.

239. This figure is based on the storms studied in this book's database and information collected from FEMA reports of cost of storms. It was adjusted based on inflation for its 2017 comparable figure.

240. Chartruk, "NOAA Meteorologist Bob Case."

241. "Storm of the Century of the Week," *The Daily Show with Jon Stewart*, Comedy Central, Episode 4031, September 16, 1999.

5. Katrina and Hurricane 2.0

1. Gian Smith, "O Beautiful Storm," poem as spoken in "Season 2: O Beautiful Storm Extended Tease," *Treme: Season 2*, HBO podcasts on iTunes, March 21, 2011.

2. Dave Walker, "How Many People Watched '*Treme*' on HBO?" Nola.com, June 27, 2010, www.nola.com/treme-hbo/index.ssf/2010/06/how_many_people_watched_treme.html.

3. Rachael Brown, "'*Treme*' Finale: The Season Ends Where It Began," *The Atlantic*, June 21, 2010, www.theatlantic.com/entertainment/archive/2010/06/treme-finale-the-season-ends-where-it-began/58446/.

4. Rolf Potts, "*Treme*'s Big Problem: Authenticity," *The Atlantic*, November 27, 2013, www.theatlantic.com/entertainment/archive/2013/11/-em-treme-em-s-big-problem-authenticity/281857/.

5. The Error Cone or Cone of Probability (formerly known as the NHC Track Forecast Cone), also known more commonly as the "Cone of Death," was introduced in in-house NWS projections starting in 2001, and unveiled publicly in 2003. It provides a five-day projection of a storm's potential path and influences evacuations, discussion of potential evacuations and storm effects, and preparation for oncoming storms. "Definition of the NHC Track Forecast Cone," National Hurricane Center, last updated 2017, www.nhc.noaa.gov/aboutcone.shtml, discussed in "How Forecasters Develop Hurricanes' 'Cone of Uncertainty,'" *CNN*, August 24, 2011, news.blogs.cnn.com/2011/08/24/how-forecasters-develop-hurricanes-cone-of-uncertainty/.

6. Johnny Ryan, *A History of the Internet and the Digital Future* (London: Reaktion Books, Ltd., 2010).

7. Internet History Podcast, "The 'First' Blogger, Justin Hall," June 11, 2017, www.internethistorypodcast.com/2017/06/the-first-blog-justin-hall/.

8. Clive Thompson, "The Early Years: Blogging," NYMag.com, nymag.com/news/media/15971/, accessed November 27, 2017.

9. Cameron Chapman, "A Brief History of Blogging," *Webdesigner Depot*, March 14, 2011, www.webdesignerdepot.com/2011/03/a-brief-history-of-blogging/.

10. Pew Research Center, "Social Media Fact Sheet," *Pew Research Center: Internet, Science & Tech* (blog), www.pewinternet.org/fact-sheet/social-media/, accessed January 12, 2017.

11. Thompson, "The Early Years: Blogging."

12. *Charlotte Observer*, "Dispatches from along the Coast," Internet Archive: Wayback Machine, preserved April 17, 2001, web.archive.org/web/20010727122443/http://charlotte.com/special/bonnie/.

13. Chip Scanlan, "Blogging Bonnie," *Poynter*, September 18, 2003, www.poynter.org/news/blogging-bonnie.

14. "Blogs Go On amid Storm—Hurricane Doesn't Stop Web Diarists," *Atlanta Journal-Constitution*, August 14, 2004.

15. "Then and Now: A History of Social Networking Sites," *CBS News*, February 4, 2014, www.cbsnews.com/pictures/then-and-now-a-history-of-social-networking-sites/.

16. Seth Fiegerman, "Facebook Is Closing In on 2 Billion Users," CNN.com, February 1, 2017, money.cnn.com/2017/02/01/technology/facebook-earnings/index.html.

17. Nathan McAlone, "Here's How Janet Jackson's Infamous 'Nipplegate' Inspired the Creation of YouTube," *Business Insider*, October 3, 2015, www.businessinsider.com/idea-for-youtube-came-from-janet-jackson-nipplegate-2015-10.

18. Ibid.

19. "Finding Weather Info on Web" in "Finding Weather Information on the Web," *Baltimore Sun*, September 17, 2003; "Webcams" in "Webcams Keep Coast in View," *Raleigh News & Observer*, September 18, 2003.

20. Between 1954 and 1979, 230 articles were printed on average for each storm. This number increased by 34 percent to 348 articles per storm between 1983 and 2008 with the introduction of 24-hour news. (Statistics from author's database.)

21. Mark Odell, "Timeline: The Rise of PayPal," *Financial Times*, September 30, 2014, www.ft.com/content/86432398-4897-11e4-9d04-00144feab7de; "History of PayPal: 1998 to Now," *Techworld*, November 25, 2015, www.techworld.com/picture-gallery/business/history-of-paypal-1998-now-3630386/.

22. eBay, "About," www.ebay.com/about, accessed November 26, 2017.

23. Civil War postcards in Alfred S. Lippman Collection, "Civil War Postal Covers," Louisiana Research Collection, Special Collections, New Orleans; framed Hindenburg Blimp photos and blimp replicas in Lori Ferber Presidential Memorabilia website, www.loriferber.com/.

24. "Beach Communities Board Up, Bail Out as Ivan Approaches," *New Orleans Times-Picayune*, September 16, 2004.

25. "Frances' Flotsam Floats to eBay," *Miami Herald*, September 7, 2004.

26. Howe, *Behind the Curve*.

27. "All of Us Share in the Sunshine and the Suffering," *Biloxi Daily Sun-Herald*, September 17, 2004.

28. Dwane Powell, "Hurricane Strength," Caglecartoons.com, image no. 11467, August 30, 2005, www.cartoonistgroup.com/subject/The-Storm-Comics-and-Cartoons-by-Dwane+Powell%27s+Editorial+Cartoons.php.

29. "Disasters Declarations (by Year)," FEMA.gov, accessed April 30, 2018, www.fema.gov/disasters.

30. US Congress, Homeland Security Act of 2002, Pub. L. No. 107-296, § 116 Stat. 2135.

31. Ivor van Heerden and Mike Bryan, *The Storm: What Went Wrong and Why during Hurricane Katrina* (New York: Penguin, 2007).

32. "Hurricane Pam Exercise Concludes," FEMA Press Release, July 23, 2004, www.fema.gov/news-release/2004/07/23/hurricane-pam-exercise-concludes.

33. "The Federal Emergency Management Agency Publication 1," Capstone Document, FEMA, Washington, DC, November 2010, www.fema.gov/media-library-data/20130726-1823-25045-8164/pub_1_final.pdf.

34. For changes in response to the definition of disaster (before 2005), see Charles Perrow for post-9/11 response in "The Disaster after 9/11: The Department of Homeland Security and

the Intelligence Reorganization," *Homeland Security Affairs* 2 (April 2006); for concerns about climate and coastal change, see James McCarthy et al., eds., *Climate Change 2001: Impacts, Adaptation, and Vulnerability* (New York: Cambridge University Press, 2001); for blurring of the lines between perceived difference of "man-made" and "natural" hazards, see Ian Burton, Robert Kates, and Gilbert White, *The Environment as Hazard*, 2nd ed. (New York: Guilford Press, 1993).

35. Tonya Adamski, Beth Kline, and Tanya Tyrrell, "FEMA Reorganization and the Response to Hurricane Disaster Relief," *Perspectives in Public Affairs* 3 (Spring 2006): 3–36.

36. "Adds muscle" in "Killer Hurricane Adds Muscle," *Houston Chronicle*, August 27, 2005; "bulks up" in "Katrina Bulks Up to Become a Perfect Storm," *New Orleans Times-Picayune*, August 28, 2005; "curls north" in "Katrina Proves More Rain for Lowcountry," *Charleston Post & Courier*, August 26, 2005.

37. "Closed in" in "Thousands Flee as Hurricane Closes In," *Los Angeles Times*, August 28, 2005; "The Big Uneasy" in "Hurricane Lashes a City Abandoned," *Los Angeles Times*, August 29, 2005; "welcome mat" in "New Orleans Pulls In the Welcome Mat," *New York Times*, August 28, 2005; "Rally and wait" in "Disaster Teams Rally & Wait," *Mobile Press-Register*, September 2, 2005.

38. Gary Rivlin, *Katrina: After the Flood* (New York: Simon & Schuster, 2016).

39. "Hurricane Katrina Kills Two in Florida," *Los Angeles Times*, August 26, 2005.

40. "Katrina: The Storm We've Always Feared," *New Orleans Times-Picayune*, August 30, 2005.

41. "New Orleans Mayor: Get Out of Katrina's way," *Biloxi Sun-Herald*, August 29, 2005.

42. "Evacuation Scramble Puts Contraflow System to the Test," *New Orleans Times-Picayune*, August 29, 2005.

43. "Perfect hurricane" in "Perfect Mix of Conditions Makes Storm a Monster," *Houston Chronicle*, August 29, 2005; "toxic gumbo" in "'Nothing but a Nightmare,'" *Raleigh News & Observer*, September 2, 2005.

44. "Hurricane Katrina: Dealing with Displacement: Geography Complicates Levee Repair," *New York Times*, August 31, 2005.

45. "Back-to-Back Storms Coming," *Charleston Post & Courier*, August 12, 2004.

46. "The Katrina Crawl," *Mobile Press-Register*, August 29, 2005.

47. "NASA Revisits Satellite Images of Hurricane Katrina," *The Atlantic*, August 29, 2011, www.theatlantic.com/national/archive/2011/08/nasa-revisits-satellite-images-of-hurricane-katrina/469659/.

48. "Katrina: The Storm We've Always Feared," *New Orleans Times-Picayune*, August 30, 2005.

49. "Not Again! FL Reels from Jeanne," *Mobile Press-Register*, September 27, 2004.

50. "Loved Ones' Cries for Help Flood the Web," *Raleigh News & Observer*, September 2, 2005.

51. Van Jones, "Black People 'Loot' Food . . . White People 'Find' Food," *Huffington Post Blog*, September 1, 2005, www.huffingtonpost.com/van-jones/black-people-loot-food-wh_b_6614.html.

52. Joshua Clark, *Heart like Water: Surviving Katrina and Life in Its Disaster Zone* (New York: Free Press, 2007).

53. Andrew Adam Newman, "A 'Weather Nerd' in Indiana Sent a Warning to the Mayor," *New York Times*, September 5, 2005, www.nytimes.com/2005/09/05/technology/a-weather-nerd-in-indiana-sent-a-warning-to-the-mayor.html.

54. National Hurricane Center, "Hurricane Katrina Advisory Archive, www.nhc.noaa.gov/archive/2005/KATRINA.shtml, last accessed December 3, 2017.

55. Douglas Brinkley, *The Great Deluge: Hurricane Katrina, New Orleans, and the Mississippi Gulf Coast* (New York: Harper Perennial, 2007).

56. Richard Knabb et al., "Tropical Cyclone Report: Hurricane Katrina," National Hurricane Center, December 20, 2005, www.nhc.noaa.gov/data/tcr/AL122005_Katrina.pdf.

57. "Katrina Lands Deadly Blow on Mississippi," *Mobile Press-Register*, August 30, 2005.

58. "Storm Smacks AL Coast," *Mobile Press-Register*, August 30, 2005.

59. "Under Water/Flooding Will Only Get Worse," *New Orleans Times-Picayune*, August 31, 2005; "Day Long Efforts to Repair Levee Fail," *New Orleans Times-Picayune*, August 31, 2005.

60. "Katrina's Aftermath—'Super Human Effort' Keeps *Times-Picayune* Publishing," *Houston Chronicle*, September 2, 2005.

61. "Gulf Coast Papers Win Pulitzer Prizes," *NBC*, April 17, 2006, www.nbcnews.com/id/12357513/ns/us_news/t/gulf-coast-papers-win-pulitzer-prizes/.

62. "3 Views on a Tragedy: Reporters Recall First Days after Katrina," *NPR.org*, August 29, 2015, www.npr.org/2015/08/29/435623921.

63. "Internet Serves Up Aid for Refugees," *Atlanta Journal-Constitution*, September 2, 2005.

64. "Today at NYTimes.com," *New York Times*, August 31, 2005.

65. "Media Coverage Takes Beating from Disaster," *Atlanta Journal-Constitution*, August 31, 2005.

66. "News, Rage, Needs in NO Blogs," *Houston Chronicle*, September 1, 2005.

67. "Under Siege," *Raleigh News & Observer*, September 1, 2005.

68. "CBD Landmarks in Tatters; Poydras Littered with Debris," *New Orleans Times-Picayune*, August 30, 2005.

69. "Stinging assault" and "smacks" in "Storm Smacks AL Coast," *Mobile Press-Register*, August 30, 2005; "stabs" in "Storm Stabs Airlines," *Mobile Press-Register*, August 30, 2005; "blasts" in "Katrina Blasts Baldwin," *Mobile Press-Register*, August 30, 2005; "knockout punch" in "What Happened to the Relief Response," *Biloxi Sun-Herald*, September 2, 2005; "upending life" in "Katrina Upends Bayou La Batre's Way of Life," *Biloxi Sun-Herald*, September 2, 2005.

70. "Horror show" in "Baldwin, Mobile Take In Evacuees," *Mobile Press-Register*, September 1, 2005; "Rampage" in "After Katrina, Some Islanders Have Little to Come Home To," *Mobile Press-Register*, August 31, 2005.

71. "On the brink of anarchy" in "Brink of Anarchy," *Biloxi Sun-Herald*, September 2, 2005; "Downtown Baghdad" in "'We've Lost Our City,'" *Biloxi Sun-Herald*, August 31, 2005; "Hiroshima" in "'It Looks like Hiroshima,'" *Biloxi Sun-Herald*, August 31, 2005.

72. "Others Look at Katrina," *Mobile Press-Register*, August 31, 2005.

73. "Katrina Bulks Up to Become a Perfect Storm," *New Orleans Times-Picayune*, August 28, 2005.

74. "Cantankerous Katrina" in "In Katrina's Sights," *Biloxi Sun-Herald,* August 27, 2005: A1; "Camille II" in "Roberts Visit Home Is Excruciating," *Biloxi Sun-Herald,* August 31, 2005.

75. "The 'Next Camille' Finally Came," *Mobile Press-Register,* August 31, 2005.

76. "Help Us, Please," *New Orleans Times-Picayune,* September 2, 2005.

77. "Superdome Became a Civic Giant," *Mobile Press-Register,* August 31, 2005.

78. JD Crowe, "Voodoo Priestess Katrina," *Mobile Press-Register,* August 30, 2005.

79. "New Orleans Inundated," *Los Angeles Times,* August 31, 2005.

80. "Life-or-Death Words of the Day in a Battered City: 'I Had to Get Out,'" *New York Times,* August 31, 2005.

81. "Media Coverage Takes Beating from Disaster," *Atlanta Journal-Constitution,* August 31, 2005.

82. "New Orleans Slides into Chaos," *Los Angeles Times,* September 1, 2005.

83. "Storm Claims at Least 55: New Orleans Spared Full Fury of Katrina; Gulf Coast Towns Deal with Devastation," *Charleston Post & Courier,* August 30, 2005.

84. "After Centuries of 'Controlling' Land, Gulf Residents Learn Who's Really the Boss," *New York Times,* August 30, 2005.

85. "Nature's Revenge," *New York Times,* August 30, 2005.

86. "Atomic bomb" in "Swept Off with a Broom," *Houston Chronicle,* September 1, 2005; "80% underwater" in "New Orleans: 80% of the City Under Water; Mississippi: Death Toll Surpasses 100 & May Go Much Higher 'Heartbreaking,'" *Houston Chronicle,* August 31, 2005.

87. "Katrina Leaves Despair as Water, Death Toll Rise," *Raleigh News & Observer,* August 31, 2005.

88. "Little Andrew" and "slapped the Florida Keys" in "Gaining Power, Katrina Heads for Land Again," *Charleston Post & Courier,* August 27, 2005; "She churned north" in "The Hot & Bothered Ask: 'Where Is FPL?'" *Miami Herald,* August 28, 2005.

89. "Menacing" in "Hurricane Lashes a City Abandoned," *Los Angeles Times,* August 29, 2005; "Monster" in "Life and Death Make Everything Else Unimportant," *Baltimore Sun,* August 31, 2005; "Wreaked havoc" and "bearing down" in "Hurricane Packs Punch on the Energy Markets," *Los Angeles Times,* August 30, 2005; "Full fury" in "Dozens Killed, Damage Heavy as Katrina Roars In," *Los Angeles Times,* August 30, 2005.

90. "Toxic gumbo" in "'Nothing but a Nightmare,'" *Raleigh News & Observer,* September 2, 2005; "Walloped" in "Hurricane Packs Punch on the Energy Markets"; "Major blows" in "Hurricane Is Felt on Many Fronts," *Los Angeles Times,* August 31, 2005.

91. "Slow and uncoordinated" in "A Diminished FEMA Scrambles to the Rescue," *Los Angeles Times,* September 1, 2005; "Deadly" and "fickle" in "Katrina Plucks 7 from Disparate Backgrounds," *Miami Herald,* August 27, 2005; "Barreled" and "ripped" in "Misery and Water Keep Rising," *Los Angeles Times,* August 31, 2005.

92. "Atomic bomb," "swept," and "a broom" in "Swept Off with a Broom"; "Strike zone" in "Katrina," *Richmond Times-Dispatch,* August 30, 2005.

93. Bob Englehart, Depiction of Katrina, *Hartford Courant,* August 27, 2005.

94. "New Orleans in Chaos; Disaster Proves Warnings True," *Atlanta Journal-Constitution,* September 2, 2005.

95. "Lawlessness Rampant as Refugees Wait," *Houston Chronicle*, September 2, 2005.

96. "Widespread Looting Hits Abandoned Businesses," *New Orleans Times-Picayune*, August 30, 2005.

97. "New Orleans Death Toll May Soar; Survivors Desperate; Looters Brazen," *Los Angeles Times*, September 1, 2005.

98. "Looting Goes beyond Essentials," *Raleigh News & Observer*, September 1, 2005.

99. "Looting Adds to Problems," *Biloxi Sun-Herald*, September 1, 2005.

100. "Chaos in the Streets," *Houston Chronicle*, August 31, 2005.

101. "Officials Throw Up Hands as Looters Ransack City," *Biloxi Sun-Herald*, September 1, 2005.

102. "Rape. Murder. Gunfights," *New Orleans Times-Picayune*, September 26, 2005.

103. "How Looters Are Made," *Raleigh News & Observer*, September 2, 2005.

104. Amanda Hess, "'I Have Made It through the Winds and Waters,'" *Slate*, August 28, 2015, www.slate.com/articles/technology/users/2015/08/please_forward_how_blogging_re connected_new_orleans_after_katrina_reviewed.html.

105. "Internet Connects Loved Ones," *New Orleans Times-Picayune*, September 23, 2005.

106. "Feds' Disaster Planning Shifts Away from Preparedness," *New Orleans Times-Picayune*, August 31, 2005.

107. "A Diminished FEMA Scrambles to the Rescue," *Los Angeles Times*, September 1, 2005.

108. "Now's Not the Time to Reduce FEMA's Responsibilities," *Mobile Press-Register*, August 31, 2005.

109. This would lead to some online commentators and newspapers to nickname FEMA, "WEMA: Worst Emergency Management Agency," for its poor response during the storm. See "From FEMA to WEMA," *New York Times*, September 20, 2005; "Out with FEMA, in with WEMA," *Mobile Press-Register*, September 21, 2005.

110. "Katrina: The Storm We've Always Feared."

111. Ibid.

112. "Hurricane Katrina at 10: The Craziest YouTube Videos," *AccuWeather*, September 12, 2015, www.accuweather.com/en/weather-blogs/weathermatrix/hurricane-katrina-at-10-the-craziest-youtube-videos/52157597.

113. "Nagin Apologizes for 'Chocolate' City Comments," CNN.com, January 17, 2006, www.cnn.com/2006/US/01/17/nagin.city/.

114. "FEMA Hotel Contracts Tied Up," *New Orleans Times-Picayune*, September 24, 2005.

115. Kanye West, "A Concert for Hurricane Relief," NBC, September 2, 2005.

116. "New Orleans Slides into Chaos; U.S. Scrambles to Send Troops," *Los Angeles Times*, September 1, 2005.

117. "City Awash in Death Faces Fight of Its Life," *Atlanta Journal-Constitution*, September 1, 2005.

118. "Ahead for New Orleans: Rebuild It or Move It?" *Raleigh News & Observer*, September 2, 2005.

119. "Share Your Memories of New Orleans," *Baltimore Sun*, September 2, 2005.

120. Ashley Morris, "FYYFF," *Ashley Morris: The Blog*, November 27, 2005, ashleymorris.typepad.com/ashley_morris_the_blog/2005/11/fuck_you_you_fu.html.

121. For examples of popular Katrina blogs, or blogs with substantial Katrina-related content, see the list created by Think New Orleans and maintained by the Rising Tide Conference blog at Mark Folse, "Rising Tide," *Rising Tide Conference Blog*, August 25, 2006, risingtideblog.blogspot.com/2006/08/rising-tide.html. Some of this author's favorite Katrina blogs include b.rox's *Life in the Flood Zone;* Mark Folse's *Wet Bank Guy*, Gina's *There's N.O. pLA.ce like Home;* RevMark's *That DAM Blog;* David's *moldy city;* Mark LaFlaur's *levees not war;* judyb's *thanks, katrina;* latin teacher's *FEMA, Katrina, and other bad words;* Scout Prime's *First Draft;* Jack Ware et al.'s *metroblogging new orleans;* and Dangle 24/7's *katrina we are not ok*. Of the 300 blogs listed on the site, 18 have Katrina listed as part of their title.

122. Bart Everson, *Please Forward: How Blogging Reconnected New Orleans after Katrina*, ed. Cynthia Joyce (New Orleans: University of New Orleans Press, 2015).

123. Chris Rose, *1 Dead in Attic* (New York: Simon & Schuster, 2007).

124. Based off of federally declared disasters by presidential order through the Robert T. Stafford Disaster Relief and Emergency Assistance Act, 42 USC §§ 5121–5207 (the Stafford Act) §401, and previous instances of federal declaration of disaster as documented by FEMA, 1953–2017.

125. Roy Rosenzweig Center for History and New Media at George Mason University and University of New Orleans, "Hurricane Digital Memory Bank," 2005, hurricanearchive.org/.

126. Mark Folse, "Rising Tide," *Rising Tide Conference Blog*, risingtideblog.blogspot.com.

127. "Hurricane Katrina Updates on NOLA.Com," NOLA.com, August 29, 2005, www.nola.com/katrina/index.ssf/2005/08/online_times-picayune_news_blo.html; Diya Chacko, "The *Times-Picayune*'s Hurricane Katrina Newspapers on NOLA.Com," NOLA.com, August 26, 2015, www.nola.com/katrina/index.ssf/2015/08/the_times-picayunes_hurricane.html.

128. Louisiana State Museum "Hurricane Katrina" textiles and costumes collection; University of Southern Mississippi–Gulf Coast Hurricane Katrina Collection and Louisiana Research Collection.

129. "Evacuees Flee New Storm," *Mobile Press-Register*, September 21, 2005.

130. Mpdoughboy153, eBay Item No. 330586178483, cgi.ebay.com/MP-Brassard-Hurricane-Katrina-worn-OBSOLETTE-1980s-90s-/330586178483?pt=LH_DefaultDomain_0&hash=item4cf878c3b3.

131. At the 10-year anniversary (2015), 80 percent of the 200 Katrina products tracked by this author since 2007 were still being sold in New Orleans or available through online marketplaces.

132. Storm Spotter Live, "Hurricane Katrina Poster," CafePress ID #58061171, May 16, 2006, www.cafepress.com; Lawrence Mercantile, "NOPD Riot Squad Mug," CafePress ID #66018077, July 15, 2006, www.cafepress.com; Remixed Propaganda Gear, "Hurricane Wall Calendar," CafePress ID # 31826201, September 20, 2005, www.cafepress.com.

133. Cathy Johnson's DopplerDuds.com website (no longer available) can be viewed as it existed in 2008 using the Internet Archive's Wayback Machine, last captured as active September 9, 2013, web.archive.org/web/20130909004511/http://www.dopplerduds.com/.

134. "FEMA: Fix Everything My Ass," and "I Stayed in New Orleans and All I Got Was This Lousy T-Shirt, a New Cadillac and a Plasma TV," as seen by author in French Quarter, New Orleans, October 16, 2008.

135. "Chocolate City Beads," "Loot 'Er Man Beads," and "Caucasian FEMA Trailer Beads" were thrown during 2006 Mardi Gras Parades and available for sale online at Millergw, "New Orleans 'Chocolate City' MG Bead," eBay Item No. B185, www.ebay.com; "New Orleans 'Loot Er Man' Bead . . . Hurricane Katrina," eBay Item No. B184, www.ebay.com; "Hurricane Katrina 'FEMA Trailer' Mardi Gras Bead," eBay Item No. B182, www.ebay.com.

136. "Katrina Gave Me a Blow Job," as seen and purchased by author in French Quarter, New Orleans, October 16, 2008.

137. "Girls Gone Wild T-Shirt," available for purchase at Mardi Gras Zone, mardigraszone.com/store/images/ggwild-hurricanes-tshirt.JPG.

138. Ernieattorney, "Magazine St. Sign—Katrina You Bitch," Flikr Album, October 17, 2005, www.flickr.com; Le Krewe d'État, "Katrina You Bitch!" Rotten to the Corps Parade, 2006, Image taken by Chuck T., Mardi Gras '06 Album, February 24, 2006, www.flickr.com; "Katrina You Bitch!" Handmade T-shirt, featured at *People Get Ready Blog,* "New Orleans Pride Displayed in T-Shirts," November 4, 2005, Image No. Prg005, peoplegetready.blogspot.com.

139. Geoffrey Nunberg, *Ascent of the A-Word: Assholism, The First Sixty Years* (New York: Public Affairs, 2012), 134–35.

140. "Bitch," *Oxford English Dictionary* Online, 2nd ed., 2013.

141. "Bitch" was used on television on *Saturday Night Live* in 1977 (Tom Shales and James Andrew Miller, *Live from New York: An Uncensored History of Saturday Night Live as Told by Its Stars* [New York: Little, Brown, 2002]); Hurricane Elena the "bitch" in article describing difference between Hurricane Andrew and other storms in "Andrew Slides By," *Biloxi Sun-Herald,* August 26, 1992.

142. Federal Communications Commission, "Program Contents Regulations," June 1, 2011, www.fcc.gov/guides/ program-content-regulations.

143. "More Than Ever, You Can Say That on Television," *New York Times,* November 14, 2009.

144. According to the *New York Times,* the use of *bitch* "is up from 30 uses on 15 shows in all of 2007 and just six instances on four programs in 2005." This equates to a 50 percent increase in the use of the word ("More Than Ever, You Can Say That on Television").

145. The author has found this true at multiple talks given between 2010 and 2018. Similarly, the prevalence of this phrase is confirmed by looking at political cartoons, such as the one by Chip Bok, a *Tampa Bay Times* cartoonist who also posts content on the Cartoonists Group site (Chip Bok, "Camille Never Did This," Image No. 11628, September 9, 2005, www.cartoonistgroup.com).

146. "Bill & Monica" and "Terri Schiavo" bumper stickers available for sale at cafepress.com.

147. As mentioned in K. Macomber, C. Mallinson, and E. Seale, "'Katrina That Bitch!' Hegemonic Representations of Women's Sexuality on Hurricane Katrina Souvenir T-Shirts," *Journal of Popular Culture* 44, no. 3 (June 2011): 525–44.

148. *Terra.Wire,* "New Orleans Waters Cede Foul, Decrepit Wasteland," September 10, 2005, www.terradaily.com.

149. "It's Time for a Nation to Return the Favor," *New Orleans Times-Picayune,* November 19, 2005.

150. Katrina Cartoons, Cartoonist Group, www.cartoonistgroup.com/, accessed April 29, 2018.

151. Karl Wimer Financial Cartoons, "New Orleans Comics and Cartoons," Cartoonist Group.

152. Julie Hernandez, "Le tourisme macabre à La Nouvelle-Orléans après Katrina: Résilience et mémorialisation des espaces affectés par des catastrophes majeures," *Norois* 3, no. 208 (2008): 61–73.

153. Steve Helber, "Not-Quite Magical Misery Tour Sells Out," MSNBC.com, January 5, 2006, www.nbcnews.com/id/10715130/ns/us_news-katrina_the_long_road_back/t/not-quite-magical-misery-tour-sells-out/.

154. "Coming Soon to New Orleans: The Katrina Tour," *NPR.org*, December 14, 2005, www.npr.org/templates/story/story.php?storyId=5053171.

155. Anna Hartnell, "Katrina Tourism and a Tale of Two Cities: Visualizing Race and Class in New Orleans," *American Quarterly* 61, no. 3 (2009): 723–47.

156. Lynnell Thomas, *Desire and Disaster in New Orleans: Tourism, Race, and Historical Memory* (Durham, NC: Duke University Press, 2014).

157. "Hurricane Katrina Tour—Gray Line New Orleans," www.graylineneworleans.com/all/tours/hurricane-katrina-tour, last accessed November 27, 2017.

158. Camille Whitworth, "Katrina Tours Spur Mixed Feelings amongst Residents, Survivors," WDSU, August 15, 2015, www.wdsu.com/article/katrina-tours-spur-mixed-feelings-amongst-residents-survivors-1/3379163.

159. "Are Katrina Tours Exploiting New Orleans' Lower Ninth Ward?" Peter Greenberg Travel Detective, October 6, 2012, petergreenberg.com.

160. WAFB Channel 9, "Police Crack Down on Katrina Tours," May 28, 2015, www.wafb.com/story/19666598/police-crack-down-on-katrina-tours.

161. Ron Agostini, "Walking Tour of Katrina Recovery in New Orleans," *Modesto Bee*, February 2, 2013, www.modbee.com/sports/spt-columns-blogs/ron-agostini/article3149241.html.

162. "Daughter Thinks Fats Domino Has Been Rescued," *Mobile Press-Register*, September 2, 2005.

163. "Jazz News: Preservation Hall New Orleans Musicians Hurricane Relief Fund," *All about Jazz*, September 7, 2005, news.allaboutjazz.com/preservation-hall-new-orleans-musicians-hurricane-relief-fund.php?width=1280.

164. Alison Fensterstock, "It Takes a Musicians Village," *Gambit*, April 25, 2006, www.bestofneworleans.com/gambit/it-takes-a-musicians-village/Content?oid=1245634.

165. *Sing Me Back Home* (New York: Sony BMG Music Entertainment, 2006).

166. Anders Osborne, "Oh Katrina," *Coming Down*, September 25, 2007.

167. Sara Bonisteel, "F— Katrina: New Orleans Hip-Hop Remembers the Hurricane," *Fox News*, August 28, 2006, www.foxnews.com/story/2006/08/28/f-katrina-new-orleans-hip-hop-remembers-hurricane.html.

168. Lil Wayne, *Dedication 2: Gangsta Grillz* (Kingwood, TX: BCD, 2008); Juvenile, *Reality Check* (New York: Atlantic, 2006).

169. Mos Def, "Katrina Klap / Dollar Day," discussed in Joseph Patel, "Mos Def among

Those Quick with Music Inspired by Katrina," *MTV News,* September 9, 2005, www.mtv.com/news/1509274/mos-def-among-those-quick-with-music-inspired-by-katrina/.

170. Jayson Rodriguez, "Mos Def Arrested after Impromptu Performance outside VMAs," *MTV News,* September 1, 2006: www.mtv.com/news/1539981/mos-def-arrested-after-impromptu-performance-outside-vmas/.

171. Chad Campbell, "Press Release: NPR's Annual New Year's Music Special to Be the First Live National Music Broadcast from New Orleans since Katrina," December 12, 2005, www.npr.org/about/press/051212.holiday.html.

172. Keith Spera, "Soundtrack of a Storm: The Most Poignant Musical Moments after Hurricane Katrina," August 27, 2015, www.nola.com/katrina/index.ssf/2015/08/hurricane_katrina_music.html.

173. Steven Mirkin, "New Orleans Jazz & Heritage Festival," *Variety,* May 1, 2006, variety.com/2006/music/markets-festivals/new-orleans-jazz-heritage-festival-1200516612/.

174. *New Orleans Times-Picayune* staff, "Post-Katrina Culture Timeline: When Restaurants, Art and Live Music Returned to New Orleans," Nola.com, August 2015, www.nola.com/katrina/index.ssf/page/katrina_culture_timeline.html.

175. Ibid.

176. "New Orleans' Post-Katrina Artistic Revival Is in Full Swing," *Christian Science Monitor,* April 15, 2012, www.csmonitor.com/The-Culture/Arts/2012/0415/New-Orleans-s-post-Katrina-artistic-revival-is-in-full-swing.

177. Amy Archerd, "'Floodgate' Opening," *Variety,* November 6, 2005, variety.com/2005/legit/news/floodgate-opening-1117932239/; "Plays—John Biguenet," www.biguenet.com/plays, last accessed November 28, 2017.

178. Le Krewe d'État, "'Katrina You Bitch!'" Rotten to the Corps Parade.

179. Alan Richman, "Yes, We're Open," *GQ,* November 3, 2006, www.gq.com/story/katrina-new-orleans-food.

180. Brett Anderson, "Parkway Bakery's Response to Katrina's Destruction: More Po-Boys," NOLA.com, August 23, 2017, www.nola.com/dining/index.ssf/2015/08/hurricane_katrina_destroyed_pa.html; "Beignets Return to New Orleans," *NBC News,* October 19, 2005, www.nbcnews.com/id/9755703/ns/us_news-katrina_the_long_road_back/t/beignets-sweet-reminder-old-new-orleans/#.Wh31uktrwxE.

181. Brett Anderson, "Shuttered Camellia Grill Gets Post-It Note Love from Its New Orleans Fans," *NOLA.com,* July 26, 2006, www.nola.com/dining/index.ssf/2006/07/shuttered_camellia_grill_gets.html.

182. "Giving Back—Abita Beer," abita.com/about/giving-back#, last accessed November 28, 2017; Danny Monteverde, "Haydel's Warming Ovens for Hubig's Replacement," *WWL,* September 2, 2016, www.wwltv.com/news/local/haydels-warming-ovens-for-hubigs-replacement/312933172; "Sugar Refinery Finally Back in New Orleans," *Chicago Tribune,* December 18, 2005, articles.chicagotribune.com/2005-12-18/news/0512180242_1_american-sugar-alliance-sugar-policy-cheaper-sugar.

183. Spike Lee, *When the Levees Broke,* HBO (40 Acres and a Mule, Filmworks, 2006); *Trouble the Water* (Entertainment Films One Canada, 2009); Greg MacGillivray et al., *Hurricane*

on the Bayou (Umbrella Entertainment [distributor], 2009); Benh Zeitlin et al., *Beasts of the Southern Wild* (Fox Searchlight [distributor], 2016).

184. *Times-Picayune* staff, "Post-Katrina Culture Timeline."

185. Sean Stephens, "Flashback: New Orleans Saints Return Home after Hurricane Katrina," *Rolling Stone*, www.rollingstone.com/sports/new-orleans-saints-2006-return-to-superdome-w442074, accessed September 26, 2016.

186. Rick Kissell, "Everyone's Watching Post-Katrina Coverage," *Variety*, September 8, 2005, variety.com/2005/scene/markets-festivals/everyone-s-watching-post-katrina-coverage-1117928712/.

187. "Why New Orleans Is the New Movie-Making Capital," *ABC News*, November 20, 2014, abcnews.go.com/Entertainment/hollywood-south-orleans-movie-making-capital/story?id=27036988.

188. For one example, see Dave Eggars, *Zeitoun* (New York: Vintage, 2010).

189. Peer-reviewed articles accessed November 28, 2017, through Google Scholar search engine, Amazon, and Google. Meanwhile, the WorldCat database lists 4,845 books; 16,012 scholarly articles; 703 DVDs; 264 CDs produced on the subject "Hurricane Katrina."

190. Disaster relief policy was revised by Congress post-Katrina through the following acts and amendments: the Post-Katrina Emergency Management Reform Act of 2006, Title VI of Pub. L. No. 109-295 (H.R. 5441); the Security and Accountability for Every Port Act of 2005, of Pub. L. No. 109-347 (H.R. 4954); the Pets Evacuation and Transportation Standards Act of 2006, of Pub. L. No. 109-308 (H.R. 3858); the Federal Judiciary Emergency Special Sessions Act of 2005, of Pub. L. No. 109-63 (H.R. 3650); the Student Grant Hurricane and Disaster Relief Act, of Pub. L. No. 109-67 (H.R. 3668); and the John Warner National Defense Authorization Act for Fiscal Year 2007, in Sections of Pub. L. No. 109-364 (H.R. 5122).

191. Gilbert F. White, *Human Adjustment to Floods*, Research Paper 29 (University of Chicago Department of Geography, 1945), 2, as cited in M. Macdonald, D. Chester et al., "The Significance of Gilbert F. White's 1945 Paper 'Human Adjustment to Floods' in the Development of Risk and Hazard Management," *Process in Physical Geography*, 2011, 1–9; Steinberg, *Acts of God*; Greg Bankoff, "Rendering the World Unsafe."

192. The phrase "natural disaster" is used extensively by the media to describe all hazards. A Google News search for the term "natural disaster" on June 4, 2018, produced articles with titles including the phrase "natural disaster" from at least five major news sources within a month of the date searched, including the *Washington Post* (June 2, 2018), *Fortune* (May 30, 2018), *ABC Online* (May 14, 2018), the *Honolulu Star-Advertiser* (June 3, 2018), and *People* (May 16, 2018).

193. The US District Court for the Eastern District of Louisiana held that a Category 4 or 5 storm was an "Act of God" in a decision regarding a marina owner and the owner of a vessel whose ship damaged another vessel as a result of Hurricane Katrina in *J.W. Stone Oil Dist., LLC v. Bollinger Shipyard*, 2007 WL 2710809 (E.D. La. 2007).

194. Chester Hartman and Gregory D. Squires, *There Is No Such Thing as a Natural Disaster: Race, Class, and Hurricane Katrina* (Abingdon, UK: Routledge, 2006).

195. Tristan Baurick, "Like the Louisiana Coast, the Gulf Seafloor Is Rapidly Eroding, Re-

search Finds," *New Orleans Times-Picayune,* April 5, 2018, www.nola.com/environment/index.ssf/2018/04/like_the_louisiana_coast_the_g.html.

196. Justin Worland, "These Are the Cities Most Vulnerable to the Next Katrina," *Time,* August 27, 2015.

197. "If You Can't Predict the Future You're in Trouble," *New Orleans Times-Picayune,* September 3, 2008.

198. "Bark Worse Than Its Bite," *New Orleans Times-Picayune,* September 2, 2008.

199. "Safe at Home: Cat. 2 Storm Strikes Nearly Empty South La.," *New Orleans Times-Picayune,* September 2, 2008.

200. "Hurricane Gustav Curtails Southern Decadence," GayCities.com, August 30, 2008, www.gaycities.com/outthere/181/hurricane-gustav-curtails-southern-decadence/.

201. Van Chew, "Gay Hurricane" in BET Comic View, July 15, 2006, www.youtube.com/watch?V=liK_knD125.

202. Jason Vincik, "Gustav Kills Southern Decadence—New Gay Lake Party Emerges in Dallas," *Anythingbutstraight,* September 3, 2008, anythingbutstraight.blogspot.com/2008/09/gustav-kills-southern-decadence-new-gay.html.

203. "Jindal, Nagin and Gustav," *New Orleans Times-Picayune,* September 11, 2008.

204. Leigh Jones, *Infinite Monster: Courage, Hope, and Resurrection in the Face of One of America's Largest Hurricanes* (Dallas: Penland Scott Publishers, 2010).

205. "Agents Face Another Flood: Damage Claims," *Houston Chronicle,* September 14, 2008.

206. "@Irene_Bitch," Twitter feed, August 26, 2011, twitter.com/irene_bitch.

207. "@HurriicaneIrene," Twitter feed, August 19, 2011, twitter.com/#!/HurriicaneIrene.

208. "Celebrities Tweet about Hurricane Irene," *Huffington Post,* August 27, 2011, www.huffingtonpost.com/2011/08/27/celebrities-tweet-about-irene_n_939008.html.

209. Jill Filipovic, "Stop Calling Sandy a Bitch: It Was a Storm, Not a Woman to Hate," *Guardian,* November 2, 2012, www.guardian.co.uk/commentisfree/2012/nov/02/stop-calling-sandy-bitch-jill-filipovic.

210. "Was Hurricane Sandy a Boy or Girl?" *Star News Online,* January 6, 2013, www.starnewsonline.com/news/20130106/myreporter-was-hurricane-sandy-a-boy-or-a-girl.

211. "'Frankenstorm,' a Mix of Hurricane Sandy and Early Snow, May Ruin Halloween 2012," *Huffington Post,* October 25, 2012, www.huffingtonpost.com/2012/10/25/hurricane-sandy-frankenstorm-halloween-2012_n_2019252.html#slide=1687842.

212. "NJ>Hurricane," seen and purchased by author at Fleurty Girl T-Shirts, Magazine Street, New Orleans, April 11, 2011.

213. "Sandy's a B*tch," CONSURV, consurv.bigcartel.com/product/sandy-s-a-btch.com, last accessed June 5, 2013.

214. "'Frankenstorm,' a Mix of Hurricane Sandy and Early Snow, May Ruin Halloween 2012."

215. Dan Nosowitz, "News Writers: Stop Trying to Scare People with Made-Up Storm Language," *Popular Science,* November 1, 2012, www.popsci.com/science/article/2012-11/dictionary-hurricane-sandy-superstorm.

216. "Disasters Declarations (by Year)."

217. Annie Colbert, "7 Fake Hurricane Sandy Photos You're Sharing on Social Media," *Mashable,* October 29, 2012, mashable.com/2012/10/29/fake-hurricane-sandy-photos/#YmMQGL5M1gqT.

218. Emily Guskin and Paul Hitlin, "Hurricane Sandy and Twitter," *Pew Research Center's Journalism Project,* November 6, 2012, www.journalism.org/2012/11/06/hurricane-sandy-and-twitter/.

219. Filipovic, "Stop Calling Sandy a Bitch: It Was a Storm, Not a Woman to Hate."

220. Bridget Coyne, "Introducing Twitter Alerts," Twitter, September 25, 2013, blog.twitter.com/official/en_us/a/2013/introducing-twitter-alerts.html.

221. "Katrina Outages Reveal Phone System Quirks," *NBC News,* August 31, 2005, www.nbcnews.com/id/9120503/ns/technology_and_science-tech_and_gadgets/t/katrina-outages-reveal-phone-system-quirks/.

222. "Facebook's Social Good Forum: Introducing Community Help and Donations in Live," Facebook Newsroom, November 17, 2016, newsroom.fb.com/news/2016/11/facebooks-social-good-forum/.

223. Bryn Stole, "Citizen-Sailors, or 'Cajun Navy,' Vital to Rescue Efforts in Sunken Baton Rouge," *Baton Rouge Advocate,* August 26, 2016.

224. Matthew Teague, "Louisianans Spurn Government and Crowdsource Aid in Wake of Floods," *Guardian,* September 2, 2016, www.theguardian.com/us-news/2016/sep/02/louisiana-floods-crowdsourcing-aid-amazon-cajun-army.

225. "A New Center for Crisis Response on Facebook," Facebook Newsroom, September 14, 2017, newsroom.fb.com/news/2017/09/a-new-center-for-crisis-response-on-facebook/.

226. Julia Zorthian, "Facebook Just Created a Crisis Response Hub," *Fortune,* September 14, 2017, fortune.com/2017/09/14/facebook-crisis-response-center/.

227. Quotes from President Donald J. Trump, @realdonaldtrump, Twitter feed, in Jason Silverstein, "Trump Keeps Tweeting about Harvey, but Is Mum on Storm Victims," *NY Daily News,* August 27, 2017, www.nydailynews.com/news/politics/trump-tweeting-harvey-mum-storm-victims-article-1.3446781.

228. Gail Fashingbauer Cooper, "Harvey Forces Weather Service to Add Two New Colors to Maps," *CBS News,* August 29, 2017, www.cbsnews.com/news/harvey-forces-weather-service-to-add-two-new-colors-to-maps/.

229. Inae Oh, "In Puerto Rico, Trump Says Hurricane Maria Isn't a 'Real Catastrophe' like Katrina," *Mother Jones,* October 3, 2017, www.motherjones.com/politics/2017/10/in-puerto-rico-trump-says-hurricane-maria-isnt-a-real-catastrophe-like-katrina/.

230. In total, the search term "Harvey vs. Katrina" on Google, performed April 30, 2018, returned 9.6 million results.

231. Historic flood and cost speculation in Shaila Dewan and John Schwartz, "How Does Harvey Compare with Hurricane Katrina? Here's What We Know," *New York Times,* August 28, 2017, www.nytimes.com/2017/08/28/us/hurricane-katrina-harvey.html; critique of response in "Posts Flood Twitter Blaming Obama for Katrina Response," *Sacramento Bee,* August 30, 2017, www.sacbee.com/news/nation-world/national/article170265837.html; productization in "Hurricane Harvey T-Shirts," www.etsy.com/market/hurricane_harvey_t_shirts, last viewed

April 30, 2018; music geared at supporting victims in Lin-Manuel Miranda and other artists such as members of the cast of *Hamilton*'s "Almost like Praying," released by Atlantic Records, October 6, 2017; and live streams in Jason Kaplan, "Hurricane Harvey Live Feeds," *WDT*, August 25, 2017, blog.wdtinc.com/hurricane-harvey-live-streams.

232. Mark Edward Phillips, "Hurricane Harvey Twitter Dataset," University of North Texas, August 18 to September 22, 2017, digital.library.unt.edu/ark:/67531/metadc993940/.

233. Maya Rhodan, "'Please Send Help': Hurricane Harvey Victims Turn to Twitter and Facebook," *Time,* August 30, 2017, time.com/4921961/hurricane-harvey-twitter-facebook-social-media/.

234. Maya Rhodan, "Hurricane Harvey: The U.S.'s First Social Media Storm," *Time,* August 30, 2017, time.com/4921961/hurricane-harvey-twitter-facebook-social-media/.

235. "The Weather Channel Delivered Its Most-Watched Year Since 2013," AdWeek.com, January 26, 2018, www.adweek.com/tvnewser/the-weather-channel-delivered-its-most-watched-year-since-2013/355957.

236. 42 Matters highlights the search for "weather"-related apps to sell subscriptions to their product, the App Market Explorer, allowing users to check on data for free and paid apps without purchasing access to their paid search functions. The results listed above come from a check of this data last performed April 29, 2018, and is expected to vary as more apps come online. It includes 1,174 paid apps; 4,953 free apps; and 6,662 total apps in Apple App Store and Google Play (42 Matters last accessed April 29, 2018, 42matters.com/app-market-explorer).

237. Adam Nagourney, David E. Sanger, and Johanna Barr, "Hawaii Panics after Alert about Incoming Missile Is Sent in Error," *New York Times,* January 13, 2018, www.nytimes.com/2018/01/13/us/hawaii-missile.html.

6. Tempest: Assessing Current Conditions

1. On October 30, 2012, the US National Weather Service issued a bulletin reclassifying Hurricane Sandy as "Post-Tropical Cyclone Sandy" (National Hurricane Center, "Post-Tropical Cyclone Sandy: Forecast Advisory Number 31," October 30, 2012, www.nhc.noaa.gov/archive/2012/a118/a1182012.fstadv.031.shtml).

2. Sandy's extenuating effects even caused the revision of disaster relief policy. In 2013, the Sandy Recovery Improvement Act and Disaster Relief Appropriations Act of 2013 further widened FEMA's ability to deliver recovery assistance to those in need (US Congress, The Disaster Relief Appropriations Act of 2013, Pub. L. No. 113-2 § 127 Stat. 4).

3. Helen Gibbons, "What's in a Name? Post-Tropical Cyclone Sandy," *USGS,* December 2012, soundwaves.usgs.gov/2012/12/fieldwork2.html.

4. "Weather Channel Names Nor'easter, National Weather Service Says Not So Fast," FoxNews.com, November 7, 2012, www.foxnews.com/weather/2012/11/07/weather-channel-names-noreaster-national-weather-service-says-not-so-fast/print#.

5. "National Weather Service: Just Say No to Athena," *Washington Post,* November 7, 2012.

6. "Winter Storm Nemo? Why Is the Northeast Blizzard Named after a Cartoon Fish?"

Latinos Post, February 8, 2013, www.latinospost.com/articles/11642/20130208/winter-storm-nemo-why-northeast-blizzard-named.htm.

7. Jillian MacMath, "TWC Winter Storm Naming 'Will Mislead Public,'" AccuWeather.com, October 10, 2012, www.accuweather.com/en/weather-news/twc-winter-storm-naming-will-m/83668.

8. Chris Ariens, "Weather Channel Releases Storm Names for 2013–2014," *AdWeek,* October 1, 2013, www.adweek.com/tvnewser/weather-channel-releases-winter-storm-names-for-2013-2014/199849.

9. The "Snowicane" label, for instance, was picked up by *ABC News,* the *Ithaca Journal,* and Gannett newspaper affiliates to label El Niño–related northeastern weather. See Robert Quigley, "The Coming Winter Storm Is Called 'Snowicane,' in Case You Were Wondering," *The Mary Sue,* February 24, 2010, www.themarysue.com/snowicane-2010/.

10. "Weather Channel's List of Winter Storm Names Takes Battering from Forecasters," *Guardian,* October 1, 2014, www.theguardian.com/world/2014/oct/01/weather-channels-list-winter-storm-names-criticism.

11. "Hogcock!/Last Lunch," *30 Rock,* NBC, January 30, 2013.

12. *Proceedings of the National Academy of Sciences,* "About," last accessed November 18, 2017, www.pnas.org/site/aboutpnas/index.xhtml.

13. Kiju Jung and Sharon Shavitt et al., "Female Hurricanes Are Deadlier Than Male Hurricanes," *Proceedings of the National Academy of Sciences* 111, no. 24 (June 17, 2014): 8782–87, doi.org/10.1073/pnas.1402786111.

14. The story first broke in the *Washington Post,* June 2, 2014. It was circulated by every major news network within hours.

15. Examples of support of the Jung and Shavitt et al. findings include Erin Gloria Ryan, "Study Shows Hurricanes with Female Names Don't Get Taken Seriously," *Jezebel,* June 2, 2014, jezebel.com/study-shows-hurricanes-with-female-names-dont-get-taken-1584970078; Alexandra Sifferlin, "Hurricanes with Female Names Kill More People, Study Finds," *Time,* June 2, 2014, time.com/2813381/hurricanes-female-names/; "Why Have Female Hurricanes Killed More People Than Male Ones?" *Phenomena,* June 2, 2014, phenomena.nationalgeographic.com/2014/06/02/why-have-female-hurricanes-killed-more-people-than-male-ones/.

16. Examples of rebuttals of the Jung and Shavitt et al. findings include Paul Frijters, "How to Lie with Statistics: The Case of Female Hurricanes," *Club Troppo* (blog), June 10, 2014, clubtroppo.com.au/2014/06/11/how-to-lie-with-statistics-the-case-of-female-hurricanes/, and "Female-Named Hurricanes Probably Do NOT Kill More People Than Male Hurricanes," *Washington Post,* June 3, 2014, www.washingtonpost.com/news/capital-weather-gang/wp/2014/06/02/female-named-hurricanes-kill-more-than-male-because-people-dont-respect-them-study-finds/?tid=a_inl&utm_term=.f4720c9872ea.

17. Eric Holthaus, James Shires, and Max Smeets, "Hurricanes Named after Women Are More Dangerous? Not So Fast," *Slate,* June 3, 2014, www.slate.com/blogs/future_tense/2014/06/03/are_hurricanes_named_after_women_more_dangerous_not_so_fast.html; Jason Samenow, "Disbelief, Shock and Skepticism: Hurricane Gender Study Faces Blowback," *Washington Post,* June 3, 2014, www.washingtonpost.com/news/capital-weather

-gang/wp/2014/06/03/disbelief-shock-and-skepticism-hurricane-gender-study-faces-blowback/?utm_term=.4e903b86908d.

18. Steve Maley, "Statistics Show No Evidence of Gender Bias in the Public's Hurricane Preparedness," *Proceedings of the National Academy of Sciences* 111, no. 37 (September 16, 2014): E3834, doi.org/10.1073/pnas.1413079111; Björn Christensen and Sören Christensen, "Are Female Hurricanes Really Deadlier Than Male Hurricanes?" *Proceedings of the National Academy of Sciences* 111, no. 34 (August 26, 2014): E3497–98, doi.org/10.1073/pnas.1410910111; Laura A. Bakkensen and William Larson, "Population Matters When Modeling Hurricane Fatalities," *Proceedings of the National Academy of Sciences* 111, no. 50, www.pnas.org/content/111/50/E5331.full?ijkey=eb3f510bf5a9797e7ba7d748736a8828e981fb11&keytype2=tf_ipsecsha, last accessed February 21, 2017.

19. Kiju Jung et al., "Reply to Christensen and Christensen and to Malter: Pitfalls of Erroneous Analyses of Hurricane Names," *Proceedings of the National Academy of Sciences* 111, no. 34 (August 26, 2014): E3499–3500, doi.org/10.1073/pnas.1411652111; Kiju Jung et al., "Reply to Maley: Yes, Appropriate Modeling of Fatality Counts Confirms Female Hurricanes Are Deadlier," *Proceedings of the National Academy of Sciences* 111, no. 37 (September 16, 2014): E3835, doi.org/10.1073/pnas.1414111111; Kiju Jung et al., "Reply to Bakkensen and Larson: Population May Matter but Does Not Alter Conclusions," *Proceedings of the National Academy of Sciences* 111, no. 50 (December 16, 2014): E5333, doi.org/10.1073/pnas.1419330111.

20. As of 2017, even the *Washington Post* has had to print additional articles revising its original position on Jung and Shavitt, et al.'s work. This has not stopped the "Female Hurricanes More Deadly Than Male Hurricanes" phrase from appearing in articles, though. "Analysis | Revision: Female-Named Hurricanes Are Most Likely Not Deadlier Than Male Hurricanes," *Washington Post*, July 11, 2017, www.washingtonpost.com/news/capital-weather-gang/wp/2017/07/11/revision-female-named-hurricanes-are-most-likely-not-deadlier-than-male-hurricanes/; Hannah Smothers, "People Literally Die Because They Don't Respect Hurricanes with Feminine Names," Cosmopolitan, July 11, 2017, www.cosmopolitan.com/sex-love/a10283959/hurricane-female-names-death/; www.facebook.com/profile.php?id=1526386.

21. See chapter 5 for discussion of social media and hurricanes, particularly sections on @Irene_Bitch and Hurricane Harvey.

22. Phillips, "Hurricane Harvey Twitter Dataset."

23. The WMO defends its practice of naming in "Tropical Cyclone Naming," World Meteorological Organization, last updated 2018, public.wmo.int/en/About-us/FAQs/faqs-tropical-cyclones/tropical-cyclone-naming.

24. Emily Wagster Pettus and Melinda Deslatte, "Louisiana Flood Damage at Least $8.7 Billion, Governor Says," September 3, 2016, apnews.com/4ebe5296e9994d8fbd51a0de579d4ab6/louisiana-flood-damage-least-87-billion-governor-says.

25. "What a Storm with No Name Has Done to Louisiana," *USA Today*, August 15, 2016, www.usatoday.com/story/news/2016/08/15/the-short-list-monday/88759280/.

26. Jason Samenow, "No-Name Storm Dumped Three Times as Much Rain in Louisiana as Hurricane Katrina," *Washington Post*, August 19, 2016, www.washingtonpost.com/news/capital-weather-gang/wp/2016/08/19/no-name-storm-dumped-three-times-as-much-rain-in-louisiana-as-hurricane-katrina/?utm_term=.58f55f27e9f4.

27. The "storm with no name" was featured as a form of art in Rachael Thomas, "Digital Album Released by Baton Rouge Recording Artists Affected by Aug. Flood," *WAFB*, December 9, 2016, www.wafb.com/story/34019388/digital-album-released-by-baton-rouge-recording-artists-affected-by-aug-flood.

28. Josh Sanburn, "Louisiana Governor: The State's 'Historic' Flooding Is Being Ignored," *Time*, August 24, 2016, time.com/4464474/louisiana-governor-flooding-president-obama-alton-sterling/; "John Bel Edwards Increases Federal Relief Request for Flood Protection Efforts," NOLA.com, September 12, 2016, www.nola.com/politics/index.ssf/2016/09/john_bel_edwards_federal_fundi.html; Alan Yuhas, "Louisiana Governor Seeks Donors and Volunteers after Floods: 'We Need Help,'" *Guardian*, August 21, 2016, www.theguardian.com/us-news/2016/aug/21/louisiana-flood-relief-volunteers-aid-governor-john-bel-edwards; Elizabeth Crisp, "Louisiana Flood Response Blasted by Congress after State, FEMA 'Fell on Its Face,' Lawmaker Says," *Baton Rouge Advocate*, April 5, 2017, www.theadvocate.com/baton_rouge/news/politics/article_d07ff7d4-1a03-11e7-8dee-a39f53622967.html.

29. "What We Don't Know about State Spending on Natural Disasters Could Cost Us," The Pew Charitable Trusts (June 2018), http://www.pewtrusts.org/-/media/assets/2018/06/statespendingnaturaldisasters_v4.pdf.

30. Phillip Molnar, "Have Homeowners Insurance? It Won't Cover Flooding," *San Diego Union-Tribune*, January 6, 2016, www.sandiegouniontribune.com/business/real-estate/sdut-flood-insurance-home-coverage-2016jan06-htmlstory.html.

31. "State Farm Already Has More Than 22,000 Louisiana Flood Claims," *New Orleans Times-Picayune*, August 19, 2016, www.nola.com/business/index.ssf/2016/08/louisiana_flood_state_farm_cla.html.

32. "Tax Relief in Disaster Situations," IRS.gov, last updated March 22, 2018, www.irs.gov/newsroom/tax-relief-in-disaster-situations.

33. See Howe's recent work, *Behind the Curve*.

34. Karla Lant, "7 Months Later, Climate Change Still Isn't Mentioned on the White House Website," *Futurism*, August 21, 2017, futurism.com/7-months-later-climate-change-still-isnt-mentioned-on-the-white-house-website/; Florida Center for Investigative Reporting, "In Florida, Officials Ban Term 'Climate Change,'" *Miami Herald*, March 8, 2015, www.miamiherald.com/news/state/florida/article12983720.html.

35. Ilan Kelman, J. C. Gaillard, and Jessica Mercer, "Climate Change's Role in Disaster Risk Reduction's Future," *International Journal of Disaster Risk Science* 6, no. 1 (March 2015): 21–27.

36. Roland Van der Meer's blog post "Climatica" marked ten years since Maher introduced the term ("Climatica," *Essential Path*, blog, March 23, 2018, essential-path.com/climatica/).

37. Anthony Leiserowitz et al., "What's in a Name? Global Warming Versus Climate Change," Yale Project on Climate Change Communication and George Mason University Center for Climate Change Communication, Report, May 2014, environment.yale.edu/climate-communication-OFF/files/Global_Warming_vs_Climate_Change_Report.pdf.

38. Brian K. Sullivan, "The Most Expensive U.S. Hurricane Season Ever: By the Numbers," *Bloomberg*, November 25, 2017, www.bloomberg.com/news/articles/2017-11-26/the-most-expensive-u-s-hurricane-season-ever-by-the-numbers.

39. Ibid.

40. "Breaking News: These 2017 Hurricanes Were So Notorious Their Names Will Never Be Used Again," *TWC App,* news alert, April 12, 2018.

41. @davidaxelrod, Twitter feed, September 6, 2017, 7:18 a.m.

42. "Harvey, Irma, Maria: Different Disasters, Different Recovery," *USA Today,* October 27, 2017.

43. "Harvard Study Estimates Thousands Died in Puerto Rico Because of Hurricane Maria," *Washington Post,* May 29, 2018.

44. "Welcome to the New Category 6 by Bob Henson," *Weather Underground,* last accessed November 18, 2017, /cat6/welcome-new-category-6.

45. "Is a Category 6 Hurricane Possible?" Weather Channel, July 28, 2016, weather.com/storms/hurricane/news/category-6-hurricane-saffir-simpson-wind-scale?_escaped_fragment_.

46. Leigh Morgan, "There Is No Such Thing as a Category 6 Hurricane," AL.com, last accessed November 18, 2017, www.al.com/news/index.ssf/2017/09/there_is_no_such_thing_as_a_ca.html.

47. Abigail Abrams, "What Do Hurricane Categories Actually Mean?" *Time,* September 19, 2017, time.com/4946730/hurricane-categories/.

48. Carol J. Friedland, "Residential Building Damage from Hurricane Storm Surge: Proposed Methodologies to Describe, Assess and Model Building Damage," PhD diss., Louisiana State University, 2009.

49. Hal F. Needham and Barry D. Keim, "A Storm Surge Database for the US Gulf Coast," *International Journal of Climatology* 32, no. 14 (November 30, 2012): 2108–23, doi.org/10.1002/joc.2425; "LSU Researchers Create First Comprehensive Storm Surge Database," www.lsu.edu/departments/gold/2012/06/storm_surge_research.shtml, last accessed November 18, 2017.

50. "Texas Hurricane Harvey (DR-4332)," "Disasters Declarations (by Year)," 2017, FEMA.gov.

SELECTED BIBLIOGRAPHY

Archival and Manuscript Collections

Bolton, Roxcy O'Neal. Papers, M94. State Library and Archives of Florida, Tallahassee.
Hurricane Collections. Louisiana Research Collections. Tulane University, New Orleans.
Hurricane Katrina Collections. Special Collections. University of Southern Mississippi, Hattiesburg.
Hurricane Katrina Ephemera Collection. Louisiana State Museum, New Orleans.
Hurricane Katrina Research Center. University of Southern Mississippi–Gulf Coast, Biloxi.
National Oceanic and Atmospheric Association Regional Library at the National Hurricane Center. Miami.
National Organization for Women. Records of the National Organization for Women, 1959–2002, MC 496 and M 152. Schlesinger Library, Boston.
Records of the Defense Civil Preparedness Agency. Record Group 397. National Archives and Records Administration, College Park, MD.
Records of the Federal Emergency Management Agency. Record Group 311. National Archives and Records Administration, College Park, MD.
Records of the National Oceanic and Atmospheric Association. Record Group 370. National Archives and Records Administration, College Park, MD.
Records of the Office of the Secretary of Defense. Record Group 330. National Archives and Records Administration, College Park, MD.
Records of the Weather Bureau, 1735–1979. Record Groups 27 and 130. National Archives and Records Administration, College Park, MD.
Stewart, George R. Papers. Storm Collection. Record Group C0128. Rare Books and Special Collections, Princeton University, Princeton, NJ.

SELECTED BIBLIOGRAPHY

Articles, Books, and Chapters

"Andrew's Name Will Be Retired." *New Orleans Times-Picayune,* August 25, 1992.

"Another Sexist Bastion Falls: Hurricanes Renamed." *New York Times,* May 13, 1978.

Arsenault, Raymond. "The Public Storm: Hurricanes and the State in Twentieth-Century America." In Wendy Gamber, Michael Grossberg, and Hendrik Hartog, eds., *American Public Life and the Historical Imagination* (Notre Dame, IN: University of Notre Dame Press, 2003), 274–75.

"At Least 9 Killed—Houses Left in Splinters." *New York Times,* August 25, 1992.

Barry, John. *Rising Tide: The Great Mississippi Flood of 1927 and How It Changed America.* New York: Simon & Schuster, 1998.

Bechtel, Stefan. *Roar of the Heavens.* New York: Citadel Press, 2006.

Bixel, Bellis, and Elizabeth Hayes Turner. *Galveston and the 1900 Storm: Catastrophe and Catalyst.* Austin: University of Texas Press, 2000.

Buhs, Joshua Blu. "The Fire Ant Wars: Nature and Science in the Pesticide Controversies of the Late Twentieth Century." *Isis* 93, no. 3 (2002): 377–400.

"Chemical Dropped on New Hurricane to Lessen Force: Position of Debbie." *Washington Post,* August 19, 1969.

Fleming, James. *Fixing the Sky: The Checkered History of Weather and Climate Control.* New York: Columbia University Press, 2010.

Funk, Ben. "Hurricane-Chaser Believes Seeding Can Tame Tempests." *Hartford Courant,* February 11, 1968.

"Georges Was an Island Hopper: The Hurricane Bypassed Most of the Caribbean; the Unlucky Few Are Now Cleaning Up." *New York Times,* October 25, 1998.

Gunther, Emil B. "Eastern North Pacific Tropical Cyclones of 1978." *Monthly Weather Review* 107 (July 1979): 911–27.

Howe, Joshua P. *Behind the Curve: Science and the Politics of Global Warming.* Seattle: University of Washington Press, 2016.

"Hurricane Juan Kills 3 as It Batters Gulf Coast." *New York Times,* October 29, 1985.

"Hurricane Packs Punch on the Energy Markets." *Los Angeles Times,* August 30, 2005.

"Hurricane Roxcy." *New Times: Miami's News & Arts Weekly* 13, no. 44 (February 22–28, 1989).

"Hurricane Watchers Now Prepare for . . . Bud, Hector, Sergio." *Washington Post,* May 13, 1978.

"Katrina: The Storm We've Always Feared." *New Orleans Times-Picayune,* August 30, 2005.

Kislow, Paul V. *Hurricanes: Background, History and Bibliography.* New York: Nova Science Publishers, 2008.

SELECTED BIBLIOGRAPHY

May, Elaine Tyler. *Homeward Bound: American Families in the Cold War Era.* New York: Basic Books, 2008.

Merchant, Carolyn. *The Death of Nature: Women, Ecology, and the Scientific Revolution.* New York: Harper & Row, 1989.

"More Than Ever, You Can Say That on Television." *New York Times,* November 14, 2009.

"National Guard Aid Asked to Protect from Looters." *New Orleans Times-Picayune,* September 11, 1965.

"New Experiments Due in Hurricane Control." *Los Angeles Times,* November 4, 1963.

"Other Nations Must Consent: Some Hurricanes May Get Men's Names." *Baltimore Sun,* December 16, 1977.

Riehl, H., and J. S. Malkus. "Some Aspects of Hurricane Daisy." *Tellus* 12 (1958): 181–213.

Rozario, Kevin. *The Culture of Calamity: Disaster and the Making of Modern America.* Chicago: University of Chicago Press, 2007.

Schwartz, Stuart B. *Sea of Storms: A History of Hurricanes in the Greater Caribbean from Columbus to Katrina.* Princeton, NJ: Princeton University Press, 2015.

Scott, Phil. *Hemmingway's Hurricane: The Great Florida Keys Storm of 1935.* New York: McGraw-Hill, 2006.

Shaw, Napier. *Manual of Meteorology.* 2nd ed. Cambridge, UK: Cambridge University Press, 1938.

Steinberg, Ted. *Acts of God: The Unnatural History of Natural Disaster in America.* Oxford, UK: Oxford University Press, 2000.

Stewart, George Rippey. *Earth Abides.* New York: Random House, 1945.

———. *Fire.* New York: Random House, 1948.

———. *Names on the Land: A Historical Account of Place-Naming in the United States.* Boston: Houghton Mifflin, 1945.

———. *Storm.* New York: Random House, 1941.

———. *Storm.* New York: Sun Dial Press, 1941.

———. *Storm.* London: Hutchinson Press, 1942.

———. *Storm.* New York: Sun Dial Press, 1943.

———. *Storm.* New York: Council on Books in Wartime, 1943.

———. *Storm.* New York: Editions for the Armed Services, 1946.

———. *Storm.* New York: Modern Library, 1947.

———. *Storm.* Lincoln: University of Nebraska Press, 1983.

———. *Storm.* Berkeley: Heyday Books, 2003.

"Swept Off with a Broom." *Houston Chronicle,* September 1, 2005.

Tao, W.-K., et al. "The Research of Dr. Joanne Simpson: Fifty Years Investigating Hurricanes, Tropical Clouds, and Cloud Systems." *Meteorological Monographs* 29, no. 51 (January 2003): 1–16.

SELECTED BIBLIOGRAPHY

"Why Gales Are Gals: Hurricane Namers (Male) Prove It's to Avoid Confusion." *New York Times,* September 26, 1954.

Woloch, Nancy. *Women and the American Experience.* 5th ed. New York: McGraw-Hill, 2011.

Correspondence and Interviews

Barris, Bernard. Phone interview and correspondence with author. August 14, 20, 22, 2013.

Bolton, Bonnie. Interviews with author. June 10, 12, 2017.

Bolton, Roxcy O'Neal. Phone interview and correspondence with author. September 1, 2011–March 2017.

Bryson, Reid. Transcript of Interview 320. University of Wisconsin Oral History Project. April 1986.

Caroff, Philippe. Email correspondence with Gary Padgett regarding SW Indian Ocean Naming. October 3, 2012.

Cerf, Vinton. Interviewed by Bernard Aboba. "How the Internet Came to Be." Posted online in 1993, www.netvalley.com/archives/mirrors/cerf-how-inet.html. Rpt. in Bernard Aboba, *The Online User's Encyclopedia.* Boston: Addison-Wesley, 1993.

Dorst, Neal. Email correspondence with author regarding Australia's 1975 tropical storm naming system change. August 16, 2012.

———. Email correspondence with author regarding contacts. August 20, 2012.

———. Email correspondence with author regarding George Stewart's impact on hurricane naming. August 14, 2012.

———. Email correspondence with author regarding lecture on hurricane names at the NOAA Regional Miami Library. October 19, 23, 24, 25, 2012.

———. Email correspondence with author regarding 1947 use of hurricane names. August 31, 2012.

———. Email correspondence with author regarding official history of naming traditions. August 14, 2012.

———. Email correspondence with author regarding *Queensland* magazine and Greek alphabet storm naming. September 11, 2012.

———. Email correspondence with author regarding Region IV meeting in 1978. August 21, 2012.

———. Email correspondence with author regarding Reid Bryson and Typhoon naming. September 26, 2012.

———. Email correspondence with author regarding the link between Clement Wragge and George Stewart. September 12, 2012.

SELECTED BIBLIOGRAPHY

———. Email correspondence with author regarding use of names in post–World War II period. August 21, 2012.

Fleming, James Rodger. Email correspondence with author regarding hurricane-naming history. August 15, 2012.

Frank, Neil. Email correspondence with Neal Dorst regarding hurricane-naming tradition, as passed on to author. August 21, 2012.

———. Telephone interview performed by Neal Dorst. August 20, 2012. Cited in email correspondence from Neal Dorst to author, August 21, 2012.

Kreps, Juanita. Interview performed by Lynn Haessly. January 17, 1986. Southern Oral History Program Collection, University of North Carolina at Chapel Hill. Interview C-0011, #4007, docsouth.unc.edu/sohp/browse/themes.html?theme_id=6&category_id=30. Last accessed October 4, 2012.

Lawrence, Miles. Email correspondence regarding naming evolution. August 20, 2012.

Norcross, Bryan. Email correspondence with author regarding Clement Wragge and other *They Call the Wind Maria* play naming story. August 14, 2012.

———. Email correspondence with author regarding Clement Wragge and Queensland newspaper articles. August 15, 2012.

Padgett, Gary. Email correspondence with author regarding Brisbane Warning Center accounts of Wragge's naming system. August 16, 2012.

———. Email correspondence with author regarding clarification of dates and regions of adoption of the naming system throughout the world. September 12, 2012.

———. Email correspondence with author regarding initial years of name adoptions as known at the time. August 14, 2012.

———. Email correspondence with author regarding 1947 and 48 storm names. August 15, 2012.

———. Email correspondence with author regarding SW Indian Ocean Naming. October 3, 2012.

———. Email correspondence with author regarding the dates of adoption of the naming system throughout the world. September 12, 2012.

———. Email correspondence with author regarding WMO naming system and suggested contacts. August 20, 2012.

Sivels, Andre. Email correspondence with author regarding NOAA collections at the National Archives and Records Administration, July 25, 2012.

Theberg, Albert J. Email correspondence with James Rodger Fleming about the hurricane-naming system history. August 15, 2012.

SELECTED BIBLIOGRAPHY

Ephemera

"The Blame Game Board Game." 2006, www.zzzinger.com.

"Blow Me." Blow Me Wearables, www.blowmewear.com/katrina.html.

BobbyofNOLA. "Chalmette Mardi Gras." Flickr Album, www.flckr.com/photos/bobby ofnola/3476848870/.

Davidson, Jim. *Camille . . . She Was No Lady*. Post-Storm Gulf-Coast Fundraising Benefit Booklet. Batesville, AK: Dav-Mac Publishing, 1969.

"DEFEND New Orleans T-shirt." Defend New Orleans, defendneworleans.com/. Last accessed June 6, 2013.

Ernieattorney. "Magazine St. Sign—Katrina You Bitch." Flikr Album, October 17, 2005, www.flickr.com/photos/ernieattorney/53461148/.

"Girls Gone Wild T-Shirt." Available for purchase in T-shirts and sweatshirts at Mardi Gras Zone, mardigraszone.com/store/ images/ggwild-hurricanes-tshirt .JPG.

Hermès. "Hurricane Katrina/New Orleans Scarf." Referenced in Deidra Woolard, "Hermes Scarf to Benefit New Orleans," www.luxist.com/tag/hurricane +relief/.

"Hurricane Katrina." CafePress.com. "Hurricane Katrina 'FEMA Trailer' Mardi Gras Bead." eBay, Item No. B182, www.ebay.ca/itm/ws/eBayISAPI.dll?View-Item&item=2003 16735540#ht_2686wt_796. Last accessed June 5, 2013.

"Katrina Gave Me a Blow Job I'll Never Forget." T-shirt. As seen by author on Bourbon Street, New Orleans, August 20, 2007.

"Katrina You Bitch!" Handmade T-shirt, featured at People Get Ready blog. "New Orleans Pride Displayed in T-Shirts." November 4, 2005. Image No. Prg005, peoplegetready.blogspot.com/2005/ 11/new-orleans-pride-displayed-in-t-shirt .html.

"Katrina You Bitch!" Mardi Gras Float. Mardi Gras '06 Album, Rotten to the Corps Parade, 2006. Image taken by Chuck T. on February 24, 2006. www.flickr.com /photos/sazerac/sets/72057594083 235628/. Accessed on August 29, 2009.

Le Krewe d'État. "Katrina You Bitch!" Rotten to the Corps Parade, 2006. Image taken by Chuck T., Mardi Gras '06 Album, February 24, 2006, www.flickr.com/photos /sazerac/sets/72057 594083235628/.

"Lakeside Shopping Mall Blue-Tarp Christmas Display, 2006." Discussed in Bayoucreole's weblog, "The Superbowl of the South." December 2010, bayoucreole. wordpress.com/category/nawlins-news/.

Mignon Faget Jewelry. "Anniversary Amulet." Product No. 5365, www. mignonfaget .com/shop/product/amulets/5365.html.

Millergw. "New Orleans 'Chocolate City' MG Bead." eBay, Item No. B185, www.ebay .ca/itm/ws/eBayISAPI.dll?ViewItem&item=110359771509.

SELECTED BIBLIOGRAPHY

Mpdoughboy153. "MP Brassard Hurricane Katrina worn OBSOLETTE 1980s–90s." eBay, Item No. 330586178483. cgi.ebay.com/MP-Brassard-Hurricane-Katrina-worn-OBSOLETTE-1980s-90s-/330586178483?pt=LH_DefaultDomain_0&hash=item4cf878c3b3.

"New Orleans 'Loot Er Man' Bead ... Hurricane Katrina." eBay, Item No. B184, www.ebay.com/itm/NEW-ORLEANS-LOOT-ER-MAN-BEAD-HURRICANE-KATRINA-B184-/110359 771821.

"New Orleans: Proud to Swim Home." From PerfectlyPinkBlogSpot, "New Orleans: Proud To Swim Home!!" July 25, 2008. jessaatpefectlypink.blogspot.com/2008/07/new-orleans-proud-to-swim-home.html.

"9th Ward Roof Tiles." Available at Fleurty Girl Store. New Orleans, April 11, 2011.

"Sandy's A B*tch." CONSURV. Last accessed June 5, 2013, consurv.bigcartel.com/product/sandy-s-a-btch.com.

Government Publications

Blake, Eric, Christopher Landsea, and Ethan Gibney. "The Deadliest, Costliest, and Most Intense United States Tropical Cyclones from 1851 to 2010 (and Other Frequently Requested Hurricane Facts)." NOAA Technical Memorandum, NWS NHC-6. Miami: National Weather Service, 2011.

"Disasters Declarations (by Year)." FEMA.gov., www.fema.gov/disasters. Accessed April 30, 2018.

Fassig, Oliver L. *Hurricanes of the West Indies*. US Weather Bureau Bulletin X. Washington, DC: US Government Publications, 1913.

Guiney, John, and Miles Lawrence. "Preliminary Report: Hurricane Mitch." National Hurricane Center, January 28, 1999.

"Hurricanes—No Slur on Women." *Irish Times*, May 27, 1971.

Interdepartmental Hurricane Warning Conference. *Report of the 1971 Interdepartmental Hurricane Warning Conference, Coral Gables, Fla., January 13–14, 1971*. National Hurricane Center: 1971, NHC Library.

International Telecommunication Union. "Appendix 16: Phonetic Alphabet and Figure Code." Geneva: ITU, 1959.

Lott, Neal. "The Big One! A Review of the March 12–14, 1993 'Storm of the Century.'" National Climatic Data Center Research Customer Service Group. Technical Report 93-1. Posted on May 14, 1993, ftp://ftp.ncdc.noaa.gov/pub/data/techrpts/tr9301/tr9301.pdf.

National Hurricane Research Project. "Project STORMFURY, 1963–1973: Annual Reports." Miami: AOML, 1973.

Norton, Grady. "Hurricanes of the 1950 Season." *Monthly Weather Review* (January 1951): 8–15.

"1 Million in Florida Flee Menacing Floyd." *New Orleans Times-Picayune,* September 14, 1999.

Perryman, Nyssa, and Sandra Theiss. "'Weather Girls' on the Big Screen: Stereotypes, Sex Appeal, and Science." *Bulletin of the American Meteorological Society,* March 2014, 347–56.

"Reorganization Plan No. IV of 1940." 5 F.R. 2223, 54 Stat. 1238, by act June 4, 1940, ch. 231, §1, 54 Stat. 230.

Rose, L. J. "Aviation's ABC: The Development of the ICAO spelling alphabet." *ICAO Bulletin.* November 2, 1956: 12–14.

US Congress. Disaster Relief Act of 1950. Pub. L. No. 81-75, § 64 Stat. 1109.

———. Disaster Relief Act of 1974. Pub. L. No. 93-88.

———. Disaster Relief and Emergency Assistance Amendments of 1988 as part of the Disaster Relief Act of 1974. Pub. L. No. 93-88, 42 USC § 5121 et seq.

———. The Disaster Relief Appropriations Act of 2013. Pub. L. No. 113-2 § 127 Stat. 4.

———. The Federal Judiciary Emergency Special Sessions Act of 2005. Pub. L. No. 109-63 (H.R. 3650).

———. Homeland Security Act of 2002. Pub. L. No. 107-296, § 116 Stat. 2135.

———. The John Warner National Defense Authorization Act for Fiscal Year 2007. Sections of Pub. L. No. 109-364 (H.R. 5122).

———. The Pets Evacuation and Transportation Standards Act of 2006. Pub. L. No. 109-308 (H.R. 3858).

———. The Post-Katrina Emergency Management Reform Act of 2006. Title VI of Pub. L. No. 109-295 (H.R. 5441).

———. The Security and Accountability for Every Port Act of 2005. Pub. L. No. 109-347 (H.R. 4954).

———. The Student Grant Hurricane and Disaster Relief Act. Pub. L. No. 109-67 (H.R. 3668).

War Department. "Practical Use of Meteorological Reports and Weather Maps." Office of the Chief Signal Officer, Division of Telegrams and Reports for the Benefit of Commerce. Washington, DC: R. Beresford Printer, 1871. openlibrary.org/books/OL23453755M. Accessed October 3, 2012.

"Weather Is the Nation's Business: The Report of the Department of Commerce Advisory Committee on Weather Services to the Honorable Secretary of Commerce." Washington, DC: Government Printing Office, 1953.

Weier, John. "Joanne Simpson (1923–2010)." *NASA Earth Observatory,* April 23, 2004. earthobservatory.nasa.gov/Features/Simpson/simpson.php.

"What's in a Name? The Phonetic Alphabet Goes International." *Topics of the Weather Bureau* 2, no. 3 (March 1952): 38.

SELECTED BIBLIOGRAPHY

Willoughby, H. E., D. P. Jorgensen, R. A. Black, and S. L. Rosenthal. "Project STORM-FURY: A Scientific Chronicle, 1962–1983." Hurricane Research Division, AOML/NOAA, vol. 66, no. 5, May 1985, NHC Library.

Online Resources

The Cartoonist Group. www.cartoonistgroup.com/.
Chartruk, Bob. "NOAA Meteorologist Bob Case, the Man Who Named the Perfect Storm." NOAA News Online, June 16, 2000, archived at web.archive.org/web/20110716220940/http:/www.noaanews.noaa.gov/stories/s444.htm.
Cooper, Alice. "Living in the Hurricane Years." Bearsville Studios, July 2, 1991.
Department of Agriculture. "A Lady Called Camille." AVA11983VNB1, 1971. Posted by Public.Resource.Org on October 5, 2008. www.youtube.com/watch?v=3XSF_V3BXWQ.
Filipovic, Jill. "Stop Calling Sandy a Bitch: It Was a Storm, Not a Woman to Hate." *Guardian*, November 2, 2012. www.guardian.co.uk/commentisfree/2012/nov/02/stop-calling-sandy-bitch-jill-filipovic.
"'Frankenstorm': A Mix of Hurricane Sandy and Early Snow May Ruin Halloween 2012." *Huffington Post*. October 25, 2012, www.huffingtonpost.com/2012/10/25/hurricane-sandy-frankenstorm-halloween-2012_n_2019252.html#slide=1687842.
"Headlines—Storm of the Century of the Week—Hurricane Floyd." *The Daily Show with Jon Stewart*. Episode 04031, September 16, 1999. www.thedailyshow.com/watch/thu-september-16-1999/headlines-storm-of-the-century-of-the-week.
"Hogcock!/Last Lunch." *30 Rock*. NBC, January 30, 2013.
"@HurriicaneIrene." *Twitter*. Live Feed, twitter.com/#!/HurriicaneIrene.
"@Irene_Bitch." Twitter Feed. August 26, 2011, twitter.com/irene_bitch.
Lerner, Alan J., and Frederick Loewe. *Paint Your Wagon: The Musical*. 1951.
New Orleans Times-Picayune staff. "Post-Katrina Culture Timeline: When Restaurants, Art and Live Music Returned to New Orleans." *Nola.com*, August 2015, www.nola.com/katrina/index.ssf/page/katrina_culture_timeline.html.
The Perfect Storm. Warner Brothers Pictures, June 30, 2000.
Phillips, Mark Edward. "Hurricane Harvey Twitter Dataset." University of North Texas, August 18 to September 22, 2017. digital.library.unt.edu/ark:/67531/metadc993940/.
Shakespeare, William. *The Tempest*. 1623. First folio ed. New York: Thomas Y. Crowell & Co., 1903, via Google Books.
Smith, Gian. "O Beautiful Storm." Poem spoken in "Season 2: O Beautiful Storm Extended Tease." *Treme: Season 2*. HBO Podcasts on iTunes, March 21, 2011.

SELECTED BIBLIOGRAPHY

Thompson, Clive. "The Early Years: Blogging." *NYMag.com*, nymag.com/news/media/15971/. Accessed November 27, 2017.

Walt Disney's Wonderful World of Color. A Storm Called Maria. November 27, 1959.

Newspapers Used to Construct Statistical Hurricane Database

Atlanta Journal-Constitution.
Baltimore Sun.
Biloxi Daily/Sun Herald.
Charleston News/Post & Courier.
Houston Chronicle.
Los Angeles Times.
Miami Herald.
Mobile Press-Register.
New Orleans Times-Picayune.
New York Times.
Raleigh News & Observer.
Richmond Times-Dispatch.

Other Newspapers Consulted

Atlanta Daily World.
Australian Queenslander.
Brisbane Courier.
Chicago Tribune.
Christian Science Monitor.
Daytona Beach News Journal.
Denver Post.
Des Moines Register.
Dublin Irish Times.
Guardian (UK).
Havana Diario de la Marina.
Havana Granma International.
Huffington Post.
Jamaica Daily Gleaner.
Latinos Post.
Louisiana Weekly.

SELECTED BIBLIOGRAPHY

Mexico City El Universal.
Nassau Daily Tribune.
Nassau Herald.
New Orleans Daily Picayune.
New Orleans Daily States/Item.
New Times: Miami's News & Arts Weekly.
New York Journal & Guide.
New York Times Magazine.
Port-au-Prince Le Nouvelliste.
San Juan El Mundo.
San Juan El Nuevo Dia.
Washington Post.
Washington Star.

Talk

Dorst, Neal. "They Call the Wind Mahina: A History of the Naming of Tropical Cyclones." Talk given October 23, 2012. Atlantic Oceanographic and Meteorological Laboratory, Coral Gables, FL.

INDEX

Notes: Individual hurricanes are listed under their names: Agnes, Alice, etc. Page numbers in *italics* refer to figures and tables; those followed by "n" indicate endnotes.

aboriginal names, 56
abortion, 105–6
"acts of God," 10, 275n193
Agnes (1974), 126–27, 131, *164*
air-conditioning window units, 40
air mass analysis, 13
Alabama: Danny (1985), 144; Frederic (1979), 139
Alice (1954), 43–44, 50, 134
Alice (1955), 52
Alicia (1983), 130, 142–44, *164*
Allen (1980), 140–42, 145
"Allen the Roulette Dealer" (*New Orleans Times-Picayune* cartoon), 141, *141*
alphabetical naming systems, 20, 26, *26*
American Dream, 39
Andrew (1992), 119, 149–55, 158, *164*, 191
antibiotics, 41
apps, weather-related, 212–13, 278n236
Armed Services Edition (ASE) ration kits, 25
Army Corps of Engineers, US, 174, 197
Army Signal Corps, US, 11–12
Arsenault, Raymond, 5, 40
atomic bombs, 26, 36–37, 179
Audrey (1957), *79*, 144

Audubon Society, 98–99
Australia, 20–21, 113, 217

"Bad Girls of '54," 43–51
Bankoff, Greg, 5, 200
Bara, Walter, 23
Barbara (1953), 56
Barbara (1954), 44
Bayh, Birch, 97, 104
Bay of Pigs, 61
Beasts of the Southern Wild (film), 198
Beaufort Scale, 123, 254n25
Betsy (1965), 35, 68–71, 125–26, 144, 176
Beulah (1963), 66–68
Bewitched, 37
Biguenet, John, 197
Bigwood, Carol, 5
Biloxi Sun-Herald, 178, 179
bird names, 98–99
"bitch" rhetoric, 190–92, 198, 204–7
Bixel, Patricia Bellis, 5
Blanco, Kathleen, 191–92
blogs, 169–71, 177, 183, 184
Bob (1979), 137–38
Bohun, Ralph, 9–10
Bok, Chip, 272n145
Bolton, Roxcy, *102;* background, 83; bird names suggestion, 98–99; ERA campaign and, 97, 104–5; Interdepartmental Hurricane Warning Conferences and media

INDEX

Bolton, Roxcy (*continued*)
coverage, 95–96, 98–104, 109–10; letter to NHC, 81–83, 90–91; letter to Simpson, 101; meeting with Simpson and media coverage, 91–95; NOW activities, 83, 88–90, 96–98, 104, 111; other feminists compared to, 111–12; Saffir-Simpson scale and, 123; senator names suggestion, 101–2
"bombshells," 38
Bonnie (1998), 169–70
Brazzell, R. J., 71–72
Brenda (1955), 52
Bud (1978), 133–34
Buhs, Joshua Blu, 5, 41
Burkart, Lohr, 67
Bush, Barbara, 184
Bush, George H. W., 153
Bush, George W., 184, 193, 195
Butler, Patricia (Twiss), 115

Cable News Network (CNN), 128–29
CafePress, 188
Cajun Navy, 208, 210
Camille (1969): Andrew compared to, 150; Bolton on language around, 90; Cold War and, 35–36; Disaster Relief Act revision in reaction to, 126; Elena compared to, 144; fears from memories of, 131; female roles in society and, 78; Louisiana coastline vulnerability and, 176; newspaper use of gender in regard to, *79;* Project STORMFURY and, 72–73; "was no lady," 73, 81, 93, 191
Cantore, Jim, 130, 178
Carfagno, Jen, 255n49
Carlotta (1978), 134–35
Carol (1954), 44–51, *79*
Carson, Rachel, 111–12
Carter, Jimmy, 112, 128
cartoons: "Allen the Roulette Dealer" (*New Orleans Times-Picayune*), 141, *141;* "Do I look like a hurricane?" (*Miami Herald*), 93, *94;* "Feminists Prevail" (*New Orleans Times-Picayune*), 114, *115;* "Gustav and the GOP Convention" (*Mobile Press-Register*), 202, *202;* "Hilda and the Gulf Coast" (*New Orleans Times-Picayune*), 64, *65;* "Meteorological Optometrist" (*Mobile Press-Register*), 53–54, *54;* and New Orleans as victim of abuse (*Mobile Press-Register*), 192–93; "Voodoo Priestess Katrina" (*Mobile Press-Register*), 179, *180*
Castro, Fidel, 61, 66
cautionary signaling processes, 12
Charleston, SC: Floyd (1999), 159–60; Hugo (1989), 147–48; vulnerability of, 126
Charley (2004), 170
Charlotte Observer Hurricane Bonnie blog, 169–70
Civil Rights Act (1964), 85, 96
Civil War, 11
"climate change," 228–29
Clinton, Bill, 153, 193
CNN (Cable News Network), 128–29
code systems, 24–27, 29
Colbert, Stephen, 161–62
Cold War: analogies for storms, 54; atom bomb and H-bomb, 36–37, 54; disaster policies and, 125, *125;* Red Menace or Red Threat, 52; satellites and, 60–61; transgressive women and, 78; weaponized nature and, 36–37
Colten, Craig, 5
Concert for Katrina, 184
Cone of Probability or "Cone of Death," 265n5
Connecticut: and Diane (1955), 53
Connick, Harry, Jr., 195
Connie (1955), 52–53, 56, *79*
Conroy, Alfred B., 21
consumption culture, disaster-related, 186–87
control, desire for: Allen and end to, 142; Civil War and, 11; postwar fight against nature, 39–41; study of hurricanes and, 41–42. *See also* hurricane modification projects

INDEX

Cook, Ann, 67
Cooper, Alice, 149
Cooper, Anderson, 178
Cressman, George, 99–100
Cronon, William, 5
CrowdSource Rescue, 210
Crowe, JD, 179, *180*
Cuba, 61
Cuban Missile Crisis, 66
cultural responses to hurricanes and storms: consumption culture, 186–87; disaster tourism, 193–94; early modern, 8–10; Katrina, culture production and consumption around, 193–200; memorabilia and disaster kitsch, 187–93, *189, 190*. See also cartoons

Dade County Chapter, NOW, 89. See also Miami-Dade Chapter, NOW
Dade County Rape Treatment Center, 104
Danny (1985), 144–45
Daston, Lorraine, 5
David (1979), 138–39, *164*
DDT (dichlorodiphenyltrichloroethane), 40–41
Debbie (1969), 73–76, 78, 90, 122, 142
declarations of disaster, federal, 125, *154*, 185, *225–27*, 225–28
Dennis (1999), 159
"Desexing the Federal Code" project (NOW), 106
Diane (1955), 53–54, *79*
dichlorodiphenyltrichloroethane. *See* DDT
digital repositories, 186
disaster fiction: in 1930s, 7; literature about Katrina, 199; *Storm* (Stewart), 6–7, 14–23, 25, 31, 33–34, 47
disaster kitsch, 187–93, *189, 190*
disaster perception and redefinition post-Katrina, 174–75, 185, 200–207; multistate hurricane-preparedness conference, 126
disaster policies, management, and relief: Cold War and, 125; declaration of disasters,

125, *154*, 185, *225–27*, 225–28; definition of "major disaster" vs. "emergency," 127; FEMA, creation of, 124; impact of names on federal funding, 224–28, *225–27*
Disaster Relief Act (1950), 125, 126, 225
Disaster Relief Act (1974), 126–27, 146
disaster tourism, 193–94
Dixon, George, 57
"Do I look like a hurricane?" (*Miami Herald* cartoon), 93, *94*
Dolly (1954), 44, 50
Domino, Fats, 194–95
Donna (1960), 63, *79*, 138
DopplerDuds.com, 188
drill, "Hurricane Pam" (Baton Rouge), 174

Eastern Pacific Ocean region and male-female naming system, 114
Eastern Seaboard: "Bad Girls of '54" (Carol, Edna, Hazel), 44–51; Connie (1955), 52; David (1979), 138; Floyd (1999), 160–61; Hugo (1989), 147–48
e-commerce websites, 172–73
Edna (1954), 44–51, 56, *79*
Edwards, Edwin, 144
Edwards, John Bel, 223–24, 226
EEOC (Equal Employment Opportunities Commission), 85–86
Elena (1979), 140
Elena (1985), 144–45, 191
Ella (1962), 66
"emergency," definition of, 127
Emily (1987), 145
Environmental Science Services Administration (ESSA), 72
Equal Employment Opportunities Commission. *See* EEOC
Equal Rights Amendment (ERA), 87, 97, 104–5, 108, 110
Error Cone, 265n5
ESSA (Environmental Science Services Administration), 72
Esther (1961), 63–64

INDEX

Executive Order 8991 (1941), 23–24
Executive Order 10980 (1961), 84
Exxon Valdez oil spill, 146

Facebook, 170–71, 207–9, 210, 211
Faith (1966), 247n136
fear of weather and storms, 7–8, 36, 131, 173–74
federal disaster declarations, 125, *154*, 185, 225–27, 225–28
Federal Emergency Management Agency (FEMA): 2004 season and, 173–74; Andrew (1992) and, 153; creation of, 124, 128; effeminacy references to, 191–92; expansion to mitigation, 153; Katrina and, 183; named, unnamed, declared, and undeclared disasters and, 225–27, *225–27*; numerical IDs for disasters, 231–32; Sandy Recovery Improvement Act and Disaster Relief Appropriations Act and, 278n2; as "WEMA" (Worst Emergency Management Agency), 270n109
"Female Hurricanes Are Deadlier than Male Hurricanes" (study by Jung and Shavitt), 218–20
female naming system: Bolton campaign against, 81–84, 90–104, 108–10; code systems during World War II, 24–27; cultural impacts of, 76–80; ended by Kreps, 112–16; newspaper editorials on, 49–51; newspaper use of gender by storm and region, *79;* Pickens and Kuchel campaign against, 55–58; and Queensland, Australia, 20–22; in Stewart's *Storm*, 18, 22–23; test years (1954 and 1955), 51; and US Weather Bureau (1948), 33; women asking names to be added to list, 99, 100. *See also* gender
feminist movement: Bolton campaign against female naming system, 81–84, 90–104, 108–10; Bolton compared to Friedan, Steinem, and Carson, 111–12; "Language Lib," 106–8; "Ms." and "Herstory," 106–7;

NOW and rival organizations, 86; public distaste for, 108–9; sexism concept, 106; term "feminist," 86; "Women's Lib Storm," 103–4. *See also* National Organization for Women (NOW)
"Feminists Prevail" cartoon (*New Orleans Times-Picayune* cartoon), 114, *115*
Fico (1978), 135
fiction on natural disasters. *See* disaster fiction
Fifth Ward Weebie, 195
Filipovic, Jill, 207
Finnegan, William, 67
Fitzgerald, F. Scott, 238n87
Fleet Weather Facility, Jacksonville, FL, 72
Fleming, James Rodger, 5, 11
flood-control structures, 40
flooding scale, consideration of, 230
Florida: "1947 Ripper," 42; Andrew (1992), 150–53; ERA and, 105; Georges (1998), 156; Labor Day Storm (1935), 12–13; Opal (1995), 155
Florida Area Cumulus Experiment, 126, 247n137
Floyd (1999), 159–63, *164*
42 Matters, 212, 278n236
Frances (2004), 170
Frank, Neil, 113–15
Frederic (1979), 138, 139–40, 143
Friedan, Betty, 82, 84–86, 90, 111–12
Fujita, Tetsuya "Ted," 124
Fujita Scale, 123–24
Fujiwara Effect, 53

Galveston, TX: 1900 storm, 12, 158; Alicia (1983), 143; seawall, 40
gay stereotypes, 157–58, 202–3
Gelbart, Larry, 197
gender: American associations transferred internationally, 78; atom bomb as male, 26; "Bad Girls of '54," 43–51; "cute" language,

298

INDEX

49; decreased rhetoric (1974 to 1983), 132–33; effeminacy, 191–92, 202; feminine descriptors, 43–44, 72–80; homosexuality and terminology of sexual deviance, 157–58, 202–3; hurricane as gendered object, 53, 77, 163; masculine descriptors, 133–34, 139–42, 145–48, 152, 156–61; in meteorology, 24; multicity newspaper study on impact of gendered names, 220–22, *221, 222;* negative gendered traits attributed to storms, 48–49, 77–78; newspaper use of, by storm and US region, *79, 164, 212;* normalizing of stereotypes, 80; opinions of men vs. women, treatment of, 57–58; psychological study on gender bias (Jung and Shavitt), 218–20; seeding projects and, 72–73; sexualized images in World War II, 25–26; sexualized language for storms, 78; ships as female, 239n89; trend of assigning to storms, 4; Weather Channel and, 130. *See also* women; *names of specific hurricanes*
Gentry, R. Cecil, 71–72, 75
"George" ("the 1947 Ripper"), 29, 42
Georges (1998), 156–59
Gilbert (1988), 130, 145–46, 149, *164*
Ginger (1971), 122
"Girls Gone Wild" storms (Katrina, Rita, Wilma), 190
Gloria (1985), 143
gods of weather and water, 8–9
The Grapes of Wrath (Steinbeck), 7
Grease (film), 205
Great Gale of 1878, 205
The Great Gatsby (Fitzgerald), 22, 238n87
Greek and Roman gods naming systems, 20, 22, 56, 216–17
"Gulflandia," 173
Gulf South: damages in, 161; Elena and Juan (1985), 144–45; levee-construction projects (eighteenth century), 11, 39; named, unnamed, and declared disasters in, *226,* 226–27, *227;* and population growth, 38, *39, 131, 131. See also* Florida; Louisiana
Gustav (2008), 201–3
"Gustav and the GOP Convention" (*Mobile Press-Register* cartoon), 202, *202*
Gutenberg, Beno, 124

Hale, Kate, 153
Hale, Todd, 205
Hall, Justin, 169
Halloween Nor'easter of 1991, 156
Harding, E. T., 72
Hartford Courant, 181–82
Harvey (2017), 201–2, 209–10, 228–29, 232
Hazel (1954), 45–48, *46,* 56, *79,* 205
H-Bombs, 52, 54
Hemingway, Ernest, 13
"Herstory," 106–7
heteronormativity, 157–58
Hilda (1961), 64, *65*
"Hilda and the Gulf Coast" (*New Orleans Times-Picayune* cartoon), 64, *65*
"himicanes," 109, 114, 132–42
historical character names, infamous, 92
Homestead, FL, 152, 155
homosexuality, 157–58, 202–3
Hoover, Herbert, 13
Horowitz, Andy, 5
Hot Tower hypothesis, 62–63
Houston Chronicle editorials on female naming, 49–50
Howe, Joshua, 5
Huff, Janice, 255n49
Hugo (1989), 130, 147–48, 149, 150, 160, *164*
Hurricane 2.0: consumption culture and, 186–87; cultural production and consumption, 193–200; disaster perception, redefinition, and hypersexualization post-Katrina, 174–75, 185, 200–207; disaster tourism, 193–94; Harvey, Irma, and Maria, 209–10; Katrina and, 166–68, 175–86; memorabilia and disaster kitsch, 187–93,

Hurricane 2.0 (*continued*) 189, 190; new fears with web-based knowledge, 173–74; role of media in construction of, 211–13; social media and, 204–11; Web 2.0 context, 168–73. *See also* Katrina (2005)

Hurricane Alley, 134, 136

Hurricane Digital Memory Bank, New Orleans, 186

"hurricane," etymology of, 8–9

Hurricane Hunters, 42–43, 48, 59–61

hurricane modification projects: Betsy, 68–71; Beulah, 66–68; Camille, 72–73; conspiracy theory about, 69–70; cultural impacts of, 76–80; Debbie, 73–76, 142; Hot Tower hypothesis, 62–63; NOTS technique, 67–68; Project BATON, 66, 70; Project CIRRUS, 42–43, 58; Project STORMFURY, beginnings of, 64–65; Project STORMFURY, end of, 121–22; reduction in speeds with Debbie, 74–75; refutation of, 122, 142; satellites and, 60–61; silver iodide crystals technology, 36, 61–64; standards and storm selection, 67, 71–72

Hurricane on the Bayou (film), 198

"Hurricane Pam" drill (Baton Rouge), 174

hurricane-preparedness conference, multistate, 126

hurricane season, official, 136

Hurricane Warning Service (Jacksonville, FL), 13

"Hurricane Years" (song), 149

Hurston, Zora Neale, 7

Ike (2008), 201–2, 203–4

Incans, 8–9

"Incredible Hulk," 146, 259n121

Ingle, Martha, 81, 82, 97

insurance companies, 227–28

Interdepartmental Hurricane Warning Conferences, 92, 95–96, 98–104, 109–10

International Civil Aviation Organization (ICAO) Phonetic Alphabet, 31, *32*

International Meteorological Organization (IMO), 28

International Phonetic Alphabet, 31

Internet. *See* Web 2.0

Irene (2011), 201–2, 204

Irma (2017), 201–2, 209, 230

Ivan (2004), 170, 174

Jamaica: and Gilbert (1988), 145

Johannessen, Karl, 99

Johnson, Cathy, 188

Johnson, Lyndon B., 89

Joint Army/Navy Phonetic Alphabet Naming System, 30–31, *31*, *32*, 42

joint Army-Navy task force, 24–25

Juan (1985), 144, 145, 258n112

Jung, Kiju, 218–20

Junger, Sebastian, 156

Katrina (2005): art and, 196; disaster consumption and, 186–87; disaster redefined following, 174–75, 200–13; documentaries and films, 198–99; as first 50-state disaster declaration, 185; as first Internet storm, 168–69, 210–11; gendered rhetoric and hypersexualization of, 179, 189–93, 201; Hurricane 2.0 and, 167–68, 210–11; landfall, 177; literature about, 199; Mardi Gras and, *197*, 197–98; memorabilia and disaster kitsch, 187–93, *189*, *190*; musicians and, 194–96; as new type of storm, 185–86; plays about, 196–97; restaurants and, 198; storm, aftermath, narration, and consumption of, 175–84; and Superdome, 179, 182; tourism, 193–94; TV shows about, 166–67, 194. *See also* Hurricane 2.0

Kelman, Ilan, 5

Kennedy, John F., 84

Kierner, Cynthia, 5

King (1947), 43

INDEX

King, Stephen, 33
Kinsey, Alfred, 37
Kirsha Kaechele Projects, 196
kitsch from Katrina, 187–93, *189, 190*
Kreps, Juanita M., 112–16, 117–18, 133
Krewe d'État parade, *197,* 197–98
Krick, Irving P., 16, 246n109
Kuchel, Thomas, 55–58

"Labor Day Storm" (1935), 12–13, 150
"Labor Day Storm" (1948), 29
Landsberg, Helmut, 14
"Language Lib," 106–8
Lanterns on the Levee (Percy), 7
Leave It to Beaver, 37
Lee, Spike, 198
Legal Defense and Education Fund (NOW), 91
Lerner, Alan, 31
levee-construction projects, 11, 39
Lewis, Dean, 86
Lil Wayne, 195
Living with Hurricanes exhibit, Louisiana State Museum, 1
Loewe, Frederick, 31
"Looterman" Mardi Gras beads, 189, *189*
Louisiana: "1947 Ripper," 29, 42; 2016 "noname storm" and floods, 223–24, *224;* Andrew (1992), 151; "Hurricane Pam" drill (Baton Rouge), 174; Juan (1985), 144. *See also* New Orleans
Loy, Brendan, 177
LSU Hurricane Center, 174

Maher, Bill, 228
"major disaster," definition of, 127
male-female naming system: 1978 Pacific list, *135;* 1979 Atlantic and Pacific lists, *137;* in Australia, 113; homosexuality and terminology of sexual deviance, 157–58, 202–3; Kreps's order and international switch to, 113–16; masculine descriptors, 133–34, 139–42, 145–48, 152, 156–61; questioning of, 163
Malkus, Joanne (later Simpson), 62–65, 68, 71, 77, 92, 245n93, 247n137
Manual of Meteorology (Shaw), 22
Mardi Gras beads, 189, *189*
Mardi Gras parade ("Rotten to the Corps"), *197,* 197–98
Maria (2017), 201–2, 209–10, 229
Maria (fictional storm), 19, 22–23, 25, 31–34, 47, 217
marketplaces, online, 172–73
Marsalis, Branford, 195
Martin, Laura, 5
Masters, Jeff, 230
May, Elaine Tyler, 5, 26
Mayans, 8–9
McPhee, John, 5
merchandizing of Katrina. *See under* Katrina (2005)
Merchant, Carolyn, 5, 10
"Meteorological Optometrist" cartoon (*Mobile Press-Register*), 53–54, *54*
meteorology: 24-hour TV and, 119; private, 16; Shaw's *Manual of Meteorology,* 22; "Weather Girl" figure, 47–48, 107–8, 130, 255n49; "Weather Man" or "weatherman" figure, 28–29, 48, 108, 130; "Weather Woman" figure, 24; women in, 24
Mexican names, 134, 136
Mexico: and Gilbert (1988), 145
Miami, vulnerability of, 126
Miami-Dade Chapter, NOW, 81, 82, 105. *See also* Dade County Chapter, NOW
Miami Herald: Bolton, characterization of, 93–94; "Do I look like a hurricane?" cartoon, 93, *94;* editorials on naming system, 50–51
Miller, Casey, 107
"Miss Hurricane Hunter," 60
Mitch (1998), 155–59, *164*
MMS (Moment Magnitude Scale), 124

INDEX

Mobile, AL: and Frederic (1979), 139
Mobile Press-Register: cartoons on New Orleans as victim of abuse, 192–93; "Gustav and the GOP Convention" cartoon, 202, *202;* "Meteorological Optometrist" cartoon, 53–54, *54;* offline during Frederic, 140; "Voodoo Priestess Katrina" cartoon, 179, *180*
Moment Magnitude Scale (MMS), 124
Moore, Vaughan, 31
Morgan, Robin, 106
Morris, Ashley, 184
Mos Def, 195–96
Mother Nature figure, 10
Ms. magazine, 106
Mulcahy, Matthew, 4–5
musicians after Katrina, 194–96
MySpace, 170–71
mythological names, 9, 56, 92, 216–17

Nagin, Ray, 176, 183–84, 189, 202
naming of hurricanes: 2016 Louisiana "no-name storm" and economic impact, 223–24, *224;* climate change and, 228–29; cultural associations attached to names, 3; disaster declaration, naming, and economic impact, 227–28; harm question, 214–16, 220, 230–32; history of, 3; multicity newspaper study on impact of gendered names, 220–22, *221, 222;* names retained in post-tropical status, 206; names vs. no names and federal disaster declaration, 224–27, *225–27;* original motivation and alteration over time, 214–16; psychological study on gender bias (Jung and Shavitt), 218–20; social media/online study, 222–23; tropical cyclone naming process, 2–3; Weather Channel winter-storm naming system, 216–18. *See also* female naming system; male-female naming system; *names of specific hurricanes*

National Conference of Commissions on the Status of Women, Third (1966), 85
National Flood Insurance Program, 126
National Flood Insurance Protection Act (1965), 125–26
National Hurricane Center (NHC): and Andrew (1992), 152; Bolton letter to, 81–83, 90–91; FEMA and, 128; founding of, 60; funding of, 126; seeding and, 74
National Hurricane Research Project (NHRP): established, 58; prediction and tracking focus, 59–60; seeding, development of, 61–64; seeding guidelines and storm selection, 65; TIROS satellites, 60–61. *See also* Project STORMFURY
National Oceanic and Atmospheric Administration (NOAA), 112–16, 177
National Organization for Women (NOW): abortion and, 105; about, 84–88; Bolton's involvement in, 83, 88–90, 96–98, 104, 111; Dade County Chapter, 89; "Desexing the Federal Code" project, 106; ERA campaign, 87, 97, 104–5, 108, 110; growth of, 86, 96, 97–98, 104; Legal Defense and Education Fund, 91; Miami-Dade Chapter, 81, 82, 105; "New Image of Women" campaign, 90; New Orleans conference (1969), 89–90; statement and letter on hurricane names, 90–91. *See also* Bolton, Roxcy
National Plan for Emergency Preparedness (1964), 125
National Weather Service (NWS): colors for rain density, revision of, 229; Error Cone, 265n5; FEMA and, 128; "Hurricane Pam" drill, 174; names retained for longer, 206; Weather Channel winter-storm naming system and, 216–18
National Women's Liberation Front (NWLF), 86
"natural disaster," 200–201
nature, postwar fight to tame, 39–41

INDEX

Shakespeare, William, 9, 15
Shavitt, Sharon, 218–20
Shaw, Napier, 22
Sherman, William Tecumseh, 147
ships as female, 239n89
silver iodide crystals technology, 36, 61–64. *See also* hurricane modification projects
Simpson, Joanne Malkus, 62–65, 68, 71, 77, 92, 245n93, 247n137
Simpson, Robert H., *102;* Betsy seeding and, 68; Bolton and, 91–93, 99, 101–4; at National Hurricane Center, 74; NHRP and, 59–65; Project STORMFURY and, 121–22; Saffir-Simpson scale and, 123; at Weather Bureau, 71
Smith, Gian, 166, 167
Smithsonian Institution, 11
"snowmageddon," "snowpocalypse," and "snowicane" labels, 217
social media, 170–72, 204–11, 222–23
Socrates, 15
South Carolina: and Hugo (1989), 147–48, 150
Southern Decadence festival, 202–3
Sputnik, 60
Stafford, Robert T., 146
Stafford Act (Robert T. Stafford Disaster Relief and Emergency Assistance Act, 1988), 146–47, 153, 225
Steinberg, Theodore (Ted), 5, 200
Steinem, Gloria, 106, 111–12
Stevenson, Adlai, 83, 89
Stewart, George R., 6–7, 14–20, 22–23, 25, 31, 33–34, 47, 217
Stewart, John, 161–65, *162*
STOP ERA, 108, 110
Storm (Stewart), 6–7, 14–23, 25, 31, 33–34, 47
A Storm Called Maria (film), 33
"Storm of the Century," 148–51, 161–65, 229
"Storm of the Century of the Week," 161–65, *162*
Storm Patrol Bill (1936), 13

storm-surge scale, 230
Strepsiddes, 15
"superstorm," 205–6, 216
Swift, Kate, 107

Taínos, 8–9
Tannehill, Ivan Ray, 33, 50
telegraph network, 11
television: "bitch" rhetoric on, 191; continuous news cycle, 119–20, 128–29, 163–64, *165;* growth of meteorology on, 47–48; Katrina coverage, 178; profitability of hurricanes and proliferation of weather segments, 155–56; shows about Katrina, 166–67, 194, 198–99; Weather Channel debut, 128–30; "Weather Man" figure, 28–29
Television Infrared Observation Satellite (TIROS), 60–61, 63
"tempest" as term, 9
"terrorist," 148
Their Eyes Were Watching God (Hurston), 7
Theiss, Sandra, 130
"They Call the Wind Maria" (song), 31–33, 34
Think New Orleans, 186
30 Rock (TV), 218, *218*
Three Mile Island nuclear disaster, 127–28, 146
TIROS. See Television Infrared Observation Satellite (TIROS)
tourism, disaster, 193–94
tracking: after World War II, 28; Beulah (1963), 60–61; blogs, social media, and, 172; continuous TV coverage and, 150; Esther (1961), 63–64; gendered descriptions of Allen and, 141–42; Hurricane Hunters, 42–43, 48, 59–61; newsworthiness and, 121; radar technology and, 41–42; Sandy (2012), 205; satellites and, 61; self-made weather videos and, 130; Stewart and, 15, 22; TIROS, 60–61
transatlantic natural language, 8–10
Treme (TV), 166–67, 194, 198

tropical convection, 62–63
Trouble the Water (documentary), 198
T-shirts, 188, 190, *190*, 192, 205
Turner, Elizabeth Hayes, 5
Turner, Marilyn, 107
Twitter, 204, 206–7, 210

US Army Corps of Engineers, 174, 197

videos, self-made, 130
"Voodoo Priestess Katrina" (*Mobile Press-Register* cartoon), 179, *180*
vulnerability studies, 174

Walters, Barbara, 107
water gods, 8–9
Weather 2000 Inc., 205
Weather Bureau, US: Bolton and, 99; conspiracy theory about, 69–70; female naming system, 33, 51, 78–79; phonetic alphabet system, 30; post–World War II, 27–31; private meteorologists, conflict with, 16; Project CIRRUS, 42–43; staffing levels and expansions, 14, 24, 27–28, 47; Steering Committee, 99; Stewart's *Storm* and, 6, 15–17, *17*; transferred to Department of Commerce (1940), 13–14; underfunding of, 13; World War II and, 23–27. *See also* National Hurricane Center (NHC)
Weather Channel (TWC), 128–30, 142–43, 216–18
"Weather Girl" figure, 47–48, 107–8, 130, 255n49
weather gods, 8–9
"Weather Man" or "weatherman" figure, 28–29, 48, 108, 130
"Weather Woman" figure, 24
Web 2.0: blogs, 169–71, 177, 183, 184; e-commerce and online marketplaces, 172–73; gender use and, 222–23; Hurricane 2.0 and, 168–69; new fears about hurricanes and, 173–74; social media sites, 170–72
Wells, Christopher, 5
West, Kanye, 184
Westbrook, Robert, 25
When the Levees Broke (documentary), 198
White, Gilbert F., 200
White, Robert M., 72, 113
"Who Murdered the Vets?" (Hemingway), 13
"Why Gales Are Gals" (*New York Times*), 51
Wilma (2005), 186, 190
winter-storm naming system, Weather Channel, 216–18
Witt, James Lee, 153
women: negative stereotypes of, 77–78; nuclear analogies for, 38; opinions, treatment of, 57–58; postwar redomestication of, 37; transgressive, cultural anxieties about, 37–38, 78; World War II sexualized images of, 25–26. *See also* gender
"Women's Lib Storm," 103–4, 110–11
Women's National Abortion Action Coalition (WONAAC), 105
Woods Hole Oceanographic Institution, 63
Woodward, C. Vann, 38
WordPress, 169
World Meteorological Organization (WMO): formation of, 28; International Phonetic Alphabet, 31, *32;* male-female naming system and, 113–14, 135–36; names list from, 2–3, 231; naming policies, new, 136
World War II, 23–27
Wragge, Clement Lindley, 20–22, 217
wrestlers, 145

Yates, Dorothy, 115
YouTube, 171–72, 211

Zee, Ginger, 255n49
Zuckerberg, Mark, 171

www.ingramcontent.com/pod-product-compliance
Lightning Source LLC
Chambersburg PA
CBHW021345300426
44114CB00012B/1092